THE HUNT

COMPLETE GUIDE
TO EFFECTIVE
JOB FINDING

TOM WASHINGTON

Mount Vernon Press
Bellevue, Washington

The editor was Tina Blade (Seattle, Washington)
The cover design and book design was by Charles Fuhrman (Forest Knolls, California)
The typesetting was by Steve Wozenski (Fairfax, California)
The illustrations and cartoons were drawn by Edith Allgood (Berkeley, California)
Inputting, editing, and proofreading has been provided by Andrew Dillman (Seattle, Washington)

ISBN 0-931213-08-8

Library of Congress Catalog Number: 92-90488

To my wife Lois, who has provided invaluable counsel and advice over the years, and particularly during the writing of both *Resume Power* and *The Hunt*. Without her support, in so many ways, neither would have been possible.

ACKNOWLEDGMENTS

I want to particularly express thanks to Bernard Haldane, the real pioneer in the field of career development and job finding. Virtually everything written today regarding transferable skills and the hidden job market comes directly from his work in the 1960s, 70s, and 80s. He is the foundation upon which so many have built. It has been my privilege to have known him for the past fourteen years. His work continues to be vibrant and important.

Besides Bernard, I have been most influenced by the work of John Crystal, Richard Bolles, Tom Jackson, Howard Figler, and Richard Lathrop.

In writing *The Hunt* I have borrowed ideas freely from Bernard Haldane (*Career Satisfaction And Success*), Richard Bolles (*What Color Is Your Parachute*), Anthony Medley (*Sweaty Palms*), Paul Green, one of the pioneers of behavior-based interviewing, Howard Figler (*The Complete Job Search Handbook*), Tom Jackson (*Guerrilla Tactics In The New Job Market*), Richard Lathrop (*Who's Hiring Who*), Donald Asher (*The Overnight Resume*), Arthur Miller and Ralph Mattson (*The Truth About You*), Jack Chapman (*How To Make $1000 A Minute: Negotiating Your Salaries And Raises*), Robert Half (*How To Get A Job In This Crazy World*), Richard Irish (*Go Hire Yourself An Employer*), and Howard Freedman (*How To Get The Headhunter To Call*). I have borrowed and synthesized ideas from these people and for that I am most grateful. Each has contributed greatly to the field of career planning, career development, and job finding.

Much thanks goes to several special people who provided extensive advice in the creation of *The Hunt.* Gary Kanter, my associate and friend for the past four years gave me many ideas which have strengthened its quality. Tim Ainge, Dick Milligan, Robin Ryan, Lois Washington, and Wanda Washington provided extremely valuable advice on major portions of the book and freely gave of their time. Diane DeWitt and Michael Grubiak have been especially supportive over the years and I owe them a great deal.

I wish to thank the many friends who willingly read portions and gave me much valuable input during various stages of writing: Howard Babroff, Greg Firnstahl, Beau Hamilton, Julie Hull, Amy Jensen, Katherine Kushell, Erick Peterson, Joan Peterson, David Roy, Bruce Thompson, Nat Washington Jr., Debbie Williams, Ron Williams, and Debbie Wilson.

Edith Allgood, Tina Blade, Andy Dillman, Charles Fuhrman, and Steve Wozenski put in many hours on the editing and production side and enabled me to meet my deadlines.

CONTENTS

Part One

FINDING THE JOB THAT'S RIGHT FOR YOU

Part Two

CREATING A HIGH IMPACT RESUME

Part Three

WINNING AT INTERVIEWING

Appendices

HOW TO USE THIS BOOK

The Hunt was written with the goal of providing a highly comprehensive and complete book on job finding. I wanted to utilize my years of experience to provide practical advice, advice that really works out there in the real world. You could say I want to give people the street smarts they need to succeed in a job search. Because I wanted *The Hunt* to be complete, that necessitated a fairly long book. This is not a book, however, to be read from cover to cover. Feel free to jump around, or if you come to something which does not apply to you, simply skip over it. Before you really get started, flip through the book to get a feel for what's in it and how it's put together.

Having worked closely with hundreds of people going through job hunts, I have a good sense of what works and what doesn't. I've tried to give you the best ideas, techniques, and strategies available today. Over the years I have borrowed ideas from many experts, tried them out with my clients, and found that some worked better than others. I have modified those ideas, techniques, or strategies so that they will work in the 90s.

I encourage you to try the ideas as they have been presented in *The Hunt*. They are time tested and they work. But if they don't work exactly as you would like them to, modify them to fit your own personality or situation. Be creative. Try new things.

Make this job search an adventure. If you do, you'll have some fun, and you'll probably wind up with a better job.

Happy hunting.

Part One
Finding The Job That's Right For You

THE HIDDEN JOB MARKET

Experience tells me that people hate job hunting. Most would rather have a root canal—without the Novocaine—than look for a job. The anxiety and frustration that most experience is enough to keep many in a job that they detest.

Job hunting doesn't have to be like that. It's impossible to eliminate all of the anxiety and frustration of a job search, but I'll show you techniques and strategies that will transform the job search into a process that is frequently enjoyable and always challenging.

This book will enable you to join the ranks of the top 5% of all job seekers. You'll be doing things your competitors do, but you'll do them better. You'll also do things which they should be doing, but don't. You'll do all the big things right, and you'll do the little things right. Because you'll track down job openings the competition doesn't even know about, you'll face less competition for those positions. You'll expend a lot of energy to obtain each interview, but you'll make the most of each opportunity and truly sell yourself. You'll get the kinds of offers you deserve.

Why is job hunting so hard, and why do people dread it so? For some reason, most people assume that the government or *someone* has created a job hunting system that helps job seekers and employers find each other quickly and efficiently. Unfortunately, there is no such system. Instead what we have are techniques and services (mailing resumes, answering want ads, and using employment agencies) which work well for a fortunate few, but poorly for most.

The Hidden Job Market

The best way to look for jobs is to access what has come to be called the *hidden job market*. First identified by Bernard Haldane in the 1950s, the hidden job market simply describes the fact that 70% of all job openings are never advertised or listed with employment agencies, headhunters, college placement offices, or state employment services. In addition, in some competitive fields like advertising and public relations, less than 5% of jobs are advertised or listed. This fact surprises many people and explains why traditional job finding strategies work so poorly for most people. *The Hunt* will show you how to find a job using the Systematic Job Search techniques. The Systematic Job Search is composed of strategies and techniques developed by pioneers in the field, including Bernard Haldane, John Crystal, and Richard Bolles. I have adapted, refined, and organized these strategies and techniques in order to make them easy for you to apply to your job search.

HUMAN NATURE & THE HIDDEN JOB MARKET

To understand the hidden job market you have to understand that it exists because of human nature. Employers like known entities. That's why so many jobs are filled internally. That's also why job hunters who succeed in meeting hiring managers get hired for jobs that the public doesn't even know exist. *The Hunt* will help you understand the variety of ways in which human nature affects the hidden job market. You'll then use this understanding to conduct a job search that is much more focused, efficient, and rewarding than the old system used by the majority of job seekers. Yes, the old system is easy. It's easy because it takes so little time and effort to mail off dozens of resumes and call an employment agency once a week. It's easy, but it doesn't work well.

The principles of human nature explain how most people really get hired. Relatively few job openings are ever advertised since advertising a position is generally a *last* resort. In fact, a major government study established that the vast majority of employers do not advertise a *single* position in any given year. When a position opens up, the supervisor immediately begins considering people he or she knows, including people who took the initiative to meet the manager weeks or months earlier. If no one comes to mind, the supervisor may ask people in the department to refer friends or contacts. If that doesn't work, the manager may contact business associates for referrals. Finally, the supervisor may choose to advertise or list the opening with an employment agency. But most jobs are filled before that need arises.

Many companies search first in their own ranks to fill a position. Because it's not uncommon for this process to take a month, if you call or get referred by someone at just the right time, you may become the only outsider to be interviewed.

I don't advocate that you ignore the traditional job hunting techniques. Instead, I'll show you when to use those techniques and how to use them more effectively. Then I'll take you beyond those techniques and show you how to use the hidden job market to your benefit. That's what the Systematic Job Search is all about.

The Importance Of Attitude

To conduct a successful job search you need the right attitude. The right attitude is one that says, "If it's going to be, it's up to me." No one can do it better than you. No one cares as much about your career as you. While you will receive a tremendous amount of help from other people, you are the one who must put in the many hours it will take to get the job you really want. Although you don't know just how or when it will happen, your efforts will set in motion a chain of events which will result in your next job. You will call just the right person, or you will be referred to someone who knows the right someone, or your resume will cross the right desk at just the right time. It is a never ending delight to me to look back at a successful job search to see how a person's efforts made everything possible. It could be a person who made a hundred phone calls and met 40 potential employers, but only one was the right one. Had the job seeker's efforts been less intense, perhaps the chain of events would not have happened. Perhaps it would have taken another two months for the right combination of events to occur.

Believing that if it's going to be, it's up to me, does not preclude faith, prayer, and trusting God. If you trust God, you will find that doors are opened and doors are closed for you. You won't like it when doors are closed, but if you truly trust God, you will realize that there is a better job out there waiting for you. You will grieve over your loss briefly and then go on. Over the years I've seen doors open up sooner for those who were willing to work harder and smarter.

Willingness To Do Things You Do Not Enjoy Doing

Another attitude you need to develop is the willingness to do things which you do not enjoy doing. Albert Gray, a wealthy businessman in the early 1900s, was often sought out to give a talk he called *The Common Denominator of Success*. In this talk he described his search to discover why some people are more successful than others. He examined whether successful people worked harder, had more education, or were smarter than those who were less successful. He rejected those and many more explanations before he discovered the answer. He concluded that people were successful simply because they were *willing* to do the things less successful people were unwilling to do. He further stated that people who succeeded did not enjoy doing these things any more than the people who were less successful. The successful people seemed to possess a vision which motivated them and gave them a willingness to do things others would not do.

In all endeavors, especially a job search, there are undesirable tasks which only some people are willing to do. I'm going to ask you to do some things which you almost assuredly would like to avoid. In fact, virtually every job seeker tries to avoid these things. I will not ask you to *like* to do these things. I will merely ask that you be *willing* to do them. These include calling employers by phone and asking for brief appointments, sending thank-you notes to everyone who has helped you, and saying positive things about yourself during interviews. Doing these things will make the difference between a short or a long job search and between a great job and a mediocre job.

In addition to a good attitude, you need awareness. You need to realize that it is not simply the best-qualified people who get hired, but the ones who *know how* to get hired. This book will help you develop that awareness.

TECHNIQUES AND TOOLS

Numerous approaches have been developed over the years to help job seekers. Some of these include mailing resumes, filling out application forms, and making cold calls by phone and in person. Services that job seekers traditionally use include employment agencies, headhunters, college placement offices, and state employment services. While these techniques, strategies and services do not work very well for most people, each has its benefits. I'll share my insights and observations to help you determine which techniques, tools, and services you might use most effectively in your job search.

THE RESUME

When people decide to seriously look for a job, they immediately begin working on their resume. Usually they pull out the old resume and simply add their latest job description, with little thought given to whether the entire, overall effect of the resume will help sell them into the types of positions they are now seeking.

I believe that everyone should have a resume. I also know that creating a strong resume will require that you spend 5–10 hours writing and rewriting. A resume is important for a number of reasons. It forces you to focus on what you want, it can open doors for interviews, it can help guide an interview by causing employers to ask questions about your results, and it can help employers remember you weeks after meeting you.

In Part Two you'll learn how to write a resume that will get you interviews at a rate many times the norm. To accomplish that, the resume must be well-written and concise, it must be visually attractive, and it must concentrate on results and contributions rather than on mere dates, job titles, and duties. Pages 237 to 241 will provide the details on how to use your resume during your job search.

The major advantage to using resumes is that once the resume is completed, it can be put to use quickly and inexpensively. People use resumes primarily to respond to want ads and to mail to employers unsolicited.

The major drawback of resumes is that most people must send out lots of them to get an interview or two, and many people fail to get any interviews, even for jobs that they thought their background matched perfectly. Very few resumes make employers eager to meet the sender. In fact, a well-documented study indicated that companies received 245 resumes for every interview offered. When you figure an average of six people interviewed for each position, it takes approximately 1,470 resumes to land a position. These are not good odds. Despite this poor success rate, people continue to mail out masses of resumes and, in turn, receive masses of rejections.

I rarely recommend the mass mailing of 250–500 resumes suggested by some. For most people there simply are not 250 organizations that they would be interested in. Furthermore, because this machine gun approach does not work for most people, I recommend instead a rifle approach with a distinct target. This strategy obtains better results. For that approach, however, a marketing letter is a much better tool than a resume. A marketing letter resembles a cover letter and typically highlights experience and results rather than dates and names of employers. See pages 254 to 259 for examples of marketing letters.

What makes the marketing letter distinct is that it is generally sent to a specific person, and it closes with a statement that the employer will be called in a few days in order to set up a brief, face-to-face appointment. If that fails (and our experience tells us it will result in an appointment 40–80% of the time), then the resume is sent with a combination cover letter/thank-you note. Because the thank-you portion makes the cover letter much more personal, and because you've gained valuable information from the call, you will be able to specify various skills and strengths that are needed and valued by that employer. Thus you will have greater impact, and are more likely to be remembered when you follow up five weeks later, or when a position becomes available any time in the next six months.

WANT ADS

Almost all job seekers should read the want ads. After a little practice you can get through the Sunday edition of a major city newspaper in under a half-hour. Read the entire want ad section from A–Z—good jobs are sometimes placed in unusual categories. For each position that looks interesting you may spend an hour preparing a customized cover letter. Looking through the want ads can get depressing at times—they are not a lot of fun to read—but they can be helpful. About 25% of the people who use the want ads will find their jobs that way.

People often feel frustrated with the want ads, and for good reason. The want ads never present a good cross-section of the jobs that are available on any given day. Instead, the advertised positions tend to be poor-quality jobs, or jobs which are so rigid in their requirements that few people qualify. These types of jobs are rarely filled by internal or external referrals, and therefore advertising becomes the option of choice. Of course there are also some good jobs advertised that are not overly specialized, but these are in a definite minority.

There are also some types of jobs that are virtually never advertised because all the potential candidates make direct contact with employers. That's what happens in industries such as advertising, public relations, television, and radio, among others. That also explains why some people are telling their friends that the reason they haven't found a job yet is because there aren't any. They know there aren't any jobs because none has been advertised. What these people *don't* know, and what you *do* know, is that those jobs do exist. And the people who get those jobs are the ones who practice the principles of the Systematic Job Search.

In fact some people seem to believe that there must be a law that requires companies to advertise positions. A client once related an interesting story which demonstrates this point. She was leaving her management position. Because she was so highly valued, the organization allowed her to handle the initial screening of applicants for the position. Three months earlier she had met two people who were interested in her type of work. She confided in them that she would be leaving in the next few months. While she was accepting applications for her position, she called the two people who had expressed interest. Both were still interested, but neither had taken any action because they had not seen the position advertised. The position had been posted internally, however, and was never going to be advertised because there were plenty of qualified people responding without advertising.

APPLICATION FORMS

Employers like application forms because they provide the type of information which makes it easy to screen people out. For example, the application form makes it easy to spot people with gaps in their employment and to discover why a person left a position. Usually so little space is provided for job descriptions on an application form that you wonder if the employer really wants to know much about what you've done. While the resume is your document and gives you the best opportunity to sell yourself on paper, the application is clearly the employer's document. Since most people treat application forms rather casually, you will stand out when you use the application to sell yourself and make the most of your background.

People fill out applications to apply for specific jobs which have been advertised or posted, or to simply let an employer know that they are available if certain types of jobs open up. Filling out applications can take considerable time. If you utilize the concepts of the Systematic Job Search, you will seldom fill out application forms except for those jobs you actually get interviews for. If most of your appointments are with the people who have the power to hire, rather than with personnel department staffers, you will rarely fill out an application except as a final formality after you have been offered the position.

My experience has shown me that merely going around filling out application forms is not an effective job search strategy and is a waste of time for most people. It can work well for some, however, particularly for clerical workers and those who work in factories.

If you intend to fill out lots of application forms, do it the smart way. First, identify all of the organizations you may be interested in and put their names and addresses on 4 x 6 notecards. When you're through filling out your cards, arrange the organizations by their geographical location. Then, target a certain area each day and concentrate on visiting organizations within that specific area.

Next, obtain an application form and take it home with you. Fill out the form carefully and thoroughly. This will be your model for all of the other forms you fill out. It will cut in half the time you'll spend filling out application forms. In addition, once you're working from a model, the forms will be more complete and neater. Since very little space is generally provided for you to describe your duties, write small, using your resume to help you compose. Even when writing small, however, you probably won't be able to include everything.

Although you should leave a resume with the application form, do not say, "See attached resume," and then leave the job description sections of the application form blank. The resume may get detached from the application. Worst of all, that tactic is often viewed by those in personnel as one of the biggest sins committed by job seekers. So, never do it. Instead, concentrate on your key duties and take your time to write your model job descriptions.

When creating your model, be sure you get the current addresses and phone numbers of your former employers and former supervisors. If a supervisor you'd get a good reference from has gone to another organization, track that person down and let him or her know to expect calls from prospective employers. If your former boss has left and you would not get a good reference from that person, identify someone else in the organization that you may have worked for at one time. Or list your boss' boss if you believe that person would give you a good reference.

If you are going to visit many organizations, make the most of it. Fill out the application on location. As you do so, see what you can learn about the organization. Are the people friendly and helpful? While you shouldn't judge the whole organization by the few people that you come in contact with, paying attention can provide you with some insight about the organization.

If you are applying for a specific position, make sure that everything you include will help sell you into that position.

Tips On Filling Out Application Forms

Take your sample application with you at all times. It eliminates your need to memorize phone numbers and addresses, and ensures that your application will be well written and thorough. Remember, an application can be filled out in half the time when you have a sample to work from.

Write or print as neatly as you can. Employers make decisions based on impressions. A messy application causes unfavorable impressions. Always write in ink. If you mess something up, ask for another form.

Be truthful in all your statements. Most applications specify that providing false information is grounds for immediate dismissal. Often there are positive ways to explain an embarrassing past such as having been fired. People often inflate their past salaries when completing applications, hoping to obtain a higher starting salary. The risk of being perceived as dishonest, however, is not worth it. Some companies will contact your last employer after you've been hired. If you've fudged on your application, it could mean losing your new position.

Most applications ask your reason for leaving each employer. Keep your responses positive with statements like, "Offered higher salary and greater opportunity for advancement," rather than using statements like, "Couldn't get along with boss," or "Wasn't getting anywhere in the company." If you have been laid off due to cutbacks, say so with phrases like "Reduction in work force," rather than using negative terms like "fired." If you have been fired from a recent position, develop as positive a response as you can. In this section of the application, employers are also looking for evidence of job hopping. If they see a number of statements like, "Boss and I did not agree on how to run the department," employers will assume that the same problem is likely to arise if you work for their organization.

If asked, "Are you willing to relocate?" indicate "yes," unless you are applying for a clerical position, or one that you know would never require you to relocate. Applications often ask if you are willing to travel. Again, indicate "yes" on the application, but in an interview determine how much travel would be involved.

It is illegal to ask certain questions on an application. Know your rights! Questions concerning marital status are illegal. An application may ask if outside activities will interfere with your work schedule, but it cannot ask how your children are taken care of or whether a husband or wife is employed. Questions about having children and questions about pregnancy are also illegal.

Some applications will ask about disabilities. Such questions may be worded in this fashion: "Describe a handicap, major illness, or injury which might require accommodation," or "Do you have any handicaps or health problems that may affect your ability to perform the job applied for?" You must list only those problems which would affect your ability to perform the job. For example, if you have a bad back, but the job you are applying for would require only light lifting, you would not mention the back problem on the application or during interviews.

Space for listing professional, trade, business, or civic activities is often provided. Most will have a statement telling you to leave off any organizations which indicate race, color, religion, sex, national origin, age, handicap, or veteran's status. Even if such a statement is not included, those types of organizations should usually be left off. Exceptions would be those you really want an employer to know about because they will help sell you. Women should feel free to list organization such as Women in Management, but would leave off politically-based organizations such as the National Organization of Women (NOW). Men would also leave off the names of controversial organizations they belong to. List offices you've held. The space can also be used to list licenses or various types of awards or honors.

Applications which ask for general information give you an opportunity to say anything you want that will sell you. The section may be worded, "State any additional information you feel may be helpful to us in considering your application." Use such sections to your best advantage.

PERSONNEL DEPARTMENTS

Many people send out hundreds of resumes addressed to the personnel or human resources departments of organizations, typically with little success. It is not surprising since personnel can respond to a resume only if a suitable opening exists. If a position is not open when the resume is received, the resume will be filed either alphabetically or by job category. And once your resume makes it to the file cabinet, the likelihood of it seeing the light of day again are about as great as winning the lottery. I won't say that resumes and applications are never sifted through, but it is rare.

With these points in mind, when conducting a systematic job search, avoid personnel as much as possible. Personnel almost never hires people; it screens in or screens out applicants—usually out. When a position is advertised, it is usually a personnel clerk who screens out the 50–250 resumes that pour in. The personnel clerk has the job description in one hand and your resume in the other. If the job description calls for five years of experience and you have three, you end up in the reject pile even though you may be ideally suited for the job. Personnel clerks are murder on career changers who have tons of related experience but no direct experience.

Deal directly with department managers and other hiring authorities whenever possible. Nevertheless, when you must deal with personnel, always be friendly and tactful. Do everything you can to make all those you deal with want to help you. If you must go through a screening interview, make the screener your ally. Demonstrate that you have all of the energy, personality, and potential to succeed in the position.

EMPLOYMENT AGENCIES

Employment agencies act as brokers by matching qualified applicants with organizations needing to fill positions. The applicant never pays a penny unless a position is accepted which was arranged by the agency. Within 30 days, a fee, typically ranging from 10–20% of the first year's salary, must be paid by the individual or the employer. Although agencies do have fee-paid positions (where the employer agrees in advance to pay the full fee), most are paid by the individual who is placed. Employment agencies are regulated in almost all states and there are certain things they can and cannot do.

Approximately 24% of the people who use agencies find their positions through the help of an agency. Agencies work best for clerical workers, placing about 17% of all clerical workers.

Not everyone should use private employment agencies. Most tend to fill clerical and entry-level positions, with a few filling other types of positions. In most cases, if you are willing to market yourself by calling employers and asking for appointments, you will do better on your own.

It will help to understand how employment agencies operate. First, an agency needs job orders. That is why most employment counselors make 30–80 calls a day and may be on the phone 75% of the time. As they call, they will typically mention a specific candidate and ask if the employer could use such a person. Usually the answer is no. Then the counselor will ask if there are any openings at the moment. If so, the counselor will ask if the organization would pay the fee for a placement. If not, the counselor will ask for permission to send candidates. With a "yes" answer, the counselor will learn as much about the job as possible. Unfortunately, the job description is often sketchy, and in fact, the employer may not even be clear on what is needed. Ideally the counselor will get a sense of the culture of the organization and discover what personality type would fit in best with the organization. Ideally, the counselor will also know what the employer truly needs in the way of skills and experience. The reality, however, is often far from the ideal.

Once a job order is obtained, any of the counselors in the agency can fill that position with one of their clients. The counselor who obtained the job order may act as the contact person and arrange the interviews. Since there is a tendency for counselors to want to send their clients out on as many interviews as possible, someone must determine who will be sent. The person who obtained the order will usually fill that role.

The counselor must then call and sell the employer on meeting each of the candidates the agency has selected. The counselor will usually sell each of the people over the phone, and if necessary, will send their resumes. Ultimately the employer decides which ones to interview.

Employment counselors also obtain job orders by looking at the want ads. When a company places its own ad, agencies will typically call and ask for permission to send candidates.

The person who got the job order and the person whose client got the job will each receive about 25% of the fee, with the remaining 50% going to the agency to cover overhead.

The jobs that agencies fill are typically in the $15,000 to $35,000 range, although they may go up to $55,000. The high end, for a firm placing office personnel, would be about $55,000 for a senior administrative assistant or executive secretary. Those placing salespeople or lower-level managers would also approach the $55,000 range, but the vast majority of jobs will be far below that.

If an agency has an exclusive on a position, the employer will take only candidates sent by that agency. More frequently, however, several agencies will be vying to fill the same position, so competition can get intense.

Employers use agencies for various reasons. When the employer is prepared to pay the fee, which would usually be $5,000 on a $25,000 a year job, it is only because the employer believes that it will be worth the investment. The employer saves on the expense of advertising and a reduction of screening time.

Of course, when the applicant will pay the fee, employers are obtaining the screening work basically for free. That's a good price *if* the quality of screening is high.

Agencies have received a lot of criticism over the years. Because of past abuses, state regulators require that any jobs that are advertised must accurately describe real job orders. Too often in the past, applicants came to an agency only to find that the job they were interested in had just been filled. Unfortunately, among some firms those bait-and-switch tactics still exist.

Agencies cannot afford to advertise all of the positions they have, so they try to draw applicants to their place of business through just a few ads. The ads are deliberately written to make the position sound exciting. Most of the positions, however, are not.

If you see a position which is interesting, call the agency and ask to speak to a counselor. Since you are interested in the position, not particularly in the agency itself, get as much information about the position as possible and find out if you would qualify. The counselor will ask that you come down to the office so you can speak in person. Only by getting you to come to their office and sign their contract can they hope to earn any money off you. Resist those efforts until you have enough information. Of course you can understand their not wanting to divulge much information, but they should be able to indicate whether you would be a strong candidate. If the person won't provide any worthwhile information I would suggest saying something like this: "I am interested in this position, but I am not willing to come to your office unless you can at least tell me something about it. I'm not asking who the employer is. If you are unable to give me some information, I'll simply look elsewhere." Say it tactfully but firmly. You could also ask to speak to the office manager. That will either cause the counselor to give you more information, or perhaps the office manager will supply the information you want.

Employment agency counselors work strictly on commission. The pressure is on and it takes a toll on counselors. Although some stay in the business for years, the average agency staffer has less than six months' experience. That's not enough time to develop valuable contacts. Because of the high turnover rate, the field has not achieved a professional status. That some desperate staffers have resorted to deception has further damaged the reputation of such agencies.

Because agencies depend on a fast turnover of applicants, they are looking for the most easy-to-place candidates. If you haven't been placed in four weeks, interest in you diminishes.

Agencies have lists of job orders to fill and all too frequently will try to push you into interviewing for known openings, whether it is really what you're looking for or not. If you show signs of being picky (which you should), many agency counselors will drop you. They simply aren't willing to make calls to locate a specialized job just for you.

Tips For Using An Agency

Even though there are certain problems associated with employment agencies, there are some highly experienced and competent agency counselors out there. Your challenge is to find one, sell yourself to that person, and establish an understanding of how the two of you are going to benefit each other.

Although some agencies have better reputations than others, you are really not looking for a specific agency, but a specific counselor. Ask friends and people you know who they've used. Don't just get names, learn about the type of relationship which was formed. Determine if that's the type of person you would work well with. If you can't get a referral from a friend, call the personnel department of a few companies and ask who they use. Get the name of the counselor they work with rather than just the name of the agency.

There are numerous advantages to finding a good counselor. A good counselor will try to identify your strengths and understand your personality so you can be better matched with the job's requirements and the culture of the organization. A good counselor will refer you only for the type of position you've indicated you want.

Unfortunately, really good counselors are too few and far between. Too often I hear stories like this: "She doesn't seem to listen when I describe what I'm looking for. The next day she'll call up to say an interview has been arranged, but the job is nothing like what I'm seeking. Then she gets angry when I turn it down and says I'm too picky." I've also heard stories where the counselor told the job seeker that he or she must be willing to accept a salary that is lower than the salary the person was seeking. If you know you're worth a certain amount, stick to that amount and simply tell the counselor to contact you only about jobs which meet your salary requirement. After experiences like these, too many of my clients say that they will never use an agency again. This type of intimidation is unfortunate. Since job seekers often have low self-esteem already, to play on this low self-esteem is cruel.

If you can't find a specific counselor to use, try to find a good agency. Study the want ads and determine which ones seem to have the most jobs similar to those you are looking for. Then ask to speak to the office manager and ask who that agency's best counselor is. Make it clear that by best you do not necessarily mean the highest paid. Ask for the person who will be most helpful to you and who will truly help you get the right job. Once you have made it clear what you want, trust the judgment of the office manager.

If you do not take this approach you will simply go to an agency, fill out their form and be assigned to the next counselor whose turn it is to see a client. That's not how you want to do it.

Once you identify the person you'll work with, set up an appointment. You'll be asked to fill out their "application" form, which, when signed, also becomes their contract with you. The counselor will then ask questions, almost like any personnel screener would. You should treat it as an important interview. If you sell yourself well, this person will be working *for* you. Present yourself as a marketable commodity. After all, the number of phone calls this person makes on your behalf will be directly proportional to how likely the counselor believes he or she can place you. In all other types of interview situations I recommend that you avoid discussing salary requirements, but when working with an employment agency counselor or a headhunter, the person simply has to know what your expectations are. Be prepared to discuss your salary needs candidly.

Ask the counselor what he or she will do on your behalf and ask what you can do to make the counselor's job easier and more productive. Set yourself apart from all the other people this counselor will meet this week. Make this counselor want to help *you*. Yes, this counselor would like to receive a commission from placing you, but it is possible to make this person take a personal interest in you as well. You will receive more attention from the counselor if you can create this type of relationship with him or her. Tell the counselor that if you get good results you will be glad to refer your friends.

Show the counselor how focused you are. Tell the counselor exactly what you want to do and what types of jobs would be attractive. Also provide a list of approximately 100 companies and indicate that those are the ones you will be contacting on your own. This will help prevent confusion later. If the counselor mentions you to a company and you also apply to that company on your own, the agency might still seek to collect a fee from you, claiming that you obtained an interview through their efforts. Tell the counselor that you are willing to consider companies other than those on your list, but you have developed this list on your own and will market yourself to those companies.

Tell the counselor you intend to stay in touch, then call weekly. Make the calls short, but ask if any interesting positions have opened up. If you see an ad which looks interesting, call the counselor and express your interest. The counselor may have had a reason for not referring you to that position, but if you indicate an interest, the counselor may recommend you for an interview.

Typically the counselor will arrange an interview with the employer and then confirm the time with you. At that point the counselor will give you details about the job and provide some vague information about the firm, but will not reveal the name. On the day of the interview the counselor will generally invite you to the office to prep you for the interview. At that time you will be told who the employer is. Agencies are very protective of their leads and often will not reveal them over the phone. Once you've been out on a couple of interviews and have demonstrated that you are committed to working with the counselor, you might ask the counselor to give you the name of the organization sooner so you can do your own research. Although the counselor will likely hesitate, he or she may give you the information.

Cooperate fully with the counselor. For example, the counselor will ask you to call shortly after the interview to discuss how it went. The counselor will then speak to the employer and ask the same thing. The counselor will be working as an intermediary to help the two of you form a sort of marriage. Your cooperation will help the counselor do his or her work more effectively.

Before an interview, learn everything you possibly can about the organization from the counselor. Ask about what types of questions you will likely be asked and what the employer's hot buttons are. If other people from the agency have already been referred, ask what types of questions were asked so you can better prepare. Also ask to be the last person interviewed. If that's not possible, at least ask not to be the first person interviewed. Being the last person interviewed is always beneficial because you are the one best remembered. It also enables the employer to compare you to everyone who went before you. Assuming you did a good job of selling yourself, you will be more likely to be invited back for a second interview than if you had been the first one interviewed.

Read the employment agency's contract carefully. Make sure you understand everything in it before you sign. Because they are regulated by the state they operate in, most agencies will have a contract that is worded very similarly to the others.

You should know whether you or the employer will pay the fee. If you will pay the fee you may be able to negotiate this point with your new employer. You might ask the employer to pay half the fee. Or you might ask the employer to reimburse you for the fee (or half the fee) after you have been with the organization for a year. It is also important that you know what you owe if you stay only 30, 60, or 90 days. Generally, you will pay 20% of your earnings if you stay under 60 days, but the full fee if you stay over 61 days. The full fee could be equal to more than a month's salary. Since terminations often take place during the so called 90-day probationary period, if you have doubts about the sincerity of the employer, your ability to handle the job, or your willingness to stay for a year, the best thing may be to turn down the position.

The contract for many agencies will read, "I agree to pay the full fee if within six months of a referral to an employer, I accept a position with that employer as a result of that referral, even though it may not be the position originally discussed." The key phrase is "as a result of that referral." Determine in advance whether the opportunity to interview for the new position was due to a previous contact that had been arranged by the counselor.

In an attempt to inform you about employment agencies, I may have sounded fairly cautionary. To all the good and reputable agencies out there, I apologize. Nevertheless, in every service business there are those who take advantage of people who are vulnerable. This is as true of career and job finding counselors as it is of car repair shops. Because of this, it is wise to subscribe to the notion, "Let the buyer beware." An educated consumer is a good consumer. Use this information to decide whether to use agencies, and if you use them, how to use them to your advantage.

Who Should Use An Agency

No one *needs* to use an employment agency. However, it may be in your best interest to use one. For instance, you may want to use an agency if you are working full-time and if you are in a field which is commonly serviced by agencies. Do not, however, limit yourself to the use of agencies. Only 25% of those who use agencies actually get a job through them.

If you use an agency, don't rely on it as your sole job search resource or strategy. My recommendation is to treat an employment agency as merely one resource among several. You should still develop a list of at least 100 employers and do your best to get in to see the person with the power to hire.

HEADHUNTERS

Headhunters are also known as executive recruiters and as executive search firms. Headhunters act as brokers for management, executive, or technical positions. Most of the jobs they fill are $50,000 and above. In most states headhunters are unregulated because employers pay the full fee, which can range from 15% to 30% of the first year's earnings.

Most headhunters have had experience in the fields for which they recruit people. They usually have an intimate knowledge of the industry or field, speak its language, and have plenty of contacts they've developed over time. They tend to specialize by industry or field. Headhunters who specialize in an industry, such as forest products or biotechnology, will recruit for all types of jobs which exist within that industry. Those who specialize in a field, on the other hand, will recruit for very specific types of jobs, such as accounting, programming, or marketing. Because headhunters' fees are paid by the client company, their loyalty is to the company rather than to the job candidate. Many recruiters do, however, form strong ties with candidates as well.

Headhunters operate in a variety of ways. Some are paid a retainer rather than a commission. They receive payment whether a placement is made or not. A client company will ask such a recruiter to locate the best person in the country for an executive position. The recruiter is guaranteed a certain fee plus recruiting expenses. The recruiter will be looking for the fast movers and will try to entice them out of one company and into the company the recruiter represents. The recruiter will initially screen applicants by phone. When the choice has been narrowed down to two or three, the recruiter will either fly out to meet the candidates or have the candidates flown in to meet him or her. These types of searches are often conducted when secrecy is essential or when a company wants the very best person for that position. Such searches usually involve positions paying over $100,000.

Most recruiters are not on retainer. They are called contingency recruiters and receive a commission only after a placement is made. Sometimes they will be given exclusives, meaning they are the only firm involved in the search for three top candidates. More often, however, several recruiting firms will have been given the same job order and are all busily trying to recruit top candidates.

Contingency recruiters usually do all of their work over the phone, and rarely meet the people they place, or the executives to whom they refer candidates. The biggest part of this type of recruiter's day is spent seeking job orders. Considerable time is also spent reviewing the 100–300 resumes which typically arrive in a week. The resumes of those with interesting backgrounds are filed using manual or computerized systems for easy retrieval.

Once a job order is obtained, considerable effort goes into locating just the right person. Occasionally, ads are placed by the headhunter, but more frequently the headhunter spends his or her time calling managers trying to get leads on who might be a good candidate. Frequently, a headhunter will call a manager on the pretense of asking for leads, when what the headhunter really wants to determine is whether that particular manager would be suitable and interested.

Headhunting firms suffer from the same turnover problems as employment agencies. Probably 80% of all recruiters drop out in their first year. Although some recruiters do very well, it's a tough way to make a living. While their 30% fees seem high, many of their searches result in no placement, which means no fee. Those who stay in the field more than two years will generally make between $45,000 and $90,000, although some make over $200,000 per year. Those who stay in the field for over five years typically make a career out of it.

How To Make Use Of A Headhunter

Before using headhunters, you need to decide whether you would be well-served by using them. Generally, they can help only those who have at least five years experience in their present industry and who intend to stay in their current field. Recruiters are virtually never able or willing to place career changers. That does not mean that career changers are not marketable, it just means that headhunters know they won't be able to charge their 30% fees to place them.

If you are going to contact one headhunter, you might as well contact several. You can find *The Directory of Executive Recruiters* at most libraries. The directory contains lists of recruiters and also indicates their specialties. Don't limit yourself to local headhunters; virtually all of them do national searches, and many of their placements will be outside of their own metropolitan areas.

Do what you can to obtain names of specific headhunters. Then, send them a resume and cover letter. Call the recruiting firm and tell the receptionist that you are sending your resume and you want to address it to the person who handles your field. Since firms are generally composed of specialists, there will usually be only one or two who handle each field or industry. Indicate in your cover letter that you will be following up with a call.

Do not be bothered if the recruiter will not take your follow-up call. If recruiters spoke to everyone who sent a resume, they would never get any recruiting done. You can be assured, however, that your resume will be reviewed. If the recruiter thinks you are marketable, your resume will be saved and catalogued for later reference. If you do speak to the recruiter by phone, take only a short time to sell yourself.

If you live in the same city as the recruiter, ask for a face-to-face appointment, but do not be offended if the recruiter declines. Just tell yourself that you did your best. You were willing to make the extra effort. If you don't get an appointment, you will be able to devote more time to something else.

If you want headhunters to call you, get active in your industry or do something to obtain some notoriety. It can be as simple as becoming a chairperson for a committee in your local trade or professional association. One step up is to become a board member. Or you might write articles for your trade publications. Find ways to get quoted in local or national business magazines. Become a recognized expert.

Don't expect too much from headhunters. I have gotten enough feedback from clients to know that many recruiters come across as blunt, self-important, and cold. There are many other recruiters who treat each person they come in contact with in a cordial and friendly manner. My suggestion is to care only about results. If you've heard that a recruiter is good, excuse his or her idiosyncrasies.

Once you have made contact with a recruiter, send a thank-you note. Beyond that, there is rarely the need for further contact. You are in the system and nothing will happen until the right job comes up. Besides, since a recruiter may work actively on only 20–40 searches per year, the odds of the right job coming up with any particular recruiter are not great. The goal is to complete this part of your job search in the first week so you can concentrate on other aspects of the search.

UNITED STATES EMPLOYMENT SERVICE (USES)

Each state runs a federally-funded employment service known as USES. Most larger cities have a branch. In rural areas they will be more spread out. About one-third of the 2,000 offices refer to themselves as Job Service. The primary service they offer is a job bank that is available to anyone who is unemployed. USES has job developers who visit employers to explain the benefits of having USES screen people for them. Employers then call to give job listings.The service is free to employers and unemployed job seekers.

USES screens applicants to make sure they possess the basic qualifications the employer is looking for. USES counselors then call the employer and sell the applicant in order to arrange an appointment.

Applicants find out about jobs by looking at the listings which are posted on a bulletin board in the USES office, or by viewing the job listings on microfiche. The job listing includes the job title, basic duties and required experience, the city or area the job is in, and the salary range. It will not provide the name of the employer.

To get referred, an applicant must then write the job on a form and wait his or her turn. The counselor will then look up the job in the counselor's microfiche, which contains additional information. If the counselor is relatively certain the person would not be accepted for an interview, the counselor will explain why. If a person insists, the counselor may call, but will probably not make a heroic effort to obtain an interview. The counselor has the name of the company, address, phone number, and the name of the contact person. The counselor also has information regarding when the job order came in and how many people have been referred to that position. Sometimes the counselor will indicate that the job is 45 days old and 32 people have already been referred for one opening. This implies that either the job is about to be filled or that the employer may not be serious about filling it.

In many states USES also runs free job-finding workshops. They provide information on resume writing and interviewing, as well as tips on how to utilize the hidden job market.

About 5% of all job seekers find jobs through USES. The quality of the jobs USES handles has often been criticized. One survey revealed that over 50% of the people who had been placed by USES were no longer on the job 30 days later. Despite their efforts, very few USES offices have managed to draw large numbers of professional, technical, or managerial job seekers, probably because they have found difficulty obtaining those types of job orders. While overall, about 5% of all job seekers obtained their current job through USES, the statistics for specific types of occupations range from less than 2% of all engineers to about 8% of all equipment operators and blue-collar service workers.

Tips On Using USES

You can only use USES if you are unemployed. The service is free. Regardless of the type of position you are seeking, I would recommend one or two visits to your local USES office to determine whether it should be a part of your job search. You will find addresses in the blue pages of the telephone book in your state government section.

On your first visit, you will fill out the forms and meet with a counselor. Ask the counselor how you can make the best use of their services, based on your background and the type of work you are seeking. You will not be assigned a counselor. Each time you go in and find a job you are interested in, your name will go to the bottom of the list and whichever counselor is available when your name reaches the top is the one you'll meet with that day.

The most frequent comment I get about USES is that it's depressing. That's not surprising; everyone waiting around the office is unemployed. The counselors usually get high marks for caring, but job seekers quickly realize there is little time for personal consulting. USES offices are typically understaffed and waits of over an hour are not uncommon. Counselors often meet with 20 or more people per day. That doesn't give them much time to provide a lot of individual attention.

If you make USES part of your regular search, I recommend that you stop by twice a week. This will give you a chance to be referred for almost all of the positions you would have an interest in. Also, by visiting that frequently, you'll miss few openings. Go first to the bulletin board since that will have the newest positions. Use a spiral binder to keep track of jobs you've looked at. Simply write down the title and a phrase or two about the job so if you see it a week later, you'll know that you've already looked into it. Then check the microfiche listings. Track those jobs just as you did the posted positions.

Jobs are listed by the Dictionary of Occupational Title (DOT) numbers. A nine-digit number has been assigned for every one of the 12,000 occupations defined in the DOT. The first three digits indicate the type of job it is. The first digit tells you the broad category it is in, and the next two digits narrow it down to a specific occupational title. I have included the following information to provide a glimpse of what is offered.

0/1 Professional, Technical, and Managerial
2 Clerical and Sales
3 Service
4 Agricultural, Fishery, Forestry
5 Processing Trades
6 Machine Trades
7 Bench Work
8 Structural Work
9 Miscellaneous

Occupations in life sciences are 04, while 041 is occupations in biological sciences. Plant paleontologist is 041.061-086. If you are going to use USES, familiarize yourself with all of the categories you may be interested in. Then you can go right to the appropriate microfiche and quickly find what you want.

Find out what days and times of the day are least busy and visit the office at those times. Work your visits into your job search. If the nearest office is ten or more miles away, stop by anytime you are in the vicinity. Because your visit is likely to involve some time waiting to see a counselor, use your time wisely with activities such as writing thank-you notes.

Some USES offices have microfiche data bases that cover job openings outside of your state. One microfiche, for example, lists jobs in the airline industry and tells you where to apply for these positions. Another microfiche lists federal job openings that do not require federal civil service exams. The offices also often collect state and local government job announcements. These data bases and the collection of job announcements do not require the help of a counselor, so even if you are employed these resources could be helpful to you.

COLLEGE PLACEMENT OFFICES

Virtually all of the 3,200 institutions of higher education have placement offices. They are often known as career planning and placement offices, but the names vary widely from school to school. About 21% of those who use their placement office find a job through that resource.

If the title contains "career planning," it indicates that at least part of their effort is devoted to helping students determine what they really want to do. Since a college of 10,000 students may have only five career counselors, you can see that their ability to spend much time with you on your career decision making will be limited. You may want to take advantage of the career planning and job finding courses many schools offer. In some cases, you can even receive college credit for taking them. As with anything, some instructors are better than others. Make sure you take your class from the best.

The placement function of career planning and placement offices often entails obtaining part-time and temporary job listings for students to look at. The major effort, however, is devoted to obtaining job listings for college seniors and to arrange for company recruiters to visit the campus to interview those seniors. Alumni will usually not be allowed to interview with campus recruiters, but they are allowed to examine the posted job listings.

Make use of the opportunity to interview with campus recruiters. Be prepared for all of the common interview questions, and by all means read the company literature which is always sent in advance of a recruiter's visit to the campus. Particularly be prepared to answer the question, "Why do you want to work for us?" and "What do you know about us?"

THE TRADITIONAL JOB MARKET
VS.
THE HIDDEN JOB MARKET

We have taken a look at what is often called the traditional job market—those resources that are generally available to the public through commonly-used and well-established means. These include the want ads, employment agencies, headhunters, and college placement offices, as well as civil service exams. The hidden job market consists of applying directly to employers on one's own, as well as getting referrals from friends, relatives, and associates. Applying directly can include sending resumes, filling out application forms, and making appointments to meet the person with the power to hire.

Over the years, a number of studies have been conducted to determine the effectiveness of various job search methods. The most extensive of these was a 1972 study conducted by the U.S. Department of Labor in cooperation with the Census Bureau. Through a survey, researchers learned about the job finding habits of 10 million job seekers who looked for jobs in 1972. Although the study is now over 20 years old, recent smaller studies have confirmed the current applicability of those findings. These statistics can help you determine the type of job search you should conduct.

The first and most obvious thing the research reveals is that no particular job hunting method is guaranteed to work for you personally. While 66% of all job seekers spent at least part of their time applying directly to employers, less than 48% of them found their job through that approach. Still, that approach had the highest effectiveness rate among all of the methods examined. By contrast, only 24% of those who responded to want ads, and only 24% of those who used private employment agencies obtained jobs through those resources.

Method	% who got job through this Method	Usage	Effectiveness Rate
Applied directly to employer	34.9%	66.0%	47.7%
Asked friends:			
About jobs where they work	12.4	50.8	22.1
About jobs elsewhere	5.5	41.8	11.9
Asked relatives:			
About jobs where they work	6.1	28.4	19.3
About jobs elsewhere	2.2	27.3	7.4

Answered newspaper ads:			
Local	12.2	45.9	23.9
Nonlocal	1.3	11.7	10.0
Employment organizations:			
Private employment agency	5.6	21.0	24.2
State employment service	5.1	33.5	13.7
School placement office	3.0	12.5	21.4
Civil Service test	2.1	15.3	12.5
Asked teacher or professor	1.4	10.4	12.1
Went to place where employers come to pick up people	.1	1.4	8.2
Placed newspaper ads:			
Local	.2	1.6	12.9
Nonlocal	.1	.5	NA
Answered ads in professional or trade journals	.4	4.9	7.3
Union hiring hall	1.5	6.0	22.2
Miscellaneous	5.9	18.0	31.5
	100.0		

In this section I will list and explain each job search method individually.

Applying Directly To Employers

Applying directly to employers includes any type of direct contact you make with an employer that is not done as a result of a want ad or referral from friends, relatives, associates, employment agencies, or headhunters. It does include applying through a resume, filling out an application form, walking in and speaking to someone in a personnel department, and talking to the person with power to hire, either by phone or face-to-face.

Approximately 66% of all job seekers apply directly to employers. Of those, about 48% find jobs using this method. Applying directly to employers accounts for about 35% of all people who get hired. It is the most frequently used and most effective job search method: more people get jobs through that method than any other.

Every job seeker should spend time applying directly to employers. Once you know what type of job you'll be looking for, you should identify 75–200 potential employers, determine who has the power to hire, and seek to meet those people. Even when you do not succeed in meeting the person with the power to hire, you will have had a higher quality contact than 95% of your competitors. Making direct contact with employers, along with associated activities such as researching companies at the library, will take up about 90% of your time. This approach is time-intensive, but it works.

Asking Friends And Relatives

Getting referrals from friends and relatives is the method that accounts for landing approximately 26% of all jobs. You'll notice that the effectiveness rate is not as high as the effectiveness rate for applying directly to employers. Nevertheless, the fact that so many people get jobs based on leads and referrals from others indicates that it is one of the methods that all job seekers should use.

One of the reasons that this method did not show a higher effectiveness rate is that job hunters often fail to use this method to their best advantage. They rarely contact people on a systematic basis, they tell only a few people that they are looking for a job, and they rarely follow up to tell their contacts how they're doing. Although talking to friends and relatives will take up a lot of time during the first couple weeks of your search, after that you will only need to follow up with them periodically every few weeks.

The figures show that friends and relatives are about twice as likely to give you leads regarding their own companies as they are other organizations. However, by giving people a list of organizations you're interested in working for, you'll get referrals to people they know who work for your target firms. Even though you may not know those people today, you can easily make an acquaintance with them. Those people will prove very helpful.

Answering Want Ads

Everyone should look at the want ads. About 13% of all job seekers find a job through the want ads. This method has one of the higher effectiveness rates: of those responding to local ads, 24% find jobs through this method. Not surprisingly, responding to ads in nonlocal papers is considerably less successful. Answering ads placed in professional and trade journals has an effectiveness rate of only 7%, but this is one of the only avenues some people have for learning about out-of-state jobs in their profession. The number of jobs advertised in professional and trade journals is fairly small. Because people from all over the country respond to these ads, your success rate will probably be low.

Once you learn how to interpret the ads you can get through them fairly quickly. Most people find two or three ads to respond to on a weekly basis. Although we know that for the better jobs, 50–200 resumes are going to pour in, the time it takes to produce a customized cover letter is probably worth the effort. Setting aside an hour or so on Sunday to write the letter will leave you free Monday through Friday to concentrate on other aspects of your job search.

Placing Ads In Newspapers And Trade Journals

I have never known anyone personally who has gotten a job by placing an ad, but apparently some do. Placing ads in local papers has a 13% success rate, while placing ads in professional and trade journals has a 7% success rate. I would place this technique in the strictly optional category. Since the success rate of placing an ad is low, and you will have to pay for the ad, do it only if you feel you want to cover all of your bases. I do know that employers rarely look for such ads. If you do run an ad, you are likely to get far more calls from employment agency counselors and people touting multi-level selling opportunities than actual job offers.

Private Employment Agencies

There are many people who simply don't benefit from using employment agencies and headhunters. If you determine that such services are not appropriate for you, you will then be able to devote your time more effectively to other methods. Approximately 21% of job seekers use either employment agencies or headhunters, and about 24% of those folks, find their job through those resources. About 6% of all job seekers find their jobs through agencies. If you decide to utilize agencies or headhunters, however, contact them quickly, within the first two weeks of your search.

State Employment Services

About 5% of all job seekers find their jobs through state employment services. The effectiveness rate is fairly low—about 14% of those seeking jobs this way find their jobs through this method. But this service does have some advantages. For one thing, it's free. For another thing, one or two visits will be enough to determine whether it is a resource you should continue using. By merely stopping in twice a week, this resource may require only one to two hours of time.

School Placement Offices

Placement offices are used almost exclusively by graduating seniors, although they are usually available to alumni. The effectiveness rate of placement offices is fairly high. Of those who use placement offices, 21% find jobs through them. If you are a graduating senior, make every use you can of the placement office. Talk to counselors and ask them how you can take full advantage of their resources. If they offer interview coaching, or critiquing of videotaped interviews, make use of these services. They can give you considerable help as you prepare to interview with campus recruiters.

Civil Service Tests

Only 13% of those who seek jobs through civil service exams find jobs by using this method, probably because the exams are extremely competitive. Typically, in order to be eligible for interviews, you have to rank among the top ten on your scores. The manager will then hire someone from that group. So, even if you are number nine on the list, you could get hired if you interview effectively. Knowing people often helps in government hiring. But, as in all job finding, who you get to know is as important as who you already know. By being focused, you can identify those department managers within the government bodies which interest you and seek to meet them even when they don't have any openings. If you sell yourself, you'll be high on their list when an opening occurs.

Getting Referrals From Professors And Teachers

About 12% of those who seek referrals from professors and teachers get a job through this method. Because this method does not require a great deal of time, it is certainly worth using.

While you're in school, make a special effort to get to know some of your professors. Sit in the front of the class, get involved in class discussions, and take advantage of faculty office hours to meet personally with your instructors. It also helps to do "A" work; professors rarely remember B- or C students. While your typical history professor is not likely to have many contacts in private industry, he or she might surprise you. Chemistry teachers may have done consulting work for firms and will have former students who work for many different organizations. It doesn't take much time to talk with your professors, so give them a try.

Miscellaneous

About 7% of all job seekers find their jobs through many different techniques which are categorized as miscellaneous.

What Does It All Mean?

People use all of the methods described because they work—at least some of the time, for some of the people. Research shows that the more methods people use, the quicker they find jobs. As a rule, the quality of the job you obtain, and the length of time it takes to obtain it, are directly related to the amount of time you spend on your search each week, the number of people you contact, the number of people you meet, the quality of your written documents, and the quality of your personal contacts.

THE SYSTEMATIC JOB SEARCH

Many people are startled to discover that only three of every ten job openings are ever advertised or listed with employment agencies. The other seven jobs have become known as "the hidden job market." This fact of life necessitates a job-finding strategy far different from those used by the average job seeker. The typical job-finding strategy consists of mailing out dozens of resumes, visiting a handful of employment agencies, and religiously reading the want ads. While 30% of all people do find jobs this way, there are many for whom this strategy simply does not work.

Finding a job that provides growth and satisfaction requires the right strategy. It takes considerable thought, time, and energy, but the payoff is tremendous.

In order to find such a job, you're going to tap into the hidden job market with the Systematic Job Search strategy. These are the requirements:

Focus - Know exactly what type of work you want and the type of organization you want to work for. Identify your strengths so you'll know you can do an outstanding job.

Resume - Develop a resume that really sells you, one that accurately describes your accomplishments and potential.

Employer Research - Develop a list of 50–200 prime organizations that match your requirements for industry, location, size, growth, and any other factors. When an interview is arranged, learn more about the organization and go prepared.

Contacts - Send your resume to friends, relatives, and business contacts. Then talk to them about the type of position you're seeking. Your network of contacts will keep their eyes and ears open for you; when positions open up in their organizations (or in their friends' organizations), they can supply you with the names of people to contact.

Calls - In the first week, call each of your top 20 organizations and ask for the name of the person with the power to hire you. He or she will usually have a position one or two levels above the position you would fill. Send a marketing letter to that person. A marketing letter is a letter that outlines your background and acts as a substitute for your resume. (See page 254 for a complete description of the functions and purposes of a marketing letter.) State in your marketing letter that you will call to set up a brief meeting. Call those you've sent letters to and ask for a brief appointment, even if there are no openings.

Appointments - Your calls should result in appointments 40–80% of the time. Before each appointment, research the organization. During the 15-minute appointment you will learn more about the organization and what they look for in their employees. Ask intelligent questions and explain how your background could be helpful to them. Create a favorable impression of yourself so if an opening occurs, you will be given top priority.

Follow-Up - After each appointment send a thank-you note and express your interest in the organization. This causes the person to think favorably of you once again. Three weeks later, call to see if any openings have developed. If not, make a brief call every five weeks. This type of contact has at least 40 times the impact of sending a resume alone.

Interviews - All of your hard work—whether responding to want ads or getting appointments with the people with power to hire you—will result in formal interviews. Because you are ready for virtually any question, you'll shine in the interviews and get more than your share of job offers.

Finding jobs in the hidden job market will require hard work and endurance, but it can be enjoyable and rewarding. There may be frustrations and down times. But remember: your efforts will pay off. Those efforts will directly determine the success of your job search.

FOCUS

You need two types of focus to conduct an effective job search. First, you need a definite career direction. You need to identify a career field which will utilize your strengths, skills, and temperament, and will match your values. It should be a field that you can envision yourself enjoying and growing in for 15 years or more. Once you achieve clarity on your career direction, you need a second type of focus. This focus centers on knowing specifically what you need in a job and organization to keep you satisfied and motivated to do your best.

Throughout this section I will be referring to jobs and careers. By job I mean a specific position held; by career I mean a set of jobs which take place in one career field. Some people go through life having a series of unrelated jobs and thus never establish a career.

This book is not designed to be primarily a career and life planning resource, but I am going to share ideas and exercises that will take you a long way toward defining what you want and need out of your career.

To select a field to pursue you must know yourself well. Without adequate self-knowledge you will likely fall into your next job. If you're lucky, you'll like it and remain in it for many years. If you're like most people, however, you'll fall into a job which is not well-suited to you. If you're typical, you'll stay in the job until you get your first raise, then until you get your first vacation, and before you know it, ten years will have passed. You'll still be complaining about your job, but not doing anything about it.

Others respond differently to a dissatisfying job. As soon as they realize the job is not right for them, they quit and move on to something else. Ten years later, they've had five to ten jobs, but with virtually no promotions or career growth.

Self-knowledge is the key to long-term career success. The type of self-knowledge required to gain career focus is exactly the same type of self-knowledge required for job focus. Thus, by being knowledgeable about yourself you can achieve both career focus and job focus.

Some people have career focus, but lack job focus. They also experience frustration. They may have chosen the right career field, and have the talent and personality to pursue it, but they keep ending up in the wrong jobs. Although they may gain promotions, they are always frustrated.

Choosing the right career field requires a great deal of personal insight. As helpful as career and personality inventories are, it is the degree of self-knowledge which you possess which will enable you to select the right career field. I have provided six exercises that can help you attain the personal insight necessary to choose the right career field and to become totally clear on what you need in your next job.

As you increase your self-knowledge, begin reading about occupations which interest you. As you narrow your choices down, begin talking to people who are already in occupations that interest you. As you do your reading and talking, a light will flash on. You'll get excited about a particular field. It may be difficult to explain why you're excited, but you'll find yourself becoming more enthusiastic as you gather more information. You will have an internal confirmation that this is the right field for you. You'll sense that you will not get tired of doing this type of work and will continually want to learn more about it.

It's important to find the right career and the right job. Most people recognize that their health and energy level are directly related to their satisfaction with work. If you enjoy what you do and are good at it, you are likely to work harder and smarter. This will result in promotions and greater responsibility and challenges in your work. Your income will rise accordingly.

Since no one cares as much about your career as you do, you must take responsibility for achieving the things you want to achieve. To achieve those goals, you must be clear what those goals are.

I have an absolute belief that everyone can be great at something. Not everyone can be a great artist, composer, or architect, but everyone can be great at something. Your task is to find out what that thing is and become it. When you're great at something and you love doing it, you will gain the financial and psychic rewards you need.

An Ideal Job And Its Ingredients

Clarifying what would make an ideal job for yourself is critical. The more clear you are on what you want, the more likely it is that you will obtain it. When I say ideal, I do not mean *perfect*. An ideal job is any job that allows you to spend most of your time doing what you do best and enjoy most. If you can spend 50% of your time doing what you love, 20% doing what you enjoy, 20% doing things that are okay, and only 10% doing things you dislike, that's a really good job, maybe an ideal job. It doesn't get much better than that.

Contrary to popular belief, most people are not unhappy in their jobs. A 1986 poll conducted for Walt Disney World revealed 41% of Americans are very happy with their jobs, 39% are somewhat happy, 14% are somewhat unhappy, and only 6% are very unhappy. A survey by Indiana University in 1983 showed that 83% of all Americans were satisfied with their work tasks, versus 53% for Japanese workers. Over 78% of American workers surveyed were satisfied with their supervisor, versus 50% for the Japanese. And 84% of Americans were satisfied with their life in general, versus 45% for the Japanese.

Other studies reveal a somewhat different story, however. When the question is worded, "If you could choose any profession you wanted, what would you choose?" most studies show that the majority would choose something different from what they are currently doing. Although most Americans are basically satisfied with their work, they also have a strong desire to achieve greater overall satisfaction.

As I've indicated, self-knowledge is the key to selecting the right career and creating an ideal job for yourself. I'm going to describe the processes and exercises which can lead to a high level of self-knowledge. These exercises will help you identify your accomplishments, transferable skills, work content skills, temperament, motivators, and values. Once you've completed these exercises, you will be able to write an ideal job description that will become for you a vision of the future. These exercises are described in detail in Appendix A.

The first step toward improving self-knowledge involves recalling past accomplishments and identifying the skills you used within those accomplishments.

Accomplishments

Accomplishments are those experiences where you did something well, you enjoyed doing it, or you got some satisfaction from it. Accomplishments need not be particularly impressive to reveal a great deal about you. Reviewing your accomplishments plays a key role in building your self-esteem and self-confidence, as well as preparing you for interviews. As you look at your accomplishments, you will begin asking yourself, "When I was enjoying what I was doing, and when I was really effective at what I was doing, what types of things was I doing?"

Examining both work- and nonwork-related accomplishments will reveal some patterns. You might begin to see that nearly every time you organize an event, you enjoy success and satisfaction. It would quickly become clear that an ideal career and an ideal job would be one that required you to spend considerable time organizing events. There are people who are professional events planners, and you would probably want to look at that occupation, but there are many more people who have events planning as just one of their many functions. Perhaps you'll discover that it would be ideal for you to spend 20% of your time planning and organizing events, gatherings, conferences, and meetings.

Within each of your accomplishments, you used at least ten skills. By recalling 30 accomplishments, and by writing about and identifying the skills in 12 of them, you are sure to increase your self-esteem. Later, as you begin reading about dozens of different occupations, you'll have a strong sense of which ones you could enjoy and be successful at. Identifying your accomplishments and skills will also play a key role in interviewing more effectively.

Below you will find an example of an accomplishment so you can get a sense of how valuable accomplishments are. The skills and qualities that were demonstrated in the accomplishment are on the right. Notice how much was revealed from just this one accomplishment.

DESIGNING A CARDBOARD TOY

The San Francisco Museum of Modern Art sponsored a contest to design a toy that was made completely out of cardboard with no fasteners and no printed graphics. I was excited about the idea of designing a toy. My first ideas were things like dollhouses, building blocks, and cars. I discarded those ideas as being too obvious and not clever enough. I tried creating an airplane but nixed that when it wouldn't fly. I was thinking constantly about ideas, even in my sleep. One idea I tried was a catapult, which

Highly creative

Able to develop many ideas

Willing to try many things

Able to visualize what will work and what won't

Put a lot of thought and energy into projects

didn't work, but the spring action had possibilities. Then I remembered the old "Kukla, Fran and Ollie" TV-show, and I thought of making a puppet like Ollie. While in the shower one day, I suddenly put the spring and puppet ideas together and came up with a jack-in-the box idea. I made a couple of models and knew this was it. The flat qualities of the cardboard didn't lend themselves to a very friendly looking puppet, so I decided to make it a dragon. I tried many different ways of getting the dragon to come out of a box, but it lacked the right action and the catch mechanism wasn't working. I took the dragon-head puppet and put it on the springy body, then added feet to it so it would stand up. This formed a kind of origami animal that had a bouncy action to it that was fun. I made the tongue into a trigger so the mouth would stay open until something was thrown into it, and then it would snap shut and bounce around like it had just eaten something. I called it "Snap-dragon" and won honorable mention. The first and second prizes were a dollhouse and an airplane.

Enjoy a challenge

Visualize effectively in three dimensions

Develop unique solutions to problems

Quickly discard ideas that don't work

Able to put together two or more widely divergent concepts and make them work

Frequently get flashes of insight and creative ideas

Can sense when an idea is "it"

Able to turn vision into reality

Once you write about several accomplishments and identify the skills and qualities in those accomplishments, the patterns will become quite apparent. Accomplishments are fun to write about and extremely beneficial.

Skills

Most people feel they know what their skills are, but if you ask for specifics, most can provide only ten or fifteen skills. In actuality, everyone has hundreds of skills. When you know exactly what your top skills are, and which ones you enjoy using most, you are well on your way to identifying your right career and defining your ideal job.

Essentially there are three types of skills: personality skills, transferable skills, and work content skills.

Your personality skills include being energetic, effective under stress, and reliable. These are skills which simply describe the way you are. If being reliable is one of your top skills, it means that you are nearly always reliable. You don't wake up in the morning wondering if you will be reliable that day. You simply are reliable. It's part of your nature. In fact it's almost impossible for you to be unreliable. The key aspect of your top personality skills is that they are part of your very nature. Usually, these skills develop early in childhood and then are refined throughout adulthood.

34

Transferable skills also develop in childhood. They include such skills as establishing rapport easily, conceptualizing ideas, analyzing information, knowing how to figure out how mechanical things work, and getting audiences to relate to you. The outstanding feature of transferable skills is that they are highly useful in many occupations. Like all skills, people improve in their transferable skills with practice.

Work content skills make up the third category of skills. Work content skills are the more technical and specialized skills that people learn by watching others, taking courses, practicing on the job, or learning through an apprenticeship. Essentially, a work content skill is any skill which some people get paid for doing. Using this definition, knowing how to polish shoes and wash dishes are work content skills because there are people who get paid to do such things. Knowing how to repair a transmission, program in COBOL, or conduct an experiment with DNA are also work content skills.

When determining what type of career to pursue, you need to know if you have the potential to be good at it. In essence, each work content skill is composed of several personality and transferable skills. It isn't enough to want to be something, you have to have the potential for it. By knowing what type of work content skills are required for an occupation, you can determine which ones you already have. Then, by examining your personality skills and transferable skills, you can determine with a high degree of accuracy your potential to become proficient at those work content skills you don't currently have.

Temperament

According to Webster, temperament is a "characteristic or habitual inclination or mode of emotional response." In other words, temperament is what makes a person respond in a consistent way in a particular situation. If you are a gregarious person, you will enjoy being around people and will be frustrated in a job that isolates you from people. If you are a big-picture person, you will be frustrated if you spend all of your time dealing with details. As these examples suggest, it is very important for you to be in a career field and in a job which allows you to be what you already are. Careers and jobs should not ask you to try to be different from what you are. Gregarious people belong in gregarious jobs, and big-picture people belong in big-picture jobs.

Because humans are adaptable by nature, people often assume that they can simply force themselves to become whatever they must be in order to fulfill a job. It may work for a time, but there is a terrible price to pay. The versatile person who needs variety can survive for a time in a highly routine, repetitive job. Eventually, however, the person will become extremely frustrated and the quality of work will decline. As a result, promotions are likely to become harder and harder to obtain.

Unfortunately, I see a lot of people trying to make it in careers and jobs that are totally contrary to their temperament. The toll such efforts take on the psyches of these people is tremendous, and it is so unnecessary. Through self-knowledge you can avoid those careers and jobs which are contrary to your temperament.

Motivators

All people are motivated to do certain things. Some of your skills, for example, are truly motivated skills. There is something within you which motivates you to use certain skills. You are good at them, and you enjoy yourself whenever you are allowed to exercise those skills.

When you are motivated you work harder, smarter, and often longer. When you are truly motivated, you may even lose track of time. Work no longer seems like work. Perhaps you've experienced losing track of time simply because you were enjoying a hobby or activity so much.

There are other things besides skills that motivate us. People are motivated by money. People will often undergo great hardships even though the only thing motivating them is money. Some people are highly motivated by helping people. In fact, many people in notoriously low-paying jobs continue only because they have the satisfaction that they are helping people and society. Others are motivated by creativity. Give people like that a project and they will invariably give it a creative twist. We seek to do those things that motivate us, and we seek to avoid those things that do not motivate us.

The primary idea to grasp here is that all of us will do what we are motivated to do. When you are asked to do something that motivates you, you will do a great job. If you are asked to do something that does not motivate you, you will usually do a mediocre job.

Values

Values also exercise a great influence on us throughout our careers. For example, if you value your family and your family time highly, you may be frustrated by working for a company that demands your soul and ten hours a day as well. While most people do not mind occasional overtime, the person who wants to spend a lot of time with family is going to be frustrated working for such a company. Another key value is integrity. The person with high integrity will be frustrated working for a company which engages in shady dealings.

Knowing your values will help you identify the career fields and types of jobs which will enable you to remain true to your values.

The Ideal Job Description

Ultimately you must bring all of the pieces together to create an ideal job description. Knowing what you want and need in a job and career will quadruple your chances of attaining your goal. An ideal job will use primarily those skills you are best at and most motivated to use. The ideal job must match your temperament and allow you to do what you are motivated to do.

Another major part of the ideal job is working for the right organization. Determining what characteristics of an organization are most important to you will enable you to identify those companies that will be most likely to satisfy you. As you research companies and interview with them, you will use your detective skills and your intuition to determine which ones would fit you best.

Over the last fifteen years, I have continually refined this process which enables clients to select the right career field and land the right job. Although I also use other exercises with clients as well, the ones I have just described form the core of the process. These exercises are extremely efficient. That is, they create the biggest impact for the amount of time devoted to them.

If you realize that you lack the focus required to carry out an effective job search, stop at this point and complete the exercises. You might easily spend 10 hours working on them, but the effort will be well worth it. All of the information and instructions you need to complete the exercises are found in Appendix A.

If you need to select a career field, these exercises, plus considerable reading on your own, may be all you need. Or you may need to seek out assistance from a professional career counselor. For more on career counselors and how to locate a good one, read Appendix D on page 465.

CAREER DECISION MAKING

Once you know what you need to be satisfied in a career, you must still determine which occupations fit you. To do that, first examine the *Occupational Outlook Handbook (OOH)*, which describes the 300 major occupational fields in our economy. The *OOH* is available at all libraries. It will provide a wealth of information on careers, including the skills and knowledge needed, educational requirements, forecasts for the future growth of the field, salary ranges, and a description of the work itself.

You may find a field that really excites you. If so, you are in a good position. If nothing in the *OOH* particularly excites you, you should study the *Dictionary of Occupational Titles (DOT)*, which describes the work performed in about 12,000 occupations. All libraries have it as well. The *DOT* does not provide salary or educational information, but it can be extremely helpful. No other resource contains so much occupation information. The descriptions are brief, but quite accurate.

If you consult the *DOT*, you should use the 1991 revised version of the 4th edition. Begin by reading pages xvii to xxiii to gain an understanding of how the occupational definitions are constructed. Then turn to xxix to review first the two-digit occupational divisions, and then the three-digit occupational groups. Pick one of the three-digit groups that looks somewhat interesting and look up that group in the *DOT*. Everything is arranged in numerical order. There will probably be at least five occupational descriptions, each with a distinct, nine-digit code. Read two or three descriptions to gain an understanding of how they are written.

At this point, you are ready to begin your career search using the *DOT*. Go back through the three-digit groups beginning at page xxx. Whenever you come to an occupational group that might interest you, write its three-digit code on a sheet of paper. Even though you won't necessarily know which occupations will be found in that category, if it seems that there might be something of interest, write down the three-digit number. When you're done recording the job titles and their codes, begin reading their definitions. When an occupational definition interests you, write down the occupational title and its nine-digit number.

Your goal is to come up with 20–50 occupations which have some appeal for you. Do not be concerned with whether you have the necessary experience or education to do that type of work. I have found that when people identify something that they really want, they will always find a way to do it. So, at this point the only issue is whether the occupation seems interesting. Photocopy the descriptions.

The next day, read through your list again and place a check by those titles that really appeal to you. If you have forgotten what is done in some of the occupations, reread their descriptions. On the following day, reread those definitions of the occupations you check-marked the day before and put another check by the six which have the greatest appeal to you. Now ask yourself whether you seem to have a genuine enthusiasm for any of these six.

At this stage, it's appropriate to let practicality begin to enter the picture. If you have selected architect, but you are lousy in math, architect may not be a practical selection for you. Before you give up this possibility, however, read as much as you can about the field and talk to people to determine whether there is a way around this issue. Perhaps computers are about to take over a function that used to require math and so the need for math has diminished. Or, you might determine that with a tutor you could at least pass the necessary courses.

If your chosen field would require a master's degree, but the very idea of going back to school gives you an anxiety attack, perhaps that field is not for you. On the other hand, before you give up, find out if there are people who have managed to get into that field without a master's degree. If they could do it, perhaps you could too.

Before you can make a decision about which occupations to pursue, you need to know a lot more about each occupation. Ask your librarian for help. All libraries have specific occupational books with titles like *Your Career in the Airline Industry.* Sometimes an entire book is devoted to a single occupation. Whatever resources your library or school has, read everything you can get your hands on. These books will describe occupations in much more detail than either the *Occupational Outlook Handbook* or the *Dictionary of Occupational Titles.* In a book such as the *Public Relations Career Directory,* you will find several occupations described. It contains such chapters as, "A Career In Public Relations," "The Growing World of Public Relations," " Ten Myths About Public Relations Firms," " Working For The Federal Government," "Breaking Into Media Relations," and "A Career In Public Affairs." This 365-page book contains complete and accurate information about the field of public relations.

It takes this kind of reading and research to determine whether a field is really for you. Your goal is to reach a point where you are absolutely sure that a particular occupation will be a great fit for you. And you want to know both the upside and downside of any occupation you're considering. You don't want to invest hours of self-study or take courses only to discover, once you are in your job search, or worse yet, on your first job, that there are major drawbacks that you did not know about.

I met a young man who completed a one-year program at a community college in medical photography, only to discover that the field paid near poverty wages. He went through an entire program and never bothered to find out how much he could make. After investing one year in school he had to look at other fields. Don't let that happen to you.

Once you've thoroughly read about your occupational interests, you will probably be ready to narrow your choices. You should reduce your list to one or two fields. Do your best to find additional books describing the fields, and also begin reading textbooks and trade journals.

One of my clients who had been in sales for three years, was interested in becoming a purchasing agent. He had dealt with purchasing agents, but he knew relatively little about the technical aspects of the job. He found an introductory college textbook extremely helpful. It was well-organized and gave him a good grasp of all the basic concepts. Since he wasn't studying for a grade, he read the book fairly quickly with the goal of getting an overview of the main ideas. Next, he visited the library and found they had a trade journal for purchasing agents that discussed the latest trends in the field.

Trade journals are excellent sources of information about specific fields. Trade journals are simply magazines designed for specialists. Almost every industry and occupation has a trade journal. It can be useful for job seekers to read trade journals because their articles cover current practices as well as new ideas being tested in a field. Because the articles are written by people who are practicing in that profession, they'll give you a sense of what the field is *really* like. You can also pick up the jargon and language commonly used by people in that field. Knowing the jargon will be important later on when you start interviewing. Also, since employers will often ask you what you think about a particular issue, it helps to be familiar with issues that are current in a profession.

Several sources and guides are available to help you locate appropriate trade journals and other useful periodicals. Each of the resources identifies thousands of magazines, newsletters, newspapers, and journals, or other periodicals you should read to better understand your industry or field. The guides will list periodicals by subject. *Ulrich's International Periodicals Directory*, for example, lists 108,000 periodicals in 554 subject areas. The other resources frequently found in libraries include *Gale Directory of Publications, Standard Periodical Directory, Newsletters in Print,* and *Oxbridge Directory of Newsletters.*

If you have completed the exercises in Appendix A, written your ideal job description, gone through the *OOH* and *DOT*, and read several books covering interesting occupational fields, but you still lack the certainty to pursue a specific field, you're going to need some additional help. For many people there are various issues in their lives which make career decision making especially difficult. If this is true of you, you may need to make use of a career counselor. Before you seek one out, however, read *The Three Boxes of Life* by Richard Bolles, one of the best career-planning books available. Bolles provides an extensive and complete framework for career decision making. He also provides additional exercises which could be very helpful. Once you read the book, return to the *Occupational Outlook Handbook* and the *Dictionary of Occupational Titles* to see if you are better able to determine what you want.

Some people are unable to come up with the right occupation because the *DOT* doesn't give them enough information. Although it has 12,000 different occupations, those 12,000 are just the tip of the iceberg in the immense world of work. My guess is that there are at least 50,000 distinct occupations—it would be nearly impossible to catalogue them all.

That is why many of my clients will design their own job. Instead of starting with a job title, we begin with a description of what the person would ideally want to do. A certain amount of flexibility is built into the description. The client is not going to demand, for example, that exactly 21% of her time is going to be devoted to a particular function. Usually the person will design a range of say, 15-25% of time spent doing a particular task or function. There might be activities that the person *wants* to perform, but is willing to forego for the right job. There may also be activities the person definitely wants to perform, but would be willing to spend 5% rather than 15% of her time doing if this is what it takes to design an overall job that is close to ideal.

Once we design the job, we determine whether there are people who already do this type of work. If so, the client needs to speak to them. If not, we have to determine what types of organizations might hire a person to do these things. Then a resume is created that will sell the person into exactly that type of job.

Designing a job is a fairly complex process. Give it a try on your own, but if you don't like your results, you may want to seek out a career counselor to help you get through this final stage. After reading *The Three Boxes Of Life*, you may also want to consider taking a career exploration class at a community college.

JOB FOCUS

If you have already established a career focus, the ideal job description will be the primary tool you'll use to obtain just the right job. The ideal job description should provide you with a vision that will guide you as you proceed with your job search. When people have such a vision, they are able to withstand many hardships and setbacks, and they usually reach their goals.

It seems that most people who have accomplished great things were people of vision. For that reason I have always loved this quote from T.E. Lawrence (Lawrence of Arabia):

> All people dream, but not equally. Those who dream by night in the dusty recesses of their minds, wake in the day to find that it is vanity. But the dreamers of the day are dangerous people, for they act their dreams with open minds to make it possible.

We need more of these "dangerous" people who have dreams and visions and the energy to make them happen.

You need such a vision. If you can visualize yourself actually doing what you've described in your ideal job description, and if that vision offers you something important and rewarding, then declare to yourself that you are willing to do anything to make it happen. With concerted effort and drive you *will* make it happen. There will be road-blocks, but you will find ways to go through, over, under, or around them. You may be blocked for a time, but by continuing your efforts, you will reach the goal. You *can* make it happen.

Even if you've selected the right career field and you know what you want in a job , that next position may not be your ideal job the day you start. Over time, however, you can alter it for a better fit. As you receive promotions, it should become closer to what you want.

You must always maintain your vision of your ideal job. If it be-comes clear that your progress toward your ideal job is stymied, you may have to try different approaches. Sometimes it means leaving your present organization for another that values more highly the skills and experience you offer.

Not everyone is able to create a *vision* by writing the ideal job description. Some people are satisfied to merely clarify what it is they want. To achieve their career goal of simply finding a *better* job, a clearer picture is sufficient. But I do believe that everyone *can* create a vision. You'll get that vision if a vision is what you need, especially if you're willing to do whatever is necessary to get that vision.

TALKING TO PEOPLE IN YOUR CHOSEN FIELD

As helpful as occupational books, textbooks, and trade journals are, there is nothing like a face-to-face conversation with a knowledge-able person to give you the information you need about a career or job. Once you've narrowed your choices to a few occupations and done your reading, begin talking to people who already work in your chosen field. Learn the positives and negatives about the field, get ad-vice, find out which are the best companies to work for, and get referrals.

People are generally easy to talk to and they like being helpful. If you want to be a buyer for a clothing store, begin by calling a store and asking to speak to a buyer. Tell the person that you are seriously con-sidering buying as a profession. Explain that you have read about the profession and need to talk to several buyers before you can make a final decision. Then ask the person if he or she would meet with you for about 20 minutes. If you are pleasant on the phone, and speak with a degree of confidence and professionalism, I guarantee that 90% of the people you call will agree to talk with you. Of course, some will be more willing and helpful than others.

The biggest problem people face when making these calls is their fear of rejection. Don't let that stand in your way. If someone is un-willing to give you some time, assume that the person would not have been helpful anyway. Remember, you're not asking anyone to do something you wouldn't be willing to do. If someone asked for 20 minutes of your time to discuss your favorite hobby, wouldn't you give it to them? Assume people will be pleasant to you, and generally they will be.

It's usually best to meet these people at their place of business to get a feel for the environment. Often, however, a conversation over the telephone will provide all the information you need. Your task will simply be to ask these people questions and listen to their answers. The questions you ask should revolve around issues left unanswered by your reading. You should also ask what they like or dislike about their occupation, how they got into it, and what their background is. Ask for suggestions regarding job-finding strategies for that field. Ask about salary ranges. Be tactful about salaries, though—people will not want to reveal how much they make. A good approach is to say, "With my education and experience, how much do you think I should expect to be offered? I know it's hard to say exactly, so maybe you could just give me a range." Ask which are the best companies to work for. Finally, ask if they can give you the names of other people in the field you might talk to.

I'm going to give you a word of advice on accepting advice from experts: Never let the advice of one person, even a noted expert in a field, dissuade you from pursuing your course of action. Just because one expert says something really negative about a field, don't assume that it is true. People often have biases and agendas that they won't tell you about. So, while you should seriously consider anything told to you by an expert, don't give up too quickly. Speak to other experts and let them confirm or dispute what the first expert told you. Never pursue or stop pursuing a field on the basis of what one person has to say about it.

Often the negative information you hear will concern education. An expert may tell you that you absolutely must have a certain degree in order to enter the field. Your response to such a statement should be, "Do you know *anyone* in this field who does not have that degree?" This person may in fact know someone who "snuck" into the profession. That person who snuck in is the next person you need to talk to. If you find someone who has blazed the trail before you, there is hope. You should continue your quest.

I say this because when you speak to people you will get lots of advice from those who don't want to see you get hurt. They will tell you how competitive the field is and how it's likely to get even worse in the future. I do the same when people tell me they want to become career counselors. I always tell them all of the negatives, but then I temper that with what I like about the field and why I continue to do it. In my own case, I will try to dissuade people because I believe that only those people who will truly be dedicated to the field should pursue it.

Doing The Research

One of my clients had recently graduated from law school and had started her own practice only to discover that she did not like being a lawyer. Two years earlier, she and her husband had acted as general contractors while building their own home. That experience plus others told her that she really liked the construction and real estate fields. After much reading and thought, she concluded that she would like to work in a title insurance company or as a right-of-way agent, purchasing land and easements for utility companies or local and state governments.

Her first contact was with a right-of-way agent for a nearby city. He was very enthusiastic about his work and gave her a lot of information and encouragement, and the names of several organizations. Next, she spoke to a manager of a title insurance company who described what she did and the different ways one might attain such a position. She was also very enthusiastic and encouraging. She not only provided the names of all the local title insurance companies, but also information about them *and* the name of a key person to contact in each company. By using the manager's name as a reference, my client was successful in getting in to see the person in each company with the power to hire her. She found the entire process surprisingly easy and very enjoyable.

It's important to note, however, that once she had decided to pursue those two fields, she no longer asked for appointments on the pretext of getting information. Instead, she began requesting 15 minutes with the person with the power to hire so that she might learn about possible openings. I make this point because some people abuse these situations. Pretending to want only information, they seek out people with power to hire, and then hit them up for a job. This can leave a bad taste in the mouth of the person who is tricked. As a result, people have become somewhat less willing to help those who genuinely want advice and information.

Who To Talk To

As you do your research, talk to people who currently do what you want to do, not those who are one or two levels above and have forgotten what the work is like. Not only can people forget what it was like doing the type of work they were doing five to ten years earlier, but the work may have changed dramatically since then.

Research The Industry

As you select your chosen profession, you should also research the industries that hire people to do what you want to do. Some fields, such as accounting, exist in all industries. Other occupations, such as forester, are found in only one or two industries. Knowing the future of specific industries is also important. You don't want to pick an industry that is becoming obsolete.

Although career decisions should not be made solely on the predicted growth of the profession or industry, future growth should certainly be a factor. A person should never pursue a profession simply because it is predicted to grow rapidly.

Nevertheless, it *is* to your advantage to work for a rapidly growing company in a rapidly growing industry. As you research your chosen field, and as you talk to people, try to determine its future growth. Also determine the growth of the industry you would work in.

There are several sources available to help you research an industry. The first resource to use is the *U.S. Industrial Outlook,* published by the U.S. Department of Commerce. It covers 350 manufacturing and service industries. It utilizes many types of information to describe the factors which will affect a particular industry in the next few years. From it, you can determine whether an industry is likely to grow or constrict.

Standard and Poor's Industry Surveys can also be helpful. Each survey contains an analysis of economic conditions, with growth projections.

Check the *Readers Guide To Periodical Literature, Business Periodicals Index, F & S Index,* or *Infotrac* to find magazine articles about an industry. A librarian can show you how to use each of these resources.

EMPLOYER RESEARCH

Employer research is one of the most important yet most neglected aspects of a job search. Researching employers consists of two stages: 1) using directories and other resources to develop a high-priority list of 50–200 employers; 2) gathering specific information about each organization before an interview, and conducting in-depth studies of organizations that offer you a job.

In many directories, companies are segregated by industry. Thus, if your type of work is done in only one industry, it will be much easier to develop your list of employers.

The size of an organization is also important to many people. Some must pursue larger companies because only larger organizations hire people with their specialty. For instance, a company will usually have at least 75 employees before a personnel manager is hired, and around 200 before a wage-and-salary administrator is hired. Since 95% of all companies have less than 100 employees, I consider an organization with 100 employees fairly large. Many resources, such as *Contacts Influential*, provide codes which help you know approximately how many employees an organization has.

Stage One: Developing Your High-Priority List of Employers

Begin with a stack of one hundred 4 x 6 cards and find a directory that will lead you to the types of organizations you're interested in. Examples of these directories include the *American Banking Directory* and the *Thomas Grocery Register*. As you come across appropriate organizations, write down whatever information the directory provides. They typically provide the name of the organization, its address and phone number, the number of employees, its products or services, and its sales volume. All of that information should go on the front side of the card, leaving space on the back to write information that you obtain from people or from newspaper articles. The card system is also useful because it makes prioritizing easier.

Then use your own telephone Yellow Pages, plus one or more of the specialized directories available at your library, to develop a list of employers that probably hire people in your field. Later, you will prioritize them into groups of 20 using the ABC method: The *A* group will be your top 20, the *B* group your second top 20, and so on. In most cases you will be prioritizing without a great deal of information to go on, but prioritizing is still very important.

Most directories will contain key information such as an organization's industry, products, size and location. At this point, that's all the information you need. You'll use this information to identify the organizations that would be most likely to hire you to do what you want to do.

In metropolitan Seattle there are 30,000 employers. Since it's difficult to work effectively with an employer list over 300, a system must be devised to enable a job seeker in the Seattle area to screen out all but 100 to 250 employers. By selecting 1-10 industries, limiting the search to a 30-mile radius, and by limiting the selection to organizations of 10-250 employees, a list of about 200 employers will result.

Begin this process by deciding which industries and products you'd like to be involved with. The Standard Industrial Classification (SIC) coding system was created to help you do that. Because every business functions in one or more industries, each is assigned one or more industry codes. This coding system will help you find your prospects quickly. In those directories which segregate organizations by

SIC, you will find a list of the industries with their codes. If you really want to dig into the different industries, use the *Standard Industrial Classification Manual* found in most libraries.

Sometimes the work you do will automatically limit you to a specific industry. For example, a person who operates large printing presses will be limited to the printing industry. If that is the case, the person would merely need to learn that 27 is the printing and publishing industries code. Code 271 is newspaper publishing and printing; 272 is periodicals publishing and printing; 273 is book publishing and printing; and 275 is commercial printing. Since many directories have SIC sections, the person would merely turn to that section in the directory. Every business listed there would fall in the printing and publishing field.

Unlike a printing-press operator, an accountant can work in virtually all industries. To help reduce the number of potential employers to a workable number, those who can work in many industries should first select those industries which have the greatest appeal to them.

Next, decide what size of organization you want to work for. Since the greatest amount of new job creation in the last ten years has been in organizations of under 50 employees, do not overlook smaller organizations.

The work some people do is available only in organizations of over 100 employees. These people would target companies with 100 or more employees. A person who wanted to avoid really large organizations would target companies with 100–250 employees.

Next, decide the maximum distance you are willing to commute. If the maximum commute you'd accept would be 35 minutes each way, you would use that as a guide to select organizations. For a truly outstanding company you might be willing to accept a longer commute, but there would be relatively few exceptions.

Once you've made your decisions, you will be ready to utilize the many directories available in your library.

Resources

The Yellow Pages. One of the most useful directories is available in your own home—the Yellow Pages. Most organizations in your area will be listed somewhere in the Yellow Pages even if they don't advertise. The "space ads" in the Yellow Pages can be particularly useful. Those ads can give you an excellent idea of what the businesses in a particular industry do. Using the Yellow Pages will give you companies to consider that you might have easily overlooked if you relied solely on other resources.

To use the Yellow Pages, go through the listings from A to Z. Scan each page and look at each of the specific categories. Rather than assuming that you don't want to work in a particular category, start with the opposite assumption. Give each category or industry serious consideration unless you can come up with a good reason why you should not. This technique opens you to possibilities that you might otherwise have been closed to.

Among all of the resources available, you will probably find two or three which provide almost everything you need. Review the resources listed on pages 52 to 62 and place a check by any that might be useful. When you get to the library, explore those resources first.

Librarians. Make use of the business or reference librarian at your library. Tell the librarian precisely what types of organizations you are trying to locate, and mention which directories you intend to use. Then ask the librarian if there are other directories you should use. The library will probably have several local directories that could provide exactly what you need. Don't hesitate to ask for help—that's what librarians love to do.

Industry-Specific Directories. Some industries have their own, specialized directories. To locate these directories, use the *Guide to American Directories* or *Directories In Print*. A good example of a specialized directory is the *World Aviation Directory*. It provides names, addresses, and phone numbers for every airline, airport, airplane or parts manufacturer, aviation insurance company, and dealer in the United States. For some people, a specialized directory is the only resource they need.

Associations. Determine whether there is an association that represents your field or industry. The *Encyclopedia of Associations* and *National Trade and Professional Associations* can provide this information. You'll also find local associations listed in the Yellow Pages under "Associations." Associations are usually formed to give an industry or profession more political clout, as well as to provide a forum for new ideas. They generally publish membership lists and news magazines, hold conventions and meetings, list job openings, and distribute free literature. Associations exist solely to be helpful. If they fail to meet the needs of members, they lose those members and their annual dues. For this reason you'll find most association employees or volunteers to be very helpful.

The Sunday Paper. Another way to build up your employer list is to review the back issues of the Sunday newspaper in your area that has the most want ads. Read through the want ads quickly to see if certain organizations seem to be hiring. Add them to your list even if you don't know much about them.

Stage Two: Researching Your Top 20 Employers

Once you have compiled and prioritized your list of 50–200 employers, it's time to do some preliminary research on each of your top-20 organizations. To research companies, your first step is to visit the nearest major library. Many libraries will have such resources as clipping files, house organs, and annual reports. These resources will be described in detail on page 60.

As valuable as written resources are, information gathered from people is often the most helpful. Talk with people who work for or have worked for your target company, people with competitors or suppliers, and people who work for a customer of the target company. All of these people can add to your insights and information about a company.

Gathering Information From People

You may be saying to yourself, "But I don't know anyone who works for my target companies." While this may be true, I can guarantee that someone among your friends and contacts does know someone who works for your target companies. An interesting study by Stanley Milgram (described in *Psychology Today*, May 1967), indicates that nearly all adults have between 500 and 1,000 contacts. "Contacts" include personal friends, relatives, present and former coworkers, schoolmates, church members, social club members, people you do business with (hair stylist, mechanic, banker), and even people you barely know. People who collect business cards (a very useful pastime) will probably have more than 1,000 contacts. Using two links in the chain (your contacts plus your contacts' contacts) could lead to between 250,000 (500 x 500) and 1,000,000 (1,000 x 1,000) contacts. Add a third link and you get between 125 million and one billion. The article went on to describe experiments in which people used contacts to communicate with a specific person thousands of miles away, usually requiring only two links.

While I'm not going to recommend that you contact your 500 contacts and ask each of them to contact their 500, the above example demonstrates the wide range of contacts that is available to you. What it boils down to is this: if you want to *badly enough*, you can get direct information about almost any organization in the country using only one to two links.

Employees And Former Employees

Once you have your list of target organizations, call your contacts and ask them who they know in those organizations. If they don't know anyone, ask them to ask around for you. It's okay to ask for favors. After all, you'd do the same for them. Once you get a name, call the person to learn as much as you can about the organization. Be sure to mention the name of the person who referred you or your new contact may be rather cool and reserved. Also try to establish rapport before asking probing questions. For instance, you might start by asking the person his or her overall view of the company.

Competitors

Competitors are valuable sources of information, but they may have some obvious biases. When talking to competitors, talk to sales and management people. Employees at lower levels seldom keep up on competitors. For example, the purchasing manager of a competitor probably belongs to the same association as the purchasing manager in your target company; they may even know each other. Sales people are helpful because it's their business to know about competitors. As you're picking up information, determine whether the person is sincere. If the person shares both positives and negatives about your target organization, instead of just negatives, the information will probably prove useful.

Suppliers/Customers

Suppliers and customers may be harder to locate than competitors, but a few well-placed phone calls can reveal them. Most of your target organizations probably fall in a few industries. Call several companies that would be likely to purchase the products or services of your target organizations and ask if they buy from any of them. It's very possible that they buy from several of your target firms since an organization rarely buys everything from just one source. Each of these companies will give you a slightly different view of your target organizations, so you will have some information to piece together when you complete your calls. Invariably, two or three organizations will be consistently mentioned as having excellent products and providing outstanding service.

Inside Information

Insiders can give you a great deal of information that you won't find in any written resources. Be aware, however, that every insider, whether employee, former employee, competitor, customer, or supplier, is likely to have some biases about the organization. Be alert to such biases. Everything you hear represents only one viewpoint and needs to be treated as such. This is true of virtually any organization: some will love it, some will hate it. You'll need to determine whether the person you're talking to with has an axe to grind (he may recently have lost out on a promotion), knows enough about the organization (she may really know only about her own department), or is even telling the truth. This is the fun part. You're a detective, evaluating motives and confirming stories.

Interviews are a very important part of employer research. During most interviews you'll learn a lot about the company and the department you would be working in. Make full use of the opportunity to ask questions. Ask about your growth potential, your duties, the interviewer's management style, and the future directions of the company.

REASONS FOR RESEARCHING AN ORGANIZATION

There are four main reasons for researching employers.

1. **To determine whether the organization is right for you.** Try to discover all the pros and cons you can. Research may reveal a serious problem that might cause you to eliminate the organization, or it may reveal some outstanding opportunities that will further encourage and motivate you.

2. **To impress the interviewer.** You'll impress the interviewer simply by explaining in concise terms why you should be hired and by demonstrating that you are full of enthusiasm, experience, and potential. Because so few people bother to research a company, you'll stand out in a very positive way if you've done your homework and go armed with information. Weave your information into the conversation appropriately. Some employers will ask, "What do you know about us?" Most people will hem, haw, and fail this question miserably. But you will shine. Even when asked this question, however, don't overwhelm the interviewer with your answer. Give a thorough but concise response.

3. **To discover problems you can help solve.** Problems you have the ability to solve could come to light before or during an interview. If you discover them before the interview, you'll have time to prepare and perhaps even develop a proposal. Otherwise, listen for clues to such problems during the interview. An employer may come right out and describe problems, but will probably only allude to them. Careful listening can help you match your abilities or experience to the problem area. By all means emphasize those strengths that can help solve the organization's problems.

4. **To identify questions that must be clarified by the employer.** An annual report or a magazine article may have mentioned an exciting new product being developed by your target company. If the interviewer doesn't mention it, you may have to ask if you would have a role in developing, marketing, or selling it. If an inside source told you that a strike could cripple the company, you might ask about the ef-

fects of such a strike. If the company has lost money three years in a row, you might ask what the company is doing to reverse the losses.

Interviewing is a continuation of your research. Keep your detective cap on and discover all you can. Ask yourself if you would enjoy working for this person. Will you respect this boss? Do your management philosophies match? Will you like each other? These are some of the important questions that can be answered, in part, by the research you conduct during interviews.

Do some research before each interview, even if it's the third or fourth interview with the same company. This is particularly important if you feel really good about the job, your potential boss, and the company. Discover all you can. Answering questions effectively and asking the right questions could make the difference between being the number-one choice and the number-two choice.

Luck—the crossroad where preparation and opportunity meet.

RESOURCES FOR EMPLOYER RESEARCH

Employer research takes place in two stages: 1) Obtaining a list of 50–200 employers, and 2) gathering information about employers prior to the first interview, as well as more in-depth research after a job offer is made. A survey of professional recruiters indicated that knowledge of the company was one of the three most significant factors in successful interviews. "What do you know about us?" is a favorite question of many employers. Fortunately, for most companies over 50 employees, information is available.

STAGE ONE—EMPLOYER LIST

In stage one, you'll be using various resources to develop your list of 50–200 employers. As with any resource that lists key company officials, always call to confirm that that person is still there and holding the position listed in the resource. Go ahead and use the resource to initially list names, but do not depend on them for the accuracy of those names or spelling.

Local Resources

Yellow Pages. The *Yellow Pages* are valuable because organizations have been categorized by industry, service, or function. Most city libraries will have dozens of *Yellow Pages* for other cities in your state plus the *Yellow Pages* for most major cities in the country.

Metropolitan Directories. *Contacts Influential,* and several metropolitan directories like *CI,* come close to being the ideal local resource. Each resource covers an entire metropolitan area, including suburbs. Virtually all businesses, even one-person businesses, are included, making these resources usually the most complete resource available for those metropolitan areas where they are published. The resources provide names, addresses, zip codes, phone numbers, key managers, and their titles. With a coded system, you can determine the number of employees, and whether it is a local, branch, or headquarter's office.

The resources each have an alphabetical section and a zip code section, but most people will find the SIC (industry) section most helpful. For most people the alphabetical section will simply be too overwhelming. For example, the Seattle *CI* lists over 30,000 employers. Even after you learn how to scan a page and look for companies of a certain size, it could take many hours.

Those who do not want to commute long distances often do well with the zip code section. A map in the resource should help you identify which zip codes are of interest to you. Since size is often a key factor, you can then scan through, stopping at those which fall within your desired size range.

Most will want to use the SIC section which arranges organizations by their industry code. I find that most people are interested in companies in 5–15 SIC codes. What that does for you is it immediately filters out all but 500–1000 organizations. It still isn't much fun reading the small print, but it can save you a tremendous amount of time.

Contacts Influential has directories in Denver, Ft. Collins/Pueblo, Kansas City, Minneapolis, Orange County (three separate directories), Orlando, Portland, St. Paul, Salem/Eugene, St. Petersburg, San Diego North, San Diego South, Seattle/Everett, Tacoma/Olympia, and Tampa.

Inside Contacts has directories in Boston, Cleveland, Phoenix, and Washington, D.C.

Inside Prospects has directories in Austin, Orange County, San Diego, and Seattle.

Business Wise has directories in Atlanta, Dallas, and San Francisco.

There may be resources similar to the ones listed which are not included. Ask your librarian for help in locating them.

Other Local Resources. People with no desire to leave their current geographical area will get better results with local, rather than national resources. It would be impossible, of course, to list all local resources, but I can help you find them. The best place to start is in the business reference section of your library. In this section you'll find *Yellow Pages* and many other directories.

After you've scouted out the reference area, talk to the reference librarian and ask about resources. You'll find reference librarians very helpful. Some libraries will have a list of useful resources and directories.

If you are looking for government, nonprofit, or social service agencies, ask the reference librarian for help. United Way generally publishes a booklet describing the agencies it funds. For state, city, or county governments there may be a telephone directory with names of departments, key staff people, and their phone numbers.

Virtually every chamber of commerce publishes information on local companies. Most of their directories cost between ten and twenty dollars but they should also be available at your library. As an example, the Seattle Chamber of Commerce produces a resource which lists the 800 companies in the Puget Sound region with over 100 employees. For those wanting to or needing to work for larger organizations, that can be the perfect resource. Another excellent local resource is called *Advanced Technology in Washington State*, which lists hundreds of high tech companies. Do not hesitate to ask your librarian for help— there may just be a perfect directory that someone else has already spent hundreds of hours compiling so you don't have to.

Don't overlook talking to people at the Chamber of Commerce or United Way; many can provide useful information about their metropolitan area.

State Directories
Every state publishes a list of manufacturers operating in that state. The alphabetical section gives names, telephone numbers, addresses (including divisions and subsidiaries), key executives, SIC numbers, products manufactured or services provided, number of employees, locations of branch offices and/or plants, whether they are importers and/or exporters, annual gross sales, and year established. State directories also have SIC and geographical sections. Many are published by private companies, but all are published in conjunction with that state's department of commerce. Arranged by state in alphabetical order, the directories are:

Alabama Directory of Mining and Manufacturing
Alaska Petroleum and Industrial Directory
Directory of Arizona Manufacturers
Arkansas Directory of Manufacturers
California Manufacturers Register
Directory of Colorado Manufacturers

Connecticut State Industrial Directory
Delaware Directory of Commerce and Industry
Principal Employers, Metropolitan Washington D.C.
Directory of Florida Industries
Georgia Manufacturing Directory
Directory of Manufacturers State of Hawaii
Manufacturing Directory of Idaho
Illinois Manufacturers Directory
Indiana Industrial Directory
Directory of Iowa Manufacturers
Directory of Kansas Manufacturers and Products
Kentucky Directory of Manufacturers and Products
Louisiana Directory of Manufacturers
Maine Marketing Directory
Directory of Maryland Manufacturers
Directory of Massachusetts Manufacturers
Minnesota Directory of Manufacturers
Mississippi Manufacturers Directory
Missouri Directory of Manufacturers and Mining
Montana Directory of Manufacturers
Made in New Hampshire
New Jersey State Industrial Directory
Directory of New Mexico Manufacturing and Mining
New York State Industrial Directory
North Carolina Directory of Manufacturing Firms
Directory of North Dakota Manufacturers
Ohio Industrial Directory
Oklahoma Manufacturers Directory
Directory of Oregon Manufacturers
Pennsylvania State Industrial Directory
Puerto Rico Official Industrial Directory
Rhode Island Directory of Manufacturers
Industrial Directory of South Carolina
South Dakota Manufacturers and Processors Directory
Tennessee Directory of Manufacturers
Directory of Texas Manufacturers
Directory of Utah Manufacturers
Directory of Vermont Manufacturers
Virginia Industrial Directory
Washington Manufacturers Register
West Virginia Manufacturing Directory
Classified Directory of Wisconsin Manufacturers
Wyoming Directory of Manufacturing and Mining

National Resources

Some of the national resources listed below cost over one hundred dollars per year and are found only in libraries with a major business section. Go to your nearest library first to find out what local and national directories they have. Eventually you may need to visit a larger library.

National resources are useful primarily for those who want to work for companies over 500 employees and are willing to relocate to do so. If you want to remain in your metropolitan area, or at least in your state, there will virtually always be local directories which will be more helpful than the national directories.

Dun and Bradstreet—Million Dollar Directory. This publication lists 160,000 companies with a net worth of $1,000,000 or more. The alphabetical section includes company names, names of parent companies, addresses, telephone numbers, SIC numbers, sales figures, number of employees, principal officers, and whether companies are involved in importing and exporting. Dun and Bradstreet also has geographical and SIC sections.

Dun and Bradstreet—Middle Market Directory. Same as above except it covers companies with a net worth between $500,000 and $1,000,000.

Standard and Poor's. This directory includes 37,000 corporations, with names, addresses, telephone numbers, products made, number of employees, and sales volume. Volume 1 has an alphabetical listing, volume 2 has biographical information on 75,000 key officers listed alphabetically by last name, and volume 3 lists corporations by SIC and geographic area.

Dun's Directory of Service Companies. It lists 50,000 organizations in the following categories: management consulting, executive search, public relations, engineering and architectural services, business services, consumer services, research services, repair services, hospitality, motion pictures, amusement and recreation. All have more than 50 employees.

The Career Guide—Dun's Employment Opportunities Directory. The guide describes several hundred companies which recruit on college campuses. It is primarily designed for recent college grads, but it can used by anyone. It describes the company, the college majors it recruits for, its training program, internships offered, and locations of facilities apart from the headquarters.

The College Placement Annual. Contains national companies and lists the college degrees they desire most. Basic information about the company is provided. One section lists college majors and the companies which are seeking those majors.

Corporate Technology Directory. Lists 35,000 high-tech firms by their products and indicates total sales, percent of sales from export, and key employees.

Mac Rae's Blue Book. *Mac Rae's* lists 50,000 firms and is primarily used by purchasing agents. It provides addresses, primary products or services, telephone sales offices and distributors, and cities and phone numbers for sales reps or outlets. Volume 1 has an alphabetical listing plus about 100,000 brand names listed alphabetically with name of company. Volumes 2 through 4 are arranged by product with manufacturers of that product listed below each heading. Volume 5 contains the catalogs of over one hundred companies.

Thomas Register. This directory is like *Mac Rae's*—it was designed primarily to assist purchasing agents locate companies that offer certain products or services. Volumes 1 through 6 list over 50,000 products and the companies that produce them. Volume 7 indexes these products by the pages they can be found on; it also lists 72,000 brand names and the companies that own them. Volume 8 is an alphabetical list of United States manufacturers. It provides names, addresses, telephone numbers, dollar values of tangible assets, subsidiaries, and affiliated companies. Volumes 9 through 14 contain the catalogs of over 800 companies.

Trade Names Dictionary. Identifies the producer of various products listed by their trade names.

Who Owns Whom. This is useful for tracing subsidiaries, parent companies, affiliations, or divisions.

America's Corporate Families. Describes 9,000 U.S. parent companies and 45,000 subsidiaries. Volume 2 lists U.S. subsidiaries and their foreign parents.

Directory of Corporate Affiliations. This directory lists 4,000 parent companies with addresses and phone numbers. Section 1 gives sales, number of employees, type of business, top officers, divisions, subsidiaries, and affiliates. Section 2 lists 45,000 divisions, subdivisions, and affiliates alphabetically and gives the parent company. This resource also has a geographical index.

Directory of American Firms Operating in Foreign Countries. Section 1 lists firms alphabetically and the countries each one operates in. Section 2 lists countries and tells which American firms operate in each.

Directory of Foreign Firms Operating in the U.S. This directory lists foreign firms operating in the United States and describes their products.

Ward's Business Directory. *Ward's* provides information on 90,000 mostly privately held companies with a net worth greater than $500,000. What makes *Ward's* distinct from *Dun & Bradstreet* and *Standard & Poor's* is that it concentrates on privately held companies (which is difficult information to obtain) and provides various rankings such as the largest pharmaceutical firms in the U.S.

Industry Directories

Thousands of directories exist which are helpful to job seekers. As an example, the *Whole World Oil Directory* lists all oil and gas companies, drilling companies, oil well services, and refineries. It may be the only resource some people would need.

Keep in mind that while being very useful, no directory is complete. Small companies are often listed haphazardly, and even large ones are sometimes left out. The information may be outdated or sometimes just plain wrong. Frequently businesses have moved or gone under. Still, these directories are great sources of information.

Several resources are available to help you locate useful directories. Most libraries will have either the *Guide to American Directories* or *Directories in Print*. Both list and describe over 5,000 directories that are divided into over 300 categories. They are quick and easy to use. They have an alphabetical section and a subject section. They will also tell you what the directories cost and where to order them. Most directories cost $15–30 but some cost in the hundreds. After you identify a useful directory, check the card catalog to see if the library has it. Even if your library does not have it, an interlibrary search with the help of your reference librarian, may help you find a library which does.

Below is a sampling of some of the more useful directories. They are listed merely to give you an idea of the types of directories available. When you use either *Guide to American Directories* or *Directories in Print*, assume that there is a directory for your field or your industry, and 99 times out of one hundred, you'll be right. Virtually every major industry has at least five directories.

Administrative
　　Consultants and Consulting Organizations Directory
　　National Trade & Professional Associations of the U. S.
　　Directory of Management Consultants
Apparel
　　Apparel Industry Magazine Sourcebook
　　American Apparel Manufacturers Association Directory
Aviation
　　Aviation Telephone Directory
　　World Aviation Directory
Banking and Finance
　　American Bank Directory
　　Polk's Bank Directory
Broadcasting
　　World Radio—TV Handbook
　　Los Angeles Directory of TV Commercial Film Producers
　　Video Industry Directory

Computers

Official Directory of Data Processing

Microcomputer Market Place

Conservation and Environment

Environmental Organizations Directory

Directory of Public Aquaria of the World

Conservation Directory

Electrical/Electronics/Communications

Telephony's Directory of the Telephone Industry

Electrical Product Membership Directory

American Electronics Association Directory

Food/Food Processing

Directory of the Canning, Freezing and Preserving Industry

Directory of Frozen Food Processors

Food Processing Guide and Directory

Thomas Grocery Register

Import/Export

Directory of United States Importers

American Register of Importers and Exporters

Metal/Metal Manufacturing

Directory of Iron and Steel Works of the U. S. and Canada

Dun and Bradstreet's Metal Working Directory

National Machine Tool Builders Association Directory

Media/Advertising/Public Relations/Marketing

Graphic Arts Buyers Guide Directory Issue

O'Dwyer's Directory of Public Relations Firms

Standard Directory of Advertising Agencies

Oil

Directory of Oil Well Supply Companies

U.S.A. Oil Industry Directory

Whole World Oil Directory

Research

Research Centers Directory

Directory of American Research & Technology

Retail

Fairchild's Financial Manual of Retail Stores

Sheldon's Retail Trade

Sales

National Directory of Manufacturers Representatives

Verified Directory of Manufacturers Representatives

Transportation/Shipping

Official Guide of the Railways

Truck Broker Directory

Warehouse Directory

STAGE TWO—OBTAINING INFORMATION ABOUT THE ORGANIZATION

Once you've landed an appointment or an interview, it's time to shift into high gear and get prepared. Since knowledge of the organization is critical for interviews, researching an organization can enable you to go in armed with knowledge. This knowledge will give you added confidence in your appointments and interviews. Avoid overwhelming the interviewer with your knowledge about products or financial figures, though. Instead, keep your information in reserve and use it only when appropriate.

The following resources will provide valuable information.

Moody's. *Moody's Industrial Manual*—Provides financial information, history, subsidiaries, products and services, sales, principal plants and properties, executives, number of employees. One to two pages are devoted to most companies. All of the *Moody's* manuals concentrate on large companies.

Moody's OTC (Over the Counter)—Same format as above but covering smaller companies.

Moody's Municipal and Government Manual
Moody's Bank and Finance Manual
Moody's Public Utilities Manual
Moody's Transportation Manual

Clipping Files. Many libraries maintain files of news articles and feature articles about local businesses clipped from local papers. While most articles are short news releases, you will also find highly informative feature articles about new developments within target companies.

House Organs. Companies publish house organs (in-house newsletters) as internal public relations vehicles and will have such things as a letter from the president describing past achievements and future goals, pictures of the bowling team and those retiring, and usually a feature article about a person, department, or a new product. House organs are especially helpful. Check with your library to see if a file of house organs is maintained.

Annual Reports. If the company is publicly owned (stock which is publicly traded), it is required by law to publish an annual financial report. Understanding the financial jargon is unnecessary. The past year's failures and achievements will be summarized along with descriptions of new products and future goals.

Recruiting Brochures. Major companies which recruit at college campuses produce recruiting brochures. The brochures describe the history and background of the company, training programs, company benefits, and desired training and characteristics of employees. College placement offices will have many on file.

Indexes. In addition to clipping files, you will want to use one or more indexes to locate articles in magazines or newspapers. First look up the company by name. If you don't find the listings you want, you could read articles about the industry that your target company falls in and possibly find a reference to your target company in that way. The indexes can also be used to research a topic, a product, a new technology, or an entire industry.

Encyclopedia of Business Information Sources. Lists trade associations, periodicals, directories, bibliographies, and an abstract index of recent articles. An outstanding resource.

Readers Guide to Periodical Literature. Lists articles found in over two hundred popular magazines, giving the periodical, date and title of article. This is the same green-covered resource you used in high school when you did research reports.

Business Periodicals Index. The *BPI* uses business periodicals which are generally not covered in the *Readers Guide to Periodical Literature.* Examples: *Human Resource Management* and *Automotive News.*

The Magazine Index. An automated system found in many libraries which indexes articles in about 400 general interest magazines. It is published by Information Access Company which, in a similar format, also publishes: *National Newspaper Index, Business Index,* and *Legal Resource Index.*

Infotrac. A computerized data base found in many libraries, it indexes 1,100 magazines, going back ten years. With the help of a librarian it takes under five minutes to learn how to use. Some libraries just have the magazine index, while others will also have the newspaper and business indexes as well. The business index indexes articles found in magazines which are not included in the magazine index. With it you can research industries, products, new technology, and companies. The business index provides information about the companies themselves, including address, products, number of employees, etc., and articles written about them. With most articles you can also read an abstract, which is a short version of the article. Both the abstracts plus the information about the article such as the name of the periodical, date, and page number, can be printed out so you don't have to write them all down. In that way you can get a print-out on many articles and then later decide which ones to look up.

ABI Inform. Same concept as *Infotrac,* it abstracts 700 business journals.

F & S Index of Corporations and Industries. Lists articles on industries and companies, including mergers, acquisitions, new products, and emerging technology. Lists trade journals, addresses and their costs.

F & S Index Europe. Same format

F & S Index International. Same format. Covers Canada, Latin America, Africa, and Asia

Wall Street Journal Index. The first section is alphabetical by company; the second section is alphabetical by subject and peoples' names.

New York Times Index. Same format

Chicago Tribune Index. Same format

Los Angeles Times Index. Same format

Washington Post Index. Same format

Libraries which carry these indexes will probably also have the newspapers on microfilm.

Your Interviewer. Search the clipping file and house organs for articles about your interviewer. Before you go to a specific *Who's Who,* look up the name of your person in *Index to Who's Who Books.* The information tends to be strictly biographical with date of birth, address, school graduated from, and offices held. Most of the information is supplied by the individuals themselves. The primary *Who's Who* include:

Who's Who In America

Who's Who In The West

Who's Who In The East

Who's Who In Finance and Industry

Who's Who Of American Women

You will also find other specialized *Who's Who In ...,* covering various subjects such as human resources: *Who's Who In HR.*

Other resources that include biographical information include:

Dun & Bradstreet Reference Book of Corporate Managements— Lists companies alphabetically, then lists executive with name, title, year born, summary of career, education.

Standard and Poor's, vol. 2—Register of Directors and Executives. Same information as *Dun's,* but executives are listed alphabetically by last name.

CONTACTS

Friends, relatives, acquaintances, and business contacts can all provide useful leads if you approach them in the right way. Before they can help, people must know what you're looking for and what your qualifications are. About 26% of all jobseekers find positions through such leads. This number could be increased substantially if people made better use of this method. Include your banker, barber, broker, and butcher. Every person who has an interest in your success can be helpful.

Use the methods described below to develop your list of contacts:

1. Start by listing the names of friends, relatives, and contacts in your area (assuming you plan to stay in your present location). Include each person's home phone and address, and, if possible, each one's employer and title.

2. Develop an *A*-list and a *B*-list. Your *A*-list includes people most likely to hear about the type of opening you're interested in and those who could refer you to other key people. If your parents live in the area, include many of their friends on your list. Perhaps you haven't spoken to them in years, but they will still be glad to help you. These people are likely to be either retired or near the end of their careers. In any case, they are likely to have high-level contacts. Your *B*-list consists of people you know who are less likely to hear of job openings in your field. You'll still want to contact them but they won't receive the same priority as your *A*-list people.

3. Mail resumes first to your *A*-list people with a short, handwritten note indicating the type of work you're seeking and stating that you'll call in a few days to explain the resume more fully. Also send a list of your 70 top employer prospects. If you include a longer list, people won't pay as much attention to it. The resume is important because most of your friends probably don't know much about your background or qualifications. The note attached to your resume might read like this:

> Janice — I'll be calling you in a few days to tell you about my career goals. I plan to move out of teaching and into sales. I don't expect you to know of any openings right now, but you may hear of some in the coming weeks. I've enclosed my list of preferred companies. If you know anyone at all who works there, please let me know. Thanks.
>
> Joyce

❖

Dear Kemper,

I'll be calling you next week to let you know what I'm up to. Please read my list of potential employers and let me know if you know <u>anyone</u> who works there.

Bob

4. When you call or visit one of your contacts, explain how they can help. Indicate that you're not asking for a job, but simply asking them to keep their eyes and ears open for leads, either within their own organization or other organizations. Also explain that you don't expect them to set up any appointments for you, but do ask them to pass leads on to you so you can follow them up on your own. Indicate that you would like to use their name whenever it is appropriate. Ask for any advice they might have for you. Get them involved in your search. After people have given advice, they feel they have a stake in your success.

5. Get referrals. Ask your contacts if they know anyone at all who works for any of the organizations on your list. Emphasize *anyone*. It's great if they know a key person in a particular organization, but the name of anyone in the organization can be useful. Don't rule out people such as secretaries, bookkeepers, janitors, and truck drivers. They will know others within the organization, and they may have insights to share with you.

Let's assume you're seeking a position as a purchasing assistant. Perhaps a contact knows the very person you need to reach in a particular organization. If so, that's excellent! Learn as much as you can about that individual—his or her likes, dislikes, management style, good points, and bad points. If the contact knows someone in a different department, by all means call that person and ask about the purchasing department and its supervisor. If you mention your friend's name, the person will most likely be open with you. If you simply make the cold call and start asking specific questions about departments or department heads without mentioning your contact, the person may react defensively and will be less inclined to give you useful information.

Establishing rapport with these new contacts is crucial. Initially, the only thing you have in common is a mutual friend. Although that will help a great deal in the first minute, in order to get the information you really want, you will need to build your own rapport. This person may be open to listening to you, and may have some desire to help because of the mutual friend, but *you* will need to take it a step further.

Begin by introducing yourself and then give the name of your mutual friend. Describe the reason for your call. Explain exactly what you want from this person. In explaining the purpose of the call, indicate that you are considering working for this company. Very briefly, describe your background, taking less than a minute to do so. Then briefly describe what you know about the organization and indicate which department you think is the best fit for you. You should have already gained the name of the person with power to hire—give that name, asking for confirmation that he or she is indeed the right person.

Feel free to spend some time talking about your mutual friend if this person asks a question about your friend. If, in fact, you barely know the person (perhaps the person is a business associate of your father's you've never met) indicate that and then move on to your request. An up-front response works best: "Actually I barely know her. But when I was speaking to her a couple days ago she suggested I call you."

Ask if the organization is a good one to work for. The person may return with a resounding yes, or you might get something like this: "This used to be a great company, but we were purchased by another firm two years ago. If I didn't already have 20 years in here, I'd probably be looking myself. For a person like yourself just breaking into the industry, I would look more at ABC and XYZ." This is extremely helpful information. Ask the person to describe what he or she likes and dislikes about the organization. As the conversation comes to a close you might say, "I really appreciate the information you've given me. I may or may not pursue a position there, but your information will be very helpful. If I do speak to Mr. Rathman, can I say you suggested I call?" Rarely will your request to use another person's name be turned down.

Occasionally, the person will not want to be mentioned by name. It may be that the two barely know each other, but more likely it will be because they don't get along. The contact is really saying that he or she would not be a useful reference. In such a case, of course, you would not use the contact's name.

When the person does permit your use of his or her name, you have a real advantage. When you call the hiring authority and get the secretary, you will be able to say, "Jeanett Horner suggested I call." The use of the name will help you get through to your person. Then when you get the hiring authority on the line, you would repeat that Jeanett Horner suggested the call. Ultimately, you will have to sell yourself, but just mentioning the person's name will raise the level of attention you receive from the employer. That attention level can make the critical difference regarding whether that person will meet with you.

The best way to illustrate the difference between giving a name and not giving one is to use some figures based on my experience. A person who is getting appointments with 75% of the hiring authorities when a reference name is given will probably still succeed in getting appointments with 60% of the hiring authorities when no reference is given.

Most of the time you will probably not be able to say that a particular person referred you. Without a doubt, giving a name as a reference is valuable, but when you don't have a name, you simply have to work a little harder at selling yourself on your own merits.

As you can imagine, the process of contacting all of these people takes time. It takes time to call all of your target organizations to determine who is the person with power to hire. It takes time to call friends, relatives, and associates and ask for assistance. It takes time to call people within your target organizations or those people who know about your target organizations. Then it takes still more time to call the employers and ask for appointments. Just remember: the results you get will make it more than worthwhile.

You've been presented with a systematic way to learn about openings and to get appointments with employers. This method is far more effective than the methods the average person uses. Even using haphazard and inconsistent techniques, 26% of all people get their jobs through the help of friends, relatives, and contacts.

Follow-up With Contacts

It is extremely important to follow-up with your contacts. For the first two or three weeks after you initially contact them, they will think a lot about you. If they overhear a conversation on the bus or in a restaurant which might be of value to you, their ears will prick up and they will take appropriate action. After about three weeks, however, their ears will become a little dull. That same conversation that three weeks earlier caused the ears to prick up now stirs up nothing. This is human nature: we tend to forget people if we don't hear from them. After about six weeks, those people you contacted who do not know you well will have almost totally forgotten you. If they happen to see a job posting, they will probably still think of you, but they will not be actively pursuing leads on your behalf.

Following up with your contacts will keep them interested and thinking about you. They need to hear from you. Your initial call usually requires the most time since you will be explaining your plans and answering any questions the person may have. It's also very likely that you will get into a conversation about old times, especially if this is a person you don't see or speak to frequently. Or the person may ask what you know about some mutual friends. Your initial call, therefore, can easily take 15–20 minutes. Your follow-up calls, however, can usually be kept to under five minutes.

In those follow-up calls, quickly bring the person up-to-date on your activities and progress. If the person gave you any referrals or ideas, you should mention what you did in response. The main thing you're doing is simply reminding the person that you are still actively and systematically conducting your job search. It's important to let people know you are both active and systematic. If people believe you are not doing all that you can, they will feel less responsibility for helping you.

In this initial follow-up, you could also ask about some additional organizations. If you have a list of 100 target companies, but on the list you sent you included only 70, you could verbally mention another 20–25 organizations and ask if the person knows anyone who works for any of those organizations.

The telephone call completes your first follow-up. About six weeks later, follow-up through the mail. Write a letter describing what you've been up to. Include an interesting story about an experience you had or someone you met. Photocopy the letter and personalize it by handwriting the person's name and perhaps add a personal paragraph. These letters will cost you postage plus the reproduction costs, but they will save time and long-distance telephone costs. Letters are an excellent way to maintain contact with your resources.

Six to eight weeks later, and every six to eight weeks thereafter, you should follow up again with a brief, three-minute phone call. Not only will your resources appreciate it, it will make them much more aware and helpful.

Many people fail to make contact with friends, relatives, and associates because they really don't want people to know that they are job hunting. Job hunting is not a sin and unemployment is not a disease. These people want to help you. Remember, you are not asking them for any great favors. They will spend next to no time on your behalf; you are merely asking them to keep their eyes and ears open to opportunities.

As I've mentioned, 26% of all people get their jobs through leads supplied by friends, relatives, and associates. The research also shows that people usually make contact with friends and relatives very haphazardly. People often tell only three of their closest friends about the job search, and over a period of time, five or six relatives may find out as well. If people can get such results from such a haphazard effort, imagine what you can do with a systematic approach that involves 30–80 people looking out for you.

You will quickly find yourself getting a lot of leads. Like a detective or salesperson, you'll need to prioritize your leads. If you start getting more that you can follow up on, prioritize them according to the likelihood that the lead will get you closer to your goal.

A few days after your calls to friends, relatives, and associates, send a thank-you letter to each one. It can be handwritten and does not need to be more than three sentences long. Even if the person was not able to help you at the time, a quality lead may still come from that person. In any case, the person gave some of his or her valuable time, and common courtesy says the person should be thanked. Furthermore, this thoughtful gesture will also cause the person to be even more impressed with you than before. As a result, the person will be more likely to pass future leads to you.

After you obtain a position you should once again send thank-you notes to all those who helped you. This one could be a form letter describing your new job, with perhaps a sentence or two at the bottom which personalizes the letter. It could be a special thank you concerning a particularly useful lead or piece of advice.

Even Haphazardness Can Lead To Job Offers

That 26% of all people have their current job because of a lead is somewhat amazing given how haphazard most people are about letting others know they are looking for a job. The following examples illustrate how most people approach the job search. These examples are quoted from *Getting A Job*, by Mark Granovetter. Granovetter performed one of the finest research projects to date demonstrating how people actually obtain their jobs.

> Carl Y. was doing commission sales for an encyclopedia firm, but was not doing well. He decided he would have to find a different job; meanwhile he started driving a cab to bring in extra money. One passenger asked to be taken to the train station where he had to meet a friend. This friend turned out to be an old friend of Carl Y's, and asked him "what're you doing driving a cab?" When Mr. Y. explained, the friend offered him the job he now holds—labor relations manager for a small company owned by his friend.

> Edward A. had graduated from high school and been in the service. After returning, he resumed his practice of driving to the local park, in the evening, where his friends hung around; bars and restaurants in the vicinity made the area a popular teen-age hangout. The usual procedure was to drive by and see if anyone was there that you knew. On one occasion he ran into an older friend who was employed by an engineering firm. The friend told him that there was an opening for a draftsman in this firm. Mr. A. applied and accepted this position.

> George C. was working as a technician for an electrical firm, with a low salary and little apparent chance for advancement. While courting

his future wife, he met her downstairs neighbor, the manager of a candy shop, a concession leased from a national chain. After they were married, Mr. C. continued to see the neighbor when visiting his mother-in-law. The neighbor finally talked him into entering a trainee program for the chain and arranged an interview for him. Within three years, Mr. C. was earning almost four times his previous salary.

So you can see what rather extraordinary things happen to people almost by chance. Of course, some people do deliberately talk to friends and relatives, and end up with excellent leads by doing so. But the vast majority of connections are made in ways similar to the examples above.

CALLS

In this phase of the process, it is crucial to meet the person who has the power to hire you. Determining who that person is and getting an appointment requires a well-planned strategy.

Determining Who Has the Power to Hire

The person with the power to hire you normally holds a position that would be one or two levels above you in the department or functional area you have focused on. Often this person will be a department head. When calling, ask for the name of the person whose job title indicates that he or she has the power to hire you. With very small companies, you might first contact the president or vice president if that seems appropriate. If that person does not hire people at your level, get a referral to the person who does. When you can, however, avoid speaking to the president, since that person is always the most difficult person to reach.

Work hard, however, to determine precisely who the person is who could hire you for the type of position you want.

Once you have your list of organizations, begin identifying the people who do the hiring. Getting their names is easy because nearly every business has a receptionist. Call and ask for the person's name, being sure to get the correct spelling and title. Most receptionists are so busy that they won't bother to ask you why you want to know.

Occasionally, the receptionist will not know the proper person, or will hastily connect you with personnel. Don't be startled, just ask your question again with confidence and assertiveness. If the receptionist or personnel clerk asks why you are calling, the most simple response is, "I have some material to send to your purchasing manager." Typical responses might be like these:

69

Receptionist:	Dearborn Insurance, may I help you?
Steve:	Hello, can you give me the name of your claims manager?
Receptionist:	Yes, that would be John Yaeger.
Steve:	Would you spell his last name, please?
Receptionist:	Sure, Y A E G E R.
Steve:	Thank you very much.

❖

Receptionist:	Medico, may I help you?
Sally:	Hello, can you give me the name of your EDP manager?
Receptionist:	EDP?
Sally:	Yes, Electronic Data Processing. Do you have someone in charge of computer programming?
Receptionist:	I think you probably want Bob Benson.
Sally:	What is his title?
Receptionist:	He's vice president of operations, but I think he's in charge of our three programmers.
Sally:	Okay, thank you very much.

❖

Receptionist:	Continental.
Kevin:	Can you give me the name of your purchasing manager?
Receptionist:	Just a moment.
Personnel:	Personnel.
Kevin:	Can you give me the name of your purchasing manager?
Personnel:	That would be James Townsend.
Kevin:	Thank you.

❖

Receptionist:	Malco, may I help you?
Holly:	Could you please give me the name of your advertising manager?
Receptionist:	Just a moment.
Personnel:	Personnel.
Holly:	Could you please give me the name of your advertising manager?
Personnel:	What is this concerning?
Holly:	I have some material to send and I want to make sure it gets to the right person. Could you give me the name of your advertising manager?
Personnel:	That would be Janet Lynn.
Holly:	What is her title?
Personnel:	She's director of marketing.
Holly:	Thank you.

Occasionally you'll find a firm that is so secretive they won't give out anyone's name. If the organization has a high enough priority for you, there is always a way to find out who you need to talk to. Usually such firms are fairly large. By putting all your contacts together, you should be able to identify someone who works there or who knows about the organization.

One client who was facing such a difficulty came up with an effective solution. When a receptionist refused to divulge the information, he would respond, "Who should I contact later if I want additional information?" He then asked for that person's area of responsibility. In that way he was virtually always able to call later and get the name of the person with the power to hire him.

Another possible solution is to call before 8 a.m., between noon and 1 p.m., or after 5 p.m. At these times a less experienced person is likely to be on the switchboard and will simply give you the desired information.

Whether you list 70 or 250 organizations, I would recommend going through the entire list in two or three days to get the names of all the hiring authorities. You can then check off that activity as being completed. You'll also need the names of hiring authorities when you send the list of your 70 preferred organizations to friends and relatives.

Calling the Person With the Power To Hire

Once you know the names of the people with the power to hire in your organizations, start setting up appointments. This part is more challenging than just getting the names. Your first task will be getting past the person's secretary. One of the secretary's duties is to protect the boss from unnecessary calls, and some exercise this duty with a vengeance. Don't be afraid, though; you can get past even the toughest secretary. Once you get to your potential boss, you must present yourself quickly and ask for an appointment. With a polished opening, you should be able to get appointments 40–80% of the time.

Getting Past Secretaries

When talking to a secretary, present yourself as a confident businessperson with legitimate business reasons for calling. Give your name immediately since the secretary will invariably ask for it. You'll also sound more authoritative. If, after trying all the styles given below, you just can't get past the secretary, try calling very early in the morning or after 5:30 p.m. A busy executive will often answer the phone when the secretary is not there. One of the techniques below will usually work:

Receptionist:	Glasgow and Associates.
Polly:	I'd like to speak to Marilyn Shelton.
Receptionist:	Just a moment, please.
Secretary:	Marilyn Shelton's office.
Polly:	This is Polly Preston. I'd like to speak with Marilyn Shelton.
Secretary:	What is this concerning?
Polly:	Don Drummer of Polycorp suggested I speak with her.

or

I have some advertising concepts I would like to discuss with her.

or

I have some personal matters to discuss with her.

or

I have some business matters to discuss with her.

Secretary:	Just a moment, I'll ring her office.

Avoid Return Calls

If the person is out when you call (or so the secretary says), avoid leaving your phone number. Say that you will be in and out yourself and ask for the best time to call back. It is much better for you to initiate contact. If the employer returns your call, you may be caught unprepared, perhaps even coming out of the shower. If you have been calling several people, you may not even recognize the person's name at first. This can be very embarrassing. Furthermore, by leaving your name and number you lose control of the situation. Once you leave your name and number, you are basically obligated to give the person two or three days to return your call. If the person never calls, you've lost three days. When you finally do get through, more days will have passed since the person read your marketing letter. The dialogue below illustrates how to handle this situation.

Secretary:	Janet Spurrier's office.
John:	This is John Bradley. I'd like to speak with Janet Spurrier.
Secretary:	I'm sorry, she's in a meeting now. Can I have her return your call?
John:	No, I'll be out most of the day. What do you think would be a good time to reach her?
Secretary:	That's hard to say, but probably about 3:30.
John:	Thank you.

Voice Mail

Now that voice mail has become so popular, new problems have arisen for job seekers. Often when you call the switchboard and ask for the specific person, the next thing you know you are listening to that person's voice mail message. Voice mail has both an advantage and a disadvantage. The advantage is that you can call as often as you like and no one will know the difference. I would recommend that you continue calling until you reach the person. If the call is long distance, you can usually be sure that if the person is available he or she will answer within two rings. If you don't get an answer within two rings, simply hang up. To do that, of course, you need the person's direct extension. Once you know the person has voice mail, I would ask the receptionist for that number. Usually it will be given to you.

The disadvantage of voice mail is that some people who have it never answer their phone. They never receive calls, they only return them. If you get one of those people, eventually you will have to leave a message and hope the person calls. When leaving a message, sound professional and give the person a good reason to call you back.

What Do You Say After Hello?

After your future boss answers, you have 20–30 seconds to sell yourself. A prepared script can give you added confidence and just the right words to make a great first impression. Since it is so easy to say "no," make it easy for the employer to say "yes" when you ask for a brief appointment.

To sell yourself, you must quickly summarize your background and present evidence that you are a highly desirable person. Upon concluding your pitch, ask for an appointment. Ask to "get together" or have a "brief meeting," but never call it an interview. You are *not* seeking a traditional job interview.

Practice by first making a few of these calls to low-priority firms. Your voice should convey self-confidence and enthusiasm. Your words should convey potential. Naturally, if you are reading from a script, you won't want the employer to sense this. Practice until you speak in a normal conversational tone. After a few calls you should keep the script by you for reference, but you should begin varying your words slightly each time to provide a sense of spontaneity. You might even record your first few calls to check your enthusiasm level. Record your portion of the call on a portable recorder. Be sure to project enough enthusiasm so that it is conveyed to the person at the other end of the line.

In the first sample script below, a recent college grad is making a cold call. It takes only about ten seconds to complete the call. Notice that the introduction is brief but sufficient for the purpose.

Mr. Crenshaw, this is Brian Dawlar. I just graduated from the University of Washington with a degree in business, emphasizing marketing. I realize you may not have any openings at this time, but I would appreciate setting up a time when we could meet for 10 or 15 minutes.

In the next example, Sandra is reminding Mrs. Garner that a marketing letter was sent. Sandra is hoping Mrs. Garner remembers, but even if she does not, Sandra will still provide only a brief summary of her background and then ask for an appointment. If the person has not received the letter, there is no need to tell the person that you will send another copy of the letter—once you have the person on the line, go for the appointment.

The example below demonstrates how a marketing letter works. It is followed by the script from Sandra's phone call.

7/22/92

Roberta Garner
District Sales Manager
ABC Corp.
1878 116th N.E.
Bellevue, Washington 98004

Dear Ms. Garner:

I have a strong sales personality. During six years as an educator teaching French and history, I have sold programs and ideas to school administrators, teachers, parents, and community leaders. Selling comes naturally to me. Because of this ability, and a desire to achieve a high income, I am now looking at sales opportunities.

I am a high-energy person with real initiative. I make things happen. I am quick to take on responsibility and I succeed at whatever I put my heart into. The people I know in sales all say I will be successful. I believe them.

I will call you next week to set up a time when we might meet briefly.

Sincerely,

Sandra Bennett

Having read the marketing letter you can see why Sandra is confident as she calls Garner and seeks a brief appointment.

Mrs. Garner? Hi, this is Sandra Bennett. I wanted to confirm that you received the letter I sent a few days ago describing my teaching background in French and history...Good...I've been teaching for the last six years, but all my sales friends tell me I'd be a natural in sales. I realize you may not have any openings at this time, but I would appreciate arranging, oh, a 10- or 15-minute get-together. I'd like to tell you a little more about me and at the same time learn about some of the directions Salvo is headed. Would early next week work for you?

Read Sandra's spiel again and notice what she did. As she introduced herself she mentioned her letter which had described her background in teaching French and history. We all know that teaching French and history are not prerequisites for a career in sales. Nevertheless, she mentioned her teaching because it would act as a "cue" for Garner. Providing a cue is an important part of making the marketing letter and the phone call result in an appointment.

Your marketing letters that are sent to local people should go out on a Friday. You can be quite certain that a letter you mail on a Friday will arrive on Monday. To allow for a delay in the postal system, or in case the person was out of the office on Monday, you should begin calling people Tuesday afternoon. If you send out 10–20 marketing letters each week, that means Tuesday and Wednesday will be your heavy telephone days. By waiting until Tuesday to call, you can be quite sure that the person will have received it, but not so much time will have elapsed that the person is likely to have forgotten it. If you send your marketing letter any other day of the week, you will not be so certain about its arrival time. Also, by beginning your calls on Tuesday, you have the rest of the week to call the people that you were not able to reach on Tuesday and Wednesday. Even those you reach on Friday should not have forgotten you.

The cue you mention in the phone call is an important way to help a person recall having seen your marketing letter. It is unlikely that the person will remember all of the details of the letter. All you are really hoping for is that the person will have some memory of having read the letter. The backgrounds of some people are so outstanding, and their letters so well written, that some employers are actually anticipating the call. For most people, however, that will not be the case. You should feel good if the person merely indicates that he or she saw it. But trust me, the letter will have had an impact and it will help you get an appointment.

In Sandra's case, the cue is not necessarily a selling point. The cue was not even intended as a selling point. She is not implying that this sales manager should want to meet her merely because she taught French and history. Those points were only made because Sandra wanted Garner to remember her letter. The selling point in Sandra's spiel is that her sales friends all think she would be great.

There are some cases in which a marketing letter may not be necessary. In the example below, Jim Thomas decided not to use a marketing letter. He has a strong background in sales and is accustomed to setting up sales appointments over the phone. By dispensing with the marketing letter he saves time and money, and he'll end up with just as high a success rate as he would if he sent a marketing letter. Anyone who feels confident in their phone skills should give consideration to skipping the marketing letter and simply making direct contact with the hiring authority.

> Hi Mr. Bradley, this is Jim Thomas. I've been selling radio advertising for the last six years and I'm seriously considering changing stations. I've been in the top 15% in sales for the last three years. I'm not in a rush to leave, but I would like to set a time when we could get together for 15 minutes or so.

Each of the scripts presented here as examples can be said in 10-20 seconds. When you've just reached a stranger on the phone, and the most the person has said is "Hello" or "This is Crenshaw," twenty seconds is quite a long time.

Below is an example of a more complete script where the applicant is going to ask for a 15-minute appointment. The employer will respond by saying he doesn't have any openings. That will be the most common response, even though you will have just said something like, "I realize you may have no openings at this time, but I would like to meet briefly with you for perhaps 15 minutes." Either employers don't hear that statement, or they choose to ignore it. Those who ignore it do so, I believe, because they know that by stating that there are no openings, 90% of all job seekers will lose interest in coming in. By asking for a meeting you'll demonstrate that you're not like all the rest.

The key to the success of this technique is that you are making such a reasonable request. Initially, you ask for 15 minutes. If that does not succeed, you make a second request, but drop the time down to ten minutes. When asking a third time you would ask either for just five minutes or for two minutes just to introduce yourself. Notice how skillfully this is done in the following example.

Jay: This is John Jay.

Sur: Mr. Jay, this is Bob Sur. I was calling to confirm that you received my letter which describes my 15 years in purchasing, including purchasing all the steel, glass, and concrete for the Columbia Center in Seattle.

Give the listener a cue so he can recall you from among the 10–30 letters received in the last few days. In this case, the Columbia Center project mentioned in the marketing letter served as the cue.

Jay: Yes, I believe I saw that yesterday.

Sur: I'm glad you had a chance to review it. I do have a strong purchasing background. For Maynard and Wyatt Construction I implemented a very effective just-in-time program. I realize you may not have any openings at this moment,

Make it easy for the person to say yes.

but I did want to set up a time when we might meet for 15 minutes or so. I'd like to tell you a little more about my background, and at the same time learn more about some of the directions you're moving in. Would early next week work for you?

Jay: Bob, I'm sure you have a very good background, but I simply don't have any opening at this time and don't anticipate any for at least six months.

Sur: I can certainly understand that. I really didn't expect that you'd have any openings. What I did want to do is to just set up a time, even ten minutes, when we might meet briefly. Would late next week work for you?

Jay: Bob, I just don't have any openings. I'm in the middle of developing my budget and it just wouldn't be worth my time or your time.

Sur: While I have you on the line Mr. Jay, perhaps I could just take a couple minutes to tell you more about my background.

(Gives two minute summary)

As you can see Mr. Jay, I do have a strong purchasing background. And I really do understand your situation. It's always helpful to me, however, when I can meet a person face-to-face. It enables them to remember me better in case something would unexpectedly develop. Or you may hear of something elsewhere and be able to refer me. Could I stop by next week to introduce myself. I promise I wouldn't take up more than two minutes of your time.

Jay: Well, I suppose we could do that. Stop over at my office at 11:55 on Friday.

Tell the person exactly what you want him to do for you.

Ask for a time in the next few days but do not try the worn out sales technique by saying something like, "Would Wednesday at four or Thursday at one work for you?" Let the employer select a time.

Show that you are not like other people. As soon as most people discover there are no openings, they are no longer interested in an appointment.

If necessary, make it even easier to meet: reduce the requested time from 15 minutes to 10.

Be tactful but be persistent. Asking for just an additional two minutes of time on the phone allows the person to relax; he or she realizes that the conversation is coming to a close.

This is such a reasonable request. Everyone understands the value of face-to-face contact. And you're only asking for a couple minutes.

The next script is one prepared by a chief financial officer who was looking for another CFO position. In fact, this person helped pioneer the use of marketing letters and the telephone script. He wrote the script with the idea that he would be prepared for any objections that an employer might raise. He was calling presidents, the toughest people to get in to see. He had a very high success rate of about 30%. When calling presidents, a success rate of 15–20% is excellent.

Terry's script helped him clarify what he would say if various objections were raised. He had no intention of memorizing the script. He merely wanted to prepare a strong statement so people would be willing to meet him. He was not trying to get them excited about meeting him, he merely wanted them to be *willing* to meet him.

Terry's specialty was finance. During his years in the field he had taken three companies public, meaning he arranged for their first stock offerings. Many young companies desire to "go public" at some point because that is how many have gained real wealth. Bill Gates of Microsoft is an example of the type of wealth that can be created when a strong, growing, young company goes public. Terry knew that most of the presidents he spoke to would not be looking for a CFO at that moment. Yet he wanted to meet as many presidents as possible, and he needed a way to make them interested enough to meet him. Since most CFOs have never taken even one company public, that was going to be his "in."

Employer: This is Mr. Tough.

Terry: Mr. Tough, hi, this is Terry Pierce. I sent you a letter last week which highlights my qualifications in finance. I've been involved in public offerings, debt restructuring, systems development, and establishing credit lines. I'd like to meet with you for perhaps 15 minutes to further discuss how my experience could be useful.

Employer: We're having severe cash-flow problems and we're definitely not hiring. There's really no need to meet.

Terry: I don't envy your situation. I've been there myself. One thing I noticed, in many instances when cash is tight, everyone concentrates on cash while no one concentrates on the day-to-day operations of the business. I could take a lot of the day-to-day pressure off you so you could focus your energy on business. If nothing else, I could give you a couple of ideas on how to avoid certain pitfalls that I'm sure you're going to face. Should we meet the latter part of the week?

Employer:	I'm really busy and I'm not sure it would be any benefit to either of us to meet.
Terry:	Mr. Tough, are you planning to come out with any public offerings or do you intend to restructure your debt as part of your solution to your cash problem?
Employer:	Well, our long-term goal is to go public after the cash situation is resolved and we are considering a complete restructure of our banking relationships.
Terry:	These are going to be exciting and trying times for your company. I'd like to make a couple of comments regarding offerings. First, you need to accept that it will cost you 10-15% of the gross offering, in offering-related expenses. Additionally, the two most important decisions are going to be the counsel you use and the brokerage house you choose. You need a strong counsel that can control the counsel used by the underwriters. It would probably make sense to restructure your debt first to show the financial strength of the company before taking it public. Let's get together for 15 minutes so I can explain more about the process and my experience.
Employer:	All right, let's do that. Let's meet at 9:00 on Friday.
Terry:	Great, I'm looking forward to meeting you.

You see that Terry was prepared for just about anything. Besides having an excellent background, his success in meeting so many presidents can be attributed largely to his ability to counter each argument and his ability to get a president to realize there might be some benefit to meeting him.

When you ask for appointments, avoid using the phrase "I was wondering if" as in "I was wondering if we could meet next week?" Instead, simply tell the person what you want by stating, "I would like to meet briefly with you next week." Or, ask a simple but direct question such as, "Could we meet early next week?" By asking in either of these last two ways you come across as more confident and professional.

Ideally the person with the power to hire will immediately arrange a time. This happens surprisingly often. You must also be prepared, however, for any objections the person might raise. The example below illustrates my point. Objections are often raised, so you must be prepared.

Employer:	We won't be hiring for at least six months.
	(How does she know? An employee may quit tomorrow.)
You:	I can understand that. Actually I'm not in a hurry to leave my present job. It would certainly be beneficial to me if we could meet for just ten minutes.

Employer:	I'm really tied up for the next three weeks.
You:	That's fine. Would the Monday following that week work for you?
Employer:	Probably you should go through personnel and fill out an application.
You:	I'd be glad to at the appropriate time. But really my goal is just to meet you and introduce myself.
Employer:	Right now we're laying off people in your field.
You:	I can appreciate your concern. I know the economy is rough right now. I think that makes it even more important that we get together. My company went through a similar situation a year ago. My money-saving ideas helped turn the company around.
Employer:	I really don't think you have the right experience.
You:	It is a bit unusual, but really, the problems I've dealt with are not much different than the ones you are undoubtedly facing. My new procedures at Silco created a 7% increase in productivity.

It's unlikely you will face all of these objections from one person, but be prepared for them. Make it easy for the person to say "yes." Asking for only ten minutes is a very reasonable request. Most people can spare at least that much time. And because you have much to offer, the interview will prove mutually beneficial. At the very least, such a meeting can give the employer a pleasant and relaxing ten minutes.

Below is an outline of the procedure you should follow when making your phone calls.

1. Speak to the person with power to hire and ask for a 15-minute meeting. Indicate that you realize there may be no openings.

2. If the person responds by saying there are no openings and therefore doesn't want to meet with you, explain again that you understand there are no openings, but that you want only ten minutes to talk about the field and your background.

3. If the person counters by saying there is a freeze on hiring, or gives some other reason why he thinks a visit would be a waste of time for both of you, say something like this: "I can sure appreciate the tough economic climate in this area. Since I have you on the phone, let me just take a minute to tell you a little more about myself." Then give a one- to two-minute summary of your strengths and experience.

4. When you finish your summary, ask once more for an appointment. Ask for a five-minute appointment, or just two minutes for an introduction. You might approach it in one of the following ways:

Mr. Belquez, I can certainly understand your situation. I'm working at this time, and what I'd really like to do is meet you and tell you a little more about myself so when openings do develop you'll be able to keep me in mind. I promise I won't take more than five minutes of your time.

❖

Ms. Baum, that gives you just a sketch of my experience and abilities. It's certainly not uncommon these days for a company to have a hiring freeze, and I can understand your reluctance to take time out of your busy schedule. But it would be very helpful to me if we could meet for just five minutes.

❖

Mr. Baker, as you can see, I have a strong background in purchasing. It would really help me if you could take five minutes to see me. And I really do mean just five minutes.

At that point you will have asked three times for an appointment. Don't give up with just two tries; many people relent on the third request. The first two requests were based on your merit. You're a very capable person and you requested an appointment because most people in management continually have their eyes open for new talent. Make the third request on the basis of a favor. When you appeal to their desire to help others, many people will consent. You should also reduce your request for time by asking for two to five minutes.

5. If you still don't get an appointment, you may yet get some valuable information if you hold the person on the phone another two to three minutes. Remember, you worked hard to get this hiring person on the phone, so don't give up too easily. Consider these: "Mr. Bledsoe, when you *do* have a position open, what can I do to make sure I'll be considered?" "Mr. Bledsoe, when you have openings in your marketing department, what do you look for in candidates?" "Mr. Bledsoe, I've briefly described my background. Is it the type of background you'd be looking for?" "If someone quit, would they be replaced?" As you are getting responses to your questions, jot notes down on the back of your 4 x 6 card.

6. In addition, you could ask about the size of the department, particularly the number of people who do your type of work. Ask about turnover. If no one has left in the last four years, that certainly tells you something. You may want to assign that company a lower priority because of the unlikelihood of an opening. Or you may give it a higher priority because low turnover often indicates employee satisfaction. You're the best judge of priority.

7. By this time you've probably convinced the person that you are a highly desirable employee. The person may know of something

happening in other companies. Do not ask the person if she knows of any openings. Instead, try this: "Mrs. Kelsoe, I think you have a pretty good feel for my background. What other companies do you think I should be contacting?" The reason for not asking about specific openings is that referrals are more important to you than knowledge of specific openings. And besides, the phrasing of the question will surely cause her to tell you about any openings she knows of. If the person says "Nothing comes to mind right now," she may need some help to jog her memory. Your response might be, "Basically, I'm looking for a progressive firm like yours in the electronics industry. I realize you may not know of specific openings, but your advice on good companies would sure be helpful." If she names some companies, ask for the name of a person to contact in each. Then ask, "Do you mind if I say you suggested I call?" Nearly always you will be given permission. You would simply say, "Beverly Kelsoe at Utalco suggested I call you. During the last five years, I've been purchasing microcircuits. I realize you may not have any openings, but I would like to set up a time when I could meet with you for about 15 minutes."

8. Thank the person for his or her time. If no appointment was made, indicate that you'll be sending your resume, and that you'll be staying in touch. If the person asks you to simply talk to his or her secretary, respond with a thank you. This employer is implying that the secretary will know in advance if any positions become available. Send a brief thank-you note with your resume to confirm your appreciation.

Your goal is still to get in and see as many hiring authorities as possible. A personal meeting always creates a much stronger and more lasting impression than just talking by phone. But think of it this way: if *you've* been unable to make an appointment, virtually *no one else* is going to, either. When you got the person on the phone, you made the most of it and sold yourself. The employer was impressed. Once the person receives your thank-you note, resume, and a follow-up phone call, you'll undoubtedly be one of the first to be informed when a position becomes available.

Your primary goal in using this strategy is to locate job openings in the hidden job market. While personal meetings with employers increase your chances of finding such positions, your telephone conversation, resume, thank-you note and follow-up are the next best things.

Let's look at an additional benefit of this telephone strategy. During a period of high unemployment, you may get appointments only 25–40% of the time, compared to the 40–80% rate most experience during better economic times. When you don't get an appointment, chances are great that it will be because there really are no openings, and when vacancies occur, they are not filled. So an appointment really would have been a waste of your time. While the employer is saving only ten minutes, you'll be saving the two to three hours it would take to research the organization, drive there, meet the person, and return home. When you get a turndown, be thankful that you just saved yourself three hours, and then go ahead and call the next person on your list.

In your phone calls, use humor whenever possible. My clients report that making the employer laugh has significantly increased their ability to get valuable information, even when they do not get in to see the person.

Tips On Getting Appointments

Despite their qualifications, and their telephone and persuasion skills, no one gets appointments 100% of the time. It helps to understand some of the reasons you won't get an appointment. Although I have seen a few people achieve a 90–95% success rate in getting appointments, most people will get appointments 40–80% of the time.

There are many reasons why a person won't meet with you. Those within your control might include the following possibilities: your marketing letter was not well written; your background was not impressive or was not sold well; you sounded nervous on the phone; your voice lacked a sense of confidence and conviction that the person really should meet you; you were not persistent to ask a second or third time for an appointment; or you sounded pushy when asking that second or third time. You have some control over these factors.

Then there are factors over which you have no control. For example, the organization may be in the midst of a hiring freeze; there may be no openings and the person knows it's highly unlikely that anyone will be quitting; the person may have just laid off people and is fearful of losing her own job; people have been laid off and now the manager is trying to do her own job plus parts of two others and is exhausted; it's a bad time and the person is extremely busy; you caught the person on her worst day in the last six months; or the person you talked to is an ego-centric person who really doesn't like helping people and would not have been helpful to you anyway.

After you've asked a third time for an appointment and have been turned down, always ask if the position would be filled if someone quit. If you get a definite no, or a hesitant yes, it may tell you that the organization is having financial difficulties. After hearing that those who leave will not be replaced, ask how long the situation is expected to continue. The answer will give you further insight and will help you determine how to prioritize the organization. Put your new-found information on your 4 x 6 card.

I've suggested that asking for a shorter meeting time is one way to overcome an employer's resistance to meet with you. That is, you start by asking for 15 minutes, then reduce that time to 10 minutes, and reduce the time again to 5 or 2 minutes if the person you're calling still hasn't agreed to meet with you. The idea is to keep making extremely reasonable requests. It's hard for a person to turn down a reasonable request.

There is another type of request you can make, however. After the person has twice turned down your request for an appointment, and after your two-minute summary, instead of asking for five or two minutes, merely request an opportunity to introduce yourself in a lobby or reception area. Indicate that you simply want to hand the person your resume so he or she can associate a name with a face. You might say: "I know you're busy, and I don't want to take up any more of your time. Could I stop by to personally give you my resume and introduce myself? I'd take less than a minute of your time."

Then, when you do meet the person for your one-minute introduction, you might say something like, "Ms. Juarez, I appreciate your seeing me. Perhaps I could tell you one reason why you should remember me. Basically I am . . ." Your spiel should take under a minute. You would then shake hands again, thank the person, and leave. The impact you have just made will be based on how you carried yourself. In one minute, the person could realize you are confident, energetic, enthusiastic, upbeat, and professional. If the whole thing is over in under two minutes, the person will be very pleased and very surprised that you really meant what you said—that you merely wanted to introduce yourself.

It does not matter if the person was ecstatic about meeting you when you called, or could barely be talked into it. My clients have met with people who were enthusiastic about meeting and then were completely uninterested and unhelpful during the appointment. Others were barely talked into it, but then were very helpful and genuinely tried to figure out how the person might find a position in their organization. One client met with a person who, after being curt on the telephone, opened up and was very cordial during the face-to-face meeting. They spoke for a half hour, and the person even made calls on the client's behalf.

Also, dropping in on people should not be completely ruled out as a strategy. I know of the president of a $100 million company who, by nature, is very reserved. In fact, he spends nearly an entire day locked up in his office handling paperwork. Yet, when people drop in and ask for him, he often meets briefly with them in a reception area, or invites them into his office and chats briefly. He is not unusual in this regard. By telling this story I am not necessarily recommending a strategy based just on cold calls, but there are people who have made this approach work.

When speaking to the person with the power to hire, it often helps to refer to others with whom you've met. You might say something like, "I'd very much like to meet briefly with you. I was up at Fluke and Eldec last week (two well-known Northwest firms) and I hoped I might also meet with you." You could also mention the names of the people, as well as the names of their companies. These people may know each other or know of each other. And it's an impressive little tidbit to indicate that these other people felt good enough about you to let you visit them.

One of my clients was convinced that his energy level and self-confidence were the two most important factors in his getting appointments. He also did better when he treated the process of making calls as a game. When he told himself that there were plenty of other fish out there and that it didn't really matter if he got a meeting or not, he had a higher success rate. Also, when he made two or three good appointments in a short time, he kept making calls even though his plan may have been to stop earlier. When he was on a roll, he wanted to make the most out of his positive responses and the momentum they gave him. This, too, increased his success rate.

The strategy of seeking brief meetings should result in appointments 40–80% of the time, except during periods of high unemployment. If you're not getting appointments 40% of the time, however, you're probably not using the telephone effectively.

Also, if you're trying to meet with presidents, you must be very sharp on the phone. Even then your expected success rate with these people will be only 10–30%. Presidents are clearly the most difficult people to meet. That's why you should avoid speaking to presidents unless they are truly the only ones who have the power to hire you to do what you want to do.

When it comes to meeting the person with power to hire, remember: you're the one making the special effort. You have offered to drive to the business, pay for parking, walk to the building, and wait until the person is available—all for just fifteen minutes of his or her time. You may have spent two hours just preparing for the appointment. In addition, you've done all this so the person with the power to hire can experience an enjoyable, relaxing time talking with you.

Tips On Cold Calling

Cold calling—that is, dropping in unannounced to see the person with the power to hire—can be particularly effective if you are seeking retail positions. In a retail environment the store manager is almost never insulated by a secretary. What's more, the manager likely spends time out on the floor selling and handling management responsibilities. That means if you walk in during a slow period when there are few customers around, you could easily get five minutes of the manager's time.

Although larger retail chains often have a personnel department, most hiring is actually done by the store manager in smaller stores, or by a department manager in large stores.

If you want to use cold calling as one of your strategies, begin by plotting out on a map the locations of the stores you are interested in. Then, based on your knowledge of the industry, determine what times during the day are likely to be slow for those businesses. Restaurants, for example, tend to be slow from 10–11 a.m., and then from 2–5 p.m. Most retail stores are slow for the first two hours after opening, between 2 and 5 p.m., and then again just before closing time. It's important to talk to the manager when the store is not busy in order to get even five minutes of his or her time.

I would suggest going into each store and scoping it out. Make observations about how clean it is and how well the merchandise is displayed. If you can, listen to a salesperson help a customer. That will give you a sense of how well trained the sales staff is. Then, when a salesperson approaches you to help you as a customer, quickly explain why you are in the store. Ask if it's a good store or chain to work for. Then ask for the name of the manager and ask to be introduced. If the manager is out on the floor, you will probably be immediately introduced. If the manager is in the back room, it may take a few minutes. In most cases, the manager will see you. If not, you would ask when a good time to return might be.

You will most likely speak to the manager while standing up, so practice your spiel while standing. Quickly describe your background in retail or describe your strong interest in a retail career. Ask whether the store will be adding staff. If not, confirm that people who leave will be replaced. Sell yourself and then leave a copy of your resume. If the manager gives you an application to fill out, accept it and say you'll return it in a few days when you come back for another visit.

Lower-level retail positions are usually filled quickly, so it is important to stay in touch with the manager. Stop by every few days and simply ask if there will be any openings soon. After the initial visit, you'll take up less than a minute of time each time you stop by. After three visits, you might call once or twice in a two-week period to find out about openings. After that you might alternate between calling on the phone and visiting in person. This process takes time, but this is how people in retail get hired.

Produce 40 Times The Impact

Meeting a hiring authority in person has many times the impact of merely sending a resume. A resume, no matter how good it is, is just a piece of paper. You will always be more impressive in person than on paper.

Your goal is to meet hiring authorities in person, even if it is for only ten minutes. Lasting impressions are made from person-to-person contact, not from resumes or even telephone conversations. The person meeting you will associate your name with a face, a voice, a personality.

In each meeting, create a lasting, positive impression so that when a job opening occurs, you'll be the first person considered. Suppose five weeks ago you spent 15 minutes with Mrs. Johnson, a key hiring authority in one of your most desired companies. No opening existed at the time, but you had a pleasant conversation. You learned more about her organization and you shared some of your accomplishments. Mrs. Johnson told you she was impressed with your background, and even mentioned three companies she felt you should look at. Two days later Mrs. Johnson received a nice thank-you note, and she once again remembered you and recalled your potential. She also felt good about herself because she knew she had been helpful. Three weeks later you called her and had a one-minute conversation asking if there had been any job developments. Not surprisingly, there had been none.

Two weeks after your call, however, someone informed Mrs. Johnson that he was leaving the company for a better position. What could Mrs. Johnson do? She could have informed personnel immediately and asked them to place an ad. She could also delve into her file cabinet and review the hundred or so resumes she has accumulated over the last six months. Instead, she thought of you. She picked up the telephone and called you for an interview.

Consider for a moment why the strategy of meeting hiring authorities works so well. During the first twelve weeks after mailing your marketing letter, you will have eight high-quality contacts. The average job seeker has one low-quality contact—a mediocre resume. These eight high-quality contacts produce at least 40 times the impact of mailing a typical resume. The eight contacts include: 1) mailing a marketing letter; 2) following up with a phone call and obtaining an appointment; 3) meeting the person face-to-face; 4) leaving a copy of your resume; 5) sending a thank-you note that evening; 6) following up with a one-minute call three weeks later; 7) a second short call five weeks later; and 8) mailing an interesting article five weeks after that. From that point on, a call would be made or an article sent about every five weeks.

Going through the strategy step by step will show you how this combined approach has at least 40 times the impact of a resume.

An excellent first impression is created when the person reads your marketing letter. The marketing letter is a nice touch because it is different from what employers are used to receiving. While your background may not be so powerful that the employer calls you on the phone immediately, a favorable impression has been created, nonetheless. The person will notice that you've indicated that you will call in a few days. While not necessarily excited about taking your call, particularly if there are no suitable openings, the person will probably speak with you. You may have to call several times because such people are often in meetings, out of the office, or out of town. But when you speak to the person you are going to come across as very confident and capable. Most people will agree to meet with you.

When you meet the person, you will have prepared a monologue. You'll use it if the first thing the person says is, "How can I help you?" Frequently the person will not even remember why you are there. The person may only know that your name is on his schedule for a fifteen-minute appointment. The "How can I help you?" question, or any one of its derivatives, are cordial ways of getting down to business right away. By having a five- to seven-minute summary of your background and strengths prepared, you'll be ready to sell yourself. When you leave the meeting, this person should be thinking, "If I had an opening, this is the type of person who could really help us."

As you leave, you will give the person your resume unless the person had already asked for it. Some people prefer not to bring a resume with them. Instead they tailor the resume to the situation after they get home. If you really do intend to tailor each resume, then this is a good strategy.

That evening you would compose a personal thank-you note. Although many notes are no more than four lines, they can be considerably longer if you want to supply additional information about your background or strengths. The person who met with you will receive the thank-you note a day or two later and think favorably of you once more.

Three weeks later you will call and reintroduce yourself so that the person will remember the conversation, if not your name. Then you will ask if there have been any developments (which there probably have not) and then state once more your interest in the organization. There is no need to feel that you are impinging on this person's time because you will take only a minute. Then five weeks later you will make yet another one-minute call. While you are only taking up one minute of the employer's time, it has probably taken you at least ten minutes to prepare and make several calls before getting through. That's okay, though. You are making an impression.

For your next follow-up, I recommend finding an article that your hiring authorities would enjoy reading but are fairly unlikely to have already seen. You would simply write, "Thought you might be interested," and then sign your name. Once again this person will think of you and realize that you are really serious about working there.

When you add up the impact of those eight contacts, I believe it has to be at least 40 times the impact of a resume alone. Let's face it, most resumes are not well written, and they have little impact. Rarely does a person read a resume and say, "We've got to have that person." When an employer speaks to a potential employee, however, and the person is self-confident and enthusiastic, and follows-up by contacting the employer again and again—that has impact.

Tips For Appointments

Your preparation for appointments will be key. Developing a five- to seven-minute summary of yourself is especially important. Some appointments consist of genuine conversation, but if the employer has no openings and wants to keep the meeting short, he or she is likely to say, "How can I help you?" When you get such a questions, respond with something like, "Mrs. Klevinger, I really do appreciate your taking time to meet with me. And I understand that you don't have any openings at this time. Perhaps the best thing I can do is simply share my background and describe some of my strengths. Basically I . . ." Then you'll give your summary.

Seven minutes may seem like a long time to talk nonstop, but it really isn't. It gives you just enough time to summarize your work history and education and then have a couple minutes left to share some strengths. Of course, while you are describing your work history you should briefly mention some of your accomplishments. This will give the employer an excellent overview of your background. It will also allow the employer to ask some questions if he or she is so inclined.

Often the employers you meet with will have no questions for you. Assuming a fifteen-minute appointment, half of your time will be gone when you've completed your monologue. If the person does not ask you to clarify or expand on anything, you should ask some questions. For instance, you might ask questions like: "Do you see any expansion in the next six months?" "Do you think there will be any openings in the next few months?" "When you have openings, what skills, qualities, and experience are you looking for?"

After the person has finished answering your questions, your time will be almost up. You should indicate the appointment is drawing to a close by saying, "Mr. Klucewski, I don't want to take up any more of your time. Maybe I should just summarize what I think my strengths are." You would then share some of your key strengths. This would all be part of a two-minute summary you should have practiced numerous times. In addition to recapping your prepared summary, you would also cover some of the points the employer mentioned just minutes earlier in response to your question about desired qualities and skills. Some of the words you use might be identical to the ones the employer used, some you would paraphrase. All the while, however, you'd be showing that you possess those skills and qualities. After sharing your points, you would then thank the person for the meeting, stand up, and say goodbye. Whenever possible, you should be the one to terminate the conversation to show that you are a person of your word: you asked for fifteen minutes and you got your fifteen minutes, so it's time for you to leave.

Unless the employer is truly keeping the conversation going, you should terminate it at the set time. This is a crucial point. Sometimes conversations go on for an hour, and I'm sure that, in most cases, the employer gladly gives the additional time. I also know that sometimes a person walks out the door and the employer is saying, "She asked for fifteen minutes and she stayed almost 45 minutes. Now I'm really behind in my work." No matter how impressive the person was, no matter how well she sold herself, and no matter how good some of her stories were, this person will be remembered primarily as the one who did not keep her word.

The way to avoid this potential problem is to be aware of time. If you sense time is drawing to a close, you should very deliberately look at your watch. Do it in an obvious way. By doing so you are demonstrating that you are concerned about taking too much of this person's time. One way to do it is to look at your watch just as you are finishing a sentence. Lift and turn your wrist in an obvious manner and glance at your watch. Since the employer has been maintaining eye contact while listening to you, the employer will definitely notice that you are looking at your watch. And the person will know why.

If you really are hoping for some additional time, and it appears that the employer is enjoying the conversation, and perhaps even keeping it alive, you might say, "Mr. Barratt, I appreciate the time you've given me. I did ask for just fifteen minutes. Do you have an upcoming appointment?" If he wants to terminate the conversation you have provided a perfect out, with the person probably saying, "Well, I do need to get back to my project in about five minutes." Or, the person may say, "No, that's fine, I've got another fifteen minutes."

If the person is clearly directing and continuing the conversation, then you may continue past the allotted time. After the appointed time has passed, however, be very alert for signals that the meeting has gone on long enough. If you notice the person looking at a clock or watch, looking away as if bored, or fidgeting, quickly draw your comments to a close and thank the person for the time.

If the person begins asking you specific questions about your experience, the appointment has probably turned from an appointment into an interview. A person who has no openings and knows there will be no openings in the next few months will rarely ask those types of questions. One of the few exceptions would be if the person were considering referring you to someone who has or may have an opening. In any case, being asked questions is a very positive sign.

The reasons why an employer would ask you questions include: 1) The person has no openings but will remember you and probably offer you an interview if something opens up; 2) the person will refer you to someone else if he learns of an opening; 3) the person is thinking of creating a position in a few months and may move that date up if a really capable person comes along; 4) the person thinks someone is about to quit; 5) the person is considering firing someone, but may do so only if the replacement is ready to be hired; 6) the person is always looking for people who can make money or solve problems for him.

During your appointment, do your best to get the employer involved in a true conversation. The more involved the person is, the more likely the person will want to talk beyond the requested ten or fifteen minutes.

Using Your Resume During Appointments

Take several copies of your resume with you to appointments. If the interviewer already has a copy, don't assume she has read it or remembers any of its contents. Avoid such statements as, "Well, as you can see in my resume, I . . ." She'll start fumbling around with the resume looking for that point and will be distracted from what you're actually saying. Feel free to discuss points that are in the resume, but talk in the same way you would if the person had never seen your resume.

Since employers will often ask for your resume, have one handy. Personally, I like to see someone's resume at the beginning of an appointment. In two minutes I can learn what might otherwise require ten minutes. If your time has drawn to a close, and the person has not asked for your resume, hand it to the employer as you leave saying: "Thanks for taking the time to see me, Mrs. Castor, you've been very helpful. Let me give you a copy of my resume in case anything should develop." If nothing else, now the employer will know how to contact you. If you made a favorable impression, she will probably keep your resume in a special folder at her desk. If a position does open up, your resume will be reviewed before the hundreds of mediocre resumes she has seen. Your resume will bring to mind the favorable impression you created while meeting face-to-face. A top-quality resume continues to work for months after you've handed it to a potential employer.

Some people prefer not to take a resume with them so they can send a customized resume the following day. They customize their resumes based on any knowledge picked up during the conversation. I'm not necessarily recommending this approach, but it has worked well for those who have used it. If you intend to customize your resume, and the employer asks for a copy, simply indicate that you did not bring one with you, but that you would be glad to send one the following day.

Referrals

At the end of each appointment, you should seek referrals unless you were interviewing for a known position or you believe a position may come up shortly. If you impressed the employer, he will be more than ready to do you a small favor.

You might try asking for referrals in the following ways:

You: Mr. Sanders, I really appreciate your taking time to see me today. Perhaps you could do one more favor for me. I'd like to leave my resume with you, and if anything would develop within Xytex, or if you hear of anything in another organization, please let me know. Can you think of any other organization I should contact?

❖

You: Mrs. Bell, I really enjoyed our chat today and I appreciate the time you've given me. In my research I've identified eight other organizations that I'd like to work for and I've gotten the names of the people I think I should be contacting. Do you know any of these people? (show your list)

Bell: I know Johnson and Coleman.

You: Could you give me just a quick sketch of both of them?

Taking Notes

Have a notepad handy when you have an appointment or interview. That way you'll be ready if the person you're meeting with refers you to someone or suggests an article to read. Although I generally recommend that people not take notes during an appointment, you can do so if you maintain good eye contact with the person and write your notes as unobtrusively as possible.

As soon as you get back to your car you should jot down some notes while the interview is still fresh in your mind. Your notes might cover these points:

1. The organization: needs, problems, size, plans, growth, etc.

2. The hiring authority: age, biases, management style, overall personality

3. Questions that were asked, including objections you may have to overcome

4. Overall impression

5. Specific points, such as the date you should call back

6. Questions you would like to ask in the future

FOLLOW-UP

Following up begins the same day as the appointment. Between appointments or when you get home, write a brief, typed or handwritten thank-you note. The five minutes it takes to write a thank-you note could be the most valuable time you spend. It will cause an important person to think favorably of you once more. A successful job search includes doing all the little things right.

The value of a thank-you note can be seen most clearly after a formal interview. Suppose Barbara is making a career change from telephone operator to sales representative. One of fifteen candidates interviewed, she was told that only *three* would be invited back for second interviews. Ten people had sales experience, but despite Barbara's total lack of sales experience, she was ranked *fourth.* She enjoyed the interview and, out of habit, wrote a nice, quick, four-line thank-you note. When the note arrived, the sales manager was getting ready to call the three top candidates. In the ten seconds it took to read the note, he began recalling the interview with Barbara. A moment later he was calling Barbara, having decided it wouldn't hurt to interview a fourth person.

A thank-you note is a perfect device. It makes you stand apart from the vast majority of job seekers who never bother with them. It says that your expression of interest in the organization was genuine. Any indication of enthusiasm and interest will be interpreted as evidence that you will work harder and stay with the organization longer than others. The reason for taking five minutes to write a thank-you note is simple—it is a common courtesy *and* it can increase the number of second interviews by 20%. Employers feel good when they know they've been appreciated, and their feeling good about you can help dramatically.

The note can be anywhere from three sentences to two pages in length. The note might read like this:

Dear Mr. Mathews,

I really appreciated the time you gave me yesterday. After talking to you, I'm even more sure that personnel is the right field for me. I'll keep you informed of my progress.

Sincerely,

John Stevens

❖

Dear Mrs. Kelser:

Thank you so much for seeing me yesterday. Our conversation confirmed what others have told me--that Dalco is an exciting company to work for. Of course, when I first called you, I did not expect you to have any openings. Since our conversation, however, I am convinced that I could be a real asset in the accounting department. Through my auditing and computer programming background I think I could really contribute to Dalco.

I will stay in touch to check on any developments.

Sincerely,

Ron Sakulski

❖

Dear Mrs. Madison:

I really enjoyed today's interview and I appreciate the fact that I was invited from among so many candidates. I just wanted to say again that I am quite excited about the prospect of working for Sentry, and especially within your department.

Sincerely,

Roberta Marsh

The first note was in response to an informational interview, the second an appointment in which no opening existed, and the third, a formal job interview. Any of these letters could have been longer, but that is usually unnecessary. Write a longer note only if you have a definite purpose in doing so. For instance, you may want to write a proposal describing a problem you discovered during the interview, along with your proposed solution. Or, if you did not have an opportunity to make an important point during an interview, a letter provides you with an excellent opportunity to cover it, even if it extends the letter's length to more than a page. If an objection was raised during the interview, and you missed it, didn't handle it adequately, or simply want to attack it from another angle, you can do so in a letter. Unlike shorter thank-you notes which may be handwritten, proposals or lengthy letters should be typed.

Everyone you interview with should get a thank-you note, so whenever you have multiple interviews or a panel interview, ask for people's business cards or write their names down when you meet them. For multiple interviews where you will meet three or more people in separate interviews, ask the person who is coordinating the interviews to supply you with the names and titles of the people you'll be meeting.

Most of your appointments will be with employers who do not have current openings. Your process of following up with them can last weeks or even months. Three weeks after your first appointment, call to ask if there have been any developments. Don't worry about bothering the person; you'll only talk for a minute. When you get the person on the phone, introduce yourself, indicate when you met, and briefly describe what you talked about. Do not assume the employer will remember you. He or she may have met 40 people in the last three weeks and will probably need a reminder.

Odds are there is still no opening. In closing, emphasize your interest in the company, and perhaps bring the person up to date on your efforts, particularly if you have contacted any of the people you were referred to. If you had not received referrals before, this would be a good time to ask for the names of organizations that this person thinks you should contact. If you think the person may have a position fairly soon, however, I would suggest that you avoid asking for referrals. By not asking for referrals in this type of situation, you will be indicating that the organization is one of your top choices

A follow-up call might go like this:

Bob: Hi, Mr. Benson, this is Bob Phillips. We met about three
            weeks ago when I came in to talk about microprocessors
            and the directions Microdata is taking. I just wanted to find
            out if there have been any new developments in your mar-
            keting department.

Benson: Bob, I remember you and I still have your resume, but there
            haven't been any openings.

Bob: I really appreciated your taking time to see me. The more I
            hear about Microdata, the more excited I get. I did call
            Mr. Jensen at Datasoft. He was very helpful. I'll probably
            talk to you again in four or five weeks. Thanks again.

When making your follow-up calls, you will frequently talk to a secretary if the person with power to hire is out or unavailable. You will generally be asked to leave a message and your number so the call can be returned. Instead, ask when a good time to call would be. After three or four unsuccessful calls, you might explain that you saw the person three weeks earlier and that you just need to talk to him or her for a minute to ask a couple questions. If the secretary has been brushing you off, that may help. *Always stay on good terms with the secretary.* On the second or third call, ask the secretary's name. You may talk to the secretary six or seven times, so you'll want to maintain your composure and sense of humor. Try to get to know this person. Make him or her want to help you.

After your first follow-up call, call every four to five weeks. Try to create and maintain enough interest so that if any openings occur, you'll be notified. Even if they don't call you, you're never more than five weeks away from discovering the opening through one of your calls. In the hidden job market, jobs frequently stay open for six to ten weeks.

If the person asks you to speak to the secretary in the future, that's okay as long as the secretary will know of openings as they occur. One advantage to you is that the secretary will be readily available. Seek to get to know this person and exchange pleasantries each time you call.

Another method of follow-up is to send a note accompanying an article the person may find interesting. This would usually occur after you have made two follow-up calls.

You should also follow up with your contacts. Every six weeks you'll need to call them to let them know about your experiences and your progress. If they referred you to someone, tell them what happened. Make them an integral part of your search and make them feel valued. This kind of follow-up will counter a psychological fact—with every passing week their ears become duller. In the beginning, you'll be notified if they hear of a job that remotely resembles the one you want. But by seven weeks, your contacts may assume you've found another job. By nine weeks they may hear about your perfect job but fail to even think of you.

OPTIONAL STRATEGIES

In addition to the main strategy I've described of meeting hiring authorities face-to-face, there are other options which deserve consideration. When using these next two options you will still eventually contact the people with the power to hire. The advantage of these two strategies is speed. In a few days, you can contact 100–200 organizations to learn if they have any immediate openings in your field. If they do, you may get some interviews that you might otherwise have missed.

Try A Large Mailing

Because I believe it is more effective for you to meet as many hiring authorities as possible face-to-face, I rarely recommend that people rely on the mass mailing of resumes. There is, however, a place for large mailings. On the chance that there may be an immediate opening with one of their 150 target organizations, some people send out resumes or marketing letters to their prospects during the first week of their job search. The attitude these people have is that they do not want to miss any immediate opportunities as they begin the long-term process of sending out 10–25 marketing letters each week.

A marketing letter, or a resume with a cover letter, have impact in and of themselves only if they arrive two weeks before or after a job has officially opened up. If your material arrives sooner, it usually ends up in a file cabinet somewhere. If it arrives later, it receives no consideration because the candidates for interviews have probably already been selected.

So, with all of this in mind, give consideration to a large mailing. This strategy still requires that you develop your list of 75–200 employers, and that you determine who the person is with the power to hire you.

Either a marketing letter or a resume with a cover letter can be quite effective. Be sure to invite the employer to call you if an opening exists.

Once you have the names of the hiring authorities, decide how the letters will be produced. If you have your own computer and "mail merge" software with your word processing software, you may want to key in the names and addresses yourself. Mail merge software enables you to merely type in the names and addresses of your prospects all at one time, then the software joins, or merges, those names and addresses with your letter. It can save hours of typing.

If you don't have your own computer with mail merge software, you should take your letter and your names and addresses to a secretarial service. It will cost you under two dollars per letter for them to type the letter and the accompanying envelope. All you will need to do is sign each letter and mail your material.

Once your materials go out, you would begin concentrating on sending marketing letters to your top-twenty group of employers. You would continue sending out about 20 each week. If you get some invitations for interviews based on your resume or marketing letter, great. If not, you'll soon be getting appointments as a result of following up on your marketing letters.

Call Your Prospects

Calling your prospects is another strategy that has the advantage of speed. This strategy works most effectively when the companies you're interested in are large and have personnel departments. Once you have your list of prospects, call their personnel departments and simply ask if they are currently looking for people with your background. If the personnel manager is unavailable, a personnel clerk will usually know what positions are open. When speaking to someone in personnel, briefly describe your background, and suggest one or more job titles that might be suitable for you. Using this strategy you will learn only of those openings that have been made known to personnel. With whatever information you have garnered, thank the person and move on to the next one.

This strategy has several advantages over just sending a resume. Two negative things can happen when you mail a resume—a rejection or no response at all. In either case, you still don't know what the real situation is. A quick call, on the other hand, can give you a great deal of information. Whether you get a clerk or the personnel manager, ask questions. If you learn that there are no suitable openings, you could confirm that the company does in fact have the types of positions you're interested in. You can also discover whether the organization is growing, and if so, whether there are any plans to expand in your specialty.

At a rate of eight calls per hour, you can get through your entire prospect list in three to five days. With this strategy, do not expect lots of interviews. Think of it instead as a way to gain some additional information about the firm. It is another way to ensure that you are not missing out on any opportunities as you begin the longer process of meeting hiring authorities.

AFTER YOU'VE MET HIRING AUTHORITIES

After talking to key people in most of your top twenty organizations, you have two main options.

For most, the next logical step will be to repeat the process with your next group of twenty. You've exhausted your top-twenty group and visited or talked to 10–15 hiring authorities. Very likely there were no current openings, but you should have the confidence that you will be contacted if openings occur. It makes sense simply to continue what is working well for you. Progress may seem slow, but you're making high-quality contacts.

If you are currently working and intend to be very particular in who you work for, a second option is available. You may choose not to contact any more firms since your were very impressed with the 10–15 firms you had appointments with. You might decide to merely maintain your follow-up with these organizations until the right opening occurs. If you've found six to twelve outstanding organizations, and if you're convinced there aren't any others that might interest you, you can stop your search and develop a creative follow-up campaign. Continue to learn as much as possible about each organization. Look for every opportunity to demonstrate that a position should be created to utilize your unique talents and experiences. Mailing really interesting articles to the hiring authorities can be one effective way of causing them to remember you.

AN IMPORTANT JOB FINDING OPTION

I typically recommend that job seekers develop a list of at least 70 potential employers and seek face-to-face meetings with the hiring authorities. There are exceptions, however. In some types of positions, particularly office and clerical jobs, you are actually better off calling the personnel department of larger companies or the office manager of smaller companies. The reason for this is that clerical people work in almost any department of an organization, so there may be many people who hire clerical staff. If you use this strategy you could still identify 10–20 organizations that you are especially interested in and meet the personnel manager or office manager. Simply walking in and meeting someone in personnel can also be effective.

When using the calling strategy, you would begin by introducing yourself, briefly explaining your background, and asking if any openings currently exist. You should be able to average 12 calls an hour. If you have 120 organizations on your list and call once a week to learn of openings, your total time expended is only ten hours weekly. The strategy should yield two to three interviews each week. Although 120 may seem like a lot of organizations, when using this strategy you need large numbers. Even 150 is not too many. If you are looking for office positions and you live in an urban area, there will probably be over 150 potential organizations within 15 minutes of your home.

If personnel informs you that no openings are currently available, carry on a conversation similar to this:.

Personnel: Personnel, may I help you?

Carol: This is Carol Prescott, I have a diploma from Harrington Business College and two years of clerical experience. Do you have any clerical positions available at this time?

Personnel: No we don't.

Carol: Do you anticipate adding any office staff in the next month or two?

Personnel: It's highly doubtful that we'll be adding any positions in the next four months.

Carol: If someone quit, would the person be replaced?

Personnel: I'm sure they would.

Carol: Approximately how many clerical positions do you have?

Personnel: Counting bookkeepers, probably around 30.

Carol: What kind of turnover do you have?

Personnel: It's nothing unusual, I'm sure it's about average.

Carol: Thanks a lot for your help, who am I speaking to?

Personnel: I'm Betty.

Carol: Betty, you've been really helpful. I plan to call once a week and if it's all right, I'll probably just ask for you. Is there anything else I can do to learn of any openings?

In less than two minutes, Carol learned so much more than if she had hung up after hearing that no openings existed. She also has a person to talk to in personnel. In a short time, Betty may actually recognize Carol's voice, and because Carol is friendly and courteous, Betty may actually go out of her way to help her. Of course, don't feel you can only talk to one person. If your regular person is unavailable, ask questions of whomever happens to be on the line. Also, notice what Carol did at the end of her call. Although she stated her intention to call periodically, she specifically asked if there was anything else she could do to ensure that she would learn about all potential openings. Although she plans to call weekly, she is prepared to do anything else that will help her.

This strategy is fast and gets excellent results—but don't use it as a shortcut if you are one of those who should be talking with the person with the power to hire.

Sometimes it's useful to write a week-to-week plan of your job search. Barbara wrote such a plan. She was tired of the 45-minute commute she had made for 14 years and wanted to work close to home. Although there were hundreds of businesses within a 15-minute drive, most were small—only about 20 had over 50 employees. We decided that if she was going to look at small businesses, she needed to be able to contact and consider a lot of companies. In her search for an office management position, she decided to contact 275 companies.

Barbara was unemployed during her job search and determined that she would devote 25 hours per week to her search. Her plan looked like this:

Week 1
1) Complete list of 275 firms using the zip code section of *Contacts Influential*. Select organizations with at least ten employees.
2) Begin making calls to find out who has the power to hire.
3) Visit A, B, C, D, E (five local employment agencies).
4) Mail out resumes and notes to 50 friends and relatives.
5) Respond to want ads.

Week 2
1) Call friends and relatives and tell them what I'm looking for. Figure 15 minutes each.
2) Call 100 companies and speak to the hiring authority or someone in personnel.
3) Mail resume to each person I speak to.
4) Respond to want ads.

Week 3
1) Finish calling friends and relatives.
2) Call 125 companies and speak to the hiring authority or someone in personnel.
3) Mail resume to each person I speak to.
4) Call each agency counselor and remind the person what I'm looking for.
5) Research the company before each interview. Practice my answers to interview questions.
6) Respond to want ads.

Week 4
1) Call the last 50 companies on my list.
2) Mail resume to each person I speak to. Tailor cover letter to what I learn.

3) Prioritize firms: Call 30 on a weekly cycle; 120 on a two-week cycle; 100 on a three-week cycle; 25 on a four-week cycle (this worked out to 130 calls per week).
4) Research each company before an interview. Practice answers.
5) Respond to want ads.

Week 5
1) Call 130 companies. Reintroduce myself and sell myself.
2) Call each agency.
3) Learn about each company before interview. Practice answers.
4) Respond to want ads.

Week 6
1) Call 130 companies.
2) Learn about each company. Practice answers.
3) Call friends and relatives. Tell them what I've done. Quick five minute calls.
4) Respond to want ads.

You can see that with this strategy Barbara was covering all of her bases. She selected the five best employment agencies and got referrals to specific counselors at three of them. If she didn't hear from them, she called at least every two weeks. She read the want ads every Sunday and usually responded to four or five positions. Those are the things that every job hunter would do.

Barbara also called 130 organizations each week and got to know the people she spoke to. After the initial call, in which she asked several questions, the conversations barely lasted a minute. She did not want to waste their time or hers. At that point she just needed to know if any positions had come open.

Her goal was to learn about jobs before they were advertised or listed with agencies. She succeeded. On her third call to one of her high-priority firms, a position came open that was ideal for her and she got it. The key to her success was consistency. She didn't care how she found out about jobs, she simply wanted as many leads as possible. She was prepared to continue the strategy each week until she landed a position. She got three interviews through the agencies and her friends gave her several leads, two of which led to interviews. She was well prepared, and she sold herself well in her interviews. Had she not gotten the position that she *did* receive, she was still being considered for several other positions. She was making things happen.

Barbara did not enjoy making the phone calls but they really didn't bother her. Her plan was to call 25 companies each day. Once she completed that task, plus any others she had set for herself that day, she worked in her garden as a reward to herself. Consistency was the key.

MAKING THE SYSTEMATIC JOB SEARCH WORK

The people who succeed with the Systematic Job Search strategies become detectives. Successful detectives never get discouraged. They follow up on each lead until the case is solved. Dozens of leads may dead end, but eventually one pays off. Remember, it only takes one good job offer, and you'll never be able to predict where the lead will come from.

The number-one cause of failure in job hunting is inaction, and the number-one cause of inaction is fear of rejection. Many people are not technically inactive; in fact they may be very busy. But they're inefficient, spinning their wheels, and making no headway. Such ineffective tactics can lead to a vicious cycle. It usually starts like this: when people lose their jobs, they start looking at the want ads. They throw their slightly revised resume around with very little success, but finally an invitation for an interview is offered. Since most people "wing it" in interviews with no research, practice, or forethought, the first few interviews go very poorly, leading to a string of rejections. Eventually, many people reach what Richard Bolles calls "Desperation Gulch," that feeling of hopelessness and depression that can lead to giving up.

By all means, avoid the vicious cycle. You will do that by: 1) following the strategy as it has been described; 2) keeping busy and using good time management; and 3) enjoying several low-stress appointments each week.

A New Definition Of Success

I have one more thought to offer you. I'd like to give you a new definition of success. For most job seekers the only success is getting the right job offer. That's *all* wrong. You can experience success each day and should reward yourself for it by feeling good about yourself. I believe success is having one or more pleasant experiences every day. Success is talking to someone who opens up to you and tells you everything about a field you're interested in. Success is completing your employer list. Success is getting in to see an employer and having an interesting conversation. Success is getting a good lead from a friend. Success is being a finalist among 50 applicants.

If you have at least one success each day, that ultimate success—a job—will come about as a matter of course. Start your day as if you had a full-time job. If you're used to getting up at 6:30 a.m., continue that habit. Put in a solid six-hour work day. You're different from the rest of your competition. While they're complaining about their rotten luck, you're doing your employer research. While they're sitting next to the telephone waiting for interviews to be arranged for them, you're on the telephone setting up your own appointments. While they're watching soap operas and game shows, you're meeting hiring authorities and getting job leads. While they're hoping for a lucky break, you're creating your own breaks.

Relaxing is one of the most difficult things for an unemployed job seeker to do. Turning your job search into a full-time job is the best medicine. If you're busy with research and appointments, you won't have time for negative thoughts. If you spend six full hours each day on your job search, you've done your job for the day. When you were employed, you didn't try to finish big projects in a single day. You knew you would get part of it done each day. In a job search you can't do it all in one day. That's what tomorrow is for. Monday through Friday stay busy between 8:30 a.m. and 4:30 p.m., then call it a day. You've done all you can do. Relax. Enjoy your family. Read a book. Go to the health club.

REAL EXPERIENCES

The following examples demonstrate some of the many ways people find out about their new jobs. These weren't just lucky breaks, the people created these situations.

I had spoken to someone in each of my top-ten companies, but there were no openings. I then developed a new list and was starting to talk to key people. One of the firms had no openings but suggested that I talk to someone in a very young but growing firm that I had never heard of. Sure enough, this firm was expanding and I got there at just the right time. The training I'm getting is excellent, and the income potential is excellent, too.

❖

I was just calling people to get information. I spoke to one person who thought his company was looking for a person with my background. The next day I went in for an interview and got the job.

❖

After I clarified what I really wanted to do, I contacted a former co-worker who had moved into the field I was interested in. We talked by phone and later had several meetings. He needed someone to assist him and he knew I had the ability and the background. We're now working together.

❖

A former supervisor went to work for a new company, and when an opening occurred he recommended me to his boss. I was hired after several interviews.

❖

I developed a list of consultants I might like to work for. I was contacting them pretty much alphabetically. With several, I just used a cold-call approach. I had talked to people in most of my top-twenty companies and had only a few left to contact. One day, I was in the vicinity of one of the firms I had yet to contact. I didn't know anything about the firm. I just walked in. One of the principals of the firm was there. We talked for over an hour. We really clicked. I started helping with some small projects and within two months I was working full time.

❖

A friend in the building where I live wanted me to help her teach a training course. I interviewed with her boss who said I'd be perfect for another job in her husband's company. I interviewed there and my experience was exactly what they wanted. I became his assistant and got a 35% pay increase.

❖

In 1975 I moved from Madison, Wisconsin to Salem, Oregon without a job. My intention was to look for work and complete my master's thesis. When I arrived, I did quite a bit of informational interviewing. I'm not quite sure how I got in to see people, but I somehow did. My main focus was state government.

I met with no success; instead, I took a temporary job as a census enumerator with the federal government. I also finished my thesis, went back to Madison to take my oral exams and returned to Salem intending to pack and move to Washington, D.C. I made my plane reservations and said my farewells to the Oregon beaches and my boyfriend. But just one week before I was to fly off, I received a call from the director of the Oregon Legislative Research Office. He was looking for a research analyst. He had received my name and resume from one of the people I had talked to nearly a year before. I got the job. It changed my whole life.

TIPS FOR THE JOB SEARCH

I want to share with you various tips that can make a difference in your job search.

Concentrate on smaller companies. The Department of Labor tells us that in the last ten years approximately 80% of all *new* jobs have been created by companies with fewer than 50 employees. That's the size of company which seems to be most dynamic in our present economy. As a result, a lot of your efforts should be aimed at organizations of 10–50 employees. Because these are not high profile organizations, your competition will be less. Not as many people will be trying to make appointments with key people in those organizations, making it easier for you to get in and meet the person who has the power to hire you. It will also make it easier for the employer to remember you, since he or she will be meeting fewer of your competitors.

I'm definitely not telling you to avoid the larger organizations, I'm only pointing out that the greatest growth is occurring with smaller organizations.

Print up 500 business cards. You will often be in situations where people typically trade business cards. Having a card of your own makes it easier to ask for another person's card. Even if you don't have a job at the moment, you should have a card that simply includes your name, address, and phone number, along with a title that matches what you are looking for. Keep your eye out for advertised specials at print shops. You can usually get 500 cards for under $30. Give your cards out freely; try to have less than 100 left by the time you get your job.

Get leads from anyone you meet. If you meet anyone who just went through a job search, get leads. Ask about any interesting organizations the person came across, as well as companies that might be hiring. Get referrals as well.

Avoid 900 numbers. There are various services out there which offer job finding assistance using 900 numbers. Most are simply recordings which cover such topics as interviewing and resume writing. Often a person can spend twenty dollars or more for a 30-minute recorded message. If you want job finding tapes, your bookstore will have one or more which will probably provide over an hour of listening and cost around ten dollars. Plus, you can listen to it many times. And let's face it, listening to a tape through a telephone is not the ideal way to listen to anything.

Get organized. Being organized during a job search is one of the most valuable things you can do for yourself. Establish systems and habits that you will use consistently throughout your job search. If you are used to getting to work by 8:00 a.m., get to your work area by 8:00 or 8:15 on a consistent basis.

At the beginning of your job search, claim a space in your home for your job search activities. If you have a den, that's great—make full use of the privacy. Working in the kitchen, dining room, or bedroom, is not ideal, but if you are well-enough organized, they can work just fine.

If you have children in the home throughout the day, or just in the afternoon, find a place where you can make your phone calls in private. Hearing a crying child is not only a distraction to you, but to those on the other end. If you have an infant, try to time your calls while the child is asleep. You'll be tempted to just relax as the child sleeps, but that's your opportunity to make as many calls as possible.

On the back of each of your 4 x 6 employer cards, write the date you should make follow-up phone calls. You'd simply write "call back on June 16." You could also design a form which enables you to just look down the list and see who you are supposed to call that day. Or you could set up a "tickler" file. You can purchase these very inexpensively at a stationery store. Basically, they are 4 x 6 cards with tabs numbered from one through thirty-one. Each day you would pull out the cards for that day and know immediately who you should call. If you don't reach the person that day, you stick the card in the space for the following day.

Keep track of the ads you respond to. The easiest way is to simply attach the ad to a copy of the cover letter you sent. In that way, you know what you said and you have the ad. This will help you prepare for an interview. Do not save reject letters. They contain no useful information, and virtually all say the same thing. Simply make note on the ad if you responded to an ad, or on your note card if you sent a marketing letter or an unsolicited resume. Then toss out the reject letter and go on to more productive things.

Tips on working out of your home. While I would not say it is necessary every day, dressing in your professional work clothes while at home can make you feel more confident and professional. Also, when you make phone calls, try standing. Many people find that they are better able to project enthusiasm while they are standing.

Keep your insurance active. Accidents or illnesses can occur at anytime, but they are more likely to occur during times of high stress. If you have a family, you are not the only one feeling the stress of your unemployment. Your whole family is feeling it. Even if you have to borrow money to pay for your insurance, keep your insurance active. Families have faced economic ruin because a serious illness or accident occurred during a period of unemployment. If you request it, many companies will keep you on the policy for several months at their expense, or will allow you to pay for it. If the company will not pay the premium for you, but you work for a larger company, you can pay for the insurance yourself under the federal COBRA program. Your personnel department will be able to explain how it works.

MAKE USE OF ALL RESOURCES
AVAILABLE TO YOU

Many resources are available to you to help you during your job search, particularly if you are unemployed. Make the most of each resource.

Family

During a job search it seems that people either draw closer to family or withdraw. My encouragement is to utilize your family in any way possible. Your family would include a spouse, parents, siblings, aunts, uncles, cousins, and even inlaws. Those who are within a one hundred mile radius should receive your resume and your list of desired firms. Once you've made your initial contact with these people, stay in touch with them. If you are employed, that may be as far as you need to go in the use of your family.

If you are unemployed you should make greater use of your family. Rather than withdrawing from family, speak to those who are closest to you and tell them how they can help you. Supplying leads is one of the best ways. Moral support is another important thing families can provide. Explain to them that you have a strategy and that you will be working consistently at your job search. Add that what you will want from them is not advice on *how* to conduct your search, but encouragement.

If you need financial help, don't hesitate to ask. Family members usually want to help, especially when they can see that you are treating your search as a real job. Of course you need to be careful who you ask to borrow money from, but don't let pride get in the way. Families are meant to be there when you need them. Having a little financial support may enable you to hold out for a good job, rather than feeling forced to accept the first mediocre job that comes along.

Unemployment Compensation

Under the umbrella of USES, each state has an Employment Security Department. It may be called by different names in various states. In addition to the service that obtains job listings (often known as Job Service), Employment Security also manages the unemployment compensation program. Even if you are not sure if you qualify for unemployment compensation, check into it by filing a claim. The brief paper work you fill out will enable Employment Security to determine whether you qualify. The determination of whether you qualify and the amount of your benefits check will be established by a formula. If you worked for an organization which did not pay unemployment compensation taxes, you will not qualify.

Unemployment compensation was designed to provide a minimum level of support to people while they conduct a job search. The benefits are significant, but still low enough that very few would feel unmotivated to obtain a job. Benefits usually last for six months, but during periods of high unemployment, extensions are sometimes available.

Once you qualify, you will be told how much your bi-weekly check will be and the total amount in your fund. This is important in case you take a temporary job, or if for some reason you don't look for a job for a week or two. In those situations, you would not receive a payment, and your fund would not be depleted.

If you think you might qualify for unemployment compensation, you should definitely apply. Your employer paid taxes for this purpose into the state fund. What's more, unemployment compensation was intended for people who have lost their jobs for any reason. It is not charity and should not be viewed as charity. Even if you receive unemployment compensation, you will be expected to conduct a thorough job search; the benefits are intended only to tide you over temporarily.

Before you receive benefits, your former employer will be sent forms to confirm your employment and the reason for your termination. Occasionally, employers will believe a person should not receive benefits. If the organization disputes the reason for you leaving, benefits may be denied. One of the more common reasons for denial would be that you quit and were not terminated. If you are denied benefits, there is an appeal process through the state. Individuals win a fair number of those cases, so it is usually worth pursuing. If you "quit with cause," you can still collect benefits. The best way to prevent problems regarding unemployment benefits is to work out an agreement with your boss or with personnel as to what you should indicate as the reason for leaving.

Financial Resources And Community Support

Unemployment is too serious a situation to let pride get in the way. If you're unemployed, you may qualify for food stamps and should probably apply. Most communities also have food banks. If things get really serious there are various state welfare programs that you might qualify for. If these resources can make the difference in whether your family has food, shelter, and medical care, check into them. Many local agencies assist people in serious financial situations. If you don't know of an agency to call, review the various agencies in the Yellow Pages under Social Service Organizations. If the first agency you call cannot help you, they will probably be able to refer to one that can.

I strongly encourage you to make full use of the resources available to you. If you are having trouble accepting such help, tell yourself that once you get back on your feet, you are going to make financial contributions to the organizations that helped you in your time of need.

If you need retraining, there are usually several agencies in a city or town that can help. The training they provide will be at no cost or very low cost if you qualify.

You must be careful if you approach a private school for job training. Sometimes they are able to qualify you for a federal education loan, but they may fail to adequately train you for your desired field. Nevertheless, they will get paid by the federal government through your federally subsidized loan, and you will be expected to pay back the loan.

Learn everything possible about the school before committing yourself to their training. Find out what their placement rate is. Then talk to graduates of the program to confirm that rate. On your own you should also determine whether there is a demand for the type of work you are about to be trained for. If you receive lousy training, or if there is no demand for your new profession, the result will be the same— you'll still be without a job and with no means to repay the loan. There are many reputable training schools. Make sure you find one.

Free Or Nearly Free Professional Help

In most cities and many towns you will find agencies which provide assistance to those out of work. The services usually include workshops on job finding, resume writing, and interviewing. These organizations may also establish support groups, which can be very beneficial.

To find an agency that could help you, look first in the Yellow Pages under Social Service Organizations. Crisis lines, United Way, YMCAs, YWCAs and other similar agencies will often know where such services are available. Your library may have a resource which lists and describes agencies that provide job finding assistance.

Unemployment is one of the most difficult experiences that people go through. After losing their jobs many people experience depression, lack of energy, marital difficulties, and other problems. There is help in the community if you experience such difficulties. Many agencies charge for services based on sliding scales determined by your income. You may be offered group counseling, individual counseling, or a combination of both. Once again, do not let pride prevent you from asking for and receiving this type of assistance.

If you have the funds or you have insurance that will cover mental health counseling, seek out a private counselor or therapist. Psychologists tell me that one problem they frequently encounter is the unemployed person who has been depressed for an extended period of time before seeking help. It is harder to help the person who has been depressed for four months than the person who is only beginning to feel depressed. It's best to seek help sooner rather than later.

Seriously depressed people do not carry out effective job searches. They tend to wait at home for a miracle to happen. When they do go out on interviews, their energy and confidence levels are so low that they are not viewed as quality candidates. With a few rejections, the depression usually gets worse. So the depression cycle must be broken, and it should be broken early on. Seek out the help you need.

Career Planning And Job Finding Workshops

For many, a good workshop provides all the information and help needed to make a career decision or to begin conducting an effective job search. Workshops and courses are available from numerous sources.

Community colleges often offer courses, many of them for college credit. Costs typically range from $75 to $200. During a ten-week career planning workshop, for example, you would usually work on several career planning exercises and take one or more career and personality inventories. The advantage to a workshop is that you are able to ask specific questions of an instructor during class, and personal questions after class. The benefit you derive from such a class is dependent on the knowledge and teaching ability of the instructor, as well as your willingness to complete the assignments. Since most classes last ten weeks, it would certainly give you time to complete the work if you spend a few hours on it each week. Because of their learning style, many people derive more benefit from a workshop or course than they do from merely reading a book.

Many organizations besides community colleges put on workshops and courses. The continuing education department of a local college will often sponsor such courses. YMCAs and YWCAs often sponsor one- and two-day career and job finding workshops as well. If such a format interests you, a call or two will usually reveal one or more resources for you. Costs for these types of programs may range from $25 to $300, depending on the extensiveness of the course.

Private Career Counselors

Career counselors go by various labels. They may refer to themselves as career counselors, job coaches, career coaches, job finding counselors, or other names. Seeking the help of a private counselor may be a good investment. A private career counselor can provide you with the individual help you need in order to make tough career decisions. They can also guide you through the often difficult process of finding a job. Counselors who work on an hourly basis will typically charge between $50 and $95 per hour. Those who charge a fee for a combination career assessment and job finding program, will typically charge $1,200 to $3,000, with a few charging over $4,000.

Because of the cost and time spent when working with a career counselor, you need to know whether using a counselor would be a wise investment for you. You also need to know how to select a counselor who would be right for you. Because of the complexity of the subject I have covered this process in much more detail in Appendix D.

Part Two
Creating A High
Impact Résumé

A TOP-QUALITY RESUME

The eye is drawn quickly to your name to establish your identity. ————————

Effective layout invites employers to read your resume thoroughly.

BRIAN SANCHEZ
11918 NE 147th
Kirkland, Washington 98034
(206) 821-3731

A clear objective reveals that you are focused and creates a positive impression. ———

OBJECTIVE: Management opportunities

The qualifications section sells you in ways that the job description alone can't do. The section summarizes your strengths and experience and sets the tone for what the reader will discover about you. ———

QUALIFICATIONS

Strong management and marketing background. Experienced in controlling costs and meeting budget guidelines. Proven ability to increase sales and productivity. Recognized as an excellent trainer and motivator.

EDUCATION

BA - History, Western Washington University (1987)

PROFESSIONAL TRAINING

Training demonstrates growth and proficiency. ———

Negotiating Skills, Simpson & Associates, 16 hours 1992
Professional Selling Skills, Sales Professionals, 24 hours 1991
Supervising People, IPC Group, 16 hours 1990

EMPLOYMENT

Arco, Seattle, Washington, 6/90-Present

Both job descriptions are filled with results. Results sell you to an employer and reveal much more about your potential than duties alone. ———

<u>FIELD CONSULTANT</u> - Work closely with ten AM/PM Minimart units to increase sales and profit margins. Hire and develop store managers. Took six corporate stores from a "poor" rating in 1989, to the top rating in 1991 and 1992. Prepare monthly and annual budgets and have full responsibility for profit and loss of each store. Have increased sales in stores over 12% per year, the second highest district average in the Northwest Region.

Eddie Bauer, Seattle, Washington 9/87-6/90

The job descriptions are short and concise, highlighting key points. Short job descriptions invite the employer to read thoroughly and help maintain interest. ———

<u>ASSISTANT FLATPACK MANAGER</u> - In the Eddie Bauer Distribution Center, oversaw the unpacking, pricing, and inventorying of merchandise. Directly supervised a staff of 20. Through effective training increased productivity of the unit by 18%.

THE IMPORTANCE OF YOUR RESUME

A top-quality resume can net you interviews at a rate ten times greater than your competitors. This chapter will help you write that resume. This section is presented in great depth for a reason—a resume is not *just* a resume. The impact of an effective resume goes far beyond the simple act of mailing it in response to want ads. There are, in fact, at least six benefits to writing a top-quality resume:

1) You will get more interviews when responding to want ads and when sending unsolicited resumes;

2) Because it emphasizes results, your resume will guide your interviews and enable you to focus on your most positive experiences;

3) Your resume becomes your calling card and helps people remember you, while also enabling them to contact you and refer you to others;

4) You will be better prepared for interviews;

5) Knowing you look good on paper helps build self-esteem;

6) It will help your prospective boss justify the decision to hire you.

I am going to show you how to create a resume with impact. You will be making dozens of decisions as you construct your resume; the information and examples provided will enable you to make the right decisions and will enable you to make them quickly. There is no single "right" way to do anything, but I can assure you that if you follow the advice, you will have a resume that looks good, reads well, and most importantly, has impact.

Remember, a resume is not just a resume. It represents you. Take the time to create a resume that presents the best you have to offer. A resume won't get you a job, but it can help get interviews. Or, put another way, a good resume won't get you a job, but a bad one will cost you jobs. Set your mind on spending whatever time it takes to produce a resume that truly sells you.

WHAT MAKES A TOP-QUALITY RESUME?

You never get a second chance to make a good first impression. —Unknown.

Eye Appeal

A resume must be visually appealing. Lasting impressions can be formed during the first five seconds your resume is read. That's how long it takes someone to view the layout, observe the quality of the typing and printing, and note the color and quality of the paper. Of course most of this takes place on an unconscious level. Resumes are usually scanned the first time through. If the reader detects misspellings, smudges, poor-quality typing or printing, clumsy or verbose writing, or a confusing layout, the resume may be set aside after just ten or twenty seconds. The result—no interview.

Positive Tone

The top-quality resume presents you in the best possible light, yet does not exaggerate your qualifications. Every item is selected carefully to promote you in the eyes of the employer. Unflattering facts are not hidden, they are either left unmentioned or carefully turned into positives. The resume that concentrates on strengths helps you obtain interviews. Make positive statements about yourself; throw false modesty aside.

Impact

Write with impact. Impact is achieved with tight, concise phrases using action verbs. Impact is achieved when you accurately describe and *project* your desired image. Your full potential will come across only when you write with impact. Effective writing requires plenty of editing and rewriting—something even best-selling authors must do. The effective resume provides valuable information quickly and is easy to read. Each sentence expresses a fact, impression, or idea which will help sell you. All unnecessary words and phrases have been removed. Concise writing is appreciated by all employers and reveals much about your ability to communicate.

Results

An effective resume is filled with results and accomplishments. You've got many results, and when described properly, will cause employers to want to meet you.

RESUME PRINCIPLES YOU NEED TO UNDERSTAND

The Laws of Resume Writing

There are no laws when it comes to resume writing. But I can share with you principles that generally work. When I feel strongly about a principle or approach I'll tell you. But any rule or principle can be ignored if doing so will help sell you to employers.

How to Begin

Before your resume is completed, you will have made dozens of important decisions. This chapter is designed to help you make those decisions quickly and easily. Each section of a resume is explained in detail and you'll learn when and how to use each section, as well as how to write it. Examples and options are provided. You'll know what will work best for you. Examples throughout the chapter explain and demonstrate particular points. Read through pages 117 to 201 quickly. Then return to study each section as you begin to write that portion. Highlight examples that are especially applicable to you.

How Interview Decisions Are Made

Have you ever wondered how employers decide who will get interviews after they've placed help wanted ads? A good job will typically attract 75–200 resumes. An employer who has a batch of resumes on her desk will usually scan each one for 5–25 seconds and place each resume in either the "I'm interested" pile or the "reject" pile. When screening resumes, people are usually looking for reasons to reject. That's why even one typo can be a killer. A resume which contains obvious typos, spelling errors, grammatical errors, or verbose writing, will most likely end up in the reject pile. Those who obviously lack the necessary background for the position will also end up in the reject pile.

Out of 80 resumes, perhaps only 20 will be placed in the "I'm interested" pile. Those 20 will be read, with one to five minutes devoted to each. Out of the initial 80 resumes, ten will generally make it through this screening process. Of the ten or so who are called, perhaps six will be invited for interviews.

There is one type of resume that gets through this process nearly every time—the one that sells potential. That's the resume you need to write. I will be showing you some of the techniques you can use to create a resume with this kind of impact.

In the rest of the chapter I'll take you through each section of a resume and show you how to pull all of the pieces together.

STATING YOUR OBJECTIVE

Most resumes should have an objective. But it's wise to avoid the common mistake of trying to cram too much into the objective with statements such as, "Seeking responsible accounting management position with a large progressive firm offering opportunity for growth and promotion, where skills in human relations and effective written communications will prove beneficial." These types of objectives are trying to combine an objective with a qualifications summary, but the combination simply does not work. The objective sounds trite and contrived. It's better to use a simple objective and then get creative in producing an effective qualifications summary.

Before starting your resume, write out your objective. Later you can change or delete it, but having an objective will keep you focused while you write. Objectives such as "Bookkeeper," "Chemist," or "Construction Superintendent" can be very effective.

Stating an objective on your resume demonstrates focus. People naturally respect you if you know what you want. A resume that says, "I'll do anything, just give me a job" will get you nowhere. If your objective states "Sales Representative" but you have never been one, everything that follows must demonstrate your *potential* for that position.

Simple objectives usually work best:

Computer Programmer
Senior Accountant
Flight Attendant
Secondary Teacher — Drama, English, ESL
Sales Manager

In the above cases, the people knew exactly what they were looking for and so they used an exact job title. If this is your case, and the title is recognized by all people in your field, use a specific job title. However, if you are considering one of several positions which are all closely related, you might try something like this:

OBJECTIVE: Office Manager/Administrative Assistant/Executive Secretary

In this example, all three types of positions—Office Manager, Administrative Assistant, and Executive Secretary—are similar. A person who is qualified for one is often qualified for all three. In fact, what one company calls Administrative Assistant, another might call Executive Secretary. This person just wants a good job with a good company, and would enjoy any of the three types of jobs. If only "Office Manager" is listed as the applicant's objective, however, an employer with an executive secretary opening might overlook the resume.

You should never pair unrelated job titles as "Secretary/Sales Representative," "Teacher/Real Estate Agent," "Flight Attendant/Bookkeeper." It's okay to be looking for both positions at the same time, but you would need two resumes with two different objectives to do so.

Sometimes an exact job title is *not* advised. This is particularly true in management. If you are currently a personnel manager considering positions such as Training and Development Specialist, Director of Training and Development, and Vice President of Human Resources, you might want to create an objective which incorporates all of these titles such as "OBJECTIVE: Human Resource Management." Using the term *management* does not limit you to a specific job title, while "Human Resource" is specific enough that it is clear you have focus.

Use an objective if your goal can be easily stated with a job title or a descriptive phrase. Occasionally you will find it better to omit an objective and let your cover letter and the tone of your qualifications section indicate your goal. I use an objective for approximately 85% of the resumes I help people write. I frequently recommend multiple versions of a resume where the only changes occur in the objective and in the qualifications section. For example, if you were interested in both sales *and* marketing, you would have two versions of your resume, one with a "Sales" objective, and the other with a "Marketing" objective. One resume would be directed to sales managers and the other to marketing managers.

THE QUALIFICATIONS STATEMENT

The qualifications section is a summary of your background and strengths. It includes positive statements about you that would be difficult to express in any other section of a resume. Since it is designed to sell your most marketable abilities and experiences, the statements must catch and hold the reader's attention or the section will be skipped. Covering too many points will also result in the section being overlooked.

The qualifications statement can do more than any other section to create a favorable impression of you and will set the tone for the rest of the resume. It can greatly strengthen your perceived worth since employers reading your resume will constantly be asking what you can do for them. Give them positive answers in those first few seconds by creating a qualifications section which truly sells you. This section should capture the *essence* of what you want to sell. Any point which is not crucial should either be eliminated or considered for inclusion in your cover letter.

Studying the following examples will help you understand the function of the qualifications section. A job has been included with each qualifications example to help you see how they fit together.

Example #1

OBJECTIVE: Marine Sales

QUALIFICATIONS

Outstanding sales record. Highly knowledgeable in all facets of sailboats, powerboats, commercial fishing vessels, and marine hardware. Strong ability to introduce new product lines to distributors, dealers, and boat builders. Top-selling rep in the country for four major marine manufacturers.

EMPLOYMENT

Bellkirk Marine, San Diego, California 6/87 to Present

MANUFACTURERS' REPRESENTATIVE - Represent 27 lines covering California, Nevada, and Arizona. Increased the number of accounts with distributors, dealers and boat builders from 35 to 96 and increased sales 85%. Since 1989 have been the top-selling rep for four major manufacturers.

Qualifications section example #1 includes a summary and an accomplishment. It starts off with a simple but bold statement: Outstanding sales record. It then goes on to describe the areas of expertise. The top accomplishment (being the top-selling representative in the country for four manufacturers) has been included twice—in qualifications and the job description. It is a valuable statement worth repeating.

Example #2

OBJECTIVE: Grocery Store Management

QUALIFICATIONS

Strong management background. With a 21-store district, increased profits 32% and oversaw the construction of four new stores. During 17 years in management, coordinated the grand openings of 13 stores and produced some of the most profitable new stores with three different chains.

EMPLOYMENT

Fine Food Centers, Tulsa, Oklahoma 5/78 to Present

DISTRICT MANAGER 9/88 to Present. Responsible for profit and loss analysis, wage and salary administration, merchandising, store layout, advertising, and buying for 21 stores in the district. Supervised the remodeling of five stores and the construction of four stores. Developed in-house cleaning and repair services, saving $150,000 annually. Through improved merchandising and customer service, increased sales per store 28% and profits 32%.

Qualifications section example #2 begins with a bold statement: "Strong management background" and then proceeds to back it up *with proof.* Immediately you realize this person has been very successful and you want to know more about her. One fact comes right out of her current position (the 32% increase in profits). The second statement (concerning the success of 13 store openings) is a summary that comes from her entire management background. If this summary had not been stated so clearly in a qualifications section it might have been easily overlooked, even during a careful reading of the entire resume.

Writing Your Qualifications Section

Write your qualifications section last. It is the most difficult section to write and requires the most care. Once you have the employment section completed you will know better what needs to be included in your qualifications.

As you prepare for writing the qualifications section, review the resume and determine what points should be covered in it. Use qualifications to introduce yourself to the reader and to give an overview of why you are qualified for your stated objective. To do this ask yourself, "Why would I be good at this occupation?" Or if you already have experience ask yourself, "What makes me successful in this field?" Remember, in qualifications it is permissible to repeat or paraphrase points made elsewhere in the resume.

If you have strong work experience, you will probably want a short qualifications section. If you are seeking to break into a new field, qualifications is usually the best vehicle for bringing in related experiences and selling an employer on your potential.

While relatively short, the qualifications section is often the most difficult to write. Because it can strengthen the overall effectiveness of the resume, it deserves a great deal of attention and effort. An hour spent writing and editing your qualifications section is not too much.

I like short, hard-hitting qualifications sections. I try to capture the *essence* of what will impact employers. As a result, most qualifications sections I write are one paragraph with three to five lines. If there are two distinct areas which need to be sold then I may have two paragraphs with three to five lines each. People making career changes or those seeking positions without having the traditional background, may need three or four paragraphs to bring out all of their related experience. Even so, the emphasis should still be on conciseness and impact.

Essence is not easy to achieve, but the impact of your resume will be significantly strengthened when you succeed. Identify those qualities and areas of experience that an employer absolutely needs to know about you—those critical points. While there may be many points you want an employer to know about you, usually only two or three are critical. Sell those effectively and the employer will feel he or she must meet you.

To write an effective qualifications section, begin by writing a "qualifications sketch." List the key strengths and assets that you want to convey to employers. After writing your qualifications sketch, determine which are critical and which are not. Simply scratch out those which are not critical and use the critical ones to compose your qualifications section.

The qualifications sketch of a quality control manager might look like this:

1. Ten years in quality control. Familiar with all techniques that have been developed for the electronics industry.

2. Saved money and reduced rejects for three different companies.

3. I work well with other department heads, particularly production, and coordinate and cooperate well with them rather than work against them.

4. I've developed creative programs that really work.

5. I like my work and enjoy a challenge.

6. I'm always looking for a better method, technique, or system; I'm open to new ideas from others.

7. I'm an excellent supervisor. I train my staff well, I listen to them, I maintain high morale, and productivity is always high.

8. I'm hardworking, loyal, reliable, creative, and efficient.

The final version of the quality control manager's qualifications section might read like this:

QUALIFICATIONS

Strong experience in quality control gained during ten years in supervision and management. For three electronics manufacturers implemented new quality control programs which decreased rejects at each plant by at least 23%.

Develop excellent relations with all department heads and work well with production personnel.

Excellent supervisor. Consistently increase productivity of quality assurance personnel, and through effective staff training, increase their technical capabilities.

If you review the eight points the person originally wanted to cover, you'll notice that everything is included here either directly or by implication (points 5 and 8 were covered implicitly). By reading the qualifications section in the context of the entire resume, you would certainly pick up that he enjoys a challenge and that he is hardworking, loyal, reliable, creative, and efficient.

In writing qualifications sections there is a tendency to use the words *strong* and *excellent,* such as "Strong experience in quality control . . ." and "Excellent supervisor." Both are excellent words, but try not to overuse them. I've searched the thesaurus and just haven't found many good substitutes. I rarely use the word *good* because it just isn't strong enough. I occasionally use the word *outstanding,* but it can seem too strong, so use it selectively.

Other phrases can also be used to make a point. If you use "Excellent experience" in one paragraph, you could use "Broad experience," Broad background," or "Excellent background," in the next. Don't be bothered if you use the word *excellent* three times, but use substitutes to avoid using it excessively. Excellent is often the best word because it is not as humble as *good,* nor is it too strong, as *outstanding* sometimes seems.

I often start a qualifications paragraph with a short statement, such as "Excellent management experience," then I back it up with further details. In this case the follow-up might be "Consistently obtain high productivity from employees," or "Consistently implement new techniques and procedures which increase productivity and lower costs." Another effective backup statement would be: "Proven ability to turn around projects which are behind schedule and over budget." Whatever general statement you make should be explained or reinforced with details. Look at the resumes on pages 194, 206, 210, and 214 and notice how percentages or other statistics have been included in qualifications. This can be very effective but is not always necessary or possible, particularly if you are making a broad statement about your entire career.

Notice how effective the various back-up statements can be when they are paired with the beginning short statement.

Excellent management experience. Consistently obtain high productivity from employees.

Excellent management experience. Consistently implement new techniques and procedures which increase productivity and lower costs.

Excellent management experience. Proven ability to turn around projects which are behind schedule and over budget.

Broad banking background with strong managerial and technical expertise. Always a top producer with the ability to establish strong, long-term customer relationships.

Strong background in trucking gained during 20 years of management experience. Recognized for ability to significantly increase market share and quickly increase profitability. At each terminal achieved one of the best on-time records in the industry.

Opening with a short statement provides impact. It hits the reader and makes the person want some evidence, which you will provide in your very next sentence. Of course, you need to be able to verify anything you say, such as "Consistently obtain high productivity from employees," either in other sections of your resume or in a personal interview.

To write effective qualifications statements study several examples. Analyze them to determine what makes them effective. When you're through writing a qualifications statement, compare what you have to some of the examples. If you're not pleased, set the resume aside for a day. You'll return to it later with a fresh perspective. Let others see it and get feedback from them. Don't use the qualifications section as filler. Include only those points which you really think will sell you.

Some people just can't come up with a good qualifications section. If you fall into that category, do what you can to improve the qualifications section, but finish the resume so you can get it out to the right people. In such a case I would recommend that you wrap it up with a short summary of 15–25 words without trying to make any hard-hitting statements. Here's an example.

OBJECTIVE: Programmer/Analyst

QUALIFICATIONS

Excellent background in data processing gained during eight years in programming and systems analysis.

Even though this qualifications section lacks punch, it serves a purpose. As soon as an employer sees an objective, he immediately asks himself what makes this person qualified. By seeing the word *QUALIFICATIONS* followed by a statement, the employer instantly assumes the person *is* qualified and goes on to seek evidence in the education and experience sections.

You can use this way out if you have difficulty with your qualifications, but use this approach only after you've spent at least two hours working solely on qualifications. Once you've used your resume for a while, try working on qualifications again. You'll probably have some new thoughts, and it may come together after all.

EDUCATION

Education should usually appear on the first page right below qualifications. If you have a college degree or a certificate in a technical field, it should be obvious why you would want education to appear early in the resume. You can design the section so that just a glance will tell the reader what degree(s) or certificate(s) you hold. Perhaps you don't have a college degree or a certificate but have very strong experience in your field. In that case, you would still place education right after qualifications because you'll want the reader to see quickly that while you don't have a great deal of education, you have a wealth of qualifying experience.

There are a number of reasons for placing education on the first page of your resume. For one thing employers are curious about education. If education does not appear on the first page they will often flip immediately to the second page. Also, not putting your education on the first page can give the impression that you are "hiding" or "burying" your education. For these reasons, I rarely place education at the end of the resume, although it can be placed at the end of a one-page resume.

I like to see education right after qualifications. Most readers will merely glance at education and notice only that a person has a degree. The more curious will note the school, major, and year of graduation. Since employers are curious about education, and since the section takes only 3–6 seconds to read, I believe it belongs at the top.

Occasionally education is left off entirely. This most often happens when a person with 20 or more years of experience in his or her field lacks a college degree and simply decides to leave it off. One option is to include an education section which lists professional seminars as well as any college courses taken.

A top-quality resume must be easy to read. The first example below is easy to read and you obtain the key information almost instantly. The next two education sections are difficult to read. Notice the difference.

Easy to read:

EDUCATION

B.A. - Business Administration, University of Washington (1978)

The above example represents the best way of describing a college degree. "B.A."—instantly a reader can see that you hold a degree.

The next most important fact is your major, then your school, followed by the year of graduation.

The following bad examples show you what *not* to do:

Hard to read:

EDUCATION   <u>Butler University</u>, Indianapolis, Indiana.

Received a B.A. in Business Administration in December, 1979. Curriculum emphasized Marketing and Financial Management, with field of specialization Real Estate. Grade point average 3.21.

Harder to read:

<u>EDUCATION</u>

Central Michigan
<u>University</u>

Mount Pleasant, Michigan

September 1975   <u>Bachelor of Arts</u>, Majored in Sociology with
      to   a minor in Psychology
June 1980

Both are hard to read. The reader has to look carefully just to learn whether the person has a degree.

HOW TO BEST DISPLAY YOUR EDUCATION

The following section reveals the best way to show your education, depending on just what your educational background is. Highlight or place a mark by the one that matches your situation.

High School Graduate, No College

EDUCATION

Graduated - Roosevelt High School, Chicago, Illinois (1976)

Some College, No Degree

If you have attended college, there is rarely a reason to include your high school.

EDUCATION

University of Nevada, Las Vegas, Business, 136 credits (1974-1977)

In the example above, credits were included to show that although a degree program has not been completed, the person was at least a serious student, accumulating 136 of 180 quarter credits necessary to graduate. A major is given to show the emphasis of study. When determining what major to include, try to make sure it is related to the type of work you're seeking. If you have 20 or more credits in each of three fields, pick the one which will best sell you.

Certificate From A Technical School

EDUCATION

Certificate - Welding Technology, Davis Technical School (1975)

or

EDUCATION

Certificate - Computer Programming, Sims Business College (1975)
Graduated - Norcross High School, Norcross Pennsylvania (1972)

No Degree, Attended Several Colleges

Some people have acquired credits at four or more schools. If this is your situation, you need not list all schools on your resume; it may give the impression of instability.

EDUCATION

Cheboit Junior College, Castlerock Community College, Riverside Community College, 98 credits.

The person in the above example actually attended three other colleges, which are not mentioned because only a few credits were obtained. The credits are included in the total, however. Attendance was very sporadic over a ten-year period, so no dates are given. There is usually no need to mention the cities and states where the colleges were located.

No Degree, Two Colleges Attended

EDUCATION

Northeastern Illinois University, Business, 70 credits (1974-76)
University of Illinois, Circle Campus, Business, 30 credits (1972)

No Degree, No or Few College Courses Taken

EDUCATION

Total Quality Management, Dreyfuss & Assoc., 24 hours (1991)
Implementing Just in Time, Bob Huston & Assoc., 40 hours (1989)
The Problem Employee, Dreyfuss & Assoc., 8 hours (1988)
Principles of Management, University of Texas, 5 credits (1985)
Motivating Employees, Dreyfuss & Assoc., 16 hours (1984)
Introduction to Marketing, University of Texas, 5 credits (1981)

This person has been taking seminars for years but has little formal education. He has taken college courses for personal benefit, but not with a degree in mind. By combining seminars with a few college courses, this type of education section works well and demonstrates that he is a growth-oriented person.

Degree, Two Or More Colleges Attended

Unless you have a special reason for including all of your schools, list only the college you graduated from. If you got an Associate of Arts (A.A.) and then moved to a four-year college, still mention only the four-year college. Everything else is superfluous. Since you did not attend four years at the college mentioned, state only the year of graduation.

EDUCATION

B.S. - Physics, Rhode Island University (1976)

Will Soon Graduate

If you will graduate in just a few months you might show education like this:

B.A. - Political Science, University of Arizona (June 1993)

In the above example the assumption is that the resume has been written in the fall of 1992, and you are scheduled to graduate in June, 1993.

If you expect to graduate in the coming year, but don't know which quarter, you might express it this way:

B.A. - Chemistry, University of Texas (Expected 1993)

Another possibility would be:

Economics, University of Maryland, B.A. to be completed by June 1993

Bachelor's Degree Plus Graduate Studies, But No Graduate Degree

EDUCATION

Graduate Studies, Public Administration, University of Georgia
(1976-78)
B.A. - Political Science, University of Georgia (1971-75)

or

M.S. Program, Psychology, UCLA, 30 credits (1977-1979)
B.A. - Psychology, Eastern Washington University (1972-1976)

Recent College Graduate, Little Work Experience

You may want to include some of your coursework to demonstrate the extensiveness of your training. If you are a liberal arts graduate seeking a management trainee position, you could list economics, accounting, and business courses. The person with a technical degree is also often benefited by listing courses. Although the reader knows your major, that information alone is not always adequate. For the person with few summer or part-time jobs, listing coursework will make your resume, and therefore your experience, look fuller.

In the following example, the person was looking for an entry-level position in advertising.

EDUCATION

B.A. - Journalism/Advertising, University of Hawaii - 3.39 GPA (1992)
Coursework included: Advertising Copywriting, Public Relations
Writing, Media Planning, Media Representation, Production
Graphics, Advertising Layout and Design, Media Aesthetics,
Principles of Design, Principles of Color

Graduate Degree(s)

In the first two examples below the people merely listed their degrees. The third is the same except that the person chose to include his thesis. A more elaborate description of the thesis can be very effective. It could be described right after the thesis title, or an entire section could be devoted to it called "THESIS."

EDUCATION

M.A. - Counseling, UCLA (1972-1974)
B.A. - Psychology, Oregon State University (1966-1970)

EDUCATION

Ph.D. - Industrial Psychology, Stanford University (1975-1977)
M.A. - Psychology, Northwestern University (1972-1973)
B.A. - Sociology, Northern Illinois University (1967-1971)

EDUCATION

Ph.D. - Physics, University of Washington (1984-1987)
    Thesis: Interlinear Regression Analysis of Wave Length Dichotomy
M.S. - Physics, University of Washington (1979-1982)
B.S. - Physics, University of Manitoba (1975-1979)

All But Dissertation

If you have completed all requirements for a graduate degree, except for the dissertation or thesis, it might read:

Master's Program, Physics, Iowa State University, completed all but dissertation (1978-1981)

or

Master's Program, Physics, Iowa State University, completed all coursework (1978-1981)

TIPS FOR MAKING YOUR EDUCATION SECTION MORE EFFECTIVE

The following tips will help you put the finishing touches on your education section.

Listing Major and Minor

You may want to list both your major and minor if you believe the minor will also help to sell you. In the case below the person wanted to become a labor relations negotiator and felt the economics minor strengthened her credentials.

EDUCATION

B.A. - Major: Industrial Relations. Minor: Economics
    Syracuse University 1971

Degrees And Abbreviations

If you hold a B.A., B.S., M.A., M.S., or Ph.D., it is best to abbreviate since everyone knows what they stand for. Many people are not familiar, however, with B.F.A. (Bachelor of Fine Arts), so it is better to spell out the term. The same is true of M.P.S. (Master of Professional Studies), B.B.A. (Bachelor of Business Administration), and others. Almost everyone knows A.A. stands for Associate of Arts, but many do not know A.S. stands for Associate of Science or that A.T.A. stands for Associate of Technical Arts. If you think some people will not know what your degree stands for, spell it out.

When to Use GPA (Grade Point Average)

Generally GPA is listed only if it is over 3.0. GPA usually is dropped from your resume after you've been out of school for five years. By that time your work record will reveal much more about you than your GPA. It's interesting to note that most follow-up studies have revealed virtually no correlation between a high college GPA and success on the job. Many who were mediocre in school begin to shine only when they enter "the real world."

When to List Honors

If you graduated with honors or with a title like Cum Laude or Summa Cum Laude, you could include it like this:

EDUCATION

B.A. - Cum Laude, History, Brigham Young University 1968-72

City and State of College

The city and state in which your college is located is usually not included in your resume. This is particularly true if your college is well known in the region in which you are conducting your job search. If you think employers might be curious, however, include the city and state.

Fraternities and Sororities

Usually your membership in a Greek organization should not be included in a resume. While mentioning the organization may score points with a member of the same or a similar organization, it can hurt you when your resume is reviewed by a "dormie," or a competitor of your fraternity or sorority. While there are no hard and fast rules, weigh the pros and cons carefully before deciding. Usually you would list membership only if you held an office and you feel the experience will help sell you. This cautionary note does not apply to the many honorary societies such as Phi Beta Kappa.

Order of Schools

Normally schools are listed in reverse chronological order, beginning with your most recent school. Typically this would also mean that your highest level degree would appear first.

Whether to List Major

People should usually include their major, even if that major did not directly prepare them for the field they are now in. There are presidents of Fortune 500 companies who graduated with degrees in history or literature. I say keep your major in, but if you feel strongly about removing it, it might look like this:

B.S. - Southern Illinois University (1982)

132

PROFESSIONAL TRAINING

It is generally best to separate education from training. Training usually includes seminars and workshops, but can also include college courses taken to help you perform better in your field, but which are not part of a degree program. Seminars include those sponsored by your employer and those offered by outside consulting firms at your place of employment. You should also list seminars and workshops you've attended away from your place of employment, paid for either by yourself or your employer. Even if you have received college credit for such courses, you would normally include them under training rather than education. Glance at the example below and you'll see why it's a good idea to separate training from education.

EDUCATION

> Total Quality Control, Rainier Group (24 hours) 1987
> Terminating Employees, Human Resources Inc. (8 hours) 1985
> B.A. - Business, University of Colorado 1980
> Supervising Difficult Employees, Townsend & Assoc.
>   (10 hours) 1979

If you hold a degree, you want the reader to spot that fact instantly. In the example above, the B.A. is hidden by the seminars. It would look better this way:

EDUCATION

> B.A. - Business, University of Colorado 1980

PROFESSIONAL TRAINING

> Total Quality Control, Rainier Group (24 hours) 1987
> Terminating Employees, Human Resources Inc. (8 hours) 1985
> Supervising Difficult Employees, Townsend & Assoc.
>   (10 hours) 1979

Listing workshops and seminars can help demonstrate your professional growth. But as valuable as seminars are, be selective about those you choose to include—be sure they are relevant. If you took a course in estate planning, but that knowledge will be of little or no value for the job you're seeking (restaurant management, say), it's better to leave it out.

Usually you should state the seminar title, the name of the organization that sponsored it, and the year you attended. If most of your seminars lasted a half day or more, it would be useful to show the number of hours spent in class. If your company sent you to seminars in different cities, it can be beneficial to list those cities. It demonstrates that your company thought highly enough of you to invest in out-of-town workshops.

Some seminars have catchy titles that really don't describe their content. If "Make The Most Of Yourself" was really about time management, it should be written as: "Time Management, Simms and Associates (1989)." Feel free to alter seminar titles so the reader will understand their content. Review the following:

MANAGEMENT SEMINARS

    Managing People, Harvard Business Workshop, four days (1992)
    Motivating Employees, Bob Collins & Associates, two days (1990)
    Management and Human Relations, California Institute of
        Technology, 124 hours (1987)

❖

SEMINARS

    Financial Management for Closely Held Businesses, 40 hours,
        Seattle-First National Bank (1992)
    Construction Cost Improvement, 20 hours, Nevett & Associates(1991)
    Scheduling, CPM, 20 hours, Nevett & Associates (1990)
    Real Estate Syndication, 10 hours, NW Professionals (1990)
    Construction Estimating, 30 hours, Lake Washington Vo-Tech (1989)
    Closing the Sale, 12 hours, Roff & Associates (1987)
    Goal Setting/Richer Life, 18 hours, Zig Ziglar (1986)

EMPLOYMENT

Every job is a self-portrait of the person who did it.
—Unknown

For most people the employment section will be the longest section of the resume. Employment has four main purposes: 1) it reveals your career progress; 2) it describes duties and responsibilities; 3) it describes results and accomplishments; and 4) it accounts for where you've been and for whom you've worked.

Employment history should not be just a recitation of duties and responsibilities. You have a definite goal in mind: you want employers to sense your future worth to their organizations. Everything in your resume should demonstrate your ability to master the type of job you are seeking. Include whatever information will create that sense of value; exclude whatever information will not.

Describing results and accomplishments in each job you've held will do more to reveal your capabilities than anything else. Each job description should consist of concisely described duties and at least one accomplishment. The employment section should begin with your most recent position and move backward in reverse chronological order.

Writing effective job descriptions can be difficult, but I've developed techniques which will ultimately save you time and produce a better resume. The most important technique is to begin by creating a *job sketch.*

USING JOB SKETCHES TO STRENGTHEN YOUR RESUME

If I had eight hours to chop down a tree, I'd spend the first
six sharpening my axe. —Abraham Lincoln

A job sketch is simply a listing of all the major duties you've performed in each job, plus a brief description of special projects, and an analysis of the results you achieved in each job.

Before you even begin to write your resume you will write a job sketch for each job you intend to list in the employment section. Since developing the use of job sketches in 1981, I have seen the quality of clients' resumes improve by at least 50%. Job sketches work because they help prevent writer's block. Without a job sketch a person is forced to stare at a blank sheet of paper or a blank computer screen. Suddenly the person is under real pressure to produce. The questions come flooding in—"where should I start, what's important, how much space should I devote to each job?"

A job sketch prevents that type of pressure and panic. Instead of beginning by staring at a blank page, you begin your resume with each job sketch in front of you. And each job sketch covers everything that could go into the resume. You produced each job sketch under low stress conditions because you were merely writing down everything that came to mind, not worrying about spelling, grammar, sentence structure, or polished writing. In other words, you were not trying to write a resume.

With your job sketch before you, it is much easier to decide what the key points really are, and what emphasis you should give to each one. Because your job sketch is so complete, you will have more information than you will actually put into the resume. But that's okay. Information which is not used may be great material to bring up in your interviews.

To produce each job sketch, review the job in your mind and then list major duties, less major duties, and even selected minor duties which might be relevant for the type of position you are seeking. Those minor duties may have taken up less than 1% of your time, but may be critical in demonstrating that you at least have exposure in a key area.

After you've listed job duties, think about any projects you worked on. Then write a brief description of them, including their results or outcomes. A project is anything that has a definite beginning and ending. Bookkeeping includes certain things that are done daily, weekly, monthly, quarterly, and yearly—bookkeeping is not a project. Analyzing the present bookkeeping system and recommending and implementing changes would be a project. Some occupations consist of repetitive duties that rarely or never involve projects. People in occupations such as engineering, programming, chemistry, and consulting, continually move from one project to the next.

Thinking through all of these duties, responsibilities, and projects for all of your jobs will take one to three hours, but taking the time now can make the difference between a mediocre resume and an outstanding one. If you save each job sketch, you will never have to go through this process again, except as you add new positions.

The key to a good job sketch is to simply write whatever pops into your mind. Don't worry about grammar, punctuation, sentence structure, or even spelling. Just get your thoughts on paper. Go for volume. Write quickly. Don't filter out or neglect to put something down because you think it is insignificant. Remember, only a small portion of your job sketch will end up in the resume, but you need plenty of data to work with.

As you read the sample job sketches, and the job descriptions that resulted from the sketches, notice the impact that results have. After reading the polished version of the job descriptions, you have the definite sense that these two people are very good at what they do.

The following job sketch of an insurance claims adjuster is thorough and detailed. It took about 45 minutes to write. Once this person was ready to start her resume, it practically wrote itself.

INSURANCE CLAIMS ADJUSTER

Read each new claim file and determine which ones to act on first.

Call claimants or the insured party to clarify what occurred and set up appointment to inspect car, write an estimate, or meet injured parties.

Go to body shop to write estimate and negotiate final cost with manager. Haggle about how many hours to give for straightening frame, fender, quarter panel, etc. Use crash book figures for time necessary to remove and replace parts, to paint panels and for cost of parts. Threaten to take car to another shop if can't reach a compromise. Come up with creative and cheaper ways for car to be repaired such as splicing in entire front or rear section.

Totals—if totaled, use *Blue Book* to calculate value. Negotiate if necessary with claimant or insured to determine amount to be paid. Get bids from Midwest Auto Auction and award car to highest bidder. Arrange to turn over title to new owner after getting payment.

When injuries have occurred visit accident scene and draw picture, visit surrounding stores or homes to locate witnesses, get statements. Get recorded statements from claimant and insured. Go to hospital if necessary and explain that I want to make a fair settlement. Try to settle on first visit for small sum and get signature on release statement.

Collect all medical and hospital bills. Request diagnosis from treating physician. Determine real extent of injury, estimate what the case should settle for and request an adequate money authorization from supervisor to settle.

Visit claimant and negotiate—explain why injury isn't worth as much as claimant thinks it is.

Negotiate with attorney by mail or phone. Explain any circumstances which weaken claimant's case, i.e., question of who was really at fault or extent of injury.

Results

1984 Set record for most claims settled in one year.

1984 Out of 15 adjusters, 3rd lowest average cost per collision settlement, 2nd lowest average bodily injury settlement.

This person had three years' experience as a claims adjuster and was looking for another claims position with an insurance company. The final version of the job description—just 77 words—is given below.

CLAIMS ADJUSTER - 6/83-7/86. Handled full range of property damage and personal injury claims. Wrote estimates on damage to claimant and insured vehicles, disposed of total losses, and handled claims on comprehensive coverage including stolen cars, tires, and glass breakage. Investigated accidents and settled injury cases with claimants and attorneys. In 1984 set record for most claims settled in one year. Out of fifteen adjusters, had third lowest average cost per collision settlement and second lowest average personal injury settlement.

The job sketch below is written somewhat differently from the previous one. It's included to show you that there is no set way to write a job sketch.

SENIOR TECHNICIAN

A. Test printed circuit boards, end items, and systems according to test procedures set by engineering. Troubleshoot down to component level.

B. Interface with clinical personnel if problems occur with functionality of units, kits, etc. Identify problems and suggest solutions.

C. Interface with design and R & D engineering regarding fit, form or functional flaws or problems. Suggest solutions. On the Y235 scanner, suggested solutions which reduced time to produce prototype by four months. On the U454 scanner, identified a problem which would have cost over $200,000 to fix in the production phase.

D. Interface with production, test, and assembly personnel to ensure a proper production flow.

E. Work with Quality Control on functional as well as cosmetic problems. Fix if necessary or show why QC documents are wrong or why specifications should be changed. Changes in specifications typically speeded up production by 10–15%.

F. Work with Material Control to ensure parts are available when needed. Expedite shipments when necessary.

G. Assist engineering in setting up pre-clinical trials for prototype products.

H. Check out functional test procedures for Test Engineering to ensure they are correct, practical, and understandable.

I. Review printed circuit board schematics and assembly drawings and make corrections where necessary.

J. Keep and maintain a file of all new product test procedures, drawings, specifications, and parts lists. This has improved access and use of all data and saves approximately 200 man-hours per year.

Notice how points in the final job description were taken right out of the job sketch, in some cases with only minor revisions.

SENIOR TECHNICIAN - 3/87 to Present. As Senior Technician for this manufacturer of CAT scanners, test printed circuit boards, end items, and systems, and troubleshoot down to component level. Rework failed equipment. Work closely with clinical personnel and design engineers to identify problems and suggest solutions. Identified and resolved a problem with one product which would have cost over $200,000 to fix in the production stage. Interface with Quality Control and frequently recommend changes in QC specifications. Recommendations typically speed up production by 10–15%.

Assist Engineering in setting up preclinical trials for prototype products. Review test procedures established by Test Engineering to ensure tests are understandable and workable. Review PC schematics, assembly drawings, and parts lists and make corrections where necessary. Developed and currently maintain a file of all test procedures, drawings, parts lists, and specifications, which has significantly improved access and use of the data, saving approximately 200 man-hours per year.

While the data and information you produce for your job sketch are important and useful, the very process of writing the job sketch also serves several valuable functions. It makes you recall *all* the duties and functions of the job and allows you to choose the most important ones for your resume. It also causes you to relive some of the experiences and makes them more vivid. What's more, it helps you recall accomplishments and results. In addition, the very act of remembering, sorting through, and writing down all of your duties, accomplishments, and experiences, prepares you for interviews.

As you write your job sketches, it is important that you make the most out of each one of your accomplishments. The next section on accomplishments will show you how to do that.

ACCOMPLISHMENTS

To write an effective resume you should look for ways to insert accomplishments into your job descriptions, special projects, and qualifications. This section will provide you with the techniques to create real impact in your resume through the use of accomplishments and results.

Accomplishments separate achievers from nonachievers. Duties alone cannot do this. Consider two people, each with ten years of experience and identical job titles. Applicant A has not had an original idea in three years. The drive and initiative that propelled A upward is gone. Applicant B, however, has demonstrated significant accomplishments each year and still exhibits great enthusiasm. Only accomplishments will distinguish over-the-hill applicant A from full-of-potential applicant B. Accomplishments make you seem more like a real person and create strong impressions. Stressing accomplishments in a resume is important for everyone, but it is absolutely critical for the person changing careers; those accomplishments will prove potential for success in the new career.

Employers make hiring decisions based on your perceived potential. Experience is frequently used to measure potential, but it is often a poor yardstick. Employers certainly want people who can come in and handle the job from day one, but other factors are also important. Employers are willing to train someone if they feel that person has the potential to become a better employee than the one with more experience. Potential is best demonstrated through accomplishments.

Accomplishments do not have to be big, knock-your-socks-off types of experiences. They are merely experiences in which you made a contribution—on your job or through a project. An employer who clearly sees that you've made contributions that go beyond just doing your "duty," immediately assumes that you will continue to make contributions in the future. That's potential. But it's not enough to have achieved certain accomplishments or to possess potential. You must present them in your resume in ways that bring them to life. Your competitors, in fact, may have accomplishments even more impressive than your own, but if they fail to describe them in their resumes, it's the same as if they did not have them. And if they don't list them in their resume, they probably will not describe them in interviews. This gives *you* the advantage.

Ideally, you will list one or more significant accomplishments for each job you've held. For some jobs, however, this is not practical. Perhaps you held the job for just a short time, or didn't enjoy the job and performed below your full potential. With jobs like these, provide only short descriptions so that the reader will concentrate on the more important jobs you held.

Describe accomplishments concisely and concretely so that they'll have impact. Every employer seeks people who can increase profits, decrease costs, solve problems, or reduce the stress and pressure they face. Specific information such as percentages and dollar figures, make accomplishments more tangible and impressive. Compare these two statements: "Implemented new personnel policies which increased morale" and "Implemented new personnel policies which

Any other accomplish-
ments since you taught
Tippy to roll over?

reduced absenteeism by 27% and reduced turnover by 24%." The specific figures given in the second sentence make the accomplishment seem more impressive and real.

You're probably thinking, "I know my idea saved time and money, but I have no idea how much." In this section I'm going to show you how to arrive at your figures. In many cases they will be estimates, but use company records to verify your figures whenever they are available. One of my clients used printed reports to verify his 63% increase in tons of aluminum sold during a two year period. Those figures were impressive in the resume; during interviews he was able to elaborate.

Arriving at a percentage or a dollar figure when you have no verifying figures requires creative thinking and sometimes creative guessing. You would not want to exaggerate the accomplishment, but you can calculate figures to the best of your knowledge. The following example illustrates how this can be done.

Saving Money in Alaska

Roger wanted to leave Alaska, where he had repaired heavy construction machinery. He felt he was a top-level mechanic but could think of no evidence to prove it. After talking with him a bit, I discovered he was constantly developing new tools and finding easier ways to make certain repairs. One of the tools he made helped him install a $500 part by aligning it perfectly in place. Without the tool the part was sometimes misaligned, but there was no way to tell until the part was clamped in; by then it was too late, the part would crack. Roger estimated he replaced the part 30 times per year and would have cracked two of them without the tool. About 20 other mechanics with similar duties copied his tool. We figured he and the 20 others each saved about $1000 annually. So on the resume we stated that he saved $20,000 per year with his tool. Actual savings may have ranged from $18,000 to $25,000 per year; we chose $20,000 as the most likely. If an employer asks Roger to verify the figure, he can explain how it was calculated. An employer would undoubtedly be satisfied with such an explanation. In an interview all you need to do is explain how you arrived at the figures and state that they're accurate to the best of your knowledge.

Using Results To Create Impact

It's great when you've got computer printouts or company documents to prove what you are claiming, but few people have that type of documentation. Nevertheless, I have never had a client tell me that their claims were not believed.

Accomplishments which cannot be translated into dollars or percentages can still have impact. Statements such as "Selected as employee of the month," or "Brought the product to market five months ahead of schedule." can have a powerful effect on employers.

In the following sample job descriptions, notice that accomplishments are described very briefly. Elaborate on your accomplishments at the interview, not in the resume.

In the Memory Academy example below notice the impression you gain, even though no figures are used. You will quickly recognize that she is responsible, creative, hard-working, and an excellent supervisor and trainer. She is the type of person who is always looking for ways to improve programs and systems.

Memory Academy, Dallas, Texas 5/85 to 6/87

> OFFICE MANAGER/EXECUTIVE INSTRUCTOR - Office manager of a 14-person office with direct responsibility for ten. Developed and wrote detailed manuals for each position and created a smooth functioning office. In 1986 redesigned the teaching techniques of the memory course. Instructors immediately experienced better results and received enthusiastic ratings from clients.

Her key accomplishment came from improving the teaching techniques at the Memory Academy. With the recognition of an accomplishment comes a better understanding of her as a person. You know that she cared about her job and invested her energy in making the business more effective and successful.

Accomplishments are loaded with powerful information. One fifteen-word accomplishment can say more and have more impact than one hundred words of a job description. Look at the following two examples and notice the impact of the accomplishments. Imagine what the impact would be without them. I have italicized key parts of the accomplishments, for your benefit. The italics did not appear in the original.

Des Moines Trust & Savings, Des Moines, Iowa 9/87 to Present

> BRANCH OPERATIONS MANAGER - Managed operations at three branches and supervised 20 employees. *Overcame serious morale problems* by working closely with the branch staffs and providing better training and supervision. Within the branches *absenteeism was reduced 42% and turnover 70%.* Customer service and marketing of bank services were strengthened. Based on customer surveys, the *customer service rating improved from 74% good or excellent, to 92%.*

❖

Central Mortgage 5/79 to Present

DIVISION MANAGER, Missoula, Montana, 9/87 to Present. Opened the Missoula office and set up all bookkeeping and office systems. Within ten months *became the number-one home mortgage lender* in the Missoula area and *obtained 54% of the mortgage market and 68% of all construction loans.* During five years *averaged 48% profit on gross income, the highest in the company among 33 offices.*

The following example vividly illustrates the need for accomplishments. The first version lacks both accomplishments and impact. The revision ultimately sold the person into a good position.

Before

SALES REPRESENTATIVE - 2/86 to Present. Develop and service established accounts as well as new accounts. Set pricing structures after determining the market. Responsible for the district's western Orange County territory. Sales have increased each year.

After

SALES REPRESENTATIVE - 2/86 to Present. In the first three years moved the territory from last in the district to first among ten territories. Aggressively went after new accounts and have significantly increased market share in the territory. By 1989 became the number one sales rep in total profits and have maintained that position. Profits have increased an average of 30% annually.

Is there any question which resume would result in an interview? In the second job description, you get a sense of a salesperson who is successful, works hard, has excellent product knowledge, and knows how to get a sale. It makes an employer want to meet him to learn if he is as good in person as he seems on paper.

Notice that the impression you get of the person is much stronger in the second version, yet it required just one more line than the first. This powerful effect can be created by presenting *what* you've done in jobs, rather than *how* you've done it. Tell *what* resulted from your efforts, but devote little or no space to describing *how* it happened. Accomplishments speak for themselves and you rarely need to go into detail regarding all the things you did to get your results. Save the details for an interview.

Sometimes you will want to allude to what was done without providing details. The bank branch operations manager above provides a perfect example. She said, "Overcame serious morale problems by working closely with the branch staffs and providing better training and supervision. Within the branches absenteeism was reduced 42%

and turnover 70%." How she got her result is merely alluded to with the statement, "Overcame serious morale problems by working closely with the branch staffs and providing better training and supervision." She did not go into detail about the morale problem, but simply stated it existed. And, she only alluded to *how* she solved it—working closely with staff and improving training and supervision. An employer who wants to know more will have to interview her.

In the resume below, a bank controller's job description does not do him justice. Because this was his most recent and most responsible position, more detail is required to show his potential. Although the second job description is longer, it is well-written and concise. It does not contain any unnecessary words. Everything mentioned is designed to sell him and give an employer a full view of his experience.

Before

CONTROLLER - Managed accounting department, seven-person staff; prepared financial statements and filed various reports with state and federal agencies; assisted and advised senior management concerning regulatory accounting, and tax ramifications of decisions and policies; worked with savings and loan divisions on operational and systems design; served as primary liaison with computer service bureau in Los Angeles.

After

CONTROLLER - Managed a seven-person accounting department and significantly increased productivity by simplifying procedures, cross-training staff, and improving morale. Prepared financial statements and advised senior management of regulatory, accounting, and tax ramifications of new policies and programs under consideration. Heavily involved in the research and planning of an investment "swap" program which resulted in a $5.3 million tax refund. Successfully directed the Association's response when the refund resulted in an IRS audit.

As financial division representative, worked closely with both the savings and loan divisions to increase interdivision cooperation related to new systems, operations, and customer service. Significantly improved communications with the Association's service bureau and implemented modifications in the general ledger system which streamlined operations and saved more than $20,000 per year.

The accomplishments he included were his increase in productivity, finding a unique approach for justifying a large tax credit and then defending it before the IRS, increasing cooperation among divisions in the bank, improving relations with the computer service bureau, and saving money on computer services. These accomplishments are likely to pique the interest of a targeted employer.

Results Sell People

Below are additional statements which effectively convey accomplishments. Read them to give you further ideas on how you might present your results.

Developed a new production technique which increased productivity by 7%.

Through more effective recruiting techniques, reduced terminations company-wide by 30% and turnover by 23%.

Edited a newsletter for an architectural association, with readership increasing 28% in one year.

Organized a citizen task force which successfully wrote a statewide initiative, adopted with a 69% favorable vote.

Reduced the data required from contractors for permit approvals. Cut the permit process from 42 days to 28 with a savings to contractors of approximately $120 per home.

Enlisted help of community groups to support construction of a new manufacturing plant. Community groups had previously blocked all new construction in and around the community. Received approval as well as favorable tax breaks from the city council, saving $92,000 in construction costs.

As chairperson for fund raising, developed a strategy which increased funds raised by 26% while reducing promotional costs.

Increased regional revenue an average of 19% per year with sales reaching $59 million in 1991.

Awarded Medal of Merit for contributions to the community.

Recognized for the ability to calm angry customers.

Set a record of 46 days without a system failure.

Which/Which Resulted In

Accomplishments and results are powerful. Everything you've done on a job has had a result. When the result is positive *and* significant, it belongs in the resume. Train yourself to look for results. Remember, you don't need computer printouts to verify your results. Your own honest estimate is sufficient. If asked about it during an interview, just describe how you arrived at the figure and then go into more detail concerning how you accomplished it. Results sell you.

I've developed a simple technique which will help you identify your results as you write your job sketches. As you list a duty or a project, add the words *which*, or *which resulted in*, and then ask yourself what the duty or project resulted in. For example, "Wrote an office procedures manual" becomes, "Wrote an office procedures manual *which* decreased training time and billing errors." After you've taken time to quantify the results and to explain it more accurately, it will become, "Wrote an office procedures manual which decreased training time of new employees by 25% and reduced billing errors over 30%."

Later, after completing your job sketches, go through the process one more time. Review each duty and project to see if you forgot something as you were writing.

The words *which* and *which resulted in* force you to take all of your activities and accomplishments to their logical conclusion. With each duty or function you list, ask yourself whether you did it as well or better than others. If better, ask yourself how you know. This process will lead you to the logical end result. You should keep going back until you have determined what the most basic result is. Once you've identified all of the results from a particular experience, you can then determine which ones will have the most impact in your resume.

The problem I have observed is that people are often quite satisfied to come up with just one result from a duty or project. Many times, however, three or more results are actually lurking in that project just waiting to be discovered. Each one is important. Even if not all of your results get into your resume, they can become highly valuable in interviews.

An example will help show what I mean. John was a production manager in the department which assembled a unit which in turn was used in a larger unit. When he first became manager of the department it had a serious turnover and productivity problem. In his job sketch John wrote "I took better care of my staff and provided better training. As a result, morale increased significantly." This was a good start. Since morale is difficult to measure, however, and since research shows that happy employees are not necessarily more productive employees, it was important to look for other results. Fortunately in John's case, the higher morale actually did result in less turnover and less absenteeism. At that point he was getting somewhere—turnover and absenteeism can be measured and they can both have a heavy impact on productivity. Turnover generally hurts a company because the company loses money on employees while they are in the training phase. In some companies it may take six months before a person becomes fully productive and begins making money for the company. If people stay longer, they not only get faster, but they also make fewer errors. Errors hurt a company in many ways—it may take time and money to fix a mistake, and it may result in losing customers.

So, let's take this experience to its logical conclusion. John's better supervision and training led to lower turnover and absenteeism, which led to greater productivity and fewer errors. The greater productivity and fewer errors led to lower operating costs and happier customers. The lower operating costs led to higher profits. The happier customers meant that they would stay loyal and would continue to buy the company's products.

Now let's do some calculating. By improving the training, as well as people's desire to learn, training time for each new employee was reduced from 30 hours of John's time to about 20. This is a 33% reduction in training time. The improved training and better supervision resulted in turnover being reduced from eight people per year in the 20-person department, to three per year, a 63% reduction. The reduction in training time saved $1,500 annually (10 hours of reduced training time X 5 people trained annually X $30/hr (John's hourly wage plus the cost of benefits)). Because John helped make work enjoyable again, and because the employees felt a loyalty toward John, absenteeism was reduced from 19 lost days per month to only five, a 74% reduction. Since these employees had received sick pay when they are absent, even though they may not have been sick, that is a major savings: 14 days (19-5) X 8 hours X $15/hour X 12 months = $20,000.

People who are well trained make fewer mistakes. John estimated the cost to repair mistakes on the assembly line at $65. The $65 represented the value of the time it took to find and fix the error, as well as the cost of replacement parts. Rejects (units which did not meet specifications) had been averaging 7% before John became manager. Within a year that rate had been reduced to 3%, which was slightly below the industry average. That 57% decrease in rejects meant that 285 fewer units needed rework each year, for a savings of $18,500.

As John started examining results, he quickly realized that productivity had gone up. Not only was there less absenteeism, but employees were producing about 10% more units per week. The cost savings was greater than the 10% increase in productivity would indicate, since he realized that the company paid less in overtime pay as a result. In fact, overtime pay was reduced about 90%. With the higher productivity and customer satisfaction, sales increased, but John was able to handle the higher work load without adding staff. Reducing the overtime, and his ability to keep up with production requirements without having to add two new assembly workers, saved over $60,000. When all the savings are totaled up, they exceeded $100,000.

Despite that significant dollar amount, John decided to indicate his improvements with percentages in the resume, and discuss dollar amounts in interviews. The identification of these results enabled John to make the statements below as part of his job description. Remember, it all started from his initial awareness that he had increased morale. By asking himself what it resulted in, he was able to do a lot of estimating. Ultimately he felt his figures were quite accurate.

As production manager of a 20-person assembly department, introduced improved training and management techniques which reduced
turnover 63% and absenteeism 76%. Established quality programs
which reduced rejects 57%. Reduced overtime pay by 90%. Increased department production over 10% without adding any production workers. Played a key role in significantly increasing customer
retention.

If John had merely stopped with his idea that he had improved morale, the resume would not have been nearly as strong. It might have read, "As production manager of a 20-person assembly depart-ment, introduced training and management techniques which signifi-cantly improved morale." Although that would not have been bad, it simply would not have had the impact of the above paragraph.

Once you've done your best at identifying results, ask a friend to review your job sketches as well. Ask the person to look for any results which you may have overlooked. It is easy to overlook your own re-sults, and it is often surprisingly easy for an unbiased third party to see things which you did not. Invite the person to ask you questions and to clarify what you did on the job. Have the person ask you, "What did that result in?" Then the two of you should keep going until you cannot come up with any more results in that duty or project.

When describing an accomplishment, be sure to include con-crete information about its effect. Don't stop short. People often write in a way which they think demonstrates a result, but does not. For ex-ample, one person wrote, "Developed a scheduling system to better schedule production and reduce late deliveries." Through the use of the word "to" the person is merely implying that the "goal" was to im-prove scheduling and decrease late shipments. The statement does not tell us for sure that it was accomplished. Look what happens when we add *which*: "Developed a better scheduling system *which* improved production scheduling and virtually eliminated late deliveries." This is a stronger statement. There is now no doubt that the new system accomplished its goal and had a real impact on the operation.

Don't assume that just because a result does not come to mind immediately, that there is no result. People are often amazed when they go over their job sketches a second time, or when a friend helps out, that there were many more results than were initially visible.

Virtually all projects which had a successful conclusion contain at least one result. Some duties, however, do not have results; you sim-ply did the work but did it no better and no worse than others. Still, you need to pause as you look over each of your duties from all of your jobs and ask yourself whether there could be a result hiding in there. The more you find, the more interviews you'll get, and with those in-terviews you'll sell yourself to the fullest.

CALCULATING RESULTS

To make the most out of your results you need to know how to quantify them. One reason we don't see more statistics in resumes is that people don't know how to calculate results, and then don't know how to use or describe them to their best effect. Usually all it takes is simple arithmetic and a little logic. I'm going to show you the methods for calculating percentages. Try to follow along, but in case it gets confusing don't worry, there are people out there who can help you. If you are at least able to pull some estimates together, you can locate friends or relatives who can help you in this critical area. I work with statistics frequently, but I still have to think twice before I can remember how to do the calculations. So, let's begin.

In the process of calculating results the first step is to identify all benefits, whether it was something improved, increased, or decreased. Start with the assumption that if you can identify it, you can quantify it. Quantifying results may require some guesstimating, but you can do it.

Review your job sketches to see what clues they might give you. Were there any functions that were left off the sketches that you now think might be valuable? Were there any projects that were not mentioned in your sketches? If a project achieved its goal, it almost assuredly had a result. That result can be quantified. Even if you think a particular result was too small to mention in the resume, still spend some time with it because it might be helpful in an interview. Since you are going to discuss a lot of things in interviews that are not included in your resume, you need lots of additional experiences to discuss. Being able to quantify them will enable you to score points.

EXAMPLES

Determining An Average Annual Increase

Often a person will bring about improvements over a period of several years. A good way to express this figure in a resume is to show the annual increase. Selling something would be a typical example. The following example shows how one client used an increase in sales to its best effect.

Susan increased sales in her territory over a five year period. Sales the year prior to her coming to the territory were $200,000. Her first year she increased sales to $240,000, then $275,000, then $300,000, then $310,000, and finally $350,000. Her first year increase was 20% since her increase of $40,000 is 20% of $200,000.

Mathematically it is figured this way:
$$\$240,000 - 200,000 = \$40,000$$
$$40,000 \div 200,000 = .20 \text{ or } 20\%$$

The second year her increase was 14%:
$$\$275,000 - \$240,000 = \$35,000$$
$$35,000 \div 240,000 = 14\%$$

The third year the increase was 9%, the fourth 3% (a recession year), and the fifth 13%.

Over the five years she increased sales 75%. To get the average annual increase add the increases from each year and total them (20+14+9+3+13 = 59). Then divide by the five years to get the figure (59 ÷ 5 years = 11.8%) of an 11.8% average annual increase. For a resume it would be rounded off to 12%, or in the resume it could be stated, "Increased sales an average of 12% per year." Although she increased sales a total of 75% you cannot divide 75 by 5 to get the average annual increase.

Once the figures have been determined, a decision has to be made as to the strongest way to present the information. Sometimes the best way is simply to present the raw figures. In this case it would be, "In five years took sales in the territory from $200,000 to $350,000." If those figures did not have the impact she wanted she could say, "Took over a mature territory and increased sales 75% in five years," or "During a serious economic downturn in the region, increased sales an average of 12% per year."

Simple Increases
Simple increases might be figured according to the following method: In 1989 advertising revenue for a magazine had been $2,560,000. By the end of 1991 it had increased to $3,180,000. The percent of increase is 24% (3,180,000 - 2,560,000 = 620,000; 620,000 ÷ 2,560,000 = .242 or rounded off to 24%)

Simple Decreases
Simple decreases can be figured and expressed similar to the example below: A manufacturing supervisor reduced rejects (parts which did not meet specifications and were therefore rejected by quality control) from a rate of 6% to 2%. On resumes people often miscalculate such figures and might report that they reduced rejects by 4%, simply subtracting 2 from 6 and getting 4. Going from 6% to 2% actually represents a 67% reduction in rejects, however. The proper way to calculate this is 6 - 2 = 4; 4 ÷ 6 = .6666 or 67%.

Another common problem occurs if something was reduced from say 15 to 7. We'll say that the average daily absenteeism in a department has been reduced from 15 people per day to 7. Some will subtract 7 from 15 getting 8; then dividing 8 by 7 getting 1.14, which they translate into 114%. On the resume it might read, "Reduced absenteeism 114%." But nothing can ever be reduced by more than 100%, or to be more accurate, 99.9999%. Reducing something from 15 to 7 equals 53% (15 - 7 = 8; 8 ÷ 15 = .53) Logic tells you that absenteeism was cut by a little more than half so you know it will be slightly above a 50% decrease.

Large Increases

With large increases you must be careful when calculating percentages. Let's say production in a plant went from 10,000 units per year to 30,000 over a five-year period. It is easy to see that units tripled, so one would tend to say that production increased 300%. The problem is that it actually represents a 200% increase. Going from 10,000 to 20,000 was a 100% increase, and going from 20,000 to 30,000 was another 100%, for a total of 200%.

If calculating numbers is still difficult, don't simply decide not to include your results—get help. Those who know how to calculate such things will enjoy helping you.

ASSISTED IN

If you feel uncomfortable taking primary responsibility for a project, you can use the phrases, *instrumental in, key person in, played a key role in,* or *played an important role in.* It might read, "Played a key role in implementing a management-by-objectives program which increased productivity 14%."

In resumes I often see the phrase *assisted in.* I rarely use it because it tends to dilute the person's actual contribution. For example, Fred wrote "Assisted in developing a quality control program which reduced rejected circuit boards 24%." In this case, the other person working on the program was a peer who contributed less to the success of the program than Fred. A more appropriate description would be, "Developed a quality control program which reduced rejected circuit boards by 24%." During an interview Fred could explain that he was the primary, but not the sole developer of the program. Fred probably also had a supervisor who had ultimate responsibility for the success of the program, but since Fred did most of the work, he should still take credit for it.

JOB DESCRIPTIONS

Job descriptions must be concise but complete. A common problem of resumes is that the job descriptions are too short and do not adequately describe duties, experience, level of responsibility, or accomplishments. As you begin, don't be concerned about limiting the resume to one page. While it is often assumed that a resume should be no longer than one page, my studies have verified that so long as it is well-written and concise, a two-page resume is perfectly acceptable, and for many people, essential.

Once you have thought through each job and listed your duties, responsibilities, accomplishments, projects, and results, you're ready to start writing a rough draft of your resume. Start by stating your objective. As we've already discussed, your objective may be as simple as a job title, or it might be a longer, more descriptive phrase, such as "An entry-level position in marketing leading to management." You'll use your objective as a guide for writing the rest of the resume.

Although the wording of the objective may change later, you know that everything which appears in the final draft must demonstrate your capability of performing the work defined by your objective.

Begin by reviewing your job sketch for your current or most recent position. What are the most important things an employer should know about the job? Try to eliminate some of the less important duties, but don't worry if your first draft seems a little too long. When you rewrite, you will be able to identify points that should be deleted or summarized more briefly.

From your resume the employer should be able to sense your positive attributes, such as diligence, efficiency, cooperation, effectiveness, and intelligence. Your duties must be adequately covered so that the employer will recognize the full range of your experience. The types of positions you will be seeking will determine which duties should be given the most attention. If employers will have no interest in a certain duty, it should be mentioned only briefly or not at all. Describing your duties effectively will help employers immediately realize that you are ready for more responsibility. Results and accomplishments will be the frosting on the cake that makes the employer want to meet you.

The examples below demonstrate these points. Read the job descriptions as the person had originally written them, then read the revision. Notice how the revisions were made and how they affected the impact of the information being presented.

Compare the following two versions of one woman's employment section. Notice how in the first version her descriptions are concise, but lacking in detail compared to the second version. Her second version provides a fuller, more vivid description of her experiences.

Also, as you study the revised job description, ask yourself what you know about the person that you didn't before. The revised job description is longer, but it had to be to adequately describe what she had done and to give an employer enough details to fully appreciate her capabilities.

Version #1

EMPLOYMENT

Employer	Wiggins Sportswear 1991-Present
Position	Marketing Coordinator
Responsibilities	Coordinate the entire clothing program Creating and utilizing Lotus spread sheets for marketing, production, and finance projections Market research Coordinating advertising with publication Work with outside contractors on special projects Fabric and notion research/purchasing Calculated preliminary and final costing of garment Approved bills relating to the clothing program
Employer	Broadway Department Store 1990 to 1991
Position	Salesperson
Responsibilities	Sales Interior layout and display Opening and closing the department Handling customer complaints and problems Issuing merchandise transfers

Version #2

EMPLOYMENT

Wiggins Sportswear, San Diego, California 4/91 to present

MARKETING COORDINATOR - Coordinate the production and marketing functions for a new line of active sportswear. Came into the project when it was two months behind schedule and in serious trouble. Worked with the designer to select colors, designs, and fabrics. Purchased fabric and accessories. Negotiated with two garment manufacturers to produce small lots, thus reducing the required unit sales to reach a break-even point. Worked out schedule arrangements with manufacturers and authorized any changes in specifications. Line was introduced on schedule with final costs one-third lower than originally projected.

Coordinated the production of the annual sales catalog. Designed order forms, verified prices, and consulted with graphics artists and printers. Had authority to make all necessary changes.

Set up the company's first computerized systems, using Lotus and other software to provide the first accurate year-to-date sales figures, as well as highly useful marketing, financial, and manufacturing projections.

Broadway Department Stores, San Diego, California 9/90 to 4/91

SALESPERSON - Sold women's clothing and had interior layout and display responsibilities. Selected as Employee of the Month for December in this store of approximately 190 employees. Selected on the basis of sales, favorable comments from customers, and taking on added responsibilities.

The revised version is slightly longer than the original, but because it provides more background, you get a clearer picture of her capabilities. By mentioning a project that was behind schedule and in serious trouble, her ability to complete it on schedule and under budget makes the accomplishment especially meaningful. Her original resume contains only a brief list of duties and gives you no information regarding whether she had been successful. The revised job description conveys a sense of her potential. It shows that she was given a lot of responsibility and that she handled it well. It suggests to the reader that she has some very interesting stories to tell about her experiences at Wiggins; but those details will be saved for the interview.

The experience at Broadway did not receive as much space because she has no intention of returning to retail work. The experience does, however, demonstrate valuable background which pertains directly to her career in marketing. It is important that she was able to demonstrate that she was successful even though it was a short-term job. Simply listing her duties provides no clues about the quality of her work, and could lead an employer to believe that she did not do well. Mentioning that she was employee-of-the month proves that she was valuable. By mentioning the basis for the award—sales, comments from customers, and taking on responsibility—she demonstrates to the employer that she was judged outstanding in each category.

As you write your resume, look for ways to tell your story that convey your value and your successes. Even if you were fired from a job it is possible to show that you were valuable. Do that by stressing what you did well; simply ignore your problem areas.

The next job description comes from the resume of a marriage and family counselor. One of his earlier positions was as supervisor for a parks department. In the first job description you get nothing but a dull list of duties. He is a very interesting person with an excellent background, but the first version of the job description fails to convey this.

Version #1

SUPERVISOR — Portland Park Department. Portland, Oregon 5/88-7/89. Overall responsibility for staff, facility, and program at a neighborhood community center; supervising, hiring, training, and recruitment; program planning, implementation, and evaluation; record keeping, budgeting, grant writing, and analyses; work with schools, local, state, and federal agencies in a variety of capacities; direct service including teaching, training, and work with adults and youth in social, educational, cultural and athletic programs; community and business presentations.

As you read the revised job description below you'll get the sense that here is a person worth meeting. There's a personal touch evident in this version that is lacking in version 1.

Version #2

Portland Park Department, Portland, Oregon 5/88 to 7/89

SUPERVISOR - Developed and promoted social, educational, cultural, and athletics programs for the community. Contracted with consultants, instructors, and coaches to provide instruction in dozens of subjects and activities at the Browser Community Center. Interviewed and hired instructors, and conducted follow-up assessments to ensure top-quality instruction. Personally taught several courses and coached athletic teams. In three years tripled participation at the Center and took it from a $1,400 deficit to a $12,000 profit.

The revised job description presents a person who has goals and ideals. It's clear that he really cared about what he did: he got involved, he took action, and he got results. This more vital, caring tone is created by using action verbs like *developed* and *promoted*. You feel the action. The programs that the community really wanted didn't exist so he went out and *developed* them. Since people don't come flocking to programs they don't know about, he *promoted* them. And he not only planned programs he also taught some. He even coached several athletic teams. This demonstrates that he is an action-oriented person in good physical shape. The ultimate result of all this effort was a tripling of participation, yet his original job description did not even mention it.

Writing a top-quality resume takes time. From these examples you can see why. Also, describing oneself in positive terms is difficult for most people, yet it is necessary. Write your job descriptions and then keep editing until they approach the examples you find in this book. Everyone can do it, but it will take time and thought. Just remember that taking the time will pay off in interviews and job offers. And that's what you're after.

EMPLOYMENT FORMAT

The format you choose for your employment section can make a big difference in the visual appeal and readability of your resume. I have tested formats extensively and find that the format below is the one that most employers prefer.

EMPLOYMENT

Balboa's Steak House 5/89 to Present

GENERAL MANAGER, Miami, Florida, 10/91 to Present. Took over a troubled restaurant which had had six managers in two years and incurred losses each month during that time. Resolved serious morale problems, instituted an effective training program, and redesigned the menu. During the first nine months increased lunch revenue 38% and dinner 29%. Losses were eliminated within two months and a consistent profit margin of 14% has been maintained.

ASSISTANT MANAGER, Ft. Lauderdale, Florida, 7/89 to 10/91. Redesigned the menu and helped introduce wine sales. Provided extensive staff training which enabled the restaurant to become number one in wine sales in the chain of twenty restaurants. Purchased all food and supplies.

Saga, Inc., Tallahassee, Florida 9/87 to 6/89

STUDENT MANAGER - For this college cafeteria, prepared food, scheduled part-time workers, purchased supplies, and oversaw lunch and dinner lines.

Following are sample treatments of various types of work histories. One of them should conform fairly closely to your own.

Same Company, Three Positions, All in the Same City

EMPLOYMENT

Douglas Bolt Company, St. Louis, Missouri 8/79 to Present

V. P. PURCHASING, 7/88 to Present. ....
....
....

DIRECTOR OF PURCHASING, 5/85 to 7/88. ....
....
....

MANAGER, STOCK PARTS PURCHASING, 8/79 to 5/85. ....
....
....

Same Company, Three Positions, Three Different Cities

EMPLOYMENT

Horizon Gear 8/78 to Present

REGIONAL SALES MANAGER, Houston, Texas 7/89 to Present
....
....

DISTRICT SALES MANAGER, Atlanta, Georgia 3/85 to 7/89. ..
....
....

SALES REPRESENTATIVE, Little Rock, Arkansas 8/78 to
3/85. ....
....

In a situation like this you might want to indicate where the headquarters is located. In that case you would show it as: Horizon Gear, Chicago, Illinois 8/78 to Present.

One Position With Each Company

EMPLOYMENT

Shannon Electric, Garden City, Michigan 5/87 to Present

INSTALLER - ....
....
....

Preston Electric, Detroit, Michigan 6/84 to 5/87

INSTALLER - ....

....

....

Work for a Subsidiary of Division of a Major Company

EMPLOYMENT

Antac, Inc., Subsidiary of A&R Industries, Buffalo, New York
5/77 to Present

It is seldom necessary to specify the parent company. If you choose to, however, this is the easiest way to do it.

PRIOR EMPLOYMENT

A prior employment section is particularly useful if you are trying to shorten your resume or de-emphasize your earlier jobs. A prior employment section is an effective way to explain how you've gotten to where you are, without making the employer spend a lot of time reading about it. Other titles for this section include *Previous Employment, Prior Experience,* or *Additional Experience.*

The example below shows the most commonly used format for the prior employment section. The Assistant Purchasing Manager position is the sixth job description position on his two-page resume.

ASSISTANT PURCHASING MANAGER - 3/77-5/78. Set up and developed an inventory control program to reduce inventory and operating costs. Over the next year reduced inventory by 20%.

PRIOR EMPLOYMENT

Counterperson, Zenith Electronics, Los Angeles, CA 3/76-9/77
Expediter, Hughes Aircraft, Los Angeles, CA 4/74-3/76
Parts Manager, High Lift Equipment, Long Beach, CA 9/72-4/74

In the example above, the person has included title, name of company, city and state, and dates. Generally this information would be included. In the remaining examples, however, you will see how personal taste varies. I generally include city and state, but if it seems like unnecessary detail for some distant jobs, feel free to leave city and state off.

In the example below, the person provides the job title, name of employer, and dates, but not the city and state.

Example (starting with the person's fifth position on a two-page resume):

National Computer Stores, Spokane, WA 5/86-6/87

SALES REPRESENTATIVE - Sold hardware and software for this IBM authorized dealer. Consistently exceeded monthly sales goals.

PRIOR EXPERIENCE

Food Service Specialist, Johnson Nursing Home (8/84-5/86); Cook, Boyd's Restaurant (7/82-8/84); Cook, Iron Pig Restaurant (6/81-7/82)

In the following example the individual did not feel it necessary to give specific time periods or list the names of employers.

Example (starting with the person's seventh position on a two-page resume):

Xytelin Electronics, Mountain View, California 1967 to 1969

INTERNAL AUDITOR - Discovered weaknesses in the parts inventory control procedures and recommended remedial action. Responsible for quarterly and yearly audits.

Prior Experience, 1960 to 1967: Airline Internal Auditor, Cost Clerk, Production Scheduler.

In the example below, the person listed dates, but did not list employers.

Example (starting with fifth position on a one-page resume):

Department of Social Services, Winston-Salem, North Carolina 3/70 to 4/71

ELIGIBILITY SPECIALIST - Assisted families in obtaining all of the Medicaid benefits they were legally entitled to. Provided psychological and social support services.

Previous Experience:

Cashier/Hostess 1/69 to 3/70; Sales Clerk 6/68 to 1/69; Long Distance Operator 7/66 to 6/68.

The remaining examples will simply give you more options.

PRIOR EMPLOYMENT

CASHIER - Pay Less Drugs, Elgin, Illinois 5/66 to 11/67
CASHIER - Don's Rexall, Carbondale, Illinois 4/65 to 5/66
STOCKER - Jewel Foodstores, Peoria, Illinois 9/62 to 3/65

Previous Employment

Truck driver (1963-1967); Warehouseman (1963); Machine Repairman (1962-1963)

Sometimes a person will choose not to describe all the positions with a particular company, especially the first company employed with. The person below has worked for Boeing since 1972.

PRODUCTION INSPECTOR - 3/80-4/82. Performed final interior, flight line modification, and wing line inspections on Boeing 767 aircraft. Verified that the production department installed assemblies according to specifications.

Prior Boeing positions: Assistant Production Inspector 4/77-3/80; Tooling Inspector 5/75-4/77; Jig Builder 3/72-5/75.

TIPS FOR WRITING EFFECTIVE EMPLOYMENT HISTORIES

The Job Description Summary

It is often helpful to begin your job description with a summary, or an overview of what you did. It typically consists of a string of items and is very effective in helping a reader quickly understand what you did. A job description summary might look something like this:

Research databases and create surveys to analyze trends and to identify opportunities for improving customer support strategies.

For this sign manufacturing company, prepared financial statements and supervised payroll, billing, and accounts receivable personnel.

Directly responsible for all phases of investment analyses, development, and property management of properties.

Coordinated all aspects of the Early Childhood Special Education Program, including hiring and training of staff and support professionals, and the design and implementation of curriculum.

Administered and trained lending staff of four in credit and business development efforts.

Interviewed, counseled, and educated patients and families preceding and following open-heart surgery.

Even before learning the details in the rest of each job description, the reader has a good overview of what the person did. It is fine to start off with "Responsible for ..." but don't overuse it. Notice that only one of our examples started with "Responsible for ..."

Several Jobs Within One Company

Sometimes a person will have five or six changes in job title within one company, during a 4–6 year period. Frequently the person was promoted and kept all or most of the previous responsibilities, and then added others. To describe each job separately would be redundant and unnecessary. Look for any two jobs which were *essentially* the same, and treat them as one.

What To Call Your Employment Section

There are a variety of words and phrases you can use to head your employment section: *Employment, Employment Experience, Work Experience, Professional Experience, Employment History, Work History,* and *Experience* are all good terms. I typically use *Employment,* and sometimes *Professional Experience.* Each of the terms is a good term so pick the one that feels right for you.

Dates

Dates should be used on nearly all resumes. If you have no time gaps between jobs or short gaps, you should usually use the months and years you started and left. If you have long gaps, you can indicate the year you started and the year you left.

When to use month and year (example: 5/87-8/92):

1. No gaps in employment.
2. Short gaps of less than five months.
3. One gap of over five months several years ago.

Employers prefer to see month and year and may wonder if you are hiding anything by omitting months. On the other hand, if you reveal long gaps between jobs, employers may question your perseverance and dedication. With this in mind, decide what is best for you.

Location Of The Job

Your resume should indicate the city and state you actually work in, not the location of your company's national headquarters. If you work out of your home, include your city as your location; if you live in a suburb, include either the name of the suburb or the more familiar name of the large city you live near.

Job Titles

In most cases, the job title on your resume should match the one assigned by your employer. If you work for a company which has not assigned job titles, you can select a title which accurately reflects what you do. This is easiest with smaller, informal companies that haven't gotten around to writing job descriptions with exact titles. For instance, if you were a secretary who ran the office and supervised one or more clerical workers, you might use the title "Office Manager." Or, if you ran construction projects, but never had a title, you could call yourself "Construction Superintendent."

The situation gets sticky if you had a title that does not accurately convey what you did. In most cases you should use the title given you. If a potential employer contacts a former employer and learns of a discrepancy in job titles, it may not look good.

To avoid changing the title, yet still give a sense of responsibility, try something like this:

FOREMAN - Functioned as construction superintendent on five commercial projects including the 280,000-square-foot Radkin Plaza Building. Established and maintained tight production schedules, set up stringent cost controls, and scheduled and coordinated subcontractors. Completed each project on schedule and under budget.

The key in the above examples is the use of the phrase "functioned as." It indicates that the person had responsibilities that were larger than the job title would normally indicate. By no means should you always use the phrase "functioned as," but it can be a good alternative to changing your actual title.

Another alternative would be:

FOREMAN (Construction Superintendent) — Managed five commercial projects..."

In this case putting Construction Superintendent in parentheses indicates that he functioned in that role.

Another alternative is to simply ignore the fact that your title does not match what you did. In other words, give the correct job title and then describe your duties and accomplishments, letting your results speak for you.

If you've been self-employed, employers will be concerned about whether you can take direction and can fit into a corporate environment. One way to minimize this concern is to not indicate that the business was yours. If the company had your name as part of the title, you may want to simply use the initials of the company. If that is not possible, refer to yourself as "Owner/Manager." Otherwise, avoid the term owner and call yourself "Manager" or "General Manager." Call yourself "President" only if that is the type of position you are now seeking.

Clarifying What Your Company Does

If you work for General Motors, General Electric, or Boeing, there is no need to explain what the company does. If your employer is Eastside Masonry Products, it is also unnecessary to elaborate because the company name explains its type of business. If you work for SLRC Corporation, though, you may want to explain in the resume. Handle it this way:

SLRC Corporation, Montgomery, Alabama 5/78 to Present

SALES REP - For this producer of food additives, opened up a new territory and increased sales an average of 32% each year.

Or this way:

CBD, Inc., Boston, Massachusetts 1978 to Present

SALES REP - Increased sales 20% each year for CBD, the Northeast's second largest distributor of electronic components.

Scope Of The Job

The scope of a job includes such things as the products and services of the company, size of company in terms of gross sales, the size of your department in terms of people and dollar budget, the budget you personally work with, and the number of people supervised. It is useful to include the scope of the job if doing so will clarify your level of responsibility or any other key point. To describe the scope of a job you might say, "Managed all finance, accounting, and data processing functions for this $80 million manufacturer of outdoor equipment." Or you might say, "Supervised a staff of four supervisors and managed a department budget of $1.2 million."

How Much Detail And Space Should You Give?

Principles (not laws) to keep in mind: 1) Your current or most recent position is described in the greatest detail as long as it is similar to the type of job you are seeking. Each preceding job is described in slightly less detail. 2) If the job you held three jobs ago is closest to what you're seeking, devote the most detail to it. 3) Jobs held many years ago and jobs that have nothing to do with what you want to do in the future can usually be described in two or three lines, or handled through "Previous Employment."

How Far Back Should Your Descriptions Go?

If you are a college graduate, go back as far as your first full-time job after graduation. If you went to work right after high school, go back to your first full-time job. If you've had a lot of jobs, you can write about your four to six most recent positions, but also include a previous employment section, which merely lists prior positions without descriptions.

Although some of your earlier jobs may not be applicable to your current occupation, employers are still curious about where you've been. Such positions require only a very straightforward two- or three-line description of duties. Or, you might present this information in a prior employment section where you would include your job title, employer, and dates, but would not use any job descriptions.

If you feel certain that it would be detrimental to include all of your jobs, simply do not list those in the most distant past. If you do so be sure not to show dates for education, or any other section which would give away your age or would indicate that some positions are missing.

Current Job Less Valuable Than A Prior Job

Generally, it's wise to devote less space to a current, but less valuable job, and more space to an earlier, more relevant job. Another option can be effective: you can separate your experience into two segments, calling one "Related Experience" and the other "Additional Experience."

The related experience section would come first and would generally have the greatest detail. Except for the fact that you have two employment sections, Related Experience and Additional Experience, it is a standard reverse chronological resume. Within each category you should list jobs in reverse chronological order and show the correct dates. Showing the information in this way makes it clear to the employer that even though you are using an atypical format, all jobs have been covered. More importantly, it means that the employer will read your relevant experience first.

SPECIAL PROJECTS/ACTIVITIES/AWARDS

A special projects section can be especially effective for a person with valuable experiences which did not occur on a job. Career changers, recent college graduates, and women reentering the work force can benefit from including a special projects section. The section can also be labeled *Selected Projects, Accomplishments, Achievements, Activities, Projects, Noteworthy Projects, Selected Accomplishments,* or *Noteworthy Accomplishments.* Volunteer experiences with clubs and associations, as well as special projects performed as part of a course, can be presented in this section.

Use these examples as guides to determine whether a special projects section will strengthen your resume.

In the example below, the person had been at home rearing children since 1973. Her special projects section helps make it obvious that she is very capable and energetic.

SPECIAL PROJECTS

As President of PTA, increased parent participation by 26% and funds raised by 34% over the previous year. (1987)

As a United Way fund raising team leader, exceeded the quota by 22%. Honored at banquet as Team Leader of the Year. (1977)

A project or accomplishment seldom requires over 45 words—20–30 words is usually best. Do not try to describe the project in detail—concentrate on results. When writing out each accomplishment in the first draft, feel free to describe it in 50-70 words. Then rewrite it by concentrating on results and include just enough detail so that the reader will understand what you did. Save all other details for an interview. List the projects and accomplishments in reverse chronological order and include the year.

The person below had been active in community affairs for several years and was seeking the directorship of a city-run agency for youth. His employment experience alone would not have even gotten him an interview.

SELECTED PROJECTS

Wrote news articles and special features for *Troy Herald, Outdoor News,* and *College Forum.* (1988-1991)

Lobbied for and obtained Troy city council support for three community parks. Played a key role on the planning committee and helped obtain matching federal funds for this "model project." (1989)

Participated as a guest expert on disadvantaged youth for a public affairs radio talk show. (1988)

Organized a basketball camp for disadvantaged youth in Troy, and obtained $55,000 in corporate and city funding. Got four coaches and seven college players from three surrounding colleges to donate one week to the program. (1987)

Below is a special projects section used by a 40-year old woman reentering the work force after completing an MBA. She had held one part-time research position in the last ten years.

SPECIAL PROJECTS

Allocated and dispensed federal monies to ten counties - CETA Advisory Board, Newark, New Jersey, 1987-1989.

Developed and coordinated budgets for YWCA and Big Sisters Program, Newark, 1983-1986.

Developed highly successful parenting, exercise, and personal growth programs for the Newark YWCA, 1982-1985.

Planned and coordinated programs for the League of Women Voters, Newark, 1979-1983.

Chaired "The Mayor's Conference on Aging," Newark, 1977.

The following example was written by a teacher who was seeking a position in private business and needed to demonstrate non-classroom abilities.

SPECIAL PROJECTS

Interned for Omaha National Bank during the summer of 1991. Received assignments working with retail credit, corporate loans, and trust departments. Developed and completed a survey which determined customer needs. (1991)

Supervised the senior class store which sold school supplies, tickets, jackets, and sweaters. The store maintained a profit each year under my management, something it had never done previously. (1986-1992)

Supervised the research and publication of the Omaha "Volunteer Directory," which helped draw new volunteers into dozens of agencies. (1987)

Developed an intern program to allow students to work in nursing homes and schools for the retarded. Dozens of students gained new skills and several now work in geriatrics. (1984-1987)

> Organized record-breaking blood drives and won trophies each
> year from 1984 to 1988. No other schools came close to matching
> the high percentage of students who willingly donated blood.
> (1984-1988)

Sometimes other section titles such as "Honors and Awards," "Publications" or "Activities" will work better than "Special Projects." This recently graduated college student had only one special project to describe so she combined it with an award and called the section, "Awards and Publications."

AWARDS AND PUBLICATIONS

> Chairperson, Task Force on Teaching Quality. Investigated teach-
> ing evaluation methods at Reed College and published position
> paper which helped initiate change in tenure decision policies.
> (1991)

> Senior Class Inspirational Person-of-the-Year Award. (1987)

Listing honors and awards can be helpful, but only if they are meaningful and will have impact. An honors or awards section can be especially useful for recent college graduates, as in the example below.

HONORS

> Received the Mary Beth Astor award as the top speech therapy
> student in the department. (1989)

> Received the John Radcliff scholarship in recognition of academic
> and community achievement. (1988)

The secretary below was very active in a professional organization. Her experiences helped demonstrate her organizational abilities in ways that her employment alone did not.

ACTIVITIES

> San Diego Secretarial Council - Member of the board of directors
> 1984 to Present. Vice President 1988 to 1990. Presented seminars
> for entry-level secretaries and worked to increase the professional-
> ism of secretaries working for the City.

> Field Rep for the San Diego Credit Union. Explained to members
> changes in loan policies and interest rates and helped promote
> special discounts with local merchants. (1985-1987)

LICENSES/CERTIFICATES

Any licenses you hold that are necessary or valuable in the field you are seeking should be listed. Be selective, though. Only list certificates and licenses which are relevant to the new position. Mentioning a real estate license when you want to be a purchasing agent for a tool manufacturer would not add to your qualifications and might cause the employer to wonder whether your preferred career was selling real estate or purchasing.

LICENSES

First Class FCC Radio Telephone Operator (1979)
Commercial Instrument Pilot rating (1978) 840 hours flight time
Private Pilot (1977)

(Electronics technologist and sales rep who flies to see customers)

LICENSES

General Electrical Administrator Certificate, California (1982)
Journeyman Electrician License - California, Nevada, Arizona (1981)
Commercial - Instrument Pilots License (1980)

(Electrician who would like to do some flying for his employer)

CERTIFICATION

Standard Elementary and Secondary, Idaho. Lifetime 1981.

(Teacher)

LICENSES

FCC, 1981

(Broadcast journalist who needs a Federal Communications Commission license to operate on the air)

ASSOCIATIONS/MEMBERSHIPS/ PROFESSIONAL AFFILIATIONS

Including associations and memberships can demonstrate you are keeping up to date in your profession and that you have developed useful contacts. For the person making a career change, listing memberships can demonstrate you are serious in making a shift in career direction. Use these categories only if they are relevant and will help you. An engineer might use the following:

PROFESSIONAL AFFILIATIONS

> American Chemical Society (1982-Present)
> American Institute of Chemical Engineers (1980-Present)

Belonging to associations and professional organizations may mean only that you paid the annual dues, or it could mean that you are active in the organization. If you want a one-page resume and you are three lines over, affiliations can be sacrificed. The section provides interesting, but not usually crucial, information. List any offices held. The examples below can be used as guides. Do not list an affiliation unless you believe its adds credibility or value to your resume. Organizations you are no longer a member of or no longer active in are usually not mentioned, unless you held an office.

Use the examples below as guides for presenting information regarding affiliations.

MEMBERSHIPS

> Pacific Northwest Personnel Managers Association (1980-Present)
> American Society for Personnel Administration (1979-Present)

ASSOCIATIONS

> Homebuilders Association, member 1979 to present
> Officer 1985 to present
> Associate of the Year 1983
> Board of Realtors, member 1975 to present
> Chairperson, Legislative Committee 1985-87
> Chairperson, Political Affairs and Education 1979-81

ASSOCIATIONS

Southeast Community Alcohol Center
    President, Board of Directors (1987)
    Member of Board (1977-Present)
Northwest Nurses Society on Chemical Dependency
    Treasurer (1987-1989)
    Member (1983-Present)
Oregon State Council on Alcoholism
    Member (1977-Present)

If you want to mention certain organizations, but you are no longer active, try this:

AFFILIATIONS

Member, National Association of Bank Women (1977 to Present)
    Program Chairperson (1988)
Member, Bank Managers International (1977 to 1988)
    Budget Committee Chairperson (1986)
Member, Business and Professional Women (1976 to 1984)

PUBLICATIONS

A list or description of publications can be used to demonstrate expertise in a particular field. Listing publications can also demonstrate your abilities in researching, interviewing, and writing. If you are widely published, include only your most relevant articles.

Publications include articles in newspapers, newsmagazines, trade journals, professional journals, school papers, anthologies, or just about anything in printed form with a circulation over 50.

PUBLICATIONS

Contributing Editor of *Retailers Northwest* magazine, writing articles covering children's clothing.

(Included in resume of manufacturers' representative who sells children's clothing)

PUBLICATIONS

"The Arts in Seattle," *The Weekly*, July 27, 1991
"Marketing A Symphony," *The Conductor*, April, 1988
"Will Bach Be Back?" *Symphony News*, November, 1986

PUBLICATIONS

"The Dismantling of Student Loans," University of Kentucky Daily, 1991
"Tenureship Under Attack," University of Kentucky Daily, 1991
"An Hour With G. Gordon Liddy," University of Kentucky Daily, 1990

PUBLICATIONS

"Robots and Production," *Chrysler Employees Newsletter*, 1990
"Automation and Its Impact on Blue Collar Workers," paper presented at the annual Industrial Psychologists Symposium, 1988

If you are going to use a special projects section and have only one publication, you could include the publication with your projects. For example:

SPECIAL PROJECTS

Volunteer Probation Counselor, King County - 1986 to Present
Authored an environmental article published in *Ecojournal* - 1990

PERSONAL INFORMATION

Using a personal data section has become outdated. During the past 15 years resumes have gone from virtually always having a personal data section, which included such information as age, marital status, height and weight, and health status, to an almost total extinction. Women began excluding it from their resumes about 15 years ago and men have followed suit. Equal Employment Opportunity legislation also helped hasten the trend. It was never a very helpful section, but it was traditional to include it. In the 1930s and 40s it was traditional to include religion and the national origin of parents in a personal data section. It was assumed that employers wanted to know and therefore it should be included. Actually, including this information merely gave employers greater opportunity to discriminate. My recommendation is to exclude it as a section. Sometimes, however, it is useful to use a section called "Personal." It can be used to cover bonding, security clearances, citizenship, willingness to relocate or travel, and any other aspects that might not fit in other categories of a resume.

Bonding

Mention you are bondable if your type of work requires it. Essentially, anyone who does not have a prison record is bondable. Bonding is a type of insurance employers take out on employees who handle large amounts of money. If an employee heads to Mexico with thousands of dollars, the employer collects from the bonding company.

Security Clearance

Many people in the military, and civilians working on military projects, have been given security clearances, typically "Secret" or "Top Secret." After leaving the military, it quickly lapses and a new investigation is conducted before reestablishing a security clearance. By including your security clearance, however, you're really saying, "My honesty and integrity were verified by a very thorough investigation; you, too, can trust me." If you held a security clearance within the last ten years, it may be helpful to mention it. Indicate the years it was active. An alternative is to mention your security clearance in your military job description.

Citizenship

Include this information only if you believe an employer might question your citizenship, or if you especially want to let an employer know that you are a U. S. citizen. If you are not a U. S. citizen, you may want to state "Permanent Resident" or indicate your status. There is no need to specify "Naturalized U.S. Citizen;" simply say "U.S. Citizen," or possibly "U.S. Citizen since 1978." Other terms could be "Canadian Citizen since 1959," or "Valid Green Card."

Health

I suggest not listing your health status. Everyone always states "Excellent Health" anyway, so it really has no purpose. Have you ever seen a resume that said "Fair Health?" If you have a disability that you believe could affect your chances of getting a job, but not your job performance, do not mention the disability in the resume, but be prepared to discuss it during an interview. Legally you do not need to divulge any illnesses or disabilities which will not affect your job performance. This is also true when filling out application forms and during interviews. If you have any questions regarding disabilities, consult a city or state Equal Employment Opportunity office.

Military experience

If you have military experience, you can include it in your employment section, under previous experience, or under personal. It can be listed under personal in this way: "U.S. Navy, 1972-74," "U.S. Navy/ E-5/1972-74," or "U.S. Navy 1972-74, Honorable Discharge."

Relocation

If you are willing to relocate and you are contacting national or regional firms, state this in the personal section or merely state at the bottom of the resume, "Willing to Relocate."

Activities

Whether you should include activities or interests is open to debate. Some insist that anything not demonstrating work-related skills or background should be excluded. Others feel a discussion of activities can become an interesting topic of conversation and helps the candidate to be remembered. Both sides make good points. I sometimes include activities because it can make you seem more like a real person, someone employers can identify with. Select your interests and activities carefully; use only those in which you really are active. Jogging is an excellent activity to include, but don't list it if you run only occasionally.

With each activity you select, ask yourself what impact it will have on an employer. Let's say you're an unemployed loan officer who loves to skydive. Most skydivers are viewed as high risk takers, but loan officers are noted for their conservative, low-risk approach to business. Even though you may be just as conservative on the job as your colleagues, listing skydiving as an activity could arouse just enough doubt to cause an employer not to interview you.

Give a consistent picture of yourself. Decide what image you want to convey and then select the appropriate activities. Office workers are wise to state interests that indicate a highly energetic personality.

ACTIVITIES

Strong involvement in marathon running, skiing, and scuba diving.

❖

ACTIVITIES

Actively involved in golf, jogging, and camping.

❖

ACTIVITIES

Avid backpacker. Enjoy flying, horseback riding, and hunting.

❖

INTERESTS

Enjoy making exotic breads, creating stained glass windows, and dance exercise activities.

SAYING IT WITH IMPACT

Producing impact through your words is crucial in a resume. Knowing which action verbs, adjectives, and adverbs to use and how to use them will significantly strengthen your resume. This section will cover all of these points and show you how to bring it together in your resume.

ACTION WORDS

A resume should sound alive and vigorous. Using action verbs helps achieve that feeling. "I changed the filing system" lacks punch and doesn't really indicate if the system was improved. "I *reorganized* and *simplified* the filing system" sounds much better and provides more accurate information.

Review the sentences below to get a feel for action words. Then quickly scan the words in the following list and check any you think you might want to use in your resume. Don't try to force them in; use them when they feel right.

Conducted long-range master planning for the Portland water supply system.

Monitored enemy radio transmissions, analyzed information, and identified enemy strategic and tactical capabilities.

Planned, staffed, and organized the intramural sports program for this 1,200-student college.

Produced daily reports for each trial and made sure documents and evidence were handled properly.

Presented seminars to entry-level secretaries and worked to increase the professionalism of secretaries in the county system.

Improved the coordination, imagination, and pantomime techniques of adults through mime and dance training.

Allocated and dispensed federal moneys to nine counties as board member of the CETA Advisory Board.

Evaluated financial health by analyzing financial statements and ratios.

Prevented the loss of numerous key accounts through effective account management and by solving long-standing problems.

Compiled extensive fisheries data from interviews with thousands of sports fishermen.

Researched and proposed a $1,000,000 project to improve warehouse storage and develop a better distribution system.

Reduced lost time due to illness 81% and reduced industrial accidents by 67%.

Negotiated a product classification change for California freight, saving $18,000 annually.

Negotiated, awarded, and administered contracts with vendors for the procurement of over 65,000 different standard parts.

Continually streamlined policies to reduce redundant procedures.

ACTION VERBS

Accomplished	Brought about	Correlated	Eliminated
Achieved	Built	Corroborated	Employed
Acquired	Calculated	Counseled	Enacted
Acted as	Clarified	Created	Encouraged
Activated	Classified	Culminated in	Enforced
Active in	Coached	Cultivated	Engineered
Adapted	Collected	Dealt	Enhanced
Addressed	Commanded	Decided	Enlisted
Adjusted	Commended	Defined	Ensured
Administered	Communicated	Delegated	Equipped
Advanced	Completed	Delivered	Established
Advised	Compared	Demonstrated	Estimated
Allocated	Compiled	Designed	Evaluated
Analyzed	Composed	Detected	Examined
Approved	Computed	Determined	Executed
Arbitrated	Conceived	Developed	Expanded
Arranged	Conceptualized	Devised	Expedited
Ascertained	Condensed	Diagnosed	Experimented
Assembled	Conducted	Directed	Explained
Assessed	Consolidated	Discovered	Expressed
Assigned	Constructed	Dispensed	Extracted
Assimilated	Conserved	Displayed	Fabricated
Assisted	Consulted	Dissected	Facilitated
Assured	Contacted	Distributed	Fashioned
Attained	Contracted	Diverted	Filed
Attended	Contributed	Documented	Financed
Augmented	Controlled	Drafted	Fixed
Balanced	Converted	Dramatized	Followed up
Bought	Cooperated	Earned	Forged (ahead)
Brought	Coordinated	Edited	Forecasted

Formed	Led	Procured	Scheduled
Formulated	Lectured	Produced	Screened
Found	Lifted	Programmed	Secured
Founded	Located	Projected	Selected
Functioned as	Logged	Promoted	Separated
Gained	Maintained	Proposed	Served
Gathered	Managed	Protected	Serviced
Generated	Marketed	Proved	Set up
Governed	Mastered	Provided	Shaped
Graduated	Maximized	Publicized	Shifted
Guided	Mediated	Published	Shipped
Handled	Minimized	Purchased	Simplified
Headed	Monitored	Questioned	Sold
Hired	Motivated	Ramrodded	Solidified
Identified	Negotiated	Realized	Solved
Illustrated	Nominated	Received	Sorted
Imagined	Observed	Recognized	Spearheaded
Implemented	Obtained	Recommended	Spoke
Improved	Offered	Reconciled	Staffed
Improvised	Operated	Recorded	Stimulated
Increased	Optimized	Recruited	Streamlined
Influenced	Orchestrated	Rectified	Structured
Informed	Ordered	Reevaluated	Substituted
Initiated	Organized	Referred	Succeeded
Inspected	Originated	Refined	Summarized
Inspired	Overcame	Regulated	Supervised
Installed	Oversaw	Rehabilitated	Supplied
Instigated	Participated	Related	Synthesized
Instilled	Perceived	Rendered	Systematized
Instituted	Perfected	Repaired	Taught
Instructed	Performed	Reported	Tested
Insured	Persuaded	Represented	Trained
Integrated	Piloted	Reorganized	Transferred
Interfaced	Pioneered	Researched	Transformed
Interpreted	Placed	Resolved	Translated
Interviewed	Planned	Responded	Treated
Introduced	Played	Restored	Unified
Invented	Predicted	Retrieved	Updated
Investigated	Prepared	Revamped	Upgraded
Judged	Prescribed	Reviewed	Utilized
Justified	Presented	Revised	Validated
Kept	Prevented	Revitalized	Verified
Kindled	Printed	Revived	Won
Launched	Processed	Saved	Wrote

DESCRIBING RESULTS WITH KEY ACTION VERBS

The typical resume merely lists duties and does little else to sell the person. One of the best ways to sell yourself is to describe accomplishments in terms of *results*. While duties are often represented by phrases such "Responsible for...," results are frequently conveyed by using the verb *developed*. For example, one might say, "Developed a secretary's manual which explained hundreds of procedures and significantly reduced clerical errors." This person's duties were typing, filing, and answering phones, so to show that she stood above the rest, she demonstrated results.

When describing projects and results, one of the best words to use is *develop*. More than any other word, it seems to be so useful and it clearly expresses what a person wants to convey. While *develop* is an excellent word, when used three or four times in a resume it becomes overworked and loses impact. You'll need substitutes. The most common are

Created	Instituted
Designed	Introduced
Established	Set up
Implemented	

Other verbs that may be appropriate substitutes for develop in certain circumstances would be

Built	Fabricated	Originated
Composed	Fashioned	Perfected
Constructed	Formed	Pioneered
Coordinated	Formulated	Planned
Cultivated	Generated	Prepared
Devised	Installed	Produced
Elaborated	Introduced	Refined
Enhanced	Organized	Revamped

Here are examples that demonstrate how to describe results in various situations. In parentheses are words that could have been used instead of *develop*.

Developed (devised, prepared, produced) a creative financing/purchasing package to obtain 1900 acres of prime California farmland.

Developed (created, designed, introduced) a new concept in women's athletics and actively promoted the program. Participation by women grew from 18% in previous years to 79%.

Pioneered a mime program for gifted children age 8-12.

Developed (built, created, established, implemented, instituted) an intern program to allow students to work in nursing homes and schools for the retarded.

Developed (designed, established) training programs for new and experienced employees and supervised the new employee orientation program.

Set up apprenticeship programs for five skilled trades at the Physical Plant Department.

Developed and implemented an information and referral service for consumer complaints and human rights issues.

Developed and implemented mail and telephone solicitation programs and word processor systems.

Coordinated the company marketing effort, including advertising and promotions.

Designed and installed cash and inventory control systems for various clients.

Developed (created, designed) a unique computerized system which has dramatically increased service to customers.

For this small, 29-year-old manufacturer of toys, implemented changes in sales, marketing, and production which enabled the company to double sales and profits in a six-year period.

Developed and supervised a medical records internship program.

Created an employee orientation program which increased employee effectiveness and helped decrease turnover.

Built a team of highly motivated employees.

Established a sales award program which substantially reduced turnover of franchise sales staff.

Designed and introduced new operating procedures which reduced labor costs from 24% of gross revenues to 14%.

Instituted a preventive maintenance program which increased combat readiness of a unit by 10%.

VERB TENSES

Describe your current job in the present tense. For all previous jobs, write in the past tense. You may need to describe an event in your current job, such as a project that has already been completed. In that case, use the past tense to describe the project while using the present tense in the remaining portions of your current job.

Example:

STORE MANAGER - 6/90-Present. Oversee total operation of the store, supervise and schedule employees, and complete monthly profit and loss statements. Designed a new inventory system which has saved over $10,000.

Since the inventory system was designed over a year ago, it must be described in the past tense.

USING ADJECTIVES AND ADVERBS

Adjectives and adverbs are words that describe actions and things. Used appropriately, they can enliven a resume and describe more accurately what you did. While using adjectives and adverbs can add sparkle to a resume, if overused, they can actually weaken a phrase. Notice how they change the tone of the sentences below. In each example the second sentence has more impact.

1. Worked with industrial engineers.

   Worked closely and effectively with industrial engineers.

2. During seven years as staff pharmacist, learned the operation of the pharmacy department.

   During seven years as staff pharmacist, became thoroughly familiar with the operation of the pharmacy department.

3. Initiate and develop working relations with local, state, and federal agencies.

   Initiate and develop outstanding working relations with local, state, and federal agencies.

4. Establish rapport with customers.

   Quickly establish rapport with customers.

Here are more examples of how to use adjectives and adverbs effectively:

Dealt tactfully and effectively with difficult customers.

Presented technical material in objective and easily understood terms.

Actively involve parents in Individual Education Plans.

Consistently maintained high profit margins on all projects.

Significantly improved communications between nursing administration and staff.

Completed virtually all apartment units ahead of schedule.

Continually streamlined policies and procedures to create a more reasonable work schedule.

A list of adverbs and adjectives is given below. Review the list and check the ones you think may be useful to you. Try to include them but don't force it. Don't use a word or phrase unless it really fits your personality and strengthens your resume. After writing each draft, go back through the list to see if still another word or two might be useful.

accurate/accurately
active/actively
adept/adeptly
adroit/adroitly
advantageously
aggressive/aggressively
all-inclusive/all-inclusively
ambitious/ambitiously
appreciable/appreciably
astute/astutely
attractive/attractively
authoritative/authoritatively
avid/avidly
aware
beneficial/beneficially
broad/broadly
capable/capably
challenging
cohesive/cohesively
competent/competently
complete/completely
comprehensive/comprehensively
conclusive/conclusively
consistent/consistently
constructive/constructively
contagious
continuous/continually
contributed toward
decidedly

decisive/decisively
deep (insight)
deft/deftly
demonstrably
dependable/dependably
dextrous/dextrously
diligent/diligently
diplomatic/diplomatically
distinctive/distinctively
diverse/diversified
driving
easily
effective/effectively
effectually
efficient/efficiently
effortless/effortlessly
enthusiastically
entire/entirely
especially
exceptional/exceptionally
exciting/excitingly
exhaustive/exhaustively
experienced
expert/expertly
extensive/extensively
extremely
familiar with
familiarity with
firm/firmly

foresight
functional/functionally
handy/handily
high/highly
highest
high-level
honest/honestly
imaginative/imaginatively
immediate/immediately
impressive/impressively
incisive/incisively
in-depth
industrious/industriously
inherent/inherently
innovative/innovatively
instructive/instructively
instrumental/instrumentally
integral
intensive/intensively
intimate/intimately
leading
masterful/masterfully
meaningful/meaningfully
natural/naturally
new and improved
notable/notably
objective/objectively
open-minded
original/originally
outstanding/outstandingly
particularly
penetrating/penetratingly
perceptive/perceptively
pioneering
practical/practically
professional/professionally

proficient/proficiently
profitable/profitably
progressive/progressively
quick/quickly
rare/rarely
readily
record
relentless/relentlessly
reliability
reliable/reliably
remarkable/remarkably
responsible/responsibly
rigorous/rigorously
routine/routinely
secure/securely
sensitive/sensitively
significant/significantly
skillful/skillfully
solid/solidly
sophisticated/sophisticatedly
strategic/strategically
strong/strongly
substantial/substantially
successful/successfully
tactful/tactfully
thorough/thoroughly
uncommon/uncommonly
unique/uniquely
unusual/unusually
urgent/urgently
varied
vigorous/vigorously
virtual/virtually
vital/vitally
wide/widely

RESUME TIPS

In this section, many important points are covered to help you make the most out of your resume.

Making It Readable

Since resumes are often scanned the first time through, it must be easy for the reader to pick up key pieces of information quickly. Long paragraphs of over ten lines or narrow margins with heavy blocks of text, can make reading the resume seem daunting, with the result that it will often be cast aside.

Honesty

Throughout your resume you should be honest and accurate—but positive. Whatever is stated should be true, but you do not need to tell everything. Both in resumes and in interviews you have a right to withhold certain information.

Multiple Resumes

In order to sell you, a resume must demonstrate focus. If you are considering more than one type of job, you may need two or more resumes. In this case you may want to write only one resume, but give it more flexibility by using more than one objective, leaving everything else the same. This is easy to do with a word processor or a memory typewriter.

An example will help. Jim is a very good computer salesperson with no desire to change fields, but we created three different objectives for him to use in three different versions of his resume: "OBJECTIVE: Computer Sales;" "OBJECTIVE: Electronics Sales;" and "OBJECTIVE: Sales." Nothing else in the resume was changed. Computer companies got one resume, electronics companies got another, and if Jim saw something interesting outside those two industries, he sent the one that said "Sales."

Changing the objective, however, may not be adequate if the types of jobs you are seeking are considerably different from each other. Writing a new qualifications section for each objective will often do the trick. Far less frequently, you may need to make small changes in the employment section. Typically that consists of adding an area of experience which was a very small part of your job, but one which will help sell you with that particular objective. You would also look for ways to get the right buzz words in.

Using Cover Letters For Flexibility

A cover letter should accompany each resume you mail out and should be individually typed. The cover letter provides an excellent opportunity to mention points you know are important to that particular employer, but are not mentioned in the resume.

Answering Want Ads

When a want ad provides specific job requirements, there are a number of ways to respond. You can 1) send your resume with a standardized cover letter; 2) send your resume with a custom-written cover letter discussing key points mentioned in the ad; or 3) customize your resume to hit all the important points in the ad and write a creative cover letter. Obviously the third approach is likely to provide the best results, and it really doesn't take much more time.

As you customize your resume, you may find that the job descriptions require few if any changes, while the qualifications section might require substantial changes. The entire process of rewriting might take one to two hours. If you are really interested in the position and know you could handle it, consider the time as an investment. Taking time to redo the resume will not guarantee you an interview, but it can *double* your chances. If you lack certain desired skills or experience that were mentioned in the ad, simply ignore those points and really sell what you do have.

What To Call It

It's not necessary to type *Resume, Qualifications Brief, Profile,* or any other such title at the top of your resume. Everyone will know it's a resume just by glancing at it.

Color And Type Of Paper

While paper is available in a variety of colors, textures, weights, and sizes, there are some standard guidelines you should follow. The color of paper you choose can definitely make a difference in the number of interviews you get. White is always a safe color, but my studies reveal that buff or off-white paper provides even better results. The best paper I have found so far is the 20- or 24-pound classic linen made by several paper manufacturers. Many people also like classic laid. Both types of paper have a texture that implies quality without overdoing it. If you prefer a paper without a textured surface, choose one with a "rag" or cotton fiber content of at least 25%. For those seeking management positions a light gray can be effective. Blues and greens have not tested well. Color should have a positive effect; this will nearly always mean you should use light shades. Dark grays and browns or bright colors are not effective. Twenty-pound paper is always a safe standard. A slightly heavier paper is fine, but avoid heavy stocks. Monarch size paper (7" x 10") is fine for thank you notes, but stick with 8½" x 11" for your resume. Good papers have a watermark, so make sure it is right side up if you copy it yourself. Photocopy shops usually check for this, but it's wise to double check this yourself.

Typing Your Resume

My studies show that clean, crisp typing is one of the most important factors in getting your resume read. Most people type their own resumes on portable typewriters and they look home-typed.

Resumes should never be typed on dot matrix printers. As yet, even top-of-the-line dot matrix printers can only approximate the quality of the type produced by letter-quality printers. Using a high quality dot matrix printer for cover letters is acceptable, but not for the resume. If you do print your cover letters on a dot matrix printer, print in the letter quality mode.

Many people have daisy wheel printers in their home. The daisy wheel printer produces true letter quality print and has been the standard for resumes for years. With it you can "bold" your name and the various resume categories such as objective, education, and employment.

A new standard is taking over, however, and that is the laser printer. A laser printer can simply do more things with a resume and make it look sharper. If you have a Macintosh or an IBM clone, you can take your disk to a copy shop or word processing organization which offers the service, and have your resume printed on a laser printer. If you don't have a computer, simply go to a word processing organization and have them type it for you. The $20–35 it will cost will be an excellent investment. Virtually all of them use laser printers.

I do not recommend having resumes typeset. Laser-printed resumes can give you virtually the same look at half the price. With a laser-printed resume it is also faster, easier, and cheaper to make multiple versions or customized versions.

One danger of using laser printers is that people are tempted to overuse such features as different fonts, bolding, underlining, and italics. This produces a resume which looks busy and is overdone. The example below is exaggerated to help you see what I mean; you'll notice your eyes going all over the place, unable to read or concentrate on the job description.

GENERAL MOTORS, Detroit, Michigan 10/87-Present

> **SENIOR ENGINEER** - As part of a team of **Software Quality Assurance Engineers,** evaluate <u>CAD/CAM</u> software and *make* recommendations for improvements before software is made available to users within the company. Review <u>functional specifications</u> to *ensure* all portions are testable and fully meet **user needs.** REDUCED time necessary to fully evaluate software from **45 days** to **18 days.**

As a rule of thumb regarding the use of such features—keep it simple.

Size of Type

There are two sizes of type which are typically used for resumes: 12 point, which is also known as 10 pitch or pica; and 10 point, which is also known as 12 pitch or elite. I recommend using 12 point, which is a little larger and more readable than 10 point. If you are using 12 point and your resume just barely goes over a page long, you may want to make minor adjustments to make it all fit on one page. Widening the length of the lines may be all you need, or you could go to a smaller type. With a laser printer, 11 point may do the trick.

Reproduction

Reproduction quality will have a lot to do with the visual impact of your resume. There are a number of advantages to having your resume reproduced at a professional photocopy shop. For one thing, the top-of-the-line copying equipment used in such shops will produce high-quality copies that are crisp, clear, and almost as good as the originals. The quality of photocopiers most have at home or in the office cannot compete with the equipment at a copy shop.

For another thing, copy shops have a variety of high-quality papers to choose from. You can produce your original resume on a plain white bond and have it copied on your choice of paper.

And finally, copy shops are fast—you can usually be in and out in about ten minutes. They are inexpensive as well. Photocopying will cost you five to eight cents per copy plus eight to eleven cents per sheet for special paper. Many people buy extra paper so their cover letter paper will match their resumes.

Mailing

Traditionally resumes are folded in thirds and sent in a standard number ten envelope. That is still perfectly acceptable, but consider spending a little more and sending the resume in a 9 x 12 envelope so the resume does not need to be folded. It is not a big thing, but if it is not folded it will look nicer in the stack. If it weighs less than one ounce you'll need to add ten cents for a surcharge that the Postal Service charges for oversized envelopes. If it weighs over one ounce, it will cost you the regular price for the first ounce plus the reduced price for the second ounce. In 1992 that cost was 52¢—29¢ + 23¢.

For a really hot job consider having it delivered by an overnight delivery service. For a super hot local job, consider having a messenger service deliver it. The extra effort is one way of saying you want the job.

Photographs

Photographs should rarely be submitted with resumes, although they may be appropriate for models, flight attendants, performers, and media personalities. Many organizations are leery of receiving photographs with resumes because it increases the likelihood of age and race discrimination charges. Employers are nearly unanimous in preferring not to receive photographs.

Confidentiality

Employers who receive your resume will rarely inform your current employer. Even if they know your boss, they understand the importance of confidentiality. I would say that only if your boss or company has a reputation for firing people for "disloyalty," should the steps listed below even be considered. If you are truly concerned about confidentiality, your options include:

1. Write "Confidential" at the top of your resume.

2. At the bottom of the resume type and underline, "Please do not contact employer at this time."

3. Replace the name of your present employer (and possibly your next-to-last employer) with a description such as, "A major manufacturer of automotive parts," "A Fortune 500 Corporation," or "A National Retail Chain."

4. Utilize an executive recruiter (headhunter). A recruiter will sell you to an employer over the phone without revealing your name and will send your resume only if the employer is particularly interested.

If your boss suspects you are looking, but you know you are considered a valuable employee, you have nothing to worry about. You are more likely to get a raise than to get into trouble. In one sense, everyone is looking for another job—some are just more active than others. When headhunters call regarding truly great jobs, I guarantee you, virtually everyone is willing to talk. The World War II saying was "Loose lips sink ships." That's good advice at work also—do not tell even your most trusted friends at work that you're actively looking.

Salary

Salary history and salary requirements should virtually always be omitted from a resume to avoid giving anyone a cause for eliminating you.

Want ads frequently ask for desired salary or salary history. I would recommend ignoring the requested information. In this country what a person earns is one of the most personal and confidential bits of information we possess. Not only are you giving away your bargaining position when you state your current salary or salary requirements, but you are giving private information to people you don't even know.

If you feel compelled to acknowledge the request, you might simply write, "Salary is negotiable."

Relocation

If you are seeking a position with a national company, you'd better be prepared to relocate. Since many people are unwilling to relocate, a statement under "Personal" or "Additional," stating "Willing to Relocate," will make you stand out in a positive way. If you don't have a personal section, merely type it in at the end of the resume.

Reason For Leaving

Everyone has a reason for leaving a job, but the resume is rarely the place for stating it. Invariably an attempt to explain the reason will simply raise more questions than it answers. Save the explanation for an interview where the issue can be handled much more effectively. The only time I ever mention the reason for leaving is if the company or department moved out of state or the company went out of business. Even then it's best to mention it subtly, so that it just seems to be a part of the resume.

Abbreviations

Avoid abbreviations that may cause confusion to readers who are not familiar with them. As a rule of thumb, if you are certain that *everyone*, from the personnel clerk who may screen the resume to the person with power to hire you, will recognize and understand it, then consider using it. Keep in mind, however, that words are more visually attractive when spelled out. For this reason I recommend spelling out the names of states, particularly in the address at the top of a resume. In the employment section I sometimes abbreviate the state, using the Postal Service's two letter abbreviation, if that is the only way the name of the company and city/state will fit on one line. The key is to be consistent throughout the resume. Some exceptions: "B.A.," "M.A.", and "Ph.D." are preferred over spelling them out.

Know The Tradition And Language of Your Field

Learn what is traditional and accepted for resumes in your industry or field. Although I have tried to give you the principles for writing a powerful resume, I can't talk about, nor do I know all the traditions in all fields. While I recommend limiting most resumes to two pages, the four or five page curriculum vitae (the term for resumes used by academics), is perfectly acceptable. There may also be certain formats which are most accepted and expected in particular fields. When you find that is the case, go along with that tradition unless you have a compelling reason not to.

Also, use the language of your field. If this is a new field to you, read the trade journals or books on your field to learn the nomenclature and buzz words. If you weave this language into all of your communications—resumes, cover letters, and interviews—the employer will be more likely think of you as a member of that profession.

Creative License

In some ways my advice about resumes follows tradition, in some ways it does not. A conservative, tried-and-true approach often works best. This, for example, is why I recommend off-white paper. At the same time I also encourage you to be creative. Can you think of something which might just give you an edge over your competition? When you come up with an unusual idea, ask yourself, "Will it work for me; can I pull it off with my personality?" An approach tried by someone with an artistic, flamboyant, personality might be readily accepted, while that same thing attempted by a more conservative, traditional person would not. If you are about to try something rather unusual or "far out," get the opinions of others first, or try it out in a few cases to see what kind of response it gets.

I mention the creative side because over the years clients have suggested trying things which I never would have thought of. Sometimes I caution against the idea, but more frequently I give my full encouragement. When clients use these creative ideas, they've usually worked.

Stragglers

A resume just does not look good with only 2–5 lines on the second page, so if your resume ends up with a few lines on the second page, you have several options. You can 1) Cut out some less important points to shorten the resume to one page; 2) Reduce your top and bottom margins (and possibly on the sides) to get it on one page; or 3) Increase the margin top and bottom and narrow your lines, so that page two has at least six lines. At the top of page two, I often type the person's name in the upper left hand corner, then drop down a line and type "Page Two." I virtually always do this when there are less than 10 lines on page two. Then drop down 3-5 lines before beginning the rest of the resume. This helps the resume look balanced and more visually appealing.

Selecting A Format

The format is essentially the layout of the resume. The sample resumes included in *The Hunt* use the layout that I prefer, after having tested many during the past 15 years. I like the format because it is easy to scan and it makes excellent use of space. Throughout the resume there is a balance of white space and text. There are literally dozens of formats with dozens of variations. If you have seen one that you like, and feel it would do a good job of presenting your background, by all means use it. If you do not have a preferred format, you cannot go wrong if you use the format used in the sample resumes. It is time tested and well accepted.

THE TYPES OF RESUMES

Essentially there are three types of resumes—Chronological, Functional and Qualifications/Chronological. Chronological and functional resumes have both advantages and disadvantages, while the qualifications/chronological resume offers the advantages of both the chronological and functional resumes, but none of the disadvantages.

Chronological resumes describe a person's work experience in reverse chronological order, with the most recent job appearing first. Traditionally they have emphasized dates, job titles, duties, and names of employers. The primary advantage of the chronological resume is that employers are used to reading it. They know how to scan it quickly and get what they need from it. Its major disadvantage is that it is difficult to show employers the "themes" which run through your experience.

The functional resume, on the other hand, excels at bringing out these themes or functional areas of experience. The job seeker identifies key areas of experience, or "functions," and labels those functional areas with titles such as Management, Design, and Computer Programming. The writer then describes the experience the person has had in those areas. The major drawbacks of the functional resume are that it is more difficult to read, and the employer typically does not know when or where the experience being described took place. For this reason it can sometimes be confusing.

The qualifications/chronological resume is essentially a chronological resume with a qualifications section included at the beginning. It combines the best attributes of both of the other types of resume, but has virtually none of their drawbacks. The qualifications section of a qualifications/chronological resume is usually shorter than the functional portion of a functional resume, but it covers the most crucial areas of experience and provides a quick introduction to the strengths of the individual. The job description section, the other main part of the resume, emphasizes results rather than just duties, making it extremely effective.

On the next two pages you'll see excellent examples of both the qualifications/chronological and the functional resume. Following the examples you will find a complete description of the functional resume, how to write it, how to determine whether you should use it, and samples to give you ideas.

Qualifications/Chronological

ROBERTA JENNINGS
1121 Peach Drive
Atlanta, Georgia 30601
(404) 574-8769

OBJECTIVE: Airline Management

QUALIFICATIONS

Excellent management and supervisory capabilities. Highly respected by subordinates and able to obtain high performance levels from employees. Created one of the best on-time performance records in the airline industry.

EDUCATION

B.A. - Business, University of Southern California (1979)

EMPLOYMENT

Air Florida 3/84-Present

CUSTOMER/RAMP SERVICE SUPERVISOR, Atlanta, Georgia 6/87-Present. Opened the Atlanta airport facility for Air Florida and created one of its most efficient and effective operations. Supervised and trained 30 Customer Service Agents and Ramp personnel. Responsible for all day-to-day operations decisions and handled all crises related to crashes, passenger deaths and illnesses, bomb threats, hijackings, and weather delays.

Established one of the top records in the industry by successfully loading planes and preparing them for departure in twenty minutes or less, 97% of the time. Effective planning and scheduling permitted up to four planes to be serviced simultaneously. Reduced lost time due to illness by 68% and industrial accidents by 71%.

CUSTOMER SERVICE AGENT, Atlanta, Georgia 3/84-6/87. Functioned as Ticket Sales Agent, Boarding Agent, and Customer Service Representative. Provided the type of service and concern for customers which made Air Florida one of the fastest growing airlines in the U. S. Became adept at solving problems and satisfying customers' complaints. Consistently maintained monthly sales in the top 10%.

Alaska Airlines, San Francisco, California 1/80-3/84

CUSTOMER SERVICE AGENT - Worked closely with customers to provide the best connecting flights and make each flight an enjoyable experience.

Typeface: Times Roman

Functional

SUZANNE HALL
18852 52nd S.E.
Bothell, Washington 98011
(206) 481-2756

OBJECTIVE: Personnel Management

QUALIFICATIONS

Personnel Management - Five years experience in Personnel, with three years as Personnel Manager of a store with 230 employees. Supervise and train a staff of four. Significantly increased morale among store personnel and successfully fought off a unionizing effort.

Recruiting, Interviewing, Hiring - Very effective interviewer. Screen and hire all sales, supervisory, clerical and support personnel. Over 80% of all people hired have remained with the store at least one year. Turnover has been reduced 22% by careful screening and by implementing other improvements throughout the store.

EEO - Perform periodic surveys and ensure all goals are met as required.

Wage and Salary Administration - Identified unfair wage differentials between recent hires and those with longer service. Removed pay scale discrepancies and nearly eliminated turnover among more experienced staff.

Promotions - Work closely with supervisors to determine those ready for promotions. Write all final recommendations for promotions.

Terminations - Arbitrate in all firing situations and participate in all firing interviews. Conduct exit interviews and identify causes for termination. By taking quick action, several terminations have been averted.

Manpower Planning - Predict staffing needs for Christmas and major sales and hire necessary personnel.

Career Counseling - Provide extensive career path counseling to store employees.

Training and Development - Developed and conduct a 16-hour training program emphasizing customer service and job training. Turnover and customer complaints have been reduced substantially after the program was increased from 8 to 16 hours. Supervise additional training during the probationary period.

EMPLOYMENT

Briggins Department Stores, Seattle, Washington (1975 to Present)

Personnel Manager (1987 to Present)
Assistant Personnel Manager (1984 to 1987)
Schedule Coordinator (1981 to 1984)
Credit Manager (1979 to 1981)
Credit Adjustment Processor (1976 to 1979)
Sales Associate (1975 to 1976)

EDUCATION

Attended Bellevue Community College (35 credits)

Typeface: Times Roman

THE FUNCTIONAL RESUME

The functional resume offers some people the best way to get their story across to employers. If your strengths can readily be put into categories, then you should seriously consider using a functional resume.

In its purest form, a functional resume includes only functions—job titles, dates, and names of employers are omitted. I rarely recommend a pure functional resume because it usually raises more questions than it answers. When dates and employers are omitted, hiring authorities tend to wonder if the applicant is hiding something, such as a long gap in employment. If you have strong reasons for not revealing details of your employment, however, consider a functional resume.

As you will notice in Suzanne's resume, employment was included but job descriptions were not. This is common in functional resumes and helps employers feel more comfortable with the functional format. The qualifications section in Suzanne's resume is devoted entirely to her duties as personnel manager and assistant personnel manager. Those were the only jobs which were relevant to the position she was seeking. In a chronological resume it would have been difficult to have devoted so much space (24 lines) to just two positions. For Suzanne the functional resume was a perfect choice.

Read the following sample functional resumes to get a feel for how they are constructed and what makes them effective. Although the backgrounds of the people will differ from yours, you should be able to determine whether your experience is better suited to the functional format or the qualifications/chronological format illustrated and discussed throughout the book.

A functional resume worked well for Paul Shupbach and enabled him to go into much more detail about his areas of experience. His job descriptions also add important information.

David Goldman's resume could be labeled a functional resume, but it is really a combination of a functional and chronological resume. It demonstrates that by remaining flexible and creative you can produce something which works best for you and your particular situation. Jason Ryerson's resume enabled an ex-military officer to sell his experience in basically nonmilitary terms.

PAUL SHUPBACH
2917 S. E. 112th
Pittsburgh, Pennsylvania 15203
(412) 579-0002

QUALIFICATIONS

Technical Expertise - Hands-on person. Capable of operating and troubleshooting virtually any piece of equipment. Understand the problems faced by machine operators and utilize engineering knowledge to effectively solve those problems.

Proposals, Contracts and Negotiations - Have written and developed dozens of proposals and negotiated over 40 major contracts. Heavily experienced in all types of contracts, including DCAS, ASPR and DAR. Consistently negotiate the most favorable terms for Cost Plus, Cost Sharing, Cost Plus Incentive Fixed, and R&D Contracts.

Cost Management, Cost Analysis, Cost Control - Over fifteen years of Cost Management experience with all types of products and components, including processing equipment, fiberglass, and sheet metal parts. Establish Program Financial Controls which pinpoint manufacturing problems and prevent cost overruns. Expert in Value Engineering.

Cost Estimating - Experience covers all facets of manufacturing including machined parts, sheet metal, plastics, fiberglass, and software. Highly experienced in all methods of estimating including Parametric Estimating.

Vendor Selection - Inspect and analyze vendor facilities, equipment, capabilities and quality. Recommendations to use a vendor have virtually always been adopted.

EDUCATION

B.A.   Industrial Management, University of Pennsylvania (1971)
B.S.   Industrial Engineering, University of Pittsburgh (1969)

EMPLOYMENT HISTORY

Davenport Engineering & Consulting, Pittsburgh, Pennsylvania 1986 to Present

INDUSTRIAL ENGINEERING CONSULTANT - Work on assignments ranging in length from 3 to 12 months in the areas of Bidding, Estimating, Selecting Vendors, Cost Management, and Manufacturing Planning. Enabled one manufacturer to obtain their first ever contract with U. S. Steel and to expand production from $40,000 to $140,000 per month with no increase in personnel. Researched and adapted a new technology which allowed the firm to underbid all competitors.

Pennsylvania Division of Purchasing, Scranton, Pennsylvania 1978 to 1986

SPECIFICATION ANALYST - Developed quality standards, specifications, and test procedures for many raw, semi-processed, and processed materials. The capabilities and sophistication of the Division were substantially increased through these efforts.

U. S. Steel, Pittsburgh, Pennsylvania 1971 to 1978

COST ANALYST - Estimated and analyzed costs of machined parts, hydraulic components, and mechanical systems supplied by vendors. Negotiated prices and engineering changes.

Typeface: Helvetica

DAVID GOLDMAN
2430 Stoneway North
Little Rock, Arkansas 72202
(501) 254-3242

OBJECTIVE: Project Management

QUALIFICATIONS

Supervising. Took over a district with high turnover and low morale and created one of the top teams in the company. Work closely with individuals to enable both company and personal needs to be satisfied.

Negotiating. Negotiate contracts that are fair, workable, and satisfactory to customer and manufacturer. Work hard to get the best for both.

Coordinating/Planning. Installations have always been completed on schedule. Maintain close contact with customers, manufacturing, and field engineering to deal with all problems as they arise. Able to get commitments and support from those not directly responsible to me.

Computers. Excellent training and broad work experience installing and maintaining computer systems.

EMPLOYMENT

Data Systems, 1969 to Present

SENIOR PROJECT MANAGER, Little Rock, Arkansas, 1986 to Present. Negotiate contracts, schedule deliveries, and troubleshoot all phases of computer installations. Work closely with customers to determine their needs, then gain contractual commitments from manufacturing and field engineering to install systems by specific dates. Monitor factory schedules and software support schedules to ensure delivery schedules are met. Despite many difficulties, all deliveries and installations have been completed on schedule.

DISTRICT MANAGER, FIELD ENGINEERING, Los Angeles, California, 1979 to 1986. Supervised and scheduled the work of 18 field engineers installing and maintaining computer systems. Took over a district with high turnover, low morale, and a poor reputation for customer service. Within one year turnover was reduced from 35% to 8% annually. Response time to down systems was reduced from six hours to two hours. Functioned as Project Manager for the installation of a branch on-line system for Security Western Bank (180 branches). All installations were completed on time.

FIELD ENGINEER, Washington, D. C., 1973 to 1979. Installed and maintained systems for banks, hotels and airlines. Customers were kept very satisfied because of extremely low downtimes.

U. S. Air Force, 1967 to 1972

COMPUTER TECH - Maintained and serviced on-board aircraft computer systems. Supervised a five-man team.

EDUCATION

Computers
Field Engineering, Data Systems Manufacturing School - 6 months, 1974
Computer Repair, Computer Learning Institute - 6 months, 1973
Electrical Engineering, Old Dominion University - 1 year, 1972-1973
Computer Tech School, U. S. Air Force - 9 months, 1967

Typeface: Times Roman

197

JASON RYERSON
14568 NE 9th Street
Redmond, Washington 98053
(206) 877-7594

OBJECTIVE: Facilities Management

QUALIFICATIONS

Over 20 years of exceptional management experience. Proven
ability to successfully complete projects cost effectively
and on schedule. Received numerous awards for completion of
high quality projects.

Implemented comprehensive programs that dramatically improved
productivity and efficiency of personnel.

PROFESSIONAL EXPERIENCE

ENGINEERING MANAGEMENT - Eight years of demanding and successful "hands on" engineering management and plant management responsibilities. Coordinated hundreds of repair jobs
conducted by both own work force and outside contractors. In
one instance increased overall plant reliability by 300%.
While providing repair support for 12 naval ships over a
three year period, reduced equipment downtime by 50%.

FACILITIES MANAGEMENT - As Chief Engineer and Material Manager, directly responsible for operation, maintenance, and
repair of steam and diesel electric power plants. Associated
equipment included heating, ventilation, and air conditioning
systems; firefighting and sprinkler systems; and various
emergency equipment. Charged also with infrastructure repair
and modifications. Supported numerous office and work station
relocations in minimal time and without loss of productivity.

CONTRACT ADMINISTRATION - Broad experience in working with
prime and subcontractors in overseeing scheduled and emergency repairs. Represented the U.S. Government in the management of an $18 million resupply contract for 76 remote sites
in the Pacific.

TROUBLESHOOTING - Volunteered to rebuild a faltering, yet
critical department of 95 personnel. Within 45 days identified all major problem areas and initiated a corrective action plan that included a comprehensive training program for
900 people. The revitalized training program improved morale
and decreased absenteeism over 60%. Received a special commendation for the project.

EMPLOYMENT

United States Navy 6/69-12/91. Completed Naval service with
rank of Commander.

EDUCATION

MA - Political Science, Naval Postgraduate School (1976)
BA - International Studies, University of Washington (1968)

Typeface: Courier

IS A FUNCTIONAL RESUME FOR YOU?

Functional resumes do have drawbacks. While reviewing functional resumes, employers often wonder where the experience occurred since dates, job titles, and employers are not specified for each particular area of experience. Their eyes tend to dart up and down the page looking for the answers. They often become frustrated because the information in the resume is difficult to read and interpret—the applicant is making them work too hard. They may also suspect that something is being hidden.

Keeping these considerations in mind, you may still want to use a functional resume under the following circumstances: if 1) You are changing careers; 2) You are changing industries and you have related experience but no direct experience; 3) You have major gaps in employment; 4) A functional resume seems to be a perfect vehicle to showcase your strengths; 5) The Qualifications/Chronological Employment format seems unsuitable for your background; 6) Your background can easily be listed in categories such as Management, Supervision, Coordinating, Troubleshooter, Motivator, or Training.

If you think a functional resume may be good for you, go ahead and write one. Test it out on friends or business associates to determine if it truly sells you and is easy to read. If you get positive feedback, you made the right decision.

Be sure to study the format of the qualifications/chronological resumes. I like the format because it has virtually all of the advantages of the functional resume *and* the chronological resume, with none of their individual drawbacks.

WRITING YOUR FUNCTIONAL RESUME

Once your job sketches have been completed, the first step in writing an effective functional resume is to list the points or experiences that you want to include. Write the points quickly, without being concerned for polished writing. Once you're through listing the points you'll begin to see that some just naturally fit together. At that point begin to select the category titles that you will use. Most functional resumes should contain three to six categories. For your highly specific or technical categories, you'll have to come up with those names on your own, but that should not be difficult. Some of the commonly used categories include: Management, Supervision, Training, Planning, Designing, Research, Coordination, Negotiating, Public Relations, Administration, Marketing, Public Speaking, Organization, Counseling, Writing and Editing, Design, and Teaching.

Next, put the categories on two pages so you'll have plenty of room to write in your points. Initially you wrote those points quickly; now rewrite them in a more polished form as you place them in their appropriate category. Once all the points have been placed in a category, determine the order the points should be in. Usually your strongest points would be listed first within each category. At that point you've done all you should for one day.

After one or two days, review what you've written. By having set the resume aside for some time, it will be fresh and you'll be better able to see ways to improve your writing. In your second draft look for ways to make each point clearer and more concise. Virtually all of the other instructions for writing a resume apply to the functional resume as well.

WRITING YOUR RESUME

GETTING STARTED ON YOUR RESUME

Having read through the material and having completed your job sketches, it's time to start writing your resume. I can't emphasize enough how valuable you will find your job sketches as you write your resume.

Once you have reviewed your job sketches, you're ready to start. Use a pencil and feel free to erase. If you compose well at a typewriter or computer, by all means use one, but double space so you can write and edit between the lines. I always begin by writing the name, address and phone number at the top. Next, I write the objective. After that I then write in "Qualifications" and skip enough space to complete it after I've written the rest of the resume. Since the qualifications section is often the most difficult section to write, I leave it until last.

At that point I have spent only about three minutes writing, but psychologically I am totally involved with the resume. Three minutes earlier I had been looking for an excuse to postpone the writing, but now I'm *into* it. Next I tackle employment, the section which nearly always requires the most time and thought. Be prepared to spend three or more hours on your first draft. It may be frustrating at times, but keep plugging away. The effort will all be worth it in the end. Once you've completed a first and second draft of your employment section, you'll be ready to work on the qualifications section.

DON'T HESITATE

You should write your first draft relatively quickly without worrying about perfection. Concentrate on getting your thoughts on paper; you can polish the phrasing later. Once you write a phrase, read it out loud to get a feel for how it sounds. When reading, most people subvocalize; while they may not move their lips, their mind is actually saying each word almost audibly. In other words, the way a phrase sounds to you when you say it out loud is the same way it sounds when read by an employer. By the time I finish writing a resume I have read every phrase aloud four to ten times. While I don't worry about perfection on the first draft, I will rewrite some phrases and add or delete words as I go along.

Frequently I will finish the first draft of a resume late in the afternoon. While I may not be satisfied with it, I do know that all the main thoughts and descriptions are there. I will simply set it aside until the next morning. When I pick it up the next day, my thoughts are fresh and I'm able to look at it objectively. Improvements often come spontaneously.

Read over the resume and ask yourself if all the important points have been made. You might think of a point that could be covered in the employment section or an important idea you want to get across in qualifications. Make those changes on the original draft. Go through the draft sentence by sentence and phrase by phrase, rereading them out loud. Cross out extraneous phrases. Ask yourself if you can make the same point with fewer words. Use action words whenever possible. Once you've finished this process, retype or rewrite the resume, incorporating the changes you've made. You have completed your second draft. Set it aside for at least half a day.

Spit And Polish

When you pick up the resume again, take care as you go through it; this may be your last draft. As you read your resume out loud, it should flow. Are there any phrases or words you have used more than twice? If so, look for alternatives. Are all of your sentences very long or all very short? A mixture of short, medium, and long sentences reads best. Too many short sentences makes the resume seem choppy and abrupt. Lots of long sentences cause a reader to forget the main point. Long sentences can often be made into two sentences. This adds clarity and punch.

Look for any troublesome phrases that sound awkward, unclear, or confusing. Your desire is to have employers read your resume completely and thoroughly. You don't want them to stop at any point and wonder what you mean. Just one awkwardly written, hard-to-understand sentence can reduce your perceived value by 10%. Don't let that happen.

Of course *you* know exactly what you mean by everything you've written, so unclear sentences may be hard for you to spot. Have others read your resume and ask if any sentences tripped them up. Also ask for their overall impression of your resume.

Avoid big, unfamiliar words. The mark of a good writer is the ability to say exactly what is meant by using everyday words. If you do choose a seldom-used word, make sure you have used it correctly. Trying to impress someone with your vocabulary and then using words incorrectly will work against you.

Spelling must be perfect. It is worth it to make one quick pass through your resume, dictionary in hand, looking up words you "know" are correct. You may be surprised to find that you have been misspelling a word for years. Do not depend solely on computerized spell checkers. If your misspelling is an actual word in the spell checker, it will go undetected. Ask someone to review it to make sure it is grammatically correct and that words are used correctly. Words such as *their* and *there*, or possessives such as *company's* or *companys'* can cause difficulty.

Type the final draft and review it one last time for phrasing, spelling, and punctuation. If you use a word processing service, presenting a typed draft will help reduce your cost and will ensure that everything is readable.

The Key

Now for my final advice on writing a resume. Once you have your job sketches completed, simply start *writing*. The biggest problem most people face is getting started. People seem to feel that when they write, the words must come out perfectly. This rarely happens, even for the most gifted writer. *Just start writing.* Don't stop even if you're not pleased. Write a paragraph, then if you're totally dissatisfied with it, throw it away. Your next attempt will be better. At least you will have started.

Even best-selling authors must write and rewrite. Still their publishers will find ways to polish and strengthen their manuscripts. By all means, try to find people who can edit your writing. You don't have to accept all their suggestions, but you are likely to find many ideas helpful. Remember, the resume is yours, so you must make the final decisions. Accept a suggestion only if it strengthens the resume. Do not do it just to please the person.

PUTTING IT ALL TOGETHER

Essentially, writing a resume consists of putting all of the pieces together. Most sections, such as education, training, special projects, and employment are independent of each other. So, if each section is well written, the entire resume will be effective when you pull them all together.

SAMPLE RESUMES TO HELP YOU

Use the following sample resumes to get ideas and to get a sense of how an entire resume fits together. Various fonts (typefaces) have been used so you can determine which you like best. The name of the font appears at the bottom of each resume. Times Roman and Helvetica are the typefaces people most commonly use for their resumes.

Because this book presents the basic principles of writing an effective resume, it does not provide examples of resumes for all job titles. The principles given here can be applied or adapted to fit any job title. Feel free to borrow a phrase here and there, but make your resume your own. Instill it with your own flavor and character. Make it personal. And sell yourself.

Because the people in some types of careers face unique issues, I have provided specific resume writing advice to recent college graduates, women returning to the work force, those over 50, people who use portfolios, military people, programmers, salespeople, and career changers.

NOTE BEFORE YOU READ THE SAMPLE RESUMES

Many of these resumes were originally two pages. They were reduced in length to enable you to concentrate on key areas.

JANICE TENSLEY
12733 169th Place N.E.
Issaquah, Washington 98056
(206) 885-8872

OBJECTIVE: Office Administration position utilizing word processing and computer skills

QUALIFICATIONS

Strong office administration background. Implement systems that significantly increase office productivity. Quickly learn word processing, data base, and spreadsheet software. Excellent supervisor. Flexible, creative, and work well under pressure.

EMPLOYMENT HISTORY

BTC Computers, Issaquah, Washington 5/87-Present

INVENTORY CONTROL MANAGER - For this manufacturer and distributor of computers, created and implemented a computerized inventory control system. Introduced the system throughout the company and within three company-owned retail stores. System has enabled BTC to continue its rapid expansion with excellent control of its growing inventory. Instructed all staff in the use of the system and act as troubleshooter when problems or questions occur. System provides excellent controls and saves over 20 hours per week in staff research time.

Introduced a computerized accounting system utilizing Great Plains and a Novell network. Oversee computer data maintenance of inventory, purchase orders, posting, and order entry modules. Also involved with the input and maintenance of the accounts payable and general ledger modules. Provide technical software support and problem solving within the organization.

L & M Investing, Seattle, Washington 4/83-5/87

OFFICE MANAGER - Supervised and trained five employees and coordinated all work flow in the office of this investment counselor and financial planner. Maintained all office information systems. Maintained files and computer data bases on several hundred clients, as well as documentation dealing with securities, mutual funds, limited partnerships, and insurance. Tracked all purchases by clients and calculated commissions. Handled accounts receivable and processed buy or sell orders by clients. Produced and edited a monthly newsletter and created all graphics. Developed data bases and spreadsheets which owner stated increased office productivity by 30%. Considered a key person in the growth of the firm.

COMPUTER KNOWLEDGE

Excellent knowledge of Wordperfect 4.2/5.1, dBase III+, Lotus 1,2,3, Great Plains, MS DOS 4.01, Q&A, Client Manager, Newsroom, PC Paint, Personal Publisher, Novell networking.

Typeface: Helvetica

PERRY CARLTON
13922 Navajo Court
New Bedford, Massachusetts 02740
(617) 823-7947

QUALIFICATIONS

Strong store management background. Rapidly promoted based on exceeding sales and profit goals. Increased sales an average of 24% per year.

EDUCATION

B.A. - English Literature, Massachusetts State University (1984)

Graduate Gemologist, Gemological Institute of America (1986)

EMPLOYMENT

Werner Jewelers, New Bedford, Massachusetts 8/84-Present

MANAGER - 8/88-Present. Maintain profitable store operations and supervise nine employees. Control all special ordering, oversee mark-up on special orders and shop repairs, and perform all accounting functions. Increased sales an average of 24% per year and have taken the store from #8 to #3 in sales for this chain of 12 stores.

ASSISTANT MANAGER - 7/86-8/88. Sold jewelry to customers and assumed responsibility of sales training and scheduling. Promoted to store manager for improving customer service in each of three stores served.

SALES - 8/84-7/86. Rose to the top 5 in sales among 150 salespeople. Became a Graduate Gemologist and was recognized as one of the most knowledgeable in gemstones within the chain.

Typeface: Bookman

JON ARNETT
19112 Edgecliff Drive
Cleveland, Ohio 44119
(216) 726-3982

OBJECTIVE: Manufacturing Management

QUALIFICATIONS

Strong background in all aspects of production supervision in the electronics industry including job scheduling, quality assurance, inventory control, purchasing, and customer relations. Consistently increase quality, productivity, and on-time deliveries.

EDUCATION

Business, Dennison Community College, 66 credits (1976-1979)

EMPLOYMENT

Advanced Circuits, Cleveland, Ohio 7/88-Present

PRODUCTION MANAGER - Supervise 16 shop personnel in the production of prototype circuit boards. Handle cost estimating, job scheduling, production control, and inventory control. Reduced turnaround time on orders from three weeks to one without adding staff or increasing overtime. Established a Total Quality program which reduced rejects 65%. Significantly reduced purchasing costs through a more effective inventory control program.

Digital Systems, Ashtabula, Ohio 5/85-7/88.

DRILLING AND FABRICATION SUPERVISOR - Supervised 12 production workers operating computer numerically controlled drilling and fabrication machines. Developed a new job scheduling system which reduced late deliveries by 30%. Researched inventory needs for raw materials and supplies and determined lead times. Data enabled company to reduce inventory on numerous items and also reduced work stoppages due to lack of parts, approximately 40%. Increased production of printed circuit boards 22% with no additional employees.

Hudson Manufacturing, Akron, Ohio 3/78-5/85

LEAD PRODUCTION SUPERVISOR - 6/82-5/85. Supervised 2 supervisors, 4 leads, and 35 production personnel. Implemented a job scheduling system which increased on time deliveries 44% with an average of 150 shipments monthly. Heavily involved in the design of a new facility and planning the actual move.

SHOP LEAD - 4/79-6/82. Assigned jobs to 18 production workers in drilling, screening, plating, fabricating, and camera work. Developed a maintenance program which reduced production losses due to breakdowns 70%.

SILKSCREENER - 3/78-4/79. Hand screened circuitry, bakeable and UV curable solder mask, and sheet metal front panels.

Typeface: Times Roman

(Person seeking further government employment)

LAURA DONOHUE

401 Eastman West   Arlington Heights, Illinois 60015 (312) 871-2652

QUALIFICATIONS

Excellent organizational ability. Successfully developed new systems which have increased productivity and quality of work.

Broad speaking experience. Frequently speak to groups of 100-500 people. Received a standing ovation at an annual convention for making a difficult subject easily understood.

Excellent public relations ability. Work effectively with organizations and individuals while solving problems and explaining policies. Quickly gain the respect of all parties.

EDUCATION

Graduated - Colville High School, Colville, Washington (1975)

EMPLOYMENT

United States Railroad Retirement Board, Chicago, Illinois 11/81-Present

CONTRACT REPRESENTATIVE - 11/87-Present. Explain and interpret complex laws and regulations related to retirement, disability, and unemployment benefits. Interview claimants and obtain necessary documents. Substantiate evidence and determine eligibility and amount of benefits. Provide training sessions for union and management groups to explain changes in regulations. Successfully introduced a group interview procedure for explaining unemployment compensation when claims rose from 250 to 2,100 per month. Developed numerous systems which decreased backlog and increased staff morale.

UNEMPLOYMENT CLAIMS EXAMINER - 11/81-11/87. Interviewed claimants and former employers to determine eligibility for benefits. Monitored job finding efforts of claimants and assisted in their obtaining new positions. Developed a new system for coding claims and won the Region Accuracy Award in 1986.

Social Security Administration, Chicago, Illinois 6/76-11/81

SERVICE REPRESENTATIVE - 4/79-11/81. Provided assistance and technical information about Social Security, Medicare, and Supplemental Security Income to beneficiaries and the general public. Resolved problems, untangled red tape, and helped make the system work. Received cash bonus award for suggesting improvements in Social Security forms.

SECRETARY - 6/76-4/79. Ran the office efficiently, answered correspondence, and compiled statistical reports.

Typeface: Helvetica

208

WILLIAM SAXTON
641 Arastradero
Palo Alto, California 94306
(415) 881-9595

OBJECTIVE: Purchasing Management

QUALIFICATIONS

Strong background in purchasing management. Consistently develop systems which cut costs and provide the timely delivery of products.

EDUCATION

B.A. - Geography, San Jose State University (1972)

EMPLOYMENT

Rapsody Clothing, Palo Alto, California 7/85-Present

DIRECTOR OF PURCHASING - For this $20 million clothing manufacturer, supervise a staff of four and have responsibility for the purchasing of all nontextile items. Developed an inventory control system which has eliminated duplication of supplies. Increased the level of buying with key suppliers and developed stronger relationships as well as larger discounts, resulting in a reduced cost of 15-35% on items purchased. Save $20,000 annually on continuous data processing forms and have increased copying efficiency 50%. Developed and implemented a departmental charge back system for supplies. System has increased accuracy and equity in calculating actual departmental costs.

Administer all aspects of national and local trade shows, including planning, purchasing new exhibits, contracting with trade people, obtaining sites and floor spaces, purchasing materials, and handling transportation. Trade show costs have been reduced $75,000 annually over the last three years.

Ryans Department Stores, Los Angeles, California 7/72-7/85

DIRECTOR OF PURCHASING - 9/81-7/85. Negotiated, awarded, and administered contracts with vendors for the procurement of over 500 items. Personally redesigned gift boxes and saved $150,000 annually in production and storage costs. Developed a unique automated packing material system which reduced labor and handling costs and saved $20,000 annually. Planned and managed an increased volume of purchasing from $1.1 million to $3.2 million as the chain increased from 6 to 14 stores in four years. Managed the paper stock warehouse and in-plant print shop.

Prior positions within Ryans: Assistant Director of Purchasing 3/78-9/81; Purchasing Agent 10/75-3/78; Purchasing Assistant 7/72-10/75.

Typeface: Times Roman

Paul Husted
406 Ash
Boise, Idaho 83702
(208) 361-2918

OBJECTIVE: Controller

QUALIFICATIONS

Strong background in accounting, finance, taxation, auditing, and cost control programs. Have established cost control programs which have cut overhead up to 30% without
decreasing production. Implemented computerized accounting
systems and supervised installations of hardware and software.

LICENSES

˙ CPA, Idaho State Certification (1972)

EDUCATION

B.A. - Accounting, University of Idaho (1970)

EMPLOYMENT

Brandon Refrigerated Service, Inc., Boise Idaho 4/88-Present

CONTROLLER - For this refrigerated freight hauler, prepared
financial statements and supervised 8 employees in payroll,
rates, billing, and AP/AR. Extensively involved in customer
relations, establishing credit ratings, approving credit,
reviewing and approving customer claims, and making collections. Manage the cash flow of the company. Developed a
major cost control program which has cut overhead 20% and
resulted in doubling a bank line of credit. Oversaw a major
conversion of accounting software.

Bestway Freight Lines, Boise, Idaho 3/83-4/88

CONTROLLER - Responsible for financial statements and tax
preparation. Supervised 10 employees handling rates, billing, payroll, claims, and AP/AR. Oversaw the payroll system
covering 6 separate union agreements. Developed the
company's first cost studies and identified areas for substantial savings. Cut the shop force from 21 to 11 with no
reduction in work completed. Worked closely with vendor and
contract programmer while installing a computerized accounting and payroll system. Implemented a computerized
system to track commodity transactions which reduced required staff time each month from 180 to 6 hours.

Robert Perkins, CPA, Boise, Idaho 7/70-3/83

STAFF ACCOUNTANT - Performed audits and developed financial
statements for a wide variety of clients. Handled state and
federal taxes for individuals, trusts, estates, partnerships, and corporations. Provided management services and
designed cost control programs.

Typeface: Courier

ADVICE FOR SPECIAL GROUPS

Some people have special issues to consider when writing a resume. To help address and solve some of these issues, this section provides specific advice and sample resumes to assist graduating college students, women returning to the workforce, those over fifty, people who use portfolios, military personnel, computer programmers, salespeople, and career changers.

GRADUATING COLLEGE STUDENTS

Don't be depressed because you don't have ten years' experience. During your job search you'll be competing with other college graduates who are in exactly the same situation—lots of low-paid summer and part-time jobs. Don't look down on those jobs though because they can reveal many of your positive attributes.

Make the most of any related experience you have. Bookkeeping, for example, is valuable experience for an accounting major. It's not the same as accounting, but it is excellent, practical experience and is recognized as such by employers. A forestry major would emphasize any work with a timber company, even if it was only menial summer work.

As a recent or soon-to-be graduate, you have four things to sell: your education, your personality and character, related work experience, and work experience in general. Since you may have little or no related work experience, most of your resume will be devoted to revealing your personality, character, and work ethic. Employers need to sense the type of employee you will be. College graduates typically remain with their first employers for less than two years, so it's fair for employers to seek those who will quickly contribute to the organization.

Make the most out of whatever work experience you have. Internships and jobs where you've had a high level of responsibility, are particularly valuable. In John Etter's sample resume on page 214, only one job was actually described because its value was so much greater than the other summer jobs. You, on the other hand, may want to describe each of your summer jobs. Do your best to identify a result in each one. It doesn't have to be big, after all, it was a part-time or temporary job.

Look for ways to reveal your personal qualities. Citing offices held in high school and college reveals leadership and responsibility. Lettering in sports indicates learning the value of teamwork and cooperation. Excellent grades indicate discipline and intellectual capacity. Participation in debate and theater can reveal speaking ability, quick thinking, and willingness to take risks. Participating in school committees and organizations reveals responsibility, willingness to put out a little extra, and loyalty.

The qualifications section of a resume is an excellent place to describe and call attention to some of the qualities you want an employer to know about, as the example below demonstrates.

OBJECTIVE: Mathematics/Statistics

QUALIFICATIONS

Excellent training in math and statistics.

Maintain excellent relations with supervisors. Always a valued employee. Loyal, cooperative, and easy to work with.

Work well under pressure, learn quickly, hard working.

You may have noticed that none of these statements was backed up with facts. The student who wrote this statement picked qualities which she knows to be true about herself; she is more than ready to give details or examples during an interview. Carefully select the qualities you mention. Be sure they are accurate—don't pick them just because they sound good. You may get an interview as a result, but you'll never get the job unless the "you" in person matches the "you" on paper.

Most graduates should expect to write a one-page resume. Students who earn more than 50% of their total college and living expenses or who are willing to relocate, should consider stating it in the resume. These items may be stated in the following way:

PERSONAL

Earned 60% of college expenses
Willing to relocate

Offices held while in college should nearly always be mentioned. If you're proud of some of your results, describe those results rather than merely listing the offices you held.

Be careful, however, about mentioning fraternity and sorority offices. Before you make a decision to include this information, remember that while most people hold neutral feelings about such organizations, many hold strong feelings against them. Therefore, mentioning them may not be worth the risk. You may, however, want to describe successes you had as a committee chairperson in charge of a special project such as a fund-raising program. In that case you would mention the program and its result, without mentioning the organization you were a part of.

Class projects are often worth mentioning in a special projects or education section. Perhaps you were in a group of business students who developed a marketing plan for a small company or in a group of industrial engineering students who solved an actual manufacturing problem. Below is a special projects section by a student who was very active on campus:

Planned and organized the University of Puget Sound 1988 Spring Parents Weekend and set a new record for attendance. Arranged programs and activities, obtained speakers, made hotel arrangements, ordered food, and headed up a four-person committee. Increased attendance 20% over the previous year. Evaluations by parents indicated it was the best organized program since its inception in 1977.

Published the first Parents Association Newsletter which was sent to 3,500 parents of UPS students. The first two editions were well-received and the newsletter has become an official school publication, published three times each year.

The following sample resume includes coursework to show how this might be handled. Seeing your coursework will be appreciated by some employers because it gives them a better sense of your training. Those employers who are not interested in your coursework will simply skip over it

In the sample resume, John was history major, but he was looking for a position in a training and development department. He wanted to demonstrate that he had an understanding and appreciation of business even though he had taken few business related courses.

Review pages 127 to 131 for examples of education sections and an explanation of when to use your GPA.

JOHN ETTER

Current Address
426 Harris Hall
Burlington, Vermont 05401
(802) 795-2631

Permanent Address
1227 Pineway N.W.
Ascutney, Vermont 05030
(802) 683-2796

OBJECTIVE: Entry-Level Training and Development Position

QUALIFICATIONS

Excellent program development skills. Developed new intramural programs and increased participation by women 220%.

Strong research and writing ability. Published an article in the *Vermont Historical Society Quarterly.*

Speak well before the public. Won numerous debate tournaments and placed fifth in the 1992 national tournament.

Cooperate well with supervisors; reliable and responsible; work hard and complete projects on schedule.

EDUCATION

B.A. - History, University of Vermont, will graduate June 1992 (3.6 GPA)

Business Courses: History of 20th Century Business, Macroeconomics, Microeconomics

PUBLICATIONS

"Effects of the Abolition Movement in Burlington, Vermont 1826 to 1866" *Vermont Historical Society Quarterly*, January 1992 edition.

AWARDS

"Outstanding History Senior" selected by the History Faculty (1992)
Fifth place, national debate tournament, extemporaneous speaking (1991)

EMPLOYMENT

University of Vermont, Burlington, Vermont 9/90 to Present

DIRECTOR OF INTRAMURAL SPORTS - Planned, staffed, and organized the intramural sports program. Working with a tight budget, assessed equipment needs, received bids from sporting goods suppliers, and purchased sports equipment. Supervised two assistants and recruited and supervised dozens of volunteers. Developed a new concept in women's athletics and actively promoted the program. Participation by women grew from 20% in previous years to 76%. Maintained the high participation rate in the men's program and organized a successful basketball refereeing clinic.

Summer Employment:

RECORDS CLERK, Stephenson Steel, Ascutney, Vermont 6/91 to 9/91
MAIL SORTER, U.S. Postal Service, Ascutney, Vermont 6/90 to 9/90
LABORER, Isaacson Contracting, Ascutney, Vermont 6/89 to 9/89
FARM WORKER, John Tyler, Ascutney, Vermont 6/88 to 9/88

Typeface: Times Roman

WOMEN RETURNING TO THE WORK FORCE

The biggest problems women face when returning to the work force are a lack of self-esteem and a belief that what they have done for the last several years is not valued in the workplace. To overcome these twin problems you must first recognize that you possess many transferable skills that would be valued in many types of positions. To begin that realization process, spend three or more hours with the accomplishments exercise described on page 380. That exercise will help you identify many skills that you've been using for years and which are valued by employers. Then rate yourself on the transferable skills list found on page 393. This will give you a good start. There should be no doubt in your mind that you have valuable skills.

If, after completing the accomplishments exercise, your confidence is still not where it should be, begin looking for a career planning and job finding program at a community college, or consider obtaining help from a career counselor. Also look for a support group made up of women who are returning to work or look for a broader-based support group that the local YWCA or some similar organization may have. If you are divorced or widowed, or must become the primary wage earner, you will probably qualify for a "displaced homemakers" program. Such programs are often available at low cost through community colleges and can really help women get through an emotionally trying period. They typically provide career exploration assistance, job finding guidance, and emotional support.

Even though you have not worked for several years, make the most out of whatever paid work experience you do have. Scour each job to find whatever results and contributions you may have had, even if it was 20 years ago. Establishing the fact that you have been a good employee in the past, even 20 years ago, will effectively convince employers that you have a strong work ethic.

Those who have been out of the work force for many years must often emphasize their volunteer experience. In actuality, volunteer activities are merely jobs you didn't get paid to do. They can be as mundane as licking stamps or as interesting and challenging as organizing a blood donor drive, or handling public relations for a small nonprofit organization. If you consistently spent ten or more hours weekly on a volunteer position, treat it as a job with a job title and a job description, with results included. In the resume there is no need to state the number of hours spent weekly. If an employer is curious you can explain in the interview. If most of your volunteer activities were of short duration, you could treat them as projects (see Special Projects page 166). Concentrate on results, but also describe duties.

Make the most out of each activity. If you held an office, say so. If you obtained excellent results, describe them. *Don't be modest.*

How good a position you get depends on the quality of your resume and how well focused you are. There is probably no need to return to school for a degree, but you may need to study your preferred field on your own or take a few classes at your local community college. Study enough to know the terms, history, and trends in your field.

I've included Sharron's resume because it is so strong in the volunteer area. Don't be intimidated by it. You may not have been as active or may not have had such quantifiable results, but it shows what can be done.

SHARRON COSGRAVE
526 South State Street
Wilmington, Delaware 19803
(302) 543-9161

(objective unstated, but basically looking to become an administrative assistant to a director of a nonprofit agency)

QUALIFICATIONS

Strong experience in developing effective new programs, motivating and coordinating large numbers of volunteers, and making office systems more efficient.

Excellent fund-raiser. Have written three successful grant proposals, one of which was funded for $20,000. Through PTA fund-raising activities increased revenue 18% above the previous record.

EDUCATION

University of Delaware, Liberal Arts, 96 credits, 1966 to 1969

PROJECTS/ACTIVITIES

PTA President, Robert Frost Elementary, 1990/91. Increased attendance at monthly meetings from 51 to an average of 107. Worked with principal and teachers to develop six new volunteer programs for parents. Participation in programs increased from 26% of parents to 58%. Because of active parent involvement, vandalism at the school decreased to almost zero.

Fund-raising Chairperson, Robert Frost PTA, 1989/90. Coordinated the efforts of over 200 children and 95 adults in six fund-raising activities. Exceeded the previous record by 18%.

Board Member, Wilmington Crisis Clinic, 1985 to Present. Analyze and approve annual budgets, interview and select new directors, and study proposed program changes. President of the board 1988 and 1989. Wrote grant proposal which obtained $20,000 in federal funds.

President, Wilmington Chapter, MADD (Mothers Against Drunk Drivers), 1984 to 1987. Organized the local chapter and tripled dues-paying membership each year. Testified as an expert witness before the Delaware Legislature. Coordinated statewide lobbying efforts and helped pass legislation which significantly strengthened laws against drunk driving.

EMPLOYMENT

McClinton, Brandeis & Nelson, Wilmington, Delaware 7/69 to 9/71

OFFICE MANAGER - Handled bookkeeping, payroll, bank statements, accounts payable, and accounts receivable. Purchased office equipment and supplies. Greeted clients, answered phones, scheduled court reporters for depositions, and developed an improved appointment and court scheduling system for 8 attorneys.

Typeface: Helvetica

The next resume is perhaps more typical of a woman returning to work. She's had two part-time jobs since she got married. In 1992 she decided to return to work on a full-time basis. From her experience at Debbie's Designs (three years, part-time) she knows she would like to own her own shop someday. Her plan is to get a full-time retail sales job at a small but classy store and eventually become the manager or assistant manager. While working there she intends to learn the business inside and out so she'll be ready when she opens her own shop.

JANICE STEVENS
4060 W. Warwick
Chicago, Illinois 60626
(312) 476-2917

OBJECTIVE: Retail sales

QUALIFICATIONS

Excellent retail experience. Work very effectively with customers - able to identify needs, tactfully answer questions, sell products and services, and solve problems.

EDUCATION

Northeastern Illinois University, Psychology, 20 credits 1979 to 1982
Bates Community College, Liberal Arts, 42 credits 1966 to 1968

WORKSHOPS

Window Dressing, Retail Merchants Association, 12 class hours (1990)
Retail Bookkeeping, Retail Merchants Association, 24 class hours (1989)
Buying for the 80's, Retail Merchants Association, 14 class hours (1988)
Retail Selling/Know Your Customer, Retail Merchants Association,
    20 class hours (1988)

EMPLOYMENT

Debbie's Designs, Chicago, Illinois 2/88 to 4/91

RETAIL SALES - Consulted with customers in the selection and coordination of furniture, fabrics, carpeting, wallpaper, draperies, and gift items. Functioned as store manager for an extended period when the store owner was on vacation. Purchased and priced all items and developed attractive displays.

Illinois Arts & Crafts Association, Chicago, Illinois 9/74 to 8/79

GALLERY ASSISTANT - Assisted customers in the purchase of art objects, explained the processes used by each artist, and trained and supervised other volunteers. Handled numerous details for the annual arts and crafts fair, including registering artists, judging art work, and overseeing sales and bookkeeping.

Typeface: Times Roman

THOSE OVER 50

The greatest concern of people over fifty years of age is usually age discrimination. While federal law prohibits discrimination on the basis of age, we know that it persists in both overt and subtle ways. With this in mind, you must decide whether you will reveal your age, since employers by law cannot ask your age or birthdate. Your resume should contain only information you choose to reveal to an employer.

Make the most of your experience and maturity. Some people unnecessarily worry that youth always has the edge. In your resume and during interviews, reveal yourself to be an energetic and youthful person, but one who has the maturity and sound judgment that comes only with age and experience. If you have planned your career carefully, you will probably be at a level where only those with similar age, experience, and results will even be considered as qualified. If that is not your case, then simply recognize that your age is another barrier that must and can be overcome.

Trenton is a 59 year old insurance executive. In his resume education was not included because he does not have a degree. Showing his one year of college was deemed unnecessary because he has so much experience. Two early jobs were left off which accounted for five years. Using a prior employment section was an effective way to concentrate on his higher level jobs.

TRENTON McGRATH
2215 Broadway North
Houston, Texas 77012
(713) 785-2761

OBJECTIVE: Sales/Marketing Management

QUALIFICATIONS

Complete knowledge of Mortgage Lending/Mortgage Finance/Secondary Markets.

Recognized as an outstanding trainer and motivator of sales staffs. Substantially increased market share in each position held.

Broad marketing experience. Developed and marketed new products and services which have consistently been accepted in the financial community.

EMPLOYMENT

Diversified Mortgage Insurance Company, Minneapolis, Minnesota 1/78 to Present

REGIONAL VICE PRESIDENT 1/87 to Present, Houston. Moved into a troubled 16-state zone and have increased market share 61% from 3.2% to 5.2%. Have aggressively marketed new services and became active with the

Bond Business, Pension Funds, Swaps, and assisting lenders with Portfolio Sales. Travel extensively and work closely with 4 district sales managers and 20 salespeople.

SENIOR VICE PRESIDENT, SALES AND MARKETING 12/83 to 1/87, Minneapolis. Developed and implemented a reorganization of the national sales force, moving from 12 divisions to 4 zones. Reorganization has been credited with strengthening DMI's national market share. Took part in the development of the Mortgage Finance Unit which has successfully moved DMI into new markets. Developed strategies for participation in Mortgage Revenue Bonds, Pass Through Certificates, Pension Funds Issues, Builder Buy-downs and Pay-through Bonds.

VICE PRESIDENT, NORTHWEST DIVISION MANAGER 9/81 to 12/83, Portland. Covering 9 western states, trained and supervised a staff of 9 account executives, 3 underwriters and 2 secondary market managers. Increased market share in the territory by 88%. Traveled extensively throughout the territory and made calls on CEOs.

PRODUCT MANAGER 1/78 to 9/81, Minneapolis. Developed and implemented marketing plans for specialized insurance products for mortgage lending financial institutions: Error/Omission Coverage, Special Hazard Coverage, and Officers/Employees Liability Coverage. Responsible for national marketing of the products. Sales volume for these products increased sevenfold in six months.

American Insurance Company, Atlanta, Georgia 6/74 to 1/78

DIRECTOR OF FIELD OPERATIONS 6/76 to 1/78, Atlanta. Had total responsibility for sales production of 6 regional and 21 state managers. Introduced new mortgage life and disability insurance programs and created a highly effective sales training program.

REGIONAL MANAGER 6/74 to 6/76, St. Louis. Supervised operations of 4 state managers and personally generated new business in metropolitan St. Louis.

Niagara Home Life Assurance Company, Palo Alto, California 8/68 to 6/74

ASSISTANT VICE PRESIDENT - Negotiated exclusive contracts with S&Ls for the sale of Niagara Home Life's Mortgage Life Plan and Disability Plan. Designed and implemented a specialized Insured Savings Plan for Savings and Loan depositors which had an excellent effect on insurance sales. Recruited and trained sales agents.

Prior Employment

SALES AGENT/TRAINER, Home Owners Security, Inc. 2/64 to 8/68
SALES AGENT, Home Security Associates 2/62 to 2/64

Typeface: Times Roman

PEOPLE WITH PORTFOLIOS

Architects, drafters, artists, designers, photographers, models, and writers, use portfolios to help sell themselves. They often make the mistake of placing too little emphasis on a top-quality resume, assuming the portfolio alone will sell them.

As important as your portfolio is, don't shortchange yourself. There are lots of talented people out there with outstanding portfolios. Taking the time to develop an effective resume will make an important difference to your job hunting success. Your resume can reveal qualities and background that won't come across in your portfolio. A portfolio can express your technical or creative ability, but a resume reveals where you've been and how you developed your ability. In fact, without an effective resume you won't often get the opportunity to show that fantastic portfolio you so painstakingly assembled.

Artistic people are stereotyped as temperamental. In your resume do everything possible to demonstrate that you are flexible and easy to work with.

Consider reproducing two or three samples of your work on 8½" x 11" paper. Then, either enclose it with your resume, or give it to employers when you meet them face to face. When reviewing the samples a week or two after meeting you, the employer will be helped to remember both you and your portfolio better. Writers should attach clippings or short pieces for a similar effect.

Graphic artists and designers should feel free to come up with creative formats for their resumes. This is one of the few groups of people who will benefit from having a resume typeset since it is an opportunity to show their graphics ability.

The most important thing to note in Bobbie's resume, is simply that employers will know much more about her than if they only saw a portfolio. Quantifying results is harder for artistic people than for many others, but do your best. In Bobbie's resume, there are no quantifiable results. Still, you get a sense that she is dedicated and very capable. If employers liked her portfolio, the resume will simply help them remember her more easily.

BOBBIE BLANE
1127 Mariposa Drive
Santa Barbara, California 93110
(805) 651-2720

OBJECTIVE: Graphics/Illustration Artist

QUALIFICATIONS

Develop excellent relations with clients and have satisfied even the most demanding. Specialty is personality portraiture used in advertising.

Excellent graphics and illustration training and experience. Skilled in design, layout, paste-up, lettering, story boards, and the use of darkrooms and stat cameras. Knowledgeable of printing procedures and experienced in preparing work for printing. Have operated printing presses and other printing-related equipment. Prepared work for black-and-white and full-color reproduction, as well as two- and three-color.

EDUCATION

Bachelor of Fine Arts, Illustration, Seymour Art Center (1985)

EMPLOYMENT

Freelance Work 1985 to Present

ARTIST - Painted and sold over 45 portraits and scenes using water color, graphite, pen and ink, egg tempura, and oil (1985 to Present).

Provided graphics and illustration for numerous projects: notebook cover, Advancetec (1991); brochure cover, Barr & Associates (1991); map and tour guide, Santa Barbara Museum of Natural History (1990); catalog and advertising design, Briton Engineering (1990); work order design, Armor Advertising (1989); logo and menu design, Silk Oyster Restaurant (1989); logo, business card design, Donner Electronics, Inc. (1989); magazine illustration, *Psychology Today* (1988); catalog design, Sunstra Inc. (1987); scratchboard portrait of DeVinci for ad appearing in *Smithsonian* (1987); layout, design, illustration, *Infoworld* (1986).

Jonathan Edwards Galleries, Santa Barbara, California 1990 to Present

ART DEALER - Assist customers in purchasing art works for both personal viewing and as investments. Help customers in understanding the artist and the art piece. In a short time, have developed an excellent reputation for knowledge, helpfulness, and tact.

Redecorate the gallery as new works are shown and touch up damaged pieces. Commissioned through the gallery to do portraits. Currently showing several personal works of children and scenes including "Cool Mist," "High Noon," "Children in the Sun." Help design the monthly newsletter and provide calligraphy and design expertise for gallery signs.

Typeface: Times Roman

MILITARY PERSONNEL

To write a successful resume, the person with 6–30 years in the military needs to have confidence that the abilities he or she possesses are marketable. Without that assurance the resume will probably come out bland and next to useless. Feel good about yourself. Regardless of your function in the military, you developed skills there which are valuable in the civilian job market. Those responsible for getting you to re-enlist have probably painted a pretty bleak picture of the difficulties of finding a civilian job. If you plan well, analyze your strengths, and are clear on what you want to do in civilian life, you should have no more difficulties than anyone else finding the job you want.

Use Your Strengths

Analyze your background carefully and emphasize the experience that will help sell you into a civilian job. There may be functions you performed in the military that are so unique to the military that they should be mentioned briefly or not at all. You've done plenty of things which civilian managers are looking for so emphasize those things.

If you have been involved in any phase of electronics, data processing, mechanics, or other technical fields, you are highly marketable. The U.S. government has invested thousands of dollars training you, and there are employers who desperately want that expertise and experience.

Many ex-pilots have gone to work for airlines and defense contractors. Don't feel limited to seeking jobs that are directly related to your military functions, however. As an officer you were assigned various command positions. Describe them properly, and you can sell yourself into a midmanagement or executive position. Whatever your background, sell your experience.

Things to Avoid

As you write your resume, scrupulously avoid military jargon, also known as militarese. Let a civilian read your resume to determine if your descriptions are understandable.

Be careful about mentioning the supervision of large numbers of people. In the military, to have responsibility for 500 people is not unusual, but most presidents of companies never have 500 people under their control. Seeing such large numbers can seem threatening. Generally you would only list the number of direct reports.

Avoid phrases like "Responsible for overseeing a $95 million budget." In the military overseeing large budgets is common, but in the private sector, only presidents of the largest companies could make such statements. Again, it can seem threatening.

The same principle would apply if you were a pilot or ship's captain: "Responsible for a $21 million piece of equipment" (pilot) or, "Had total responsibility for operating and maintaining a $260 million piece of equipment" (captain of a destroyer). The statements may sound impressive, but they are actually counterproductive.

Using Evaluations And Letters Of Commendation

As a military person you have undoubtedly saved your fitness reports, evaluations, and letters of commendation. Selected short quotations can be included in your resume to make positive statements about yourself. Praise coming from an objective third party, especially from a superior, will carry more weight than if you made the same statement about yourself. Rarely should anyone include more than one or two quotes in the resume, so choose them wisely. See page 228 for an example of a retired military person who used extensive quotes from evaluations as an addendum to his resume. In places where the evaluation would have said "Captain Handle," it simply states "Handle," in order to remove as much military terminology as possible. These quotes were heavily edited, with only small portions of each evaluation included. When skipping portions of the evaluations there was no attempt to use ellipses (...) to signify a gap. Instead, it was all woven together to make a strong statement about Handle and allowing commanding officers to say things he couldn't say about himself.

Generally you should take your addendum (label it "Portions of Annual Evaluations") with you on interviews so that if it seems appropriate you could give a copy to your interviewer. Occasionally you might include it with your resume when you send it in the mail, but our research indicates that people with professional or technical experience are usually better off not including letters of recommendations or evaluations with their resumes.

For some military people a functional resume works best because no matter how they describe their jobs, they don't sound like anything that goes on in the civilian world. See page 198 for an example.

In the first sample resume, Sanders does an excellent job of convincing the reader that he is totally dedicated to safety. It is clear that the record he set for the most consecutive months without a major accident, came by his dedication and the development of a comprehensive safety program.

In the second sample resume, Handle clearly sells his technical ability.

PETE SANDERS
237 Durham Way
Durham, California 95938
(213) 628-9714

OBJECTIVE: Safety Administrator

QUALIFICATIONS

Developed a comprehensive safety program which resulted in six years without a serious accident to any of the 800 personnel.

Proven ability to set up effective, low-cost, industrial safety programs which rely heavily on instilling a safety consciousness in all employees.

Totally familiar with OSHA regulations and compliance procedures and have worked closely with OSHA inspectors.

Certified to administer all forms of emergency medical aid.

WORK EXPERIENCE

U. S. Army 1963 to 1990

SAFETY OFFICER - 1971 to 1990
While Safety Officer at Ft. Bradley for ten years, was responsible for the safety of 800 air field personnel ranging from mechanics, machine operators, and vehicle operators to supervisors and management staff. Developed a comprehensive safety program which set a Ft. Bradley record for safety. Awarded a six-year safety award for 72 consecutive months without a major accident (over $500 property damage or loss of life).

Directly supervised three safety technicians and coordinated the efforts of 20 officers responsible for safety in their immediate areas. Held monthly safety seminars to promote and enhance safety awareness within each specialized group.

Made daily and weekly inspections of offices, maintenance facilities, and mechanical, paint, electrical, and machine shops, to ensure compliance with safety regulations and performed on-the-spot corrections for minor infractions. Identified potentially hazardous practices and recommended changes.

Formulated and administered safety policies and procedures to ensure compliance with federal and state safety acts. Worked closely with OSHA inspectors and developed excellent knowledge of OSHA regulations. Instrumental in starting an effective noise protection program which included annual hearing tests. Very involved with identifying hazardous materials. Wrote, filmed, and edited videotaped safety training films for the base fire department.

AIRFIELD SAFETY OFFICER/PILOT, Ft. Bradley, California 1981 to 1990

AIRFIELD SAFETY OFFICER/PILOT, Munsun-ni, Korea 1979 to 1981

AIRFIELD SAFETY OFFICER/PILOT, Ft. Bradley, California 1972 to 1979

PILOT/SAFETY OFFICER, Da Nang, Vietnam 1971 to 1972

PILOT, Chu Lai, Vietnam, 1967 to 1971

PILOT, Ft. Benning, Georgia 1966 to 1967

ARMOR CREWMAN, 1963 to 1966

EDUCATION

Business - California State University, 85 credits (1981-1984)

SAFETY EDUCATION

Accident Prevention, U. S. Army Agency for Aviation Safety, 640 class hours (1975).

U. S. Air Force Crash Investigators School, 320 class hours (1975)

Aviation Safety Officers Course, University of Southern California Safety Center, 960 class hours (1974). Course covered metal fatigue, reconstructing accidents, investigative procedures, evidence acquisition, analysis of causation factors, methods of accident prevention, and gaining employee cooperation.

Accident Prevention Management, 40-hour correspondence course, U. S. Army Agency for Aviation Safety (1973)

Typeface: Bookman

PAUL HANDLE
3715 Pearl Ave. N.
Everett, Washington 98206
(206) 954-3721

OBJECTIVE: Electrical, Electronic, Mechanical Maintenance

QUALIFICATIONS

Consistently rated superior in both technical expertise and supervisory ability. Constantly finding more effective methods of making repairs and reducing downtime of equipment.

EDUCATION

Graduated - Sheppton High School, Sheppton, Pennsylvania (1965)

EMPLOYMENT

US Navy, 10/65 to 12/91

ELECTRONICS INSTRUCTOR 2/87 to 12/91. Provided comprehensive instruction to maintenance technicians and pilots covering aircraft electrical and electronic systems. Courses ranged from basic electricity and electronics to advanced solid state theory and repair. Taught 13 separate courses averaging 80 classroom hours each. Course Manager for 5 of the 13 courses. Took difficult courses and made them more practical and easier to understand. Wrote numerous manuals and lesson guides which simplified previous courses. Students consistently outscored the students of other instructors.

SENIOR SUPERVISOR 7/75 to 2/87. Supervised 2 shift supervisors and up to 35 technicians. Developed work schedules for personnel, scheduled maintenance, and provided overall management of a large maintenance shop. Trained new technicians and personally performed many repairs on state of the art aircraft electrical systems, automatic flight control systems, and navigational systems.

Took over one command position where outdated maintenance and record keeping procedures had created serious maintenance problems. Reorganized the reporting and maintenance procedures and streamlined the operation. In 36 months the unit moved from "poor" to "excellent" in readiness reports.

ELECTRONIC MAINTENANCE SUPERVISOR 6/69 to 7/75. Supervised up to 20 technicians in the repair of electrical and electronic aircraft systems.

AVIATION ELECTRICIAN 10/65 to 6/69. Maintenance and service technician on aircraft electrical and navigational systems.

TRAINING - Navy Schools (completed over 75 courses with a total of 2,400 classroom hours)

Advanced Electronics Courses (1970 - 1989)
Polyphase power and control systems (200 hours)
Advanced magnetic devices (240 hours)
Analog, solid-state and T.T.L. devices (400 hours)
Advanced syncro/analog/solid state control and indicating systems (400 hours)
Hybrid solid-state inertial navigation systems (200 hours)
High resolution hydraulic/electronic T.T.L. control systems (160 hours)
Component/miniature component repair, including P.C.B (160 hours)

Aviation Electrician Course, 1965 (320 hours)

Typeface: Times Roman

Paul Handle
PORTIONS OF SEMI-ANNUAL EVALUATIONS

Handle's broad qualifications and maintenance know how on A6A electrical systems have enabled him to become a particularly valuable instructor. He is always striving to make difficult courses easier for the students to comprehend by ensuring that proper maintenance procedures are included in his lessons. His willingness to work at any task, no matter how large or small, has contributed materially to the mission of NAMTD. His conduct sets an example worthy of emulation by other officers. He has amply demonstrated a fair and unbiased attitude, readily accepting each and every man as an individual. Handle is industrious, thorough, and accurate in this work and extremely conscientious in all duties and endeavors. He is alert and stable, displaying a creative mind. He shows great ability to develop effective procedural methods and to prepare excellently written and easily understood lesson guides. He secures the attention and respect of his students whom he guides and directs with understanding and tact. He is frequently called upon by other rate groups of this detachment to help solve technical problems in the writing of lesson guides. He attacks these problems with a cheerful and aggressive nature, seeing any problems through to a successful conclusion. Success in his work is shown by the students' final grades and their comment sheets. January, 1991

Handle is intelligent, exceptionally quick to learn, with the ability to grasp pertinent details rapidly. Given broad guidelines, he accomplishes assigned tasks in an enthusiastic and exemplary manner. Handle is a conscientious and concerned instructor who demonstrates a sincere feeling of responsibility towards his students and works very hard to ensure they receive maximum benefit from his instruction. He is equally at ease before a group of juniors or seniors. He is very effective in conveying his thoughts clearly and fluently, both in casual conversation or when presenting a formal lesson. During this reporting period, he has been assigned the task of writing the avionics portion of AZF under the individualized instruction format. He willingly assisted other instructors with this new format and readily assumed the responsibility of insuring that uniformity was met by all rate groups. He spent many hours researching instructions. Acting as liaison between rate groups, he arranged and conducted meetings to achieve this goal. January 1989

Handle has been extremely instrumental in the training of the less experienced men assigned to the branch. He can be counted on to do any assigned task correctly, efficiently and safely. January 1987

Handle is a dedicated, knowledgeable First Class Electrician who strives to ensure work is completed safely and that the proper maintenance procedures are utilized. He keeps his superiors informed of all potential trouble areas and draws on his vast experience to propose viable solutions. He leads with an easy-going, unobtrusive manner, never interfering with the personal initiative of those he supervises. He plans the work load efficiently and utilizes a smooth rapport with the men to carry out the work. January 1985

Handle has demonstrated a high proficiency in his field and is very adept at putting his knowledge and experience to good use. He has an ability to quietly evaluate difficult situations and to arrive at practical solutions while working under trying conditions. He is a very thoughtful and sincere person who has the ability to communicate with the younger men and to define some of their problems. January 1983

Handle is a calm and reserved supervisor who receives the full support of his subordinates without haranguing or berating them. His assigned tasks are never too insignificant to warrant his total attention. The capable manner in which he plans and assigns work to his men is further enhanced by his cheerful and pleasing personality. These traits, coupled with his willingness to work with others, make for a smooth running crew on his shift. January 1981

PROGRAMMERS/ANALYSTS

Data processing is a unique field and requires a special type of resume. Since the average programmer stays only 18 months with an organization, managers usually look for someone who can step right in and do the job, based on past experience with the computer, language, and operating system used in that organization. This is a source of great frustration for programmers because many feel that in two to three weeks they can master any new system—all they need is an opportunity to prove it. Your task is to make the most out of the experience you have and to demonstrate your adaptability.

The DP resume is actually fairly simple to write because it consists of several distinct sections that practically write themselves. Start with Areas of Experience. Typically, it will consist of Languages, Systems, Special Programs, Computers, Conversions, and Applications. Applications can be further divided into New Applications and Maintenance. It should be easy, almost like filling in the blanks.

Because programming is so project-oriented, it is often better to place more emphasis on projects than on job descriptions. A special projects section will work great. Provide just enough information in each project description to give an employer a feel for what you did, then concentrate on results. This section is very important and will probably require three drafts. Start by listing the projects you feel would be most impressive. Since employers usually use resumes as a basis for interviews, be sure to choose projects that you would want to explain and describe in more detail in an interview.

For the first draft of your projects section, don't worry about length, just get your thoughts down on paper. In the second draft look for unnecessary words or phrases. The employer does not require a complete understanding of all the details, just enough information to indicate the degree of complexity and what was required to complete the project. Finish the project by describing the result. Your third draft will simply be a finer tuning of the second.

By emphasizing your areas of experience and special projects sections, your job descriptions will probably be quite short.

KEN WANDER
119 Tri-Cities Way
Richland, Washington 99352
(509) 454-4413

QUALIFICATIONS:

More than nineteen years experience in analyzing and solving complex problems involving electronic data processing and engineering. Consistent track record of systems analysis and programming applications that are maintained easily and run quickly.

Demonstrated ability to apply sound knowledge of data processing concepts to diverse applications. Use structured approach in programming.

EDUCATION:

B.S. - Mechanical Engineering, Ohio State University (1971)

AREAS OF EXPERIENCE:

Languages: COBOL, RPG II, FORTRAN, QUIKJOB, BAL, Macro Assembler, APL, OS and DOS JCL, ADASCRIPT, GE Command Language.

Special Programs: CRJE, SPF, PANVALET, ICCF, OS and DOS Utilities, S/3 Utilities, POWER, ASAP, HASP, JES, ADABAS.

Computers: IBM 360/30,40,50; IBM 370/135,145,158; IBM 3031,4331; IBM 1130/1800; IBM System/3,7,32.

New Applications: Program Inventory Reporting; Budget Updating and Reporting; Auto Engine Emission Analysis; Contact Resistance Analysis; Cash Flow Reporting; Data Decoding/Translating Systems; Automated Record Updating Systems; Records Management System Updating; Payroll Accounting; Mailing Label System Program Generator.

Maintenance: Billing, Inventory Control, Accounts Receivable, and Sales Analysis; Purchase History Reporting; Bill-of-Material Updating and Reporting; Finished Goods Processing and Reporting; Mortgage Loan Reporting.

FUNCTIONAL EXPERIENCE:

Business Applications:

Developed in six weeks a versatile system of RPG II programs for budget revising and reporting to reduce Daytex corporate budget preparation time from 12 man-weeks to 1.

Developed a translator in RPG II to convert S/7 prepared order entry data to fixed format for S/3 processing. Installed Billing, Inventory Control, Accounts Receivable, and Sales Analysis Systems.

FUNCTIONAL EXPERIENCE (continued):

<u>Information Management Applications</u>:

Developed in three weeks a series of COBOL programs to inventory COBOL application programs directly from compressed records in DOS source library.

Developed for WPPSS an ADABAS utility replacement which dynamically formats records and cuts run time from three hours to less than thirty minutes.

Enhanced and simplified complex reporting system accessing ADABAS files via dynamically callable modules.

Automated record updating using QUIKJOB for 80% of Iowa registered voters from state drivers license tapes and telephone company directory listing tapes.

Developed an ALC program generator which reduced time to fill special mailing label requests from three days to less than thirty minutes.

<u>Research Applications</u>:

Developed system to analyze research data via GE Information Systems at Palmer College of Chiropractic.

Developed a system for the EPA to analyze data for engine emission testing.

<u>Financial Applications</u>:

Developed complex, request-driven cash flow reporting application at WPPSS using COBOL report writer.

Maintained ALC programs for mortgage loan applications at FIS.

<u>Manufacturing Applications</u>:

Responsible for enhancing and final testing of Olympic Stain Corp. Inventory Control System.

Installed several plastic injection molding control packages on S/7.

CHRONOLOGICAL EXPERIENCE:

Consultant, Wander Consulting 1981- Present. Programmer/analyst responsible for new applications and program maintenance in Dayton, OH; Davenport, IA; Richland, WA.

Systems Engineer, IBM 1976 - 1981. Responsible for filling SE Services Contracts with sensor-based computer installations; marketing and technical support for customer installations.

Mechanical Engineer, IBM 1971-1976. Worked on various APL analysis applications for test equipment design and had line engineering responsibilities.

Typeface: Helvetica

SALESPEOPLE

Salespeople typically hate to write. That fact is generally quite evident in their resumes, most of which are poorly written, poorly designed, and reveal very little of substance. Taking just four to five hours of your time to write a quality resume could net you an extra $100,000 in your lifetime earnings.

The sales resume is usually one of the easiest to write because it is so results oriented. Sales resumes rarely require extensive details about duties because sales managers already know what you do. What they care about is the bottom line. Don't tell a sales manager how hard you worked or how many phone calls you made or how many sales calls you went on. Did you sell? That's all that counts.

There are a number of ways to show results: sales awards, your ranking within your sales organization, improving the position of your territory compared to other territories in the company, increasing sales, increasing profits on sales, or increasing market share. Use whatever is most appropriate. If you know your market share or can estimate it pretty closely, use that figure. Market share is effective because it provides an excellent means of comparison. During an economic boom with high inflation, the gross sales of even a mediocre salesperson will increase 5-8% annually. To increase market share, however, means you have taken business away from competitors and increased your share of the pie. It means you're doing something right. Employers won't know if you've done it on the basis of your great personality, your outstanding closing techniques, your strong product knowledge, your hard work, or your excellent time management, but it won't matter. Sales managers care only about results.

Showing increases in market share is great, but most companies simply don't do the research to know what those figures are, territory by territory. Use whatever figures will work best for you. During the last recession even many outstanding salespeople were not able to say that they increased sales. In some industries just holding steady was the mark of a great salesperson.

To show yourself in the best light you might use a combination. Let's say from 1978 to 1981 you sold office machines. Those were recession years in some parts of the country. You took over an established territory and only increased gross sales 14% in three years, slightly less than inflation. You obviously won't brag about your sales increases. Out of a sales staff of 18, you were second in sales, since no one else sold well either. That would be the result you would use. In 1981 and 1983 you sold photocopiers. You were in the right place at the right time and sales really took off and increased 20% each year for an actual increase of 44% over two years. Assuming you didn't know what market share was, nor how you did compared to the rest of the sales staff, you would certainly want to use the sales increases.

In 1984 through 1986 you decided to sell cars. You did well and each year won an award from the manufacturer. You were also Salesperson of the Month eight times during your 34 months with the dealership. You were competing with 12 other salespeople. For that job you would mention the awards and the number of times you were Salesperson of the Month. In 1986 you went to work for a tractor manufacturer which paid a research firm to determine the market share in each territory. Between 1986 and the end of 1989 the market share in your territory increased from 15% to 20%, a 33% increase in market share. In 1990 you joined a heavy equipment distributor and moved the territory from seventh to second. Sales were flat due to the recession. The resume might look something like this:

B & N Machinery, Tempe, Arizona 1/90 to Present

MARKETING REPRESENTATIVE - Developed and implemented marketing strategies to increase heavy equipment sales to the construction industry in Arizona. Took the territory from 7th (out of 8) in the company to 2nd during the first 15 months.

John Deere, Phoenix, Arizona 10/86 to 12/89

DISTRICT REPRESENTATIVE - Assisted 26 dealers in Arizona and New Mexico in marketing John Deere products. Set up 5 new dealers and developed their sales, parts and service departments. Moved 7 dealers from near bankruptcy to very strong financial positions. Increased market share 33%.

Gerald Lincoln Mercury, Phoenix, Arizona 1/84 to 10/86

SALESMAN - Each year won the Professional Sales Counselor award for sales excellence. With a sales force of 12, was salesperson of the month 8 times in 34 months.

Canon Corporation, Trenton, New Jersey 11/81 to 12/83

SALES REPRESENTATIVE - Sold a full line of photocopiers to end users. In 2 years increased territorial sales 44%.

Olivetti Corporation, Trenton, New Jersey 1/78 to 11/81

SALES REPRESENTATIVE - Sold typewriters, calculators and dictating equipment to office equipment stores throughout metropolitan Trenton. Worked closely with store managers and sales staffs and provided excellent training in selling Olivetti products. Ranked 2nd in sales in 1981 with a regional sales force of 18.

If you haven't been doing so up to this time, begin collecting and saving all the sales data you can. Whenever you start a new position, get data on what the territory was doing prior to your taking over. In the absence of cold, hard figures, rely on your memory and your knowledge of the territory. Estimate and guesstimate when you must, but do come up with some figures which you feel are accurate, and be sure you can explain how they were derived.

GAIL SHUMWAY
2928 Sunset Blvd.
Phoenix, Arizona 85004
(602) 755-2428

QUALIFICATIONS

As Division Manager and Area Marketing Manager, increased market share each year by effectively identifying new markets, recruiting and developing successful sales teams, and obtaining quantifiable results through Total Quality programs.

EDUCATION

MBA - Marketing, University of Colorado (1978)
BS - Electrical Engineering, California State Polytechnic University (1974)

EMPLOYMENT HISTORY

Dyatech Inc. 11/85 to Present

DIVISION MANAGER - Phoenix Division 7/89 to Present. Responsible for the total operation and profits for this distributor of electronic components and systems, with sales to industrial users, original equipment manufacturers, and federal and state agencies. Supervise 45 employees. Introduced an effective Total Quality program into an organization with low morale and loose controls. As a result, market share has increased from 10% to 14%, while customer retention has been increased 65%.

AREA MANAGER - Denver Division 11/85 to 7/89. Managed the 22-employee Colorado Area in the four-state Denver Division. Created and implemented a new concept in technical marketing which doubled sales and increased market share from 12% to 22%.

Insofen Corporation 5/81 to 11/85

FIELD ENGINEER - Denver, Colorado. Covering Colorado and Utah, sold high technology semiconductor products to major manufacturers of electronic equipment. Worked closely with engineers to get proprietary devices designed into new products. Increased sales from $60,000 to $210,000 per month.

Xytex Corporation 7/74 to 5/81

ENGINEER - Boulder, Colorado. Designed power systems and interfaces for data processing peripheral equipment.

Typeface: Bookman

CAREER CHANGERS

I applaud people making career changes. Career changers can find greater job satisfaction and a lifestyle more in tune with their current values. Career changers, however, have the most difficult and frustrating experiences with resumes. When they use the traditional approach of mailing out 100 or more resumes, career changers experience very little success. While having an effective resume is still necessary for career changers, the resume *must* be used in a way that takes advantage of the hidden job market.

If you are a career changer, the first thing you must do is determine the type of position you'll be seeking. Then pick out every experience even remotely related to that line of work and insert it in some form into the resume. The qualifications section is often an excellent place to do this.

When you start describing your employment, you have two main goals: 1) show you were successful at what you did; and 2) emphasize any parts of your jobs which are related to your current objective. Your successes are important. Employers are dubious enough about hiring a career changer; they certainly want a person with a proven record of success. Essentially you'll be saying through your resume, "I've been successful in the past, and I'll be successful for you, also." Emphasizing related experience in each job is important. In most cases you should provide an adequate and accurate overview of your entire job, but that can usually be covered in one or two sentences. The remaining space should cover those functions which are related to your objective. In other words, duties which took up only 10% of your time may get 90% of the space.

Career changers tend to have longer qualifications sections than those who have years of experience in the same field. Career changers sometimes do better with a functional resume. Read pages 192 to 200 for a full explanation and several examples.

I also recommend that you join appropriate associations and volunteer to head up committees or special projects. Associations are usually begging for people to spend time on projects and you don't need to have been a member for five years. It is an excellent way to get recognized and to meet the top people in your field. Those projects or committee assignments could then go in a special projects section.

In the following resume, notice how this career changer emphasized everything she had ever done that was related to training and development in any way.

ROSALYN RODRIQUEZ
2315 Dixie Avenue
Charleston, South Carolina 29406
(803) 976-4204

OBJECTIVE: Position in Training and Development

QUALIFICATIONS

Broad background in planning and developing programs. Skilled in determining program needs through task analysis. Planned and organized numerous programs, including the Council for Exceptional Children 1989 State Conference.

Extensive knowledge and experience in determining needs, setting behavioral and learning objectives, and developing assessment tools. M.A. in Curriculum and Program Development.

Expertise in selecting appropriate teaching techniques to match the audience. Quickly establish rapport with groups.

Outstanding record in education. Received ratings of excellent to outstanding in all evaluations.

Evaluated and selected speakers and consultants for educational topics and conventions.

Extensive budgetary and purchasing experience with instructional materials.

Excellent writer. Wrote three successful grant proposals and published two articles on curriculum development for the *Journal of Education.*

Extensive knowledge of statistics and research methodologies for determining effectiveness of programs.

Strong abilities in performing and graphics arts. Directed, stage-managed, and designed sets and costumes for numerous theatrical productions.

Designed and produced newsletters, manuals, and brochures using desk top publishing.

Extensive experience writing, producing, and editing video programs.

EDUCATION

M.A. - Curriculum and Instruction, University of South Carolina (1976)
B.A. - Art, Arkansas State Teachers College (1971)

EMPLOYMENT

Teacher, Charleston Public Schools, Charleston, South Carolina 9/78 to Present
Teacher, Greenville Public Schools, Greenville, South Carolina 9/71 to 9/78

ASSOCIATIONS

Member - American Society for Training and Development
Member - Council for Exceptional Children; State Bylaws Chairperson 1986 to Present; Chapter President 1985; Chapter Vice President 1984

Typeface: Times Roman

HOW TO USE A RESUME

WANT ADS

I recommend reading the want ads. In cities with two or more newspapers, one paper usually predominates and gets 95% of all jobs advertised. Of course, some employers will advertise in more than one paper, but typically only about 5% of the jobs will be advertised in the secondary paper and *not* in the primary one. In addition, about 95% of all jobs advertised will appear in the Sunday paper. For the sake of time, read only the primary paper, and read only the Sunday edition. Scan it from A to Z. Some very interesting jobs can be listed with job titles you would never expect.

If a want ad is vague, mail out your standard resume and hope for the best. If the ad is fairly explicit concerning the desired qualifications and experience, you must decide whether to mail your standard resume with a custom cover letter, or whether you will take the additional time to tailor your resume to the position. If you feel strongly enough about a position, and your standard resume does not adequately cover some key points, it is worth modifying the resume. It can double your chances of getting an interview.

Blind Ads

Blind ads are rarely productive, but may be worth trying. A blind ad is a help-wanted ad in which the name of the employer has been omitted, and all you are given is a box number in care of the newspaper. Most are legitimate, placed by companies that for one reason or another want to maintain anonymity. Unfortunately companies sometimes use these want ads to gather salary information and in fact have no position. No one knows how frequently it occurs. The problem is, there is no way to tell which are legitimate and which are not.

Since blind ads usually draw fewer responses than ads that include the name of the employer, you'll have an excellent shot at an interview if your background is ideal.

To respond to a blind ad follow the instructions that each paper prints in the want ad section. If you are concerned about the blind ad being placed by your own company, or merely one that you don't want to receive your resume, follow the instructions for that situation. If you were responding to an ad placed in the Seattle Times you would address your envelope to the Seattle Times and include the box number for that ad. You would also write on the envelope, **Confidential Desk.**

That alerts those sorting the mail that there are certain companies which should not receive your resume. Inside the outer envelope you would enclose a second envelope which would contain your resume. That envelope would also have the box number for that ad written on the outside. Along with your resume your inner envelope would also contain a separate sheet of paper which would indicate those companies you would not want your resumes to go to.

Responding to blind ads rarely gets results because the companies placing them are highly particular and may interview only three people instead of the more typical six to eight. Unless your background is almost a perfect fit for the job, blind ads are rarely worth responding to.

Sources Of Want Ads

In addition to your local paper, other good sources of want ads are the *Wall Street Journal* (Tuesdays and Wednesdays contain the most ads) and the *National Business Employment Weekly*, which carries most of the ads from all four regional editions of the *Wall Street Journal*. Both are found in most libraries. The *National Business Employment Weekly* can be found at some newsstands and costs $3.95 a copy. You can also subscribe—$22.00 for six weeks. *The National Ad Search* contains want ads from all major newspapers from around the country. Read these resources in your library to determine if a subscription would be beneficial to you.

You might wonder what kind of competition should you expect when you respond to an ad? An ad for a good position can draw up to 500 applicants (50-150 is most typical); rarely will more than eight people be interviewed. Your results will depend on how closely the job matches your qualifications and how much time you spend tailoring your cover letter. If you emphasize accomplishments and potential, you will certainly get a better response than average. According to a Department of Labor study, about 20% of all managers, sales workers, professionals, and clerical workers who answer ads, get their jobs through a help-wanted ad.

UNSOLICITED RESUMES

Unsolicited resumes are frequently sent to employers in hopes that a position may be available at the time the resume is received. Resume campaigns typically result in less than one interview for every hundred resumes sent out. If you use the strategy I'm about to discuss, you should get eight to ten interviews for every hundred resumes you mail.

You must start this type of campaign with an absolutely top-notch resume. Then develop a list of 50–200 employers of the right size, in the right industry, and in the right geographical area. (See Employer Research on page 52 to locate the best resources for obtaining names of employers.) Determine the department in which you would most likely work. Next, making about 20 calls an hour, call each organization and ask the receptionist for the name of the appropriate executive or department head. Be sure to get the correct spelling and title. Then and only then are you ready to send out resumes. Address each cover letter and resume to the specific person who has power to hire you. Addressing your letters to those with the power to hire should double your interviews compared to merely addressing it "Dear Mr. President," "Dear Marketing Manager," or "Dear Personnel Manager."

Usually you will know the typical title of the person with the power to hire you. In those cases simply ask the receptionist for the name of the person with that title. Sometimes you will be told, "We don't have anyone here with that title." Your response would then be, "Can you give me the name and title of the person who would typically hire (your job title)?" If that does not work, ask using a different job title or ask for the personnel department.

If you simply cannot identify who your resume should go to, address it to the president *by name*. The resume may still wind up in personnel, but it is just as likely to be delivered to the most appropriate person.

Decide whether you will follow up with a phone call to each person or simply wait for interview offers. Calling and asking for an appointment will usually result in appointments 30–60% of the time, while waiting for interview offers (assuming you have a top-quality resume and sent it to a specific person) should result in an 8–12% success rate. Of course your actual percentage will be determined by the quality of your resume, the amount of experience you have in the field you are seeking, the impressiveness of your accomplishments and results, the job market, and the care with which you select potential employers.

The decision to call or wait is important because it will affect the wording in your cover letter. If you will be calling for an appointment, you simply state in the letter, "I will call you next week to set up a brief appointment." This statement will cause the reader to pay more attention to the resume, to be prepared for your call, and it likely will be kept close at hand rather than filed or discarded. With the waiting approach, you can end your letter with something like, "I look forward to hearing from you soon."

It's wise to send your chosen batch of employers a second mailing of your resume. A surprising finding, first described by Carl Boll in

Executive Jobs Unlimited, is that resumes sent to the same organizations, six or more weeks after the first batch, will usually obtain results equal to the first mailing. In other words, if one hundred resumes netted you eight interviews, the second batch of one hundred should provide another eight. Give serious consideration to a second mailing.

RECEIVING CALLS

Employers generally arrange interviews by phone. If they fail to reach you after two or three tries, they may simply give up. With a top-quality resume, you'll make employers want to meet you, but don't press your luck—make it easy for them to reach you. If you're rarely home and there will be no one else to answer your phone, consider a telephone answering machine or an answering service. Answering machines can be purchased for between $60 and $200. An answering service will take messages for you just as a secretary would. Setting up your own personal voice mail through your telephone company is another option. It will cost around $8 per month and many find it more convenient than using an answering machine. If you use an answering service, include it like this:

BETTY BABCOCK
2452 165th NE
Redmond, Washington 98052
(206) 883-0629 or 883-5907

The second number would usually be the answering service. I prefer not to identify the second number as an answering service or a message phone. An alternative would be to include the number of a friend or relative who is usually home in addition to your own phone number. It may make sense to include your work number, but only if you have privacy. If you use your work number you would usually indicate it like this:

(206) 883-0629 (H) or 883-5800 (W)

Another option is to install another line. You can hook up an answering machine to that phone and that is the number that would appear in your resume. That way you know that the only people who will call that number will be prospective employers or others who happen to have received your resume. Your greeting and your request that they leave a message can then be tailored to your job search. Have others listen to your message and get feedback. You should sound upbeat and your message should be crystal clear. State your name at the beginning of the message. It might go something like this: "Hi, this is Robert Gardner. I'm not available at the moment, but I would like to get your message, and will return your call just as soon as possible. Please leave your name, phone number, your organization, and the best times to call you today. Thank you."

If you have truly confidential voice mail at work, you might list your home phone on one line and the following information on the next line: 24-hour private voice mail (213) 764-8976.

FAXING

Do not fax a resume unless an employer has specifically asked you to do so. The quality at the other end looks like a poor quality dot matrix printed resume, and the paper will be typical fax paper. If you do fax a resume, also send one through the mail so the person will see its quality. If you want it there fast, but have not been asked to fax it, use an overnight express service. This approach will have more impact.

REFERENCES

Before listing people as references, check with them to make sure they are willing to do it. Then ask them what they would feel comfortable saying about you. More than a few job seekers have been surprised to learn that an expected glowing recommendation turned out to be anything but. You can also suggest things you would like your references to say about you. Most will be happy to accommodate you.

References should virtually never be listed on a resume, even when those references are well-known people. Some people, however, like to write at the bottom, "Personal and Professional References Available Upon Request," based on the rationale that even though all employers know they can get references if they want, seeing it printed at the bottom of the page is psychologically reassuring. I recommend leaving this information off for the same reason I don't type "Resume" at the top of page one. The information simply is not needed since the reader already knows or assumes it.

References are nearly always required on application forms, however, so you should have a list of your references ready. Each reference should include the person's name, title, name of organization, address, and phone number. You might want to type up your list of references and make four or five copies. That way, if it seems appropriate, you can give a copy to an employer during an interview. Since employers rarely ask for references during interviews, you'll still have most of your copies left when you get your next job, but at least you'll be prepared.

References usually go into one of two categories—personal or professional. Although it is generally assumed by employers that personal references will say nice things about you, they are still often contacted. Therefore, choose your references carefully. John may say great things about you, but if he speaks in a monotone, gets easily flustered, and often lacks tact, I would choose someone else. Personal references should be those who know you well or have observed you for several years. It doesn't help your cause when someone says, "I don't know her well, but ..." Use influential people as references only if they can speak first hand about you and know you well enough to answer personal questions about you.

Your most important references are former bosses. Although companies are increasingly refusing to provide more than dates of employment—due to a rash of defamation of character suits in the 80s—those who really want information can usually get former bosses to reveal something. So while company policy may require your former boss to refer such calls to personnel, your boss may still supply information—good or bad.

With former bosses that you had good to satisfactory relationships with, you should at least call them and tell them that they may get calls from prospective employers. Explain what you've been up to since you worked together and thank the person for any positive contributions the person made to your career or personal growth. Find something positive to discuss, even if overall, it was not a good experience for you.

Don't be afraid to take an active, directive approach with your references. Give them a copy of your resume. Review it with them so there won't be any discrepancies between what they say about you and what you say about yourself. And don't give out your list of references until a company requests them. Usually companies will call references only when you are one of the top three choices. Still, you don't want your references called any more often than necessary. Also, keep your references updated on your job search. You would hate to find out that one of your references said, "Hasn't he found a job yet?"

LETTERS OF RECOMMENDATION

Whenever you leave a job, get a letter of recommendation. You may never use it, but it has real worth for you. A strong letter of recommendation assures you that the person will say positive things about you. It also assures you that you can make positive statements about yourself, knowing that you can back up what you say with the letter.

The letter of recommendation is especially important for the person who has been terminated. In such a case you are not seeking a glowing letter, but one which at least emphasizes your positive qualities and contributions. If you can get your former boss to say positive things in a letter, the person will almost certainly say positive things when called by prospective employers. Obtaining a positive letter of recommendation, or at the least, one which is not negative, can be very reassuring to you throughout your job search. Obtaining such a letter almost assures you that nothing negative will be said if a potential employer calls for a reference check.

Feel free to suggest to the person the points or ideas you would like covered in the letter. You may even want to list the points that you would like people to mention, and then ask each reference to cover some of those specific points. In that way, with three or four letters of recommendation, all of your desired points will be covered at least once. Do not give any one person all of the points, spread them out among those writing the letters. These people are likely to appreciate your help because most people find letters of recommendation difficult to write. Depending on the circumstances, you could even send a sample letter and suggest that the person adopt the portions he or she is comfortable with, or just use it for ideas. People will often use a sample letter as it was presented, or make only minor modifications, and have it typed on their own letterhead.

I rarely encourage people to enclose letters of recommendation with resumes. My research shows that it may be helpful for people in entry-level jobs and for those seeking office work, but most should save letters of recommendation for appropriate points during an interview. When I tested the effectiveness of letters of recommendation with engineers, their resumes were rated more highly when the resume was *not* accompanied by a letter of recommendation. Thus it seems that for professionals, the inclusion of such letters with resumes is not generally appropriate.

Never use a letter of recommendation unless it is glowing. Avoid using the typical letter which says, "Rosalyn worked for me for six years in such and such a capacity and she is an excellent employee. I can recommend her without reservation. Should you have any questions feel free to call me." Such a letter is simply not strong enough. It appears to have been written with little heart in it. Such a letter will have no positive impact—don't use it.

The glowing letter points out some of your specific strengths and uses terms like *excellent* and *outstanding*. The letter may even mention a project where you worked above and beyond the call of duty. That type of letter can help, but even in such a case, use it only if it seems appropriate.

Some people like to bring letters of recommendation or performance reviews to interviews. That's fine; I encourage people to take whatever they believe may be helpful to them. Take a briefcase or something similar so that your portfolio, letters of recommendation, performance reviews, or examples of past work, will fit neatly inside. Arrange everything so that you are able to quickly find what you are looking for and can present it in a way that does not seem awkward.

Present your materials only if it seems appropriate. For any given interview, assume that you will not be showing your materials. But if they are needed, you'll have them with you. You should never feel obligated to show your stuff just because you have it with you. For most people the best way is to tell the employer what it is you have and ask if the person would be interested in seeing it. If there seems to be no interest, you can simply summarize the contents. This will still be effective because the employer knows that you are able to back up what you are saying with the materials.

If you are going to show something, I suggest that you describe it first and then hand it to the person. If the employer must do any reading, stop talking so the person can concentrate on your materials. If you are showing a portfolio of drawings or photographs, provide some background to it as the person is reviewing it.

COVER LETTERS

The cover letter is merely a letter which introduces you to an employer. All resumes sent through the mail should be accompanied by a cover letter. The cover letter personalizes your resume and gives it greater flexibility. If your resume does not contain an objective, the cover letter is the place to express it. A cover letter gives you an opportunity to share points that are not easily covered in a resume. So a resume plus a cover letter represent the ideal vehicle to get across all of the key ideas and points that you want an employer to know about you.

A resume which arrives without a cover letter gives a jolt to the receiver and makes a loud statement about the sender—the person could not even take a few minutes to make a personal statement or sign his or her name. It begs the question, "Is this the type of person we want to hire?"

When answering a want ad, specify the exact job title in the cover letter. It is not necessary, however, to specify the source of the ad or its date. The exact title will provide all the information personnel needs. When a want ad explicitly requests certain types of experience which you have, but which is not adequately covered in the resume, use your cover letter to fill in the details. The alternative would be to rewrite your resume slightly to include the necessary details. A highly specific cover letter with a modified resume will always provide better results.

If an ad does not provide a name and you are unable to obtain the name of the person with power to hire, it is generally accepted that it should be addressed Dear Sir/Madam. If you are sending your resume and cover letter to personnel you could address it, Dear Personnel Manager, but do your best to get the name of the person.

View your cover letter and resume as a team. Each performs a different function, but they must work well together. Cover letters generally consist of two to four short paragraphs and seldom total more than twenty lines. The first paragraph should open with a strong statement about you that arouses interest and curiosity. Devote a middle paragraph to an accomplishment that will further arouse interest. The accomplishment can come from your resume but should be slightly reworded. When I write cover letters, I usually pick the strongest accomplishment from the resume and include it in the cover letter. Notice how this can be done:

> I can save money for your firm by utilizing my experience in cost control. At Standard Products I reduced paper usage by 24% and photocopying costs by 30%.

❖

I can help increase the impact of your agency. While at Family Services I wrote a proposal which was funded for $22,000. This allowed us to significantly increase the quantity and quality of our services.

Appeal to the employer's self-interest by indicating that you are a problem solver and that hiring you will lead to increased production, greater efficiency, better planning, less waste, higher profits, and more satisfied customers.

Begin the process of responding to want ads by creating a "standard" cover letter; then modify it for each response. An electronic typewriter or a dedicated word processor will prove very helpful. If you believe that "time is money," you'll save a great deal if you can modify your cover letters yourself rather than going to a word processing outfit each time you want to produce a customized cover letter. You can also rent a computer by the hour at some copy shops and then print out your work on their laser printer. Charges are generally quite reasonable. Most have Macintoshes and offer several word processing software packages. If you have your own computer, but all you have is a dot matrix printer, go ahead and use that for your cover letters but be sure to put it in letter quality mode.

To create an effective response to an ad, begin by writing down or underlining all of the key points mentioned in the ad. Check off those points which are clearly and effectively covered in your resume. If several points are not covered in your resume, determine whether you should modify your resume, or merely cover the points in your cover letter. If you decide to modify your resume you should make sure the resume covers all of the desired experience mentioned in the ad.

In using the Systematic Job Search methods you will want to meet the person with power to hire, even if no openings currently exist. Indicate in your cover letter that you will be calling to arrange a meeting. Avoid using the word *interview*. Instead say, "I'll call next week to arrange a brief meeting," or "I will call next week to arrange a time when we can meet." The word *interview* is always associated with formal hiring procedures; what you want is a relaxed meeting in which both parties learn more about each other.

Cover letters should be individually typed. Some people, however, print up 200 cover letters and then type in the employer's name and address. It doesn't look good and it does not make a good statement about you. The reader can tell that you said exactly the same thing to everyone who received your resume. Even if you develop a standard cover letter to be sent to 100 or more companies, you can still personalize it. Write the cover letter so you can insert the name of the company somewhere in the body of the letter. With today's word processors and memory typewriters, you can easily do it yourself. Secretarial services can type your letters and address your envelopes for less than two dollars each, and each one will look perfect.

If you know the company by reputation or your research has revealed some interesting information, don't hesitate to include it in the cover letter. This was done quite effectively in the following excerpts from cover letters:

> One of your competitors told me Alpa has the best quality control of any winch manufacturer in the country. The quality control system I established at Braddigan Gear also became recognized as tops in the industry.

❖

> Your recent acquisition of Marley & Sons indicates to me that you could use someone with my international marketing background.

❖

> John McNamara at IBM believes you are one of the top management consulting firms in the country.

❖

> The recent article in *The Seattle Times* about your rapid expansion was of great interest to me.

Review the sample cover letters, then simply start writing.

> June 20, 1992
>
> Mr. John Travis, Director
> Home Energy Department
> N. W. Center for Energy Efficiency
> 323 Sixth Avenue
> Seattle, Washington 98021
>
> Dear Mr. Travis:
>
> Your recent efforts to promote energy conservation are of great interest to me. My experience as Energy Consultant for Seattle City Light would make me an excellent candidate for several positions in your organization.
>
> While at City Light, I have inspected and provided energy savings estimates on over 500 homes. Eighty percent of the homeowners have acted on one or more of my suggestions and have averaged over 17% in energy savings.
>
> I will call you next week to arrange a brief meeting.
>
> Sincerely,
>
> Brad Tolliver

August 11, 1992

Leslie Acosta
Regional Sales Manager
Peoples Pharmaceuticals
5825 146th Avenue S.E.
Bellevue, Washington 98006

Dear Ms. Acosta:

I was attracted to Peoples Pharmaceuticals when I read your annual
report. My medical background and my customer service experience
make me an excellent candidate for a sales/marketing position in your
organization.

While at Danton Instruments, I was a key person involved in the writing
and organization of new product manuals. My oral presentations to the
sales force were always valuable and well received. District sales managers and the sales representatives themselves consistently expressed
appreciation for the sales aids and information given to them. In addition, a large part of my time was spent working closely with our customers, successfully troubleshooting problems, answering questions and
informing them of new products or instrument applications that might
better serve their needs.

I will look forward to hearing from you soon.

Sincerely,

Sandra Gulliver

❖

November 30, 1991

Bob Pruitt
Superintendent of Construction
Handler & Case Construction Company
1127 - 15th N.E.
Houston, Texas 77069

Dear Mr. Pruitt:

During twenty years of construction experience, most of it in project
management, I've created a record of success I'm proud of. Often working in extremely difficult circumstances, I have always completed
projects on schedule and within the budget.

My experience with fast-track projects and my proven ability to save
money through value engineering should make me valuable on any
projects you may have at this time or in the near future.

As General Superintendent of Structures on the huge $1.3 billion
Ramon Air Base in Israel, my abilities were at times stretched to the

limit--training inexperienced workers to become craftsmen, working in heat that nine months out of the year exceeded 100 degrees, constructing facilities for 4,000 employees, and completing a five-year project in three years.

I will be calling you in a few days to learn more about your projects and to tell you more about my background.

Sincerely,

Layne Sencen

P.S. I'd be very interested in any foreign projects you may have. I proved very effective at training Portuguese and Israeli workers, and I developed excellent relations with Israeli inspectors, engineers and vendors. I pick up languages quickly, and this has been a real asset.

Next is an example where the applicant has spoken to the employer by phone and is thanking the person for having given him some time. There was no opening, so the cover letter is also acting as a thank-you note. Notice that the first paragraph was written strictly for this one letter. The other paragraphs are part of the standard cover letter.

August 30, 1992

Paulette Meyers
National Sales Manager
San Sebastian Winery
San Sebastian, California 95476

Dear Ms. Meyers:

I very much enjoyed our conversation yesterday. As I indicated, I have always been impressed with San Sebastian Winery. At the Blue Panda in Portland, I was instrumental in taking San Sebastian wines from our sixth most popular wine to number two. I totally agree with you that a top sales rep must be highly knowledgeable about wines. I frequently invite wine reps to give wine tastings at the restaurant, both for my own benefit and for the staff. I think you would be impressed with both my knowledge and my palate.

At the Blue Panda Restaurants I have always been a producer. I run what has become one of the most profitable restaurants in the chain, and our wine sales are ranked number one. At each of the four restaurants I've managed, wine sales experienced dramatic increases. I am committed to remaining in the Northwest and am confident I can substantially increase your wine sales in this region.

I will call you in a few weeks to learn about any developments.

Sincerely

Tom Reston

Dear Mr. Ronagen

Your ad for a Western Region Dealer Representative was of great interest to me. I am very impressed with the Mitsubishi Company and the cars it produces. I would very much like to be a part of Mitsubishi, particularly in the area of dealer servicing. I can help Mitsubishi establish the reputation it wants for parts and service.

I know what is required to make service and parts departments run smoothly and profitably. I have always developed close working relations with dealership owners as well as parts and service managers.

In Oregon I worked closely with 16 VW dealerships. Most were poorly managed and barely making money. The service departments were all losing money. Within a year their appearances were tremendously improved, mechanics and service managers had received additional training, and quality control and inventory control systems had been established. Parts sales jumped 85%, and sales of new cars rose from 900 per month to over 1200 per month.

I am committed to the automotive industry. My experience in Oregon is just one example of what I have been able to do with dealerships. Please feel free to contact me so I can tell you more about my background.

❖

Dear Mr. Swenson:

As a Project Manager and Construction Manager for Danson Construction, I have overseen both large and small projects. As an architect I can design projects or work with an architect to come up with the best and most cost effective design. I have hired contractors and have been very successful in making sure the projects were completed on time and were of high quality.

My degree in architecture, along with four years experience in designing, cost estimating, and managing construction projects, plus nearly one year of drafting, make me an ideal candidate for your Facilities Engineer position. I am a person of high energy, which has enabled me to watch the many details of a construction project and make sure everything was completed correctly. That same energy and hard work will prove most helpful as I oversee projects at your many facilities along the East Coast.

❖

Dear Ms. Povich:

During my sixteen years in the dental industry, I have become very familiar with the Wilson Gold Refinery Company. Without a doubt the quality of your products is among the best.

Since 1985 I have sold gold and dental products for K. L. Dental covering Washington, Oregon, Idaho, Montana, and Alaska. Throughout this territory I have established a reputation for integrity and service. My technical knowledge in the dental field is among the highest. During my seven years with K.L., gold sales in the territory have increased from 120,000 pennyweights to over 200,000 pennyweights per year.

I have recently left K. L. Dental and would be very interested in talking to you about covering the Western States. My customers are very loyal to me personally, making me certain that I could significantly increase your sales.

I will call you next week so we can arrange a time and place where we can get together.

❖

Dear Ms. Glasser:

Since age eleven I have wanted to work as a flight attendant. I've been working in restaurants the last four years because I believed it would give me the best training possible for being a flight attendant.

I moved up into restaurant management so quickly because I proved I could handle the responsibility. I mix very well with customers and make each one feel important. This has increased the number of steady customers at each restaurant I have worked.

I am also a problem solver. At Leo's I helped reduce operating costs significantly. At J. K. Jake's I reduced turnover by working more closely with the staff. At both Wooden Lake and Ashki's I helped lay the groundwork so these restaurants could be successful from the day they opened.

I am very much looking forward to interviewing for a flight attendant position.

❖

Dear Ms. Preminger:

I have had a very exciting nine years in hotel sales, six of those years as Director of Sales. During that time I have developed highly effective techniques for attracting association and corporate business.

I would enjoy very much the opportunity to describe in more detail why those techniques have worked so well, and why I would function effectively as your next Sales Manager.

❖

Dear Mr. Black:

Can you use a production manager with the ability to:

Increase productivity 14% per employee through the introduction of Total Quality Programs?

Decrease absenteeism 19%?

Decrease lost time due to industrial accidents 26% through a low-cost but highly effective safety program?

Reduce rejected parts 21%?

During four years with Alliance Screw my staff and I achieved these documented results. Because of the exciting changes you have introduced at Benson Industries since becoming president, I would very much like to be a part of your management team.

On the assumption that you may soon need abilities of this type, I will call in a few days to learn when we might get together to discuss opportunities.

❖

Dear Mr. Brzenski,

During 14 years in the Navy I've dedicated myself to getting things done right and on time. At the Bremerton Naval Shipyards I oversaw all refitting of missile firing systems on naval vessels. Based on documented studies our average completion time was 30 days ahead of schedule and 6% under budget.

I will be leaving the Navy next month. During the last year I have gathered information on many firms I thought I might be interested in joining. Kidder Industries is one of only 20 that I am now actively considering. I have been impressed with your past record, and three former colleagues of mine are currently very happily employed by your firm.

During a visit to San Diego next week I will call to arrange a time when we could meet briefly. I realize you may have no current openings suitable for my background. I would, however, very much appreciate the opportunity to tell you more about myself and at the same time learn more about the directions Kidder Industries is taking. When I arrive in San Diego I will call your secretary to arrange a time convenient for you.

MARKETING LETTERS

Being different often brings positive results. Marketing letters are successful for that reason—they're different. The marketing letter presents your strongest accomplishments, usually those with quantifiable results, to entice the reader. Dates and names of employers are seldom mentioned. The marketing letter acts as a substitute for a resume with cover letter. It can even be used when responding to want ads requesting resumes. In essence, the marketing letter is more like a lengthened cover letter than a resume. Compared to resumes, marketing letters are more personal in tone and more like business correspondence in appearance. Consequently, they are rarely screened out by secretaries.

Less than 5% of all job seekers use marketing letters, yet nothing I know of can lead to more appointments and job interviews. By sending only the marketing letter, your resume is held in reserve for later use. The key to success is addressing it to a specific person and informing that person that a phone call will follow. Your goal is to meet as many people with the power to hire as possible, regardless of whether any openings exist at the moment. This is accomplished by requesting just fifteen minutes of their time.

The use of marketing letters has revolutionized the way my clients find jobs. In the past I had clients cold call potential employers to ask for brief appointments. They understood the importance of the calls, knew they would work, and had practiced what they would say. However, some failed to make their calls, and those who did call, often procrastinated. Sending a marketing letter makes placing those calls easier now. Knowing that a person is expecting your call and is already convinced that you have something of quality to offer, makes a substantial difference psychologically. Using the marketing letter should get you in to see people with the power to hire, 40–80% of the time. Those needing to speak to presidents of companies should expect to make appointments 10–20% of the time. Notice the impact of the following marketing letter and you'll begin to see why these letters get results.

The following marketing letter is especially strong because each accomplishment has been quantified. Marketing letters always have more impact when results are quantified, and most people can easily come up with at least four solid accomplishments. You sense that an employer would want to meet such a person even if no position currently existed.

1121 65th S.W.
Red Rock, California 92006
(916) 456-9874

January 21, 1992

John Campbell
Executive Vice President
Diversified Products Inc.
Redding, California 96001

Dear Mr. Campbell:

When I joined my current employer two years ago as Production Super-intendent, our quality control department was rejecting 6% of all printed circuit boards. Today that figure is less than 1% and continuing down-ward.

You may be interested in a person who has broad experience in solving production problems. Here are some other things I've done:

Reduced absenteeism 42% and turnover 31%. With less turnover we were able to invest more in training, with a corresponding increase in quality and productivity. While rejections dropped from 6% to less than 1%, productivity increased 22% per employee.

Introduced an idea program with incentives. The number of sugges-tions that were implemented grew from 11 in 1989 to 65 in 1991. In 1991 bonuses cost $15,000 while documented savings amounted to $197,000.

Implemented an inventory control system. We increased production 34% with only a 6% increase in inventory. Production delays due to unavailable parts dropped from 72 in 1986 to 11 in 1988.

Instituted a company-wide safety program. Lost time due to acci-dents was reduced 21% during the first six months. Reductions in insurance premiums will save $85,000 in 1991.

I graduated from the University of Wisconsin in 1968 with a degree in Business. Since then I have experienced rapid promotions during 23 years in manufacturing.

I'll call you next week to arrange a time when we might meet for fifteen or twenty minutes.

Sincerely,

John Gaddly

The next two examples demonstrate the flexibility of marketing letters. While they use a more narrative format and are less quantifi-able, they also have a strong impact on the reader.

11918 Northeast 143rd Place
Kirkland, Washington 98034
(206) 821-3830

June 24, 1992

Peter Phillips
Sahalee Development Corp.
2119 Fourth Avenue
Seattle, Washington 98124

Dear Mr Phillips:

In anticipation of the next development upsurge, you may be looking for a person with a broad background in land development and marketing. I have saved projects from failure, reduced development costs, and increased project marketability.

Recently, at the developer's request, I was retained to save a mobile home project that had been rejected during preliminary hearings. By creating a new marketing strategy, employing a more imaginative design, and representing the client throughout the remainder of the public hearings process, I was able to negotiate the project's approval.

As part of a team of consultants for a 1900-acre/$680 million dollar new town development, I prevented costly delays by reducing agency review time and ensuring project approval with appropriate planning and design concepts. This saved the developer hundreds of thousands of dollars in additional consultant fees and penalty payments for an extension of the land-purchase option.

I have nine years' combined experience in civil engineering, land planning, and urban design. I graduated from the University of Washington with a B.A. in Urban Planning.

I will call you next week to arrange a time when we might meet briefly to discuss my background and your future needs.

Sincerely,

Roger Cricky

❖

1298 N. Rosewood Avenue
Portland, Oregon 97211
(503) 682-9874

March 8, 1992

Don Harris
Vice President, Sales and Marketing
MicroCad
4309 Sepulveda Blvd North
Los Angeles, California 90030

Dear Mr. Harris,

I am currently looking at sales management positions with medium-sized high tech manufacturers. During the last 15 years I have worked for Datacomp and Syngestics and am currently district sales manager for a major manufacturer of teleprocessing equipment.

I was given a mandate three years ago to strengthen the Pacific Northwest district. During that time we have increased sales an average of 35% annually, the highest rate in the company. I'm known as a motivator. I work closely with my staff to develop marketing strategies and I give them the independence they need to be effective. In 1987 we led the six districts in the region in gaining new accounts, with 84.

I've been successful in both sales and sales management. As a senior account manager for six years with Datacomp, I took my territory from a ranking of 19th nationally to 7th and exceeded quota each year. I got my start in the industry with Syngestics. As a field marketing support rep for two years, my district exceeded its sales quota each year. Then as area supervisor for three years, I supervised six field marketing support engineers. The staff was rated number one in the region for providing technical support, two years in a row.

With a history of success behind me, I believe I can contribute to the further growth of MicroCad. I am strong in marketing, sales training, staff recruiting, and staff development. I will call you next week to learn about your future plans.

Sincerely,

Paul Sanderson

Writing an effective marketing letter requires that you first have a results-oriented resume. Once the resume is complete, the marketing letter almost writes itself. In fact, the results statements used in the marketing letter can come almost word for word from the resume.

The primary portion of any marketing letter is a description of your results and experience. To write a strong marketing letter, review your resume and think through how you want to summarize your background. If you have four to six key projects or results that can be quantified, simply describe them, as was done in the first sample marketing letter. If your background does not lend itself to that approach, the more narrative form will work best for you. Although names of companies are usually not mentioned, you can mention them if you so choose. Sometimes people will mention only well known companies. Even dates or time periods can be mentioned, but are not usually necessary.

Remember, the marketing letter is not a resume. The reader is not expecting to know everything about you. Your goal is to have impact. Your letter should cause the person to recognize your value and to remember you when you call. Write like you would in a letter. Let it flow. Take a look at your qualifications statement in your resume. Perhaps it can be included almost as is. If you are going to emphasize results, they can be lifted almost word for word from your resume, although you'll probably want to make some minor changes. Since your resume was written in telegraphic style, with incomplete sentences and certain words removed, you'll need to adapt the resume to the marketing letter. All sentences should be complete sentences.

Lead-ins for your results could be worded:

You may be interested in my labor negotiating experience. Some of my additional accomplishments are:

❖

My six years in customer relations could be valuable to you. This experience includes:

❖

If your advertising department needs a person with strong experience, you may be interested in what I've done.

If you choose to describe past jobs, as in the third example, phrases can again be lifted from the resume. Since this is a marketing letter, you may choose to describe only the last three jobs, even if in the resume five were described. Don't be concerned if your resume and marketing letter have similar phrases in them; no one will notice.

A good closing paragraph for your marketing letter might include a summary of your background, such as the number of years in your field, and information about your degree and alma mater. The final paragraph then prepares the reader for any follow-up contact you might make. In most cases this will be a follow-up phone call.

If the person is local you would usually request a 10–15 minute meeting and indicate so in the letter. If the person is out of state, but is likely to be in your area in the next two or three months, you would request an appointment when the person is in the area. If the person is out of state and would unlikely visit your area, you'll have to sell yourself by phone.

Each marketing letter should be individually typed and addressed to the person with the power to hire. By supplying a word processing service with ten or more names at a time, you should be able to keep your costs down to about two dollars for each letter and envelope. There will be an initial inputting charge for the letter, but after that you'll be paying primarily for printing time, plus the inputting time for the additional names and addresses.

OTHER USES OF THE MARKETING LETTER

The marketing letter is a very flexible tool. It can even function as a substitute for a resume when responding to a help wanted ad. Sometimes, no matter how well written your resume is, it may not work well in response to a particular job listing. Perhaps the job would make an excellent use of your talents, but requires experience you don't have. Traditionally one would write a customized cover letter and possibly even modify the resume. Using the marketing letter approach the entire letter would be geared to the specific job. Of course you would probably keep in major sections of your standard marketing letter, but it would be customized throughout.

Perhaps your most applicable experience occurred five years ago. With the marketing letter you could mention it first and indicate how many years you did that work. The exact dates would not be mentioned.

Although I recommend that you send marketing letters to specific people, with the intention of following up by phone, they can also be used in mass mailings. Even if you do not intend to follow up with a phone call, I still recommend that you invest the time to identify the person with the power to hire. However, if you choose not to do so, address the letter to a specific title, such as Personnel Director, Chief Engineer, or Accounting Manager. Because it is a letter, and does not have the appearance of a traditional resume, it is more likely to be delivered to the most appropriate person. With this approach it is easy and fast to send out the same mailing two months later if you have not accepted another position by that time. Your success rate will be lower with this method than if you followed up by phone—quick and easy is its main selling point. Please, however, do not use this method just as an excuse to avoid the more productive and effective follow-up methods discussed.

RESUME, COVER LETTER, AND MARKETING LETTER WORKING TOGETHER

The best way to see how a resume, marketing letter, and cover letter work together is to see a sample of each for the same person. The resume was written first, followed by the marketing letter. The greatest time was spent on the resume, making the marketing letter quite easy and quick to write. The cover letter borrowed some elements from the marketing letter, and it also was easy and quick to write.

RANDAL JOHNSON
4045 NW Abilene
Denver, Colorado 80239
(303) 765-8967

OBJECTIVE: Regional Manager

QUALIFICATIONS

Strong background in trucking with 18 years of management experience. Consistently increase market share and profitability. In a sales capacity, bring in large national accounts and significantly increase revenue from established accounts.

EDUCATION

A.A. - Business Management, Reginald Community College (1971-1974)

EMPLOYMENT

Ryan Freight 12/81-Present

TERMINAL MANAGER, - Denver, CO 7/85-Present. Responsible for the total operation and sales throughout Colorado. Planned and implemented a break bulk operation in 1986 and within two years, reduced shipment time through break bulk to 16 hours per shipment, versus the industry average of 28 hours.

Expanded the account base to include major national accounts such as Bendix, Control Data, Goodyear, and Motorola, and ultimately attained "prime general commodity status" with each of them. Through improved sales and customer service efforts, have increased revenue from $4 million to $19.5 million. Terminal has consistently ranked among the top five performers in customer service and on-time deliveries within the 42 terminal system. Won the 1991 award for the "best average revenue per shipment."

TERMINAL MANAGER - Portland, OR 12/81-7/85. Managed sales and operations for Oregon and increased revenue 74%. Significantly improved the transit service for Oregon accounts into the Rocky Mountain and Southwest regions. Took Ryan from 8th in market share to 4th in the Oregon market.

Longrider Lines 8/73-12/81

TERMINAL MANAGER - Scranton, PA 2/78-12/81. Established primary general commodity carrier status with numerous accounts including GTE, Sears, Ralston Purina, and Mattel. Terminal received annual regional awards in '79, '80, and '81 for exceeding revenue and on-time delivery goals. Took the terminal from the 3rd lowest rated terminal in the 15 terminal region, to 4th highest.

Prior positions with Longrider: Operations Manager, Scranton, PA 2/76-2/78; Supervisor, Terminal Operations, Scranton, PA 1/75-2/76; Management Trainee, Pittsburgh, PA 1/74-1/75; Checker/Loader, Reading, PA 8/73-1/74.

Typeface: Times Roman

With the resume in place the marketing letter below was easy to write.

4045 NW Abilene
Denver, Colorado 80239
(303) 765-8967

5/7/92

Ron Pitts
President
B&N Freightlines
1287 Wacker Drive
Chicago, Illinois 60626

Dear Mr. Pitts,

I have a strong background in the trucking industry gained during 18 years of management experience. With each company and at each of the three terminals managed, I significantly increased market share and quickly increased profitability. At each terminal I achieved one of the best on-time delivery records in the industry. I am now looking for a regional management position.

I have broad sales and marketing experience. At each terminal I devoted 40-50% of my time to marketing, sales, and sales management. Throughout my career I have brought in large national accounts and substantially increased the revenue from established accounts. I have achieved primary carrier status with such accounts as Bendix, Control Data, Goodyear, Motorola, GTE, Sears, Mattel, and Ralston Purina.

With my current employer, our Denver terminal won the annual award for the "best average revenue per shipment" in competition with the 42 terminals in the system.

I have turned problem terminals completely around and I have strengthened those already doing well. I took one terminal from being the 3rd lowest rated terminal (out of 15) to 4th highest in a three-year period. I will call you next week to learn more about any opportunities which may come up in the next few months.

Sincerely,

Randal Johnson

With the marketing letter in place, Randal's standard cover letter was a snap.

4045 NW Abilene
Denver, Colorado 80239
(303) 765-8967

5/17/92

Jeff Smalwun
President
RoadRider Freightlines
2312 Hennepin Avenue
Minneapolis, Minnesota 55403

Dear Mr. Smalwun,

I have a strong background in all aspects of trucking line management. At each of the four terminals I've managed, I have significantly improved on-time records, revenue, market share, and profitability. I am now looking for a regional manager's position with responsibility for 4-8 terminals.

I have broad experience in both sales and operations. I have brought in large national accounts, and increased revenue with existing accounts. On the operations side I have taken over two terminals which were among the worst in the company. Within 10 months both were profitable for the first time in years. I came up through the ranks in the trucking business, so I have hands on experience in virtually all aspects of operations. I also have extensive experience with budgets and working with state and federal agencies.

I would very much like to meet with you to describe my background in more detail. I look forward to hearing from you.

Sincerely

Randal Johnson

Using marketing letters is a very effective way of getting appointments with those who have the power to hire. Be sure to send your marketing letter to a specific person by name and title. Your marketing letter is always sent alone. It is never accompanied by a resume.

Part Three
Winning At
Interviewing

WINNING AT INTERVIEWING

Elbert Hubbard, a nineteenth century writer once wrote, "There's something rare, something finer far, something more scarce than ability. It's the ability to recognize ability." That quote summarizes the entire interviewing process. The interviewer's challenge is to recognize ability; your challenge is to sell yourself so thoroughly that the interviewer cannot possibly fail to recognize *your* ability.

This chapter is about learning how to sell yourself. While the typical job hunter gets sweaty palms just thinking about interviews, you can go into each interview with confidence, looking forward to the challenge that each interview presents. You'll know how to answer all of the difficult questions. You'll know how to overcome objections. Most importantly, you'll know how to get job offers.

This chapter will give you a thorough understanding of the psychology of interviewing as well as the principles of interviewing. You will understand what is going on in the mind of the interviewer, enabling you to respond effectively to both predictable and unpredictable events. When you've gained the self-assurance that comes from interviewing well, you will begin enjoying interviews.

THE INTERVIEWING SCALE

It is useful to think of interviewing as a process in which your skills, attributes, and potential will be weighed on a balance scale against those of other candidates. At the end of the interviewing cycle, whoever has the most weight on his or her side of the scale will get the job offer. During an interview, weights are continually being added or subtracted from the scale, depending on the quality of your answers. By answering each question as effectively as possible, each of your answers will carry a little more weight than the answers of those who are less prepared than you. After the final interview there will be no doubt who should get the job.

The balance scale metaphor also demonstrates the importance of always using your best example and telling it vividly. Assume that you have a great example that would add two pounds to your side of the scale, but under the stress of the interview, you're not able to recall it. Instead, you remember an example that's worth only one pound. Repeatedly forgetting your best examples and substituting them with less impressive examples, could easily cost you several pounds on your side of the scale. Unless your background has placed you head and shoulders above the competition, this failure to present your best examples may cost you the job offer.

INTERVIEWING PRINCIPLES

Effective interviewing is an art which can be learned, and the pay-offs can be tremendous. You'll work so hard to get each interview that it would be a shame to go into an interview unprepared. By knowing what to expect and by preparing for all of the difficult questions you'll encounter, you will greatly enhance your chance of receiving the job offer. The following fourteen principles provide you with an overview of things you should consider before going into an interview.

1. An interview is simply an opportunity for two people to meet and determine whether an employer-employee relationship will prove beneficial to both parties.

2. Interviewing is a two-way street. You're not begging for a job, you're an equal.

3. The employer is actually on your side. He or she has a need and has every reason to hope you are the right person to meet it. Keep the employer on your side. This requires active listening. Try to detect what the employer's real needs are.

4. An objection is not a rejection, it is a request for more information. If the employer states, "You don't have as much experience as we normally want," the employer is not rejecting you. In fact, the person could be totally sold on you but for this one concern. Your task is to sell yourself and overcome that objection. You will do this by emphasizing your strengths, not by arguing.

5. Let the employer talk. You listen. The longer the employer talks at the beginning, the more you can learn

about the organization. This will help you formulate positive responses.

6. Increase your chance for a second interview by dressing properly, being on time, listening intently, demonstrating potential and enthusiasm, appearing relaxed, providing brief, well thought-out responses, and asking a few intelligent questions.

7. Hiring decisions are based mostly on emotion. Do I like her? Will we get along? Will she accept criticism and be a good team worker? Being liked by the employer is just as important as having the qualifications.

8. Concentrate on giving examples of your accomplishments. Accomplishments demonstrate your potential. Stress how you can benefit the organization.

9. Be yourself, but also be your best. If you tend to be overly aggressive, consciously tone it down during the interview. If you have strong opinions on everything and like to express them, keep them to yourself. If you tend to be too quiet and reserved, try to be a little more outgoing and enthusiastic during the interview.

10. Use examples to back up any statements you make. Be prepared for questions like "Are you good with details?" "Are you a hard worker?" "Can you handle difficult people?" You can begin your response with, "Yes, I *am* good with details. For example ..."

11. Be able to explain any details included in your resume, such as accomplishments or job duties. You can use your resume to predict many of the questions that will be asked. Practice describing your job duties in the most concise way possible.

12. Showing confidence in yourself will create a favorable impression. Such confidence can come only from truly knowing yourself and recognizing your own potential.

13. Send a thank-you note the evening of the interview. Some employers have never received a thank-you note, yet this simple courtesy frequently makes the difference between selection and rejection.

14. Relax and enjoy your interviews.

INTERVIEWING TIPS

Know the time and place. Leave nothing to chance. Know the exact time and location of your interview. Purchase a pocket calendar and put all of your appointments in it with the name and correct spelling of the person you'll be meeting, as well as the person's title, and the name and address of the organization. If you're unsure about the location, drive by the day before so you'll know exactly how to get there. Leave early for the appointment to allow for traffic tie-ups or other problems.

Dress appropriately. Stories abound about men who have gone to interviews in jeans, obviously unbathed, with dirty fingernails or unkempt hair, and women who have attended interviews wearing curlers or low-cut cocktail dresses. Those folks did not get job offers. Some use their clothing to make a statement, justifying such dress with the self-defeating logic, "If they don't like what I wear, I don't want to work there anyway." Such an attitude, however, only hurts the applicant.

The emphasis is on appropriate dress; there is no rule which fits all people. For male and female professionals, a conservative and properly-fitting business suit is recommended. Pant suits for women may be acceptable on the job but should rarely be worn for interviews. If in doubt, dress up. You may know in advance that office dress is casual, but don't use that as a cue to dress down. It's fine to be dressed

Robert read Dress For Success *and had his hair styled. He just forgot one thing.*

in a suit while being interviewed by someone dressed casually. Everyone knows that when appropriate, people can dress down, but they have much less confidence that people are willing to dress up. Scents used by men or women should be subtle, with just a *touch* used. Jewelry should be conservative and limited. Unless you know it is highly accepted, a man's earring should be removed for the interview. Beards and mustaches are generally accepted when nicely groomed. Shower before a day of interviewing and make sure your shoes are well shined.

Bring pen and pad. When the interviewer gives you some key information, you'll want to have a pen and pocket-sized note pad handy. As soon as you get back to your car, jot down your impressions about the job and the organization. List any questions that you feel did not get adequately answered. While I prefer the approach of taking notes immediately after the interview, some people would rather take notes during the interview. If you take notes during the interview, do it as unobtrusively as possible and maintain eye contact as you take your notes. Your notes may be a little hard to read as a result, but you can always rewrite them later. The important thing is to give total concentration to what is being said by the interviewer.

Remember the interviewer's name. Nothing is so important to people as their name. Anthony Medley, in his book *Sweaty Palms,* recalls an applicant who kept referring to him as Mr. Melody. She didn't get the job. My pet peeve is people who insist on putting an r in Washington, making it Warshington. If you're unsure of the pronunciation of the interviewer's name, ask the receptionist. Do not call the person by his or her first name unless invited to do so. When meeting a woman, ask the receptionist if the interviewer prefers Mrs. or Ms.

Shake hands firmly. Offer your hand as soon as the interviewer makes the first move. If you are a woman, offer your hand first if you feel comfortable doing so since men are sometimes cautious about offering a hand to a woman. Most people like a firm handshake but detest both the limp and bone crushing types.

Wait before you sit. Allow the interviewer to invite you to be seated and to indicate where to sit. If no indication is made, you can ask or simply sit down in the chair which is most obvious.

Look for clues about interests. Photographs or mementos on a desk or wall can often provide clues regarding a person's interests. Discussing a shared interest can help build rapport at the beginning of an interview. For example, if a person's office has a nautical theme, it may mean that the person loves to sail or study the subject, or it may simply mean that this person likes the visual effect of such a theme. Rather than assume too much, broach the subject with an exploratory question such as, "Do you sail?" The person may respond with, "I love to sail, how about you?" If you share a love of sailing, the two of you will probably have an interesting conversation and the interviewer will begin with the belief that the two of you share numerous values and interests. That will help you. If you don't sail, you might respond with, "No, I don't sail but I've always wanted to," or "No, but I love to watch sail boats. It must be an interesting sport." The interviewer might then share a few past experiences before getting fully into the interview. Listen attentively. Avoid overstating your interest or experience in a hobby, however; it could come back to haunt you.

No smoking or gum chewing. If you're a smoker and your interviewer lights up a cigarette and offers you one, tactfully decline. You cannot fully sell yourself with a cigarette in your hand. Gum chewing during an interview is considered rude.

No profanity. Even if your interviewer uses salty language, keep yours totally free of profanity. Even among those who swear themselves, hearing it out of the mouth of an interviewee is a turnoff. Some interviewers will even use profanity as a test to see if you will join in. Don't.

Keep it interesting. Throughout the interview you must keep your responses interesting. One of the worst sins of interviewing is to bore the interviewer. Long-winded, rambling responses will cause the interviewer to lose interest. Responses that are concise and packed with key information, however, will maintain the interviewer's interest. When you're through, the interviewer may be so interested in the experience you've just described that he or she will want to know more and will ask a follow-up question. Anytime you see evidence that you've lost the interviewer, finish your response as quickly as possible.

Go in with an agenda. The employer has an agenda and so should you. In your pocket-sized notebook, using your own shorthand, list the points you want to get across and the examples you want to give. List a few questions that you can ask if the employer invites you to ask them. Toward the end of the interview, you can glance at your agenda to see if you've missed anything.

Practice your intuition. Throughout the interview try to detect the biases of the interviewer. Everyone has biases, and sensing the biases of your interviewer can be a real advantage to you. For example, if your interviewer appears to be quite conservative, you as a liberal would be careful during any discussion of social issues. Other biases might include a belief that teamwork in projects is the secret to greater competitiveness, or a belief that if quality is emphasized, profit will follow. When you detect a bias that you personally hold as well, look for opportunities to demonstrate that you share those beliefs. It is human nature that most managers prefer hiring people who are like them.

Ask about needs. If you are interviewing with someone other than the hiring manager, ask about the needs or challenges being faced in the department. Such people are often less reticent to share these types of things than hiring managers.

Detect the problems and challenges being faced. By listening intently and by using your intuition, you'll perceive problems which the interviewer had no intention of revealing. Employers avoid revealing their "dirty laundry," so you must use your intuition to detect it. You need not be absolutely certain that a particular problem exists before you share a pertinent example from your past. If you address the suspected problem by sharing an accomplishment, you'll score points. If you hit a bull's-eye, you'll score more points. Be subtle about it, however. You would not say, "It sounds like you have some real serious problems with inventory control. Let me tell you about some of the things I've done in that area." Instead you might say, "It sounds like you may have some challenges in the inventory control area. Perhaps I could share some similar challenges I've faced." Referring to something as a challenge rather than a problem is a much more tactful way of discussing an issue.

Don't ask throwaway questions. In the first and second interview you will usually have the opportunity to ask only a few questions, so they should be questions which are truly important to you. Never ask a question just because you think it will show how smart or knowledgeable you are. Often people will pick up an interesting tidbit during their research and then will try to squeeze in a question about it in order to look good. The problem with this, however, is that most employers can detect the true intent behind such a question. Instead of scoring points, such questions can actually cause you to lose points.

Don't assume. Many an interviewee has gotten into trouble by assuming too much. Don't assume the interviewer knows exactly what he wants or needs in an employee. And don't assume the interviewer knows all the right questions to ask. Help the interviewer decide that you are the right person by revealing as many strengths as possible during the interview. Don't assume that you did well or poorly in the interview. People have left an interview feeling they performed masterfully only to learn that the interview was a disaster. Others, who felt certain they'd blown it, have been surprised to get an offer. After each interview, spend a few minutes evaluating how you did, determine how you'll do better next time, and then drop any consideration of how poorly you did. The energy you could spend beating yourself up over what you assume has been a poor interview is totally self-defeating.

Leave the interview on a positive note. As you exit the interview, express your interest in the position. Do not ask how you did, as doing so can be embarrassing to both you and the interviewer. It is fine, however, to ask what the next step will be and how soon you might expect an answer.

Get invited back for a second interview. Your goal during the first interview is to get invited back for the second round. Everything you say and do should be geared to that purpose.

Send a thank-you note. Sending a thank-you note, even one as short as three sentences, can be one of the most important things you do. When employers receive thank-you notes, they immediately remember you. Sending a note also makes you stand out positively because so few people send them. Most of all, you should send a thank-you note because it is the courteous thing to do. Thank-you notes can be handwritten or typed. Stationery that is monarch-sized (7" x 10"), or the standard 8½" x 11", is generally preferred to sending a card, especially one that says "thank you" on it. A typical thank-you note might read like this:

> Thank you for the opportunity to meet you on Thursday. The position sounds quite (enjoyable, interesting, challenging, etc.). I believe I can make a significant contribution. (You could then expand on how you would contribute). If you would like any additional information, please contact me at ...

> Thanks for the interview. I would welcome the opportunity to work for (name of company).

This is just one example. It's hard to go wrong as long as you say thanks.

Follow-up phone calls may be appropriate. Do not even consider a follow-up phone call unless you've already sent a thank-you note. A follow-up call can be made to express interest and thanks, or to clarify a point. You can come right out and say, "I just wanted you to know how interested I am in the position." Because you may be interrupting the person, keep it short. You can also ask about the status of the position, but don't do this unless it is past the date when you were told a decision would be made.

KEY INTERVIEWING SKILLS

Active Listening

Active listening is perhaps the most critical interviewing skill you need to develop. Active listening can be defined as high-level listening in which your entire attention is focused on the person speaking—your body, face, and eyes all confirm you are listening. Through active listening you'll pick up the cues and clues that the interviewer is consciously and unconsciously giving you. If you are well prepared for the interview, you will be able to process the clues to determine the interviewer's needs and biases. This will enable you to respond appropriately to those needs or biases at an opportune time. Attentive listeners are more highly regarded by employers than inattentive listeners.

Do not allow your mind to wander. Not only will you miss key information, but more than one interviewee has been embarrassed by not hearing a question and then having to ask that it be repeated.

To be an active listener you must truly want to hear everything the person is saying. Too often people feign listening and simply wait for a break so they can jump in with their opinions. Allow the person to pause, collect his or her thoughts, and then continue. Your willingness to allow the person to continue sends a strong, positive message to the person, and will cause the person to provide you with more information. After you ask a question it is particularly important to let the person know you are actively listening to the response.

Do not be concerned if the interviewer does a lot of talking at the beginning of the interview. That's exactly what you want. You'll have plenty of opportunities to speak. In the meantime, listening carefully will give you an opportunity to learn valuable things about the person, the job, and the organization.

"Listen" with your body. Be relaxed, but don't slouch. You should always be looking at the speaker, but with a gentle look, never a stare. When people speak, they often look away from the listener for 5–20 seconds, but when their eyes return to you, your eyes should be gently looking at them. When the speaker's eyes return to you, they should not catch you looking at your watch, looking out the window, or looking at objects in the office.

As you listen, you should be taking in and interpreting everything. While listening, part of your brain is deciphering the information and deciding what to do with it. For example, employers are often cautious about mentioning serious problems that exist, yet will often allude to them in obscure ways. If you aren't listening actively the words might go right past you and an opportunity would be missed. The interviewer might indirectly indicate that the company is experiencing high turnover and, thus, is looking for evidence of strong company loyalty. By sensing the need, you could provide evidence that demonstrates you have the kind of loyalty the company desires.

You will approach each interview with your own agenda, looking for opportunities to sell certain skills which you feel are important for the job. You must also be flexible. You may pick up clues from the interviewer that the skills you had planned to emphasize are not as important as some other skills you possess. Only a person who has been actively listening will recognize the need for a change in strategy, then make the appropriate shift.

By concentrating on what the interviewer says, you'll be better able to use the information later in the interview. For example, the interviewer may have presented evidence that the position requires an ability to quickly gain the confidence of customers. A half hour may pass before you have the opportunity to cover that talent. Because you listened, you'll remember.

Do not assume that just because you have years of experience you are a good listener. Most of us have learned how to appear attentive with the appropriate nods, uh-huhs, and an occasional "I know what you mean." You undoubtedly can recognize fake listening, and you don't like it. A good listener makes the speaker feel that everything said is of great interest to the listener and that there is a desire to hear the whole story. Real listening occurs when you hear and understand the words, you properly interpret the feelings behind the words, and the person feels he or she has been listened to.

Preparation

Where interviewing is concerned, there is no substitute for preparation and practice. Fortunately for you, most people spend little time preparing for interviews. They will get a good night's sleep, polish their shoes, take a shower, and hope for the best. Their attitude is, "Since I don't know what the interviewer will ask, I'll just give it my best shot."

But you can anticipate and prepare for the questions that will be asked in an interview. There are approximately 75 basic questions, all others being variations of these. Then there are the technical questions that can be asked of people in your field. These too can be predicted. Questions will also arise from information you've provided in your resume, particularly your accomplishments.

A complete discussion of the most commonly asked questions follows this introduction on interviewing. In each case, the principle behind answering the question is discussed, with an example often included.

To prepare your responses, simply jot down the points you want to make. Do not try to develop word-for-word responses. That would require memorization which is not recommended—if you forget a point during an interview, you could become flustered and completely blow the response. Giving memorized answers can also make you seem mechanical. Instead of memorizing, you should practice your responses several times. This will help you feel confident and relaxed. Say your answers slightly differently each time so they have a ring of spontaneity.

Thorough preparation takes time. Preparing and practicing your responses to the 75 basic questions, the 5–8 technical questions you suspect could be asked, and the 8–10 questions likely to come off your resume, might require 10–15 hours. The effort spent, however, will pay big dividends.

Be Yourself, Be Your Best

The material in this chapter will provide you with many techniques to help you perform successfully during an interview. When you're using techniques, however, there is a danger of becoming too mechanical in your responses. As you use these techniques remember to **Be Yourself**. By acting natural, relaxed, and confident, you will do well. My advice is also to **Be Your Best**. It is important, for example, to show enthusiasm during an interview. However, you may not be a naturally enthusiastic person. During an interview then, you must consciously turn up the enthusiasm a notch or two. You are still being you, but you are being the best you are capable of. You should not try to raise your level of enthusiasm four or five notches above what is natural for you. That would be asking too much and would be self-defeating.

Control The Content, Not The Interview

Job seekers are sometimes advised to take control of interviews, but using that tactic on an experienced interviewer can backfire. My advice is to let the interviewer control the questions while you control the content. Controlling the content means that you will be deciding what to say and which examples to give. That is all the control you need.

You can greatly influence the questions by having a resume filled with results. You'll be asked to expand on those results. This will give you wonderful opportunities to add weight to your side of the balance scale.

Develop a game plan and know the points you want to cover and the experiences you want to describe. Then look for the earliest opportunity to "slide" that information comfortably into the interview.

Getting More Information About The Job

Interviewers generally spend several minutes at the beginning of an interview describing the job and its requirements. Too frequently, however, the information you have about the job is still sketchy when the interviewer suddenly asks a really tough question. Without knowledge of where the organization is headed or what challenges it's facing, providing an effective answer will be difficult.

Let's say that the interviewer begins by asking about your strengths without providing you with much background information about the job or the organization. Since you have many strengths and want to emphasize the right ones, it is important to have more information. You could respond by stating, "I've got a lot to offer, but in order to cover just the right points, it would help a lot to know more about the position and what your needs are." This will cause the interviewer to realize that further information is needed. Even after the interviewer gives you more information, you can still ask two or three questions to further clarify the job requirements. Practice how you will respond when such difficult questions arise early in the interview. This will give you the confidence to request more information. The success of your interview may depend on it.

Let Others Speak For You

When you're answering questions in an interview, let what others have said illustrate positive things about you. For example, in response to a question you might say, "My boss felt some of my most valuable attributes were..." Granted, that person is not there to confirm what you've just said, but if you have successfully established your credibility, your statement will be accepted.

Learn To Talk About Yourself

During an interview you will spend 40–60% of the time talking about yourself. Much of that time will be spent describing experiences, but you will also be describing the *type* of person you are. The interviewer will try to learn what type of person you are by asking questions like, "Tell me about yourself," and "How would you describe yourself?" or "What would your friends say about you?" The problem with this is that most people spend very little time talking about themselves. People spend a lot of time talking about what they do—the restaurants, plays, concerts, sports events, and vacation spots they've been to—but they rarely discuss the *kind* of person they are. No wonder interviewing is difficult for most people.

Think about it. When was the last time you discussed whether you are a pragmatist or an idealist, or whether you are compassionate, easy-going, flexible, or resourceful? Since you're not used to it, you may not be very good at it. It takes practice. For that reason I strongly suggest that you first complete the personality skills exercise on page 317, as well as the temperament and motivators exercises found in Appendix A. After you write about yourself, find someone you can share your thoughts with. If you can't find someone, simply share your thoughts with a tape recorder. Just hearing yourself talk about yourself will help you feel more comfortable and will improve your effectiveness in interviews.

Research The Company

Researching an organization can yield big dividends during an interview. Research can reveal problems or challenges the organization is facing, and can enable you to select in advance appropriate experiences you should describe in the interview. At the minimum you should know what the organization's products and services are, how long they've been in business, and something about their growth and reputation. If you're working with a recruiter or agency counselor, they should be able to supply you with valuable information. Even with that help, however, you should gather information on your own as well. Researching the organization will help you determine whether it is right for you. It will also enable you to answer questions more effectively. Employers commonly ask: "What do you know about us?" Harold, a graduating senior, once suffered through this question. As the very first question, a campus recruiter asked Harold, "What do you know about us?" Harold paused and squirmed. When the recruiter finally asked, "Did you read our recruiting literature?" Harold had to admit he had not, and the recruiter then coldly stated, "This interview is over." Although this was an extremely embarrassing experience, the recruiter actually did Harold a big favor—he never made that mistake again.

Sometimes it is even possible to learn about the interviewer. Check with your contacts to determine whether they or anyone they know is acquainted with the interviewer. Try to learn about the interviewer's education, biases, hot buttons, and general background. Then weave the information you gather into the interview. Do this carefully so you don't give the impression you are merely trying to make a good impression.

Julie learned from inside sources that her prospective boss was a sailing nut, but she didn't quite know how to weave her knowledge into the interview.

THE NINE TYPES OF INTERVIEWS

There are nine basic types of interviews: telephone screening interviews, screening interviews, nondirected interviews, stress interviews, group interviews, board interviews, lunch interviews, behavior-based interviews, and series interviews.

TELEPHONE INTERVIEWS

Telephone interviews are always screening interviews. In five minutes the interviewer can often gather all the information necessary to determine if a full interview is warranted. When local employers call, the telephone interview is usually quite short, typically no more than five or ten minutes. Employers calling from out of state, on the other hand, may talk to you for half an hour. Those they choose to interview will be flown in and put up in a hotel for the night, so they must do everything possible to determine in advance that the person is a solid job candidate.

Job seekers are often told in job finding books to completely avoid telephone screening interviews. While not impossible, this is often difficult to do and really serves no purpose. While the process may seem unfair in that it may screen you out before you've had a chance to demonstrate your worth, the telephone screening interview is with us nonetheless.

So if you can't avoid it, determine to sell yourself. Make the interviewer want to meet you. Let your enthusiasm sparkle. Sell your expertise, your related experience, and your potential. Tell the person you are very interested in the position and that you would like an interview.

Telephone interviews often catch people by surprise. For that reason, don't hesitate to tell the person that you've been concentrating heavily on other matters and that you'd like a few minutes to get yourself ready. Then offer to call the person back within five or ten minutes. The first thing you would do is go to your employer cards and read the information you have on the organization. Then get mentally prepared to sell yourself.

SCREENING INTERVIEWS

If the company is large enough to have a human resources department, the first interview will often be conducted by a personnel specialist, recruiter, or interviewer. These people interview frequently and often have extensive training in interviewing techniques. Their interviews will generally be planned in advance, and applicants will typically be asked the same questions. The screening interview is generally quite short—its purpose is to eliminate those applicants who are obviously not qualified. The problem is that the screener rarely has a full understanding of what the job entails. This can be particularly frustrating for applicants who have lots of potential but not much direct experience, since they are usually screened out during the resume phase or after the screening interview. There are numerous things you can do, however, to make it past the screening stage.

It helps to understand the motivation of the screener. A screener will never be criticized for screening out someone who has potential but lacks the desired background. If someone slips through, who a manager feels was completely unqualified, the screener is going to hear about it. That screener will not take such a chance a second time. With this in mind, your challenge is to show that you meet or exceed the minimum qualifications. Your only goal is to be passed on to the hiring manager.

A screening interview will consist primarily of probing questions designed to determine your technical competence. The screener may even have a checklist which will be gone through quickly to determine how much experience you have in each area. Questions will also be asked to reveal inconsistencies. These screeners will also be the ones most likely to check out your references. While the emphasis is on technical competence, they will also screen out those whose personalities are obviously not right or those who clearly would not fit in that organization's corporate culture. Don't be concerned if the screener seems rather impersonal—you may be the twentieth person interviewed that day. Simply do everything you can to gain the screener's seal of approval.

NONDIRECTED INTERVIEWS

Nondirected interviews rely primarily on open-ended questions. The interviewer is generally untrained and is simply asking a series of questions without a specific goal in mind. To do well in these interviews, remember that while you do not control the direction of the interview, you do control the content. Even if the interviewer seems unfocused, you should be very focused. You should enter the interview with your own agenda, making sure you share the experiences that will sell you. Interviewers have been known to run out of questions during this type of interview. If this happens, you might take some degree of control by saying, "Perhaps I should share with you some of my strengths that might prove helpful in this position." If the interviewer indicates a willingness for you to share this information, take it from there.

STRESS INTERVIEWS

Stress interviews, which are rarely used these days, consist of questions and situations designed to put the interviewee under stress. The theory behind this type of questioning is that the interviewee will reveal how he or she will actually handle stress when it occurs on the job. The stress applied, however, is usually so artificial that little is learned. Classic examples from the 50s included making the person being interviewed sit in a chair that had one leg significantly shorter than the others, or positioning the interviewee so a bright light was shining directly in his or her eyes.

Another form of stress questioning involves asking rapid fire questions so a person barely has time to think. A client once had an interview in which two interviewers sat at opposite ends of a rectangular table. While answering one person's questions, his back was turned to the other. These two interviewers would each ask yet another question before the interviewee had finished the previous one, so he was constantly turning one way and then the next. Had he realized that he was being put through a stress interview, he could have simply turned to the one asking the fresh question and stated, "That's an important question and I would like to answer it, but before I do I feel I need to fully answer Mr. X's question." Using this approach once or twice would have stopped their childish game. Another form of stress is to ask impossible questions and then observe how the person handles it.

Although the pure stress interview is seldom used, we find that employers still like to put people under stress at different times during an interview.

A common form of stress is to use silence. You may have just completed an answer, yet the interviewer maintains silence and simply looks at you. If you break the silence, you lose. If you were truly finished with your answer you should remain silent. Maintain a soft look at the interviewer and begin to silently count the seconds. It is almost guaranteed that the interviewer cannot hold out for more than 15 seconds. If you find it difficult to maintain eye contact during the silence, look down, but do not show any nervousness or discomfort with the situation.

The primary antidote to the stress interview is to simply recognize it. As soon as you realize the interviewer is intentionally putting you under stress, say to yourself, "Aha, I know what you're doing, and you're not going to get me to panic or get angry or become defensive." Then become assertive, as the person receiving the rapid fire questions should have.

GROUP INTERVIEWS

In a group interview you will find yourself with a group of candidates who are being observed by company officials. Although there will generally be a person who is leading the group interview, there may be other company employees who appear to be candidates. You won't know who they are, but they'll be closely observing what you say and how you behave. In some group processes the observers may be watching you from behind a one-way glass. In the group interview the observers are trying to determine how you interact with people. They may divide the candidates into groups and give them a task to work on. They will then observe who the natural leaders are and which people actively participate in the group process. Generally, the candidates who offer the least to the group receive lower ratings. One question some airlines have used when interviewing flight attendants was, "Why would you make a better flight attendant than the person to your right?" The best way to answer that question, or questions like it, is not to put the other person down, but to emphasize your own strengths.

BOARD INTERVIEWS

In the board interview two or more people interview you simultaneously, usually taking turns asking questions. Sometimes the questions have been determined in advance. In other board interviews you may be interviewed by five individuals who have their own separate agendas. In a board interview you'll often find that the only person really listening to your answer to a question is the person who asked it. Your primary goal is to make each member feel totally involved in the interview and all of your responses. You can do this by resisting the tendency to make eye contact only with the questioner. Keep each person involved by looking at each one and making each one feel important and attended to. Governments frequently use the board interview to narrow a field of candidates down to three. The department head then makes a final selection from among those three.

LUNCH INTERVIEWS

Lunch interviews tend to be more relaxed than other interviews, but they also require you to be more alert. Because of the relaxed nature of lunch interviews, it is all too easy to simply chat and talk about topics that may be interesting, but do not help you sell yourself. You must be sure to take the opportunity to sell yourself whenever possible. There is also a tendency to let down your guard during a lunch interview. While it is important to come across as genuine and willing to reveal yourself, you must also remember that even in this informal interview you are being judged, and therefore must take some care in what you reveal.

BEHAVIOR-BASED INTERVIEWS

Behavior-based interviewing consists of asking questions which enable the interviewer to know how you have actually reacted or behaved in certain types of situations. It has been confirmed that employers can more accurately determine those who will succeed on the job by identifying actual past behavior. Behavior-based interviewing is based on the concept that future behavior is best predicted by past behavior, and that future success is best predicted by past success. About 150,000 managers are being converted to this style of interviewing each year, and entire companies, Hewlett-Packard and Microsoft among them, are training all of their managers in the techniques.

While standard interviews consist of questions like, "Tell me about your last job," or "Why did you leave your last job?" behavior-based questions include:

Tell me about a time when you worked under an extremely tight deadline.

Tell me about a situation where you were particularly proud of the creativity you demonstrated.

Describe a situation where you had to deal with a difficult customer or coworker.

Can you see the difference in the responses that will be obtained in the behavior-based interview?

The behavior-based interview is one of the toughest types of interviews you will face, but if you are prepared, it can be the most enjoyable and challenging. Behavior-based interviews are usually conducted by people who have received extensive training in interviewing techniques. Every question is asked with a specific purpose and has been selected with great care. Managers prepare for the interviewing process by first analyzing the job and its requirements. During the analysis stage, the manager determines which technical skills and personal qualities are most needed to do the job.

The person who does best in behavioral interviews is the one who has taken the time to recall dozens of past experiences, and is prepared to share them in a vivid, yet concise manner. Practitioners of behavior-based interviewing report to me that most interviewees provide responses which are simply too general and sketchy. For example, a typical response to a question like, "Tell me about a time when you responded well to a high-stress situation," would be:

> Well, as you know, I work for Alaska Airlines, and we are constantly under pressure to meet the needs of customers who have lost their luggage or missed a connecting flight. You just can't survive here if you can't handle stress well. I think I do my best work under stress.

The response of the behavior-based interviewer to such an answer would be to push for specifics by saying something like "I appreciate your overview, but what I'd like is for you to give me a specific example when you were under a lot of stress and you really rose to the occasion." The behavior-based interviewer is like a bulldog who won't give up until the question has been properly answered. Those who are prepared to share specific examples really shine in these situations.

The behavior-based interviewer will typically have a list of 8–12 personal qualities and 5–10 technical skills which are deemed crucial to success on the job. Questions will have been selected to reveal that you have or don't have the required skills, knowledge, or experience. Because many of the questions will be difficult to answer, the interviewer will often encourage you to take as much time as you need to think of an example.

Another unique aspect of behavior-based interviewing is that you will be asked to describe situations in which you were not successful. In traditional interviews you may be asked one question about your greatest weakness, but that is usually the full extent of it. In a behavior-based interview, the positive question will usually be asked first, followed by a negative question. For example, a line of questioning may begin, "Tell me about a time when you faced a difficult interpersonal conflict with a boss or coworker and you were able to improve the situation." That question may be followed with, "No one is able to overcome all interpersonal conflicts. Describe a situation where no matter what you did, you just weren't able to resolve the conflict." You can see that this second question is particularly difficult. First, it may be very difficult to even think of such an example. Second, you may have serious reservation about sharing such an example, because it may show you in a bad light. Remember, everyone will be asked the same question; no one will be allowed to dodge it. The interviewer is using questions like these to determine whether you dealt with the conflict in a mature way, or whether you allowed your emotions and insecurities to get in the way of resolving it.

Another type of behavior-based interviewing places great emphasis on having you give extensive information about each job you've held. When using this style, the interviewer will ask for particular information about each position you've held. The information requested typically includes: job title, duties, major challenges you faced and how you handled them, most and least enjoyable aspects of the job, your greatest accomplishments, and your significant mistakes or disappointments. You will also be asked to describe each of your supervisors, including their strengths and weaknesses. Finally, you will be asked your reason for leaving. Then you will be asked focused questions about your learning ability, analysis skills, judgment, innovativeness, oral communications skills, management style, and many more. Not surprisingly, this type of interview can last as long as 2–3 hours, especially when interviewing for a management position.

As in any interview, preparation is the key to selling yourself effectively in a behavior-based interview. That preparation consists of recalling 30–40 accomplishments, expanding on 8–15 of your top accomplishments, and jotting down notes to help you recall dozens of other experiences, many of which may not have been accomplishments. In behavior-based interviews, you must be able to quickly recall many experiences, select the most appropriate one, and then describe it effectively. Recalling negative experiences is difficult but also necessary in this type of interview. People tend to forget negative experiences; when we do remember such experiences we resist talking about them.

There is a price to be paid, however, for not taking the time to recall dozens of experiences you've had. Interviewees are frequently caught unprepared when asked to describe a negative experience. Typically, the interviewee will be sifting through his or her experiences looking for an example, only to realize that time has just about run out. Suddenly an example comes to mind and the unprepared interviewee selects it, mostly out of desperation. As soon as the experience is described, the person realizes it's a bad example. The interviewee is now faced with a serious case of foot-in-mouth syndrome. The next several minutes can be spent trying to remove that foot—usually not very successfully.

The best way to prevent foot-in-mouth syndrome is to jot down notes about dozens of experiences. Begin by simply thinking about your current job. Then, in your own shorthand, list both the positive and negative experiences which pop into your mind. Allow yourself several writing sessions to compile your list. Come up with at least 50 experiences. These will be different from the 30–40 accomplishments which you will also have listed. By recalling so many positive and negative experiences, you will more easily recall an appropriate negative experience.

In behavior-based interviews you will always be given adequate time to think of an example. So once an example comes to mind, take five to ten seconds to quickly walk yourself through the experience to determine what the ramifications of using it will be. Those extra five to ten seconds could save you from sharing a story that you really did not want to tell.

Preparing for behavior-based interviews can take many hours, as you can readily see. The behavior-based interviewer wants you to be well prepared and wants to hear the very best example you have for each question. The better your responses, the better the interviewer can predict your success on the job. Since most people are not prepared to tell vivid stories which clearly demonstrate specific strengths and qualities, you can really set yourself apart by your preparation.

SERIES INTERVIEWS

The series interview consists of consecutive interviews with two or more people in the organization. Four or five interviews in one day is common. Typically, the interviewers have not met to determine who should ask certain questions or even to discuss the goal of the interview. After the interviews are completed, all of the interviewers will meet to discuss each person interviewed. While you certainly want to sell yourself to each person, the person who counts most is the hiring manager. Be sure you know in advance who that person is. It is rare to be interviewed by fewer than two people for anything other than entry-level positions.

You need to muster lots of energy to go through a series interview. It can be grueling to meet with four people over a 3–6 hour period. There is a tendency to forget what you said to whom. You may find yourself wondering, "Have I already shared that accomplishment with this person?" Except for one or two significant experiences that you might share with each interviewer, try to share a variety of stories and examples.

Before the interviewing begins, find out from the person arranging the interviews who you will be meeting with, and how much time to set aside. This is particularly important if the interviews will require that you take time off from work.

The most torturous interview I have ever heard of was told to me by a client. He flew in for his interview on Wednesday, and beginning Thursday morning, he interviewed with ten partners in a law firm over an eight-hour period. That evening he attended a party at the home of one of the partners and was in the spotlight throughout the party. He got back to his hotel room after midnight. At 7 a.m., he hopped a flight to another city where he began the interviewing process all over again with six partners at the home office of the law firm. Except for his five hours of sleep, this person was either on the hot seat (during the interviews) or on stage (during lunch and at the party) for 20 hours. He survived the experience, however, and is currently with that firm.

INTERVIEWING SECRETS

OVERCOMING OBJECTIONS

Performing well in interviews requires an ability to recognize the important difference between rejections and objections. Virtually everyone must overcome several objections during the interviewing process before a job offer is made. People who perceive an objection as a rejection, however, may become defensive or simply give up and assume all is lost. Thus, the failure to understand objections and differentiate them from rejection can cause some interviewees to sabotage their own success in an interview.

An Objection Is Not A Rejection

An objection is *not* a rejection. It is simply a request for more information. Good interviewees, like good salespeople, must learn to anticipate objections. Since cost is a common objection salespeople face, an effective salesperson might open with, "This is not the least expensive lawnmower on the market. But a recent survey showed that the average lawnmower lasts eight years, while ours are averaging over twelve years of trouble-free service." This way the objection may be overcome before it is ever expressed. It is important to anticipate an objection because once an objection is stated, it is much more difficult to neutralize or overcome.

The first step in overcoming objections is predicting what they will be and developing appropriate, effective responses to them. The following circumstances are likely to give rise to some types of objections: you were fired from your last job; you appear to be a job hopper; there is a major gap in your work history; you're changing careers; you don't have a college degree and you're applying for a position that normally requires one; you have three or more years of college education but never received a degree; you're over 50 years of age; or you have too little or too much experience. The list could go on. Objections can also arise if you lack a certain type of knowledge or experience the employer is looking for in an ideal candidate.

Sensing a potential objection is exactly what Pat did. Pat was interviewing for a job in which she would be training the staffs of client companies in how to use an accounting software package which cost several thousand dollars. The concern, which was never spoken directly but which was implied, was whether Pat could learn the package quickly enough to meet the employer's needs. Pat looked for the earliest opportunity to address this objection. Before the objection was directly mentioned, Pat shared that she had learned a complex accounting software package very quickly at her current job. As a result, the invoice error rate had decreased by 80%. Pat never stated that because she had learned the one package so quickly she could learn theirs as well. She didn't need to. Since the employer had not stated the objection, Pat was subtle in the way she dealt with it. She did, however, let them know how she had managed to learn the package so quickly—she had taken the manual home with her and studied it on her own time. Pat recalled that as she told her story, she could sense that her future supervisor was gaining confidence in her.

Since you will probably lack some desired skill or knowledge, look for ways to sell the fact that you learn quickly. If you are convinced that you have successfully conveyed the idea that you learn quickly, it may not be necessary to point out directly that the experience demonstrates your ability to learn quickly.

The value of anticipating objections is further demonstrated by John. His story was told to me by the person who hired him. Very early in the interview, John used an opportunity to reveal something about himself while at the same time selling himself. He knew that eventually in the interview it would come out that he had spent a year in prison for assault. When he was invited to talk about himself, he described how he had taught an English course while he was in prison. John emphasized that what made him feel really good was making valuable use of his prison time. Because of his candidness and the realization that he had a strong work ethic, this potentially disastrous piece of information was turned into something positive. He was offered a material handler position with a Fortune 500 company and became a valued employee.

When overcoming an objection, don't argue with the employer. If the employer states, "You really don't have enough experience in this field," a good response might be:

> I realize there may be others with more years of experience, but I really feel the quality of my experience is the key. Because of the variety of things I've done, and the level of responsibility I was given, I think my five years are equivalent to most people with ten. There's no question in my mind that I can do an outstanding job for you.

Another way to deal with this concern is to describe all of your *related* experience. Related experience is similar to what the employer is looking for, but not exactly the same. Your challenge is to get the employer believing that your experience is close to what they need. The more successful you are at making the employer see this similarity, the more likely you are to overcome the objection and get the job offer.

A classic story told by John Crystal reveals the importance of recognizing related experience in order to overcome objections. In the mid 70s, Bill was interviewing for a middle mangement position. During the interview he was told that the person who got the job, in addition to the many other management duties, would manage the company-owned cafeteria. Bill had never managed a cafeteria before, and neither had the other remaining candidate. In this position, others such as the head cook and cafeteria manager would actually run the day-to-day operations, but Bill would be responsible for the budget and approving major decisions made by the staff. If Bill had been like most job seekers he would have said, "Well, I've never run a cafeteria before, but I am an excellent manager, and I learn quickly. I know I could do an excellent job." He could have said that, and it would not have been a bad answer, but he had a better idea. In a flash Bill recalled that while he was stationed in Vietnam during the mid 60s, he was responsible for the transporting of warm food from the mess hall to troops in the field by Jeep, truck, tank, or even helicopter. Bill realized that his experience was not exactly what the employer had in mind, but he recognized that it was *related* to what they were seeking, so he decided to make the most of this example.

Bill also realized that he faced an objection if he did not successfully get the employer to buy his story. So he told the story with flair and vividness. He got the job and was convinced that his story had tipped the balance in his favor. He didn't get the job *because* of his Vietnam experience. But when the employer had to decide between two very qualified people, Bill had demonstrated that he had related experience regarding cafeterias. This had tipped the balance scale in his favor. I also believe that by telling a vivid tale, full of strong visual images, Bill revealed many qualities that also helped sell him. I am sure that the executive hiring Bill realized that Bill cared so greatly about his customers—those soldiers out in the trenches—that he provided a service far beyond what was expected. The executive knew that Bill would do the same in the position he was being interviewed for. Bill was obviously the person for the job.

Clearly, Bill overcame a potential objection by selling his related experience. Pat overcame a potential objection by selling her ability to learn new systems quickly. Both succeeded in heading off an objection caused by their lack of particular experience. Sometimes, however, the employer will state that you lack some experience before you've had an opportunity to anticipate or deal with the objection. In that case, you should sell your related experience *and* your ability to learn quickly. Use a highly vivid story to demonstrate your willingness to do whatever is necessary to become proficient quickly.

PROJECT ENTHUSIASM AND POTENTIAL

Enthusiasm and potential will land you more job offers than any other qualities. The two are inseparable.

Enthusiasm

Employers seek enthusiastic people who really want to get involved in the job. You should demonstrate genuine enthusiasm—enthusiasm for yourself, enthusiasm for the job, enthusiasm for your future boss, and enthusiasm for the company.

Suppose the field has been narrowed to two equally qualified people. The employer will ask many questions to determine who is the best choice. A common question is "If we offered you the position, would you accept it?" Notice the difference in the following two responses.

Sandra: Yeah, I definitely would accept it. The job seems interesting.

Susan: I'm excited about this job. I like the philosophy of top management, I like the steady growth of XYZ in the last five years, and I really look forward to working for you. This job will utilize my strengths and interests. I'm ready to get started.

If the choice came down to these two people, there is little question as to who would be hired.

The best way to appear enthusiastic is to genuinely *be* enthusiastic about the job. If you've considered your long- and short-term goals, and this job would help you attain those goals, it will be easy to demonstrate enthusiasm.

Enthusiasm is not demonstrated in just one response to one question, however; it must be demonstrated throughout the interview. It starts with listening. Really listening to the interviewer shows respect as well as enthusiasm. You can also show enthusiasm by speaking positively about previous jobs or supervisors. Describe how you put all of your energy into a job and describe the results you've achieved.

I am convinced that enthusiasm has gotten more people jobs than any other single quality. But because of the stress of interviews, most people tend to speak in a monotone and to appear unenthusiastic. Some reduce their level of enthusiasm even further because of the mistaken notion that they should play "hard to get." At the end of an interview, if you truly want the job, tell the interviewer so. Be enthusiastic. When it comes down to two people who are equally qualified, the person most enthusiastic about the job will almost always get the offer.

Because enthusiasm is so important I encourage people to perform an enthusiasm check about every ten minutes during an interview. If you are well prepared for the interview, you can use part of your thinking process to check your enthusiasm level even while you are in the midst of answering a question. If you realize your enthusiasm has waned, you should not try to instantly raise it several notches; that might seem obvious and contrived. Instead, since enthusiasm usually drops as you get too relaxed, you can begin by merely sitting up straighter in your chair. Over a period of two or three minutes, you should then introduce more hand gestures, raise the level of your voice slightly, and add more feeling to what you say. When you are saying something particularly important, raise your voice slightly, speed up your words a bit, and clip certain words for emphasis. As you practice interviewing with yourself or others, record and notice your enthusiasm level. If you can tell it is low, the interviewer will detect it also. It's something you need to work on.

I don't ask anyone to try to manufacture that bubbly enthusiasm some possess, if such enthusiasm is not natural for you. But no matter how unenthusiastic you feel you are, you can always raise your enthusiasm a notch or two. While raising it three or four notches may be too much and might sound unnatural and phony, everyone can elevate their enthusiasm level at least slightly.

You can also express your enthusiasm through your self-confidence. If you are confident you can do the job and you really want it, a degree of enthusiasm will express itself spontaneously.

Potential

Your potential is your future worth to an organization. Demonstrating enthusiasm without demonstrating potential will seldom lead to a job offer. The two must go together. Your enthusiasm will give the employer confidence that you want the job and that you will work hard at it. But if you don't also demonstrate your potential, you will not receive an offer.

Although companies occasionally use elaborate personality tests to determine potential, past success is still the best predictor of future success. If you are a top salesperson at your present company and you are interviewing for a new sales position, your past success will give the sales manager the confidence that you will continue to sell well. If you've been fired from four sales positions because of poor results, you'll have your work cut out for you as you try to convince a sales manager that you really do have potential.

Potential is best demonstrated by telling the employer about your accomplishments. For example, consider Paula, who is returning to work after 20 years out of the job market. She is applying for Administrative Assistant with a small association that represents pharmacists. Membership in the association has dropped because pharmacists feel they have not been effectively represented. In walks Paula, with no paid work experience and only one year of college, to compete with college graduates who have experience working with associations. Even with this competition, Paula lands the job, thanks to her one-year term as president of the PTA. During that year, attendance at meetings increased 60% over the previous year, and fund-raising activities brought in twice as much money. Paula also organized a banquet that people are still talking about. And she was considered to be the primary lobbying force for new state legislation that benefited her school district. By sharing these accomplishments, she proved that she could help turn the pharmacists' association around. That's potential.

Selling potential can get you job offers when others have more direct experience. Tim, who has been the chief financial officer of three companies, states that among the 30 or more people he has hired, he has never hired the "most qualified" person. He is quick to say he always hires qualified people. In fact, candidates are not even interviewed unless they have demonstrated competence in all key areas. But after narrowing the field down to two or three, he usually finds himself drawn to the person who shows great drive and desire. That person has never been the one with the most direct experience. It seems that those with the most experience generally fail to fully demonstrate enthusiasm and potential.

An interesting thing occurs during an interview as you sell your enthusiasm and potential. It begins with the employer's decision to interview you. Perhaps out of the six who were invited for interviews, you were rated number six, merely because you lacked some experience that was desired which the other candidates had. As you learned about the job, you knew it would be a challenge for you, but you also knew you could do it, and you knew you would enjoy experiencing a steep learning curve. As a result, your enthusiasm came out spontaneously during your interviews. You also related some interesting stories which demonstrated your strong work ethic, your desire for growth, and your ability to successfully take on new challenges. You came across as a person who would fit in well with the team. Three others who had more experience did not demonstrate such qualities and did not get second interviews.

When you learned you were being invited back for a second interview, your desire for the job motivated you to do more research on the organization. You learned about some problems (or challenges) you felt you could really tackle and help solve. In the second interview, you maintained your high level of enthusiasm and you sold your potential by sharing experiences that demonstrated your ability to contribute in these problem areas. You weren't aware of it yet, but the employer began to actually picture you in the job. The employer began "leaning" toward choosing you. As the employer's preference for you became stronger, she realized that she actually liked you better than the other two candidates. She hesitated hiring you, however, because on paper you were not as strong as the other two. But then she began a justification process: granted, she might have to spend more time training you, but at least you would be trained in her methods. The other two could come in tomorrow and handle the job from day one, but they might insist on using their old methods.

Your ability to sell both your potential and your ability to learn new processes quickly made the employer realize that even though the other two candidates could do the job better for the first several months, your drive and ambition would probably put you ahead of them after six months. Can you see how this process unfolds during two or three interviews? It accurately describes the thought process that occurs in the minds of employers.

Being able to demonstrate enthusiasm and potential is just as crucial to the experienced person as it is for the less-experienced person. If you are experienced, let your enthusiasm come through as you explain how much you enjoy your field of work. Demonstrate your potential by discussing recent, solid, work-related accomplishments. This will indicate to the employer that there are many future accomplishments yet to come.

MASTER THE ART OF STORY TELLING

Aloof as they may seem, employers are actually begging you to get them excited. Show that you can make or save them money, solve their operational problems, or ease their workloads, and they'll be thrilled to hire you. Merely saying you can increase productivity or get staff members to work as a team isn't enough. You must support your claims with vivid examples. People remember best those things that are stored in their minds as pictures. In fact, the latest brain research reveals that memories are stored as holographs, or 3–D pictures. That means that if words pass from your mouth and do not create any images or emotions in the minds of employers, those words will literally pass through one ear and out the other—there will be no impact or long-term memory.

Consider what happens when a person is asked to describe himself. He may declare that he is hard working, energetic, a true leader, and a person who can successfully juggle multiple tasks. The problem here is that he is trying to sell too many things at once and doesn't do a good job with any of them. Because he doesn't back up any of the claims with examples, none of the points will be remembered after he leaves the interview.

Using anecdotes to describe job skills is a highly effective interview technique. In less than three minutes, you can tell a powerful story that will make interviewers remember you favorably for days, weeks, or even months after the interview. Since employers know that the best predictor of future success is past success, tell stories which vividly describe your successes.

Stories are important because they can say so much about you in an evocative, concentrated way. Paul Green is the founder of Behavioral Technology in Memphis, Tennessee, a firm which teaches corporations how to utilize behavior-based interviewing. Paul gives an excellent example of how telling stories in an interview can make a difference. While he was conducting an interview he asked the candidate for an example that would demonstrate a strong commitment to completing tasks. The candidate described a time when he had had his appendix removed on a Thursday and was back in the office on Monday—to the dismay of everyone. His explanation was that work was piling up and he might as well do everything he could, even though he could not work a full day for the first week. The story provided strong evidence that he was a driven, hard-working person. The memory he created was that he was "the appendix guy." To this day, when Paul

Well, to begin with I'm trustworthy, loyal, helpful, friendly, courteous, kind, obedient, cheerful, brave, clean, and reverant.

Green thinks about this person, all he has to say to himself is, "the appendix guy," and a flood of memories and emotions return. The beauty of stories is that they can evoke a recollection of many skills, qualities, abilities, and characteristics.

When telling stories, provide all of the key information. Describe the situation and the challenges you faced. Then describe your analysis and the recommendations you made. Next, describe what you implemented and the results you obtained. Look for interesting tidbits and details which, though not crucial for understanding, will provide a stronger visual image of what you did.

A client shared a story with me that included vivid details and tidbits; it is a story I'll never forget. Ron had worked for 25 years in the management of seafood-processing plants in Oregon, Washington, and Alaska. Because of his reputation for working effectively with unions, he was asked to take over a plant in the Caribbean which was experiencing serious labor unrest. Always one for a challenge, Ron took it on. One day, about a week after he arrived at the Caribbean plant, he found himself surrounded by about ten workers. When they began accusing him of trying to destroy the union, he simply faced them down and reiterated the changes he felt needed to be made. When he finished speaking, he walked through the crowd and began heading back to his office. As he walked away, he knew that one of the leaders had pulled out a gun and had pointed it at his back. Although his heart was racing, he kept walking and did not turn around. He was sure that at any moment he was going to have a bullet in his back. He had never been more frightened in his life. When he got back to his office he realized he had been so scared he actually wet his pants. He said it with laughter, of course, and we both laughed together. I heard that story over three years ago, yet I still recall it most vividly.

Whenever I recall this story, I have very strong memories about Ron. The story didn't end there. Ron showed the workers that he could not be intimidated. The workers began to end their work slowdown, and they began to have confidence that he would be fair with them. Within six months the unrest was a distant memory and the plant began making a profit again. I'm not necessarily suggesting that in an interview Ron should always mention his incontinence, but I'm pointing out how this detail makes the story more memorable and amusing. Actually there were several vivid details which made this a memorable story. By imprinting vivid images in the brains of employers, you will be better remembered and more highly regarded.

Most people require practice to be able to tell vivid, effective stories. Once you have recalled 10–15 accomplishments, write brief descriptions of them. Then practice giving a three-minute version, a two-minute version, and a one-minute version of each one. With the longer versions, you can add details which provide a greater richness and make each story more memorable. The shorter versions take the most effort because you must decide which information is most crucial. Then, tell a story into a tape recorder. When you play it back, ask yourself: Is it a well-told story? Is it interesting? Does it create mind pictures?

Software engineers and other technical people tell me that their projects simply don't translate into colorful stories like the one described above. I agree with them to some extent—few of us have such dramatic stories to tell. But anyone can still tell a vivid story by emphasizing the challenges faced and by graphically describing how the problems were overcome. It's the details of a story that create strong visual images and strong emotional memories.

There are several techniques for effectively telling stories. One is to combine a nonwork experience with a work-related experience. The nonwork-related experience may be especially vivid or have a particularly useful "hook" in it which will help the employer remember you. A hook is any word-picture or imagery that will help a person recall a story. While the hook need not be a critical point of the story, it may be. The nonwork experience might be selected simply because it is the best experience you have which demonstrates a certain skill. Combining the nonwork experience with a recent work experience can help create a vivid picture of you that communicates a lot about your skills and qualities.

Combining a distant experience (work-related or nonwork-related) with a recent experience can also enrich your images and stories. It demonstrates that you have mastered that skill over time. If, for example, you are selling your ability to organize events, a related story from 5–15 years ago, when told in conjunction with a recent story, would clearly demonstrate that you've had the ability to organize events for a long time.

When telling stories that demonstrate how you've solved a problem or overcome an obstacle, create before and after pictures that highlight your impact on the situation. Paint the before picture as bleak as you can. Make the employer feel how bad the situation was. If you were dealing with a quality control problem, you might describe how angry your customers were and describe how some threatened to stop buying from your company or how some actually did. Don't exaggerate, but give the employer the full sense of the problem. As you complete your story, describe how smooth or effective things became. Create the strongest contrast possible without exaggerating. Bruce shared this story about his experience with a mobile home manufacturer:

> Before I took over the parts department, it was taking a month from the time we received a dealer's order until the dealer actually got the part.

Because of this we had two problems—most dealers simply obtained their parts from other sources, while those who did order from the factory got their kicks out of yelling at me and telling me to get the parts to them pronto. The problem was simply that no system had been established. Orders either got lost or they didn't get down to the traffic department for days. And no one even knew if the parts were in stock. When they weren't in stock, no one bothered to notify the person who had placed the order. After a week on the job, I decided things had to change.

The first thing I did was create forms for recording orders, something which had never been done even though the manufacturing facility had been operating for four years. My predecessor either wrote things down on scraps of paper or tried to remember things in his head. He was really a smart guy, but he couldn't remember everything. I established a hookup with the warehouse so our two computer systems could talk to each other. This system told me immediately whether the parts were available.

Next, I got the warehouse and the shipping and receiving managers together and we found ways to help each other rather than squabble over turf. Within four months we got our delivery times down from four weeks to five days. We haven't lost an order for at least two years. Now I'm not wasting time tracking down lost or late shipments. And my hearing is getting better since people don't yell over the phone anymore. The best thing is that parts sales to our dealers have increased from $12,000 per month to over $60,000. Our dealers are happy, so they don't need to go to other suppliers anymore.

Didn't you actually picture this person on the phone getting his ears burned? Did you imagine the orders getting written down on scraps and then getting misplaced? Could you visualize these three managers who were working at cross purposes? If so, the story was successful. But you were not merely left with a picture. You were left with a result. It wasn't just that Bruce didn't get yelled at anymore, but that sales increased dramatically. Remember that employers get excited when you demonstrate that you can make money, save money, solve problems, or reduce the boss's daily stress and pressure. Bruce demonstrated through this one story that he could do all four. The final point he made was that he could make money. After all, sales increased from $12,000 per month to $60,000. That did some very nice things to the company's bottom line.

Begin by describing the situation as you entered it. If the situation was something that existed before you became involved, describe all of the negatives. If you are describing a project that you oversaw, describe the problems or challenges in the most graphic terms possible. Describe your analysis of the situation and whatever research you applied to it. Then describe your recommendations or the conclusions you came to. Next, explain what you implemented and developed, and paint a picture of what things were like after they improved. If it was a project, concentrate on describing those parts of the project which met or exceeded objectives. Complete the story by describing how your work benefitted the company. As you end the story, remind the interviewer what skill or strength the story demonstrates, and you might add another two or three points as well. This could be done by stating: "So I really do believe that experience demonstrates my ability to manage projects effectively (the originally stated strength), as well as motivate employees and find solutions to really difficult problems."

Many questions neither invite nor demand a story. Questions such as "What did you like best about your supervisor?" or "What frustrates you about your current job?" do not invite examples. While one could use specific examples for these questions, typically a person would answer them in a very brief and straight forward manner. If you had indicated that your supervisor often did not keep his staff well informed, the interviewer might possibly ask for a specific example, but that is unlikely. There are other questions which would never require a story, such as asking what public figure you most admire.

Even though many questions do not invite stories, you need to be prepared so that when an opportunity to tell a story presents itself, you'll be ready with the best example possible.

Most people speak in generalities when asked about their strengths. Five minutes later, the interviewer will not even remember what was said. When you take advantage of the opportunity to tell a story, you will create impact and cause the interviewer to know a great deal about you. Your challenge is to bring in stories whenever they are appropriate. Any time a question is asked about a strength or asset, back up what you say with an example. If you've never done exactly what they are asking for, you might start with "That's not too different from what I did at..."

To tell effective stories:

1) Provide all of the key information.

2) Describe the situation as you came into it—problems and challenges included.

3) Describe your analysis and recommendations.

4) Describe what you implemented and the results you obtained.

5) Create vivid images.

6) Provide interesting details, but keep the story concise.

7) Make the story interesting.

DESCRIBING ACCOMPLISHMENTS

By now you should recognize the importance of telling stories. The next step is to identify your best stories and write about them. Writing about them will enhance your memory of what occurred. It will also enable you to make each story as vivid as possible. You'll start by writing about 12 of your accomplishments. An accomplishment is anything you've done well, enjoyed doing, or received satisfaction from doing. If you have several years of work experience, you should write on your 12 top work-related accomplishments. If you are trying to break into a new field, choose your 12 top work-related or nonwork-related accomplishments that best demonstrate your ability to handle the new job.

It is always best to describe accomplishments in terms of dollars or percentages. One of my clients was able to tell employers that in the two years since she had taken over her territory, she had increased the sales of shoes by 54% and profits on her sales by 68%. The company had been marketing in that area for 20 years. You can see how impressive this would be to an employer.

Other examples include: "I received a $600 bonus from Boeing for suggesting an idea that saved $6,000 the first year." "I developed a simplified computer program for a client which reduced the computer runtime by 40% and saved over $17,000 per year."

Dollar figures and percentages are so valuable in accomplishments that you should even estimate them when necessary. The computer programmer in the second example above had to estimate or guesstimate the dollar savings. She knew the runtime was reduced by 35–45%, so she chose 40% as her figure. She knew how frequently the program was run, and she knew the cost of the computer time. Thus, the $17,000 figure was calculated using simple arithmetic.

While not all accomplishments can be quantified, many can. When I'm talking with people to gather information for their resumes, I'm frequently told, "There's really no way to estimate it, I just improved it." I will then ask questions from different angles and we invariably arrive at a figure we can use.

See pages 140 to 152 for more on accomplishments. The ideas expressed there for resumes are just as applicable for interviewing.

If you are seeking an entry-level position, describe the accomplishments that are most closely related to the job you're applying for. Accomplishments enable the employer to assume that if you've done well in one field, you can do well again in another field.

Here are some examples for those seeking entry-level positions:

I haven't missed a day of work in three years.

At 19, I became one of the youngest assistant store managers Mc-Donald's ever had. My boss said she had never seen anyone learn so fast or who showed as much maturity as I did.

During the summer after I graduated from high school, I worked as a stocker in a small grocery store. I got three raises in three months because the owner said he had never had anyone who could shelve so fast.

I led my basketball team in assists. I really enjoy being part of a team.

Once you list your accomplishments, practice sharing them out loud. This will help prepare you to select the most appropriate accomplishment during an interview—the one that shows you doing work closely related to the job you're interviewing for, or one that demonstrates some of your most desirable characteristics.

PLAYING THE INTERVIEW GAME

There are rules to playing the interview game. Job seekers who know and understand the rules recognize that there are ways to make themselves stand out from the rest. Knowing how to handle ambiguous questions, when to pause, how much eye contact to maintain, and how to handle offensive and illegal questions, will make a major difference in your interviewing success.

The Pregnant Pause
Interviewees often feel they must give instant responses to every question. While you certainly would not want long pauses after every question, a significant pause is often the best response to a difficult question. If you answer an obviously difficult question too quickly, you can leave the impression of being a person who "shoots from the hip." A pause can demonstrate that you are a thoughtful person who wants to provide the most appropriate response. Pausing also gives you time to select the best example and therefore provide the best answer possible. When the question is asked and you realize it is going to be difficult, look away from the interviewer and begin to consider a response. Looking away is the natural way all people ponder a question. To try to maintain eye contact while thinking is unnatural. With difficult questions, a pause of 10–15 seconds is reasonable. If you need to buy some time you might say, "That's a good question," "That's a difficult question," or "That's a tough one." This will give you another few seconds to think.

Anthony Medley tells a classic story about Jackie Robinson. Branch Rickey, general manager of the Brooklyn Dodgers, asked

Robinson if he was willing to become the first black player in Major League Baseball. Robinson knew that if he accepted, he would face harassment from fans throughout the league. Robinson also knew that if he did not respond well to that pressure, it might prevent other black players from coming into the league for another decade or two. After pausing several minutes, Robinson said he felt he was mature enough to handle the taunting and ridicule he would face in the coming years. Had Robinson responded immediately with, "Sure, I can handle it," Rickey would have had serious doubts and might have sought another player.

Eye Contact

Interviewees are frequently told to maintain constant eye contact during an interview and that anything less will be interpreted as weakness. Actually, that type of eye contact is completely unnatural. Studies reveal that in normal conversation, the speaker typically looks away 30–70% of the time. As a person begins to speak, he turns away while speaking, then periodically returns his eyes for several seconds to the person being spoken to, and then looks away again. It is the extremes that should be avoided. Appearing to stare at the person being spoken to makes that person feel uncomfortable and proves the speaker lacks social graces. On the other hand, I've also seen people who speak for several minutes at a time and look at the person being

Getting and maintaining eye contact can be overdone.

*Darren had read about the importance of
maintaining strong eye contact.*

spoken to only as they finish speaking. That also is unnatural and needs to be corrected.

Eye contact must be maintained, however, by the listener. Whenever the speaker returns his or her eyes to you, your eyes must be on that person. The interviewer should not catch you looking around the room, looking out the window, or staring at the floor. Active listening requires you to keep a soft look on the interviewer to demonstrate interest and attentiveness.

Personal And Offensive Questions

Occasionally you will be asked personal questions which, while they are not illegal, are certainly inappropriate. If you are asked such a question, you must quickly decide whether you will answer it or tactfully decline. Because the interviewer will generally realize he's touching a sensitive area, a gentle rebuff will usually cause the person to back off. It could be "Mr. Hanson, I try not to get into personal issues during interviews." Examples of such personal questions might include, "Do you have a boyfriend?" "Are you planning to get married?" or "Are you living together?" These questions are inappropriate and should not concern the interviewer. Just knowing that you don't have to answer such questions often helps. Tactfully declining is the key. Don't try to make the person feel ashamed, since that certainly would not help you. And don't make too many negative assumptions about the person or the company because of the questions.

It may help to put yourself in the employer's position. While the question itself offends you, try to understand why it is being asked. For example, perhaps you're a woman, and you are asked a question about your plans for children. If you're interviewing for a critical position in a small company, you could understand why the person would not want to hire you for a few months and then lose you. On the other hand, you may still be offended and angry about the question. You could respond with, "Well, I do intend to have children, but I would be off work for a very short period of time. I'm the type of person who needs to be working." Or you might say, "We plan to have children, but not for several years." Or you could say, "Mr. Hanson, I really prefer not to discuss my personal life in interviews."

Illegal Questions

Because most interviewers are unsophisticated in the art and legality of interviewing, it is still not uncommon for interviewees to be intentionally and unintentionally asked illegal questions. Other questions may not, strictly speaking, be illegal, but they inappropriately pry into people's private lives. You should know your rights and know in advance how you plan to handle illegal or inappropriately prying questions. Virtually all states have laws or regulations prohibiting discrimination on the basis of race, color, religion, national origin, ancestry, medical condition, physical handicap, marital status, and age (40+), particularly as it pertains to application forms and interviewing.

Generally, questions about your or your spouse's national origin, including questions about your native language, are illegal. Employers cannot ask about your marital status or the number or ages of children or dependents. Nor can they ask questions regarding pregnancy or birth control use, or plans for having children. Employers are allowed to ask questions about disabilities in the following form: "Do you have any physical condition or handicap which may limit your ability to perform the job applied for? If yes, what can be done to accommodate your limitations?" They cannot, however, ask questions regarding an applicant's general medical condition or illnesses, or receipt of Worker's Compensation. Nor can they ask questions such as, "Do you have any physical disabilities or handicaps?"

Employers are not allowed to ask questions regarding religion. A question such as "Are there any holidays or days of the week you can't work?" would probably be held illegal, even if religion was not specified. However, it would probably be acceptable to ask, "We often work holidays and weekends. Is there anything that would prevent you from doing so?"

You'll notice that there is often a fine line between acceptable and illegal. Those who really want to find out a particular piece of information can probably find a legal way to do so.

Employers can ask if you have ever been convicted of a felony, but cannot ask if you have ever been arrested. In some states even the question about a felony would have to be worded very carefully. In those states the question about a felony conviction must be job related. The question posed to a controller might need to be, "Have you ever been convicted of embezzlement?" rather than "Have you ever been convicted of a felony?"

Generally, employers cannot ask about your past or current assets, credit rating, bankruptcy, or whether you own a home. They generally cannot ask you to "List all organizations, clubs, societies, and lodges to which you belong." They could, however, ask you to list job related organizations or professional associations if they specify that you should not list those which may indicate race, religion, national origin, sex, or age.

One way to deal with illegal or prying questions is to simply answer them without revealing that you are the least bit offended. For most such questions, that is my recommendation. To respond in that way, simply assume that the person meant no harm, is simply curious, and is unaware that some people might be offended by such questions.

The alternative to answering an illegal questions is to tactfully remind the interviewer that the question is illegal. You might say: "That's not a legal question. I would just as soon cover other points." If you do respond in this way, it is important to continue the interview by demonstrating the same professional manner you had prior to the asking of the question. The interviewer may already feel somewhat foolish for having asked such a question, or may feel perturbed at you. So it's important to proceed with the interview as if nothing happened. In a sense it has become your responsibility to put the interviewer at ease so both of you can concentrate on the key issues of the interview. Because you've demonstrated both your assertiveness and your knowledge of the law, it is highly unlikely you'll be asked another illegal question.

Just because asking a certain question is illegal does not preclude you from revealing certain information, even if you have not been asked about it. Parents will sometimes tell an interviewer that they do have children, but then go on to explain that because of their ages, there will be no problem with overtime or travel. It might be stated like this: "I have two teenagers who are both very independent. I'm able to travel, and I have never hesitated to work overtime when that was necessary." A person in a wheelchair might indicate that she drives a car, is an athlete, or that she has no work limitations. As with any issue, your challenge is to remove any objections an employer may have, whether the objections are fair or not.

If you feel you may face discrimination, be very clear on the laws and regulations of your state. Most states have a Human Rights Commission, or an equivalent agency. Each organization will have published examples of questions it considers legal and illegal.

Truthfulness

A reputation for integrity and honesty is one of the most priceless possessions a person can have. Never say anything in an interview that would cause an interviewer to question your integrity or honesty. Lying in a resume, application form, or during an interview is simply too risky, and any short-term gain you might achieve would not be worth it. Besides, being able to sleep well at night is a great asset. As John Wooden, the great basketball coach put it, "There is no pillow as soft as a clear conscience." Those who have lied about having college degrees often admit that they always worried about being found out. Most application forms have a stipulation at the end stating: "I understand that any false answer or statement on this application or any other required documents may result in denial of employment or discharge." Another application states: "I certify that answers given herein are true and complete to the best of my knowledge. In the event of employment, I understand that false or misleading information given in my application or interview(s) may result in discharge." These comments are pretty serious stuff, and they are not idle threats.

It's not uncommon to hear of a person who's been fired because some disgruntled employee decides to check up on a boss or colleague, only to discover that the person never actually graduated from college. It's so easy to verify college graduation that no one should ever falsify that information. Granted, most companies do not check up on such things, but enough do that it just isn't worth it to lie.

Mark Twain put it best when he said "If you tell the truth you don't need such a good memory." During the stress of an interview it is hard for the person who is stretching the truth to remember what has been said to whom. Interviewers can spot inconsistencies. If they catch you, they may not bring it to your attention—they simply won't invite you back for another interview.

There may be other situations in which interpretation, not truth, is the issue. Opinions and interpretations of events cannot be proved or disproved. For example, during an interview you may be asked what you liked most and least about your last boss. Even though the person may have been a total jerk, don't say that in the interview. Instead, find a major quality about him that you liked, and a fairly minor quality that you disliked. Bite your tongue if you feel the urge to say more. Are you being dishonest? I don't think so. You're being discreet.

Another common question asks about your reason for leaving each position. Whether you left of your own accord or were asked to leave, there were probably several reasons, not just one. My recommendation is to mention only one or two reasons. Those reasons should be described in such a way that the interviewer believes he would have left under those circumstances also.

Really touchy areas need a lot of thought. A client of mine was "semi-terminated." That is, he was given an option of going to another department, but there was no promise of it being permanent. The position was not desirable, so he chose to resign. In one sense he was terminated, but in another sense he quit. When he was asked why he left this job, he mentioned the impact the recession had on his company and stated that his position, as well as several similar positions at other branches, had been eliminated. He also described the position within his company that was offered to him, and explained why he had declined it. All of these statements were true, and the interviewers were satisfied with the explanation.

Along with being truthful, it is important to remain consistent. Once you decide how you are going to deal with a certain issue, maintain consistency in the way you describe and talk about it.

Employers want people they can trust implicitly. Therefore, during the interview demonstrate openness and genuineness. Make positive statements about yourself but avoid exaggeration. Such demonstrations of openness and genuineness will foster the sense that you are trustworthy. Being consistent will allow the employer's trust in you to build throughout the interview.

Skeletons And Other Touchy Subjects

Many people have a skeleton or two in the closet. It's important, therefore, to know how you're going to respond if they are brought up. If the very thought of having to explain a particular fact or issue gets your heart racing or causes you to break out in a cold sweat, you'll need a lot of thought and practice, and perhaps some professional assistance to learn how to handle the situation. Your challenge is to put the situation in the best possible light to minimize its negative effect. Depending on the situation, there may be no way to look good. Your goal may simply be to minimize and control the damage.

These skeletons include situations such as being fired from a job, having spent time in prison, having failed at a business venture, going through bankruptcy, and having been out of work for over a year. If there were five reasons for the situation, pick the two or three reasons that are easiest to discuss. It is important to provide enough information so the interviewer does not feel compelled to probe further. Practice discussing the situation until you sound confident and can explain everything without getting tense or defensive.

ASKING QUESTIONS

Employers like being asked questions. In fact, most are disappointed if you don't ask a few questions; they may even interpret a lack of questions as a lack of interest. Giving the interviewer a chance to answer your thoughtful questions makes the interview interesting and makes you seem more interesting as well. Asking questions also gives you the opportunity to gather useful information and clear up any confusing issues.

Ask your questions selectively since asking too many questions can leave a negative impression. Also, avoid a probing or belligerent tone which could make the interviewer feel under interrogation. Don't ask the questions too early in the interview. Instead, give the employer an opportunity to cover them first. Later in the interview, if some key points have not been covered, that is the time to ask your questions.

When asked properly, questions reveal that you've done your homework. For example, "What will the impact on exports be if the World Bank cuts loans to Taiwan?" Or, "What will the impact be if you have a long labor strike in June?" Or, "I saw that ATL is coming out with a complete new line of ultrasound equipment. What will you do to counter it?" These can be good questions.

When asking questions, be careful not to overwhelm the interviewer with your knowledge. Don't try to wow the person with your knowledge of earnings per share if you're interviewing with the purchasing manager. Such questions may be perceived as obvious and deliberate attempts to impress.

If you need to ask a few questions in order to remove confusion or clear up a misinterpretation, you might say, "Do you mean that earnings this quarter will determine whether you can expand next year?" Or, "Does that mean I could complete the training program in three months instead of six if I learn the process quickly?" Or, "I'm not sure I know what you mean by _____."

Some of your questions can be planned, but ask them only if they seem appropriate. Good general questions to ask might include: "Would you describe your management style?" "Would you describe your management training program?" "Where is the company (department) strong and where does it need to be strengthened?" "If I'm as effective as I think I will be, where could I be in five years?" "Is there anything else I should know that would help me understand the position?"

Ask only those questions you really care about. When you have a clarifying question, ask it as soon as it comes up. Either wait for the first opportunity or tactfully interrupt if you need clarification on a key point. Often all you need to ask is, "Would you elaborate on that?"

Ask your questions in such a way that they invite full and complete answers. Closed questions, which can be answered with a yes or no, or with a very brief, incomplete response, won't work for this purpose. A closed question might be, "Are you going to implement a computer network?" An open question would be, "If you're going to implement a computer network, how would you go about doing it?"

Ask questions your interviewer can answer. Do not ask questions the interviewer could not reasonably be expected to know. That can be embarrassing and seem threatening. For instance, asking the sales manager a technical question about inventory control would be inappropriate. Also, do not ask questions that would result in giving away trade secrets. The employer probably won't tell you anyway, and it will appear that you lack discretion.

If you do ask a question the interviewer is obviously sensitive about, back off and perhaps even apologize. This is true for all questions *except* those tough questions you must ask after the job has been offered to you. At that time, you will need a lot of data to help you decide whether to accept the position.

Do not ask dumb questions! An IBM recruiter shared a story with me that illustrates this perfectly. Right after the interview began, the interviewee asked, "What does IBM stand for?" Although the interview continued for a few minutes, it was over at that moment. Had this person really wanted to know what the initials IBM stand for, she should have found out on her own. Not only was this a dumb question, it also revealed that the interviewee was unwilling to do even a minimum amount of employer research. So, before asking a question, determine whether it's something you need to know or should know, and whether it is something an interviewer would normally have told you by that stage of the interview. If the answer is something you could come up with fairly easily on your own, don't ask the question.

Do not ask questions which make it seem as though you only care about yourself. Every employer wants to get a sense that you care about the company and its success. Some people, by their attitude and questions, reveal a self-centeredness which totally turns off employers.

Be careful when you ask, "Why?" Asking why can often feel like a probe and may seem threatening. Before asking, determine if you really need to know. Often such questions are asked merely to satisfy some curiosity.

Beware of asking loaded questions that reveal strong beliefs or feelings and imply you already know the answer. Such questions can convey a sense of superiority or even contempt. A typical loaded question might be, "Do you really believe you should be operating plants in South Africa?"

Avoid asking questions in a rapid fire manner. Rarely should you ask more than two questions at a time. Give the person an opportunity to fully respond to each question and show genuine interest in the answer.

If you've asked a question to get clarification on a point, but it is still not clear, it may be better to drop the question. You could get the interviewer frustrated, and that won't help you. If you get the job offer and the question is still an important issue, ask it again at that time.

Avoid shifting the topic away from something your interviewer is obviously interested in. Wait until it seems appropriate before asking a question which might disrupt the interviewer's train of thought.

It is proper for the employer to ask probing questions throughout the interview process. A probing question from an employer might come after you explain the reason you left your last company, with the employer asking, "Is that the only reason you left?" That is a probing question, and it may feel uncomfortable, but it is not an improper question.

If you ask probing questions in the first or second interview, it gives the impression that you don't trust the employer. If you ask a question and the interviewer appears evasive, make a mental note of it and try to get the answer through your own research or save the question until the job is offered. Try to determine whether the person was being intentionally evasive or perhaps did not fully understand the question.

Your probing questions should be withheld until the job has been offered to you. Then it is your *duty* to ask whatever questions are necessary to help you determine whether the job is right for you. While you never want to offend an employer, you may need to ask probing questions to get the information you need. Just as you may sometimes seek to withhold information, an employer may resist giving you these details. Therefore you may need to ask follow-up questions in order to obtain it. You need to ask tactfully, but if you really do need the information, you must also ask assertively. The answer to your question must be important enough that if the true answer is what you suspect, you would turn down the offer. Continue asking until you get a satisfactory response.

Many candidates have paid the supreme price for not asking enough questions once the job offer was made. The supreme price is getting fired because of misunderstandings, or feeling obligated to quit because promises were not kept. Terminations have occurred because expectations were never clarified. Typically in such circumstances, the new employee feels he or she is doing fine, while the manager does not. Be sure you know what the expectations are and be sure you can meet them. Clarification before accepting a job is critical.

Be prepared so that when the time is appropriate, or when you are invited to ask questions, you'll be ready to do so. Before the interview, jot down some things you hope to learn about the job and company. If those issues don't arise during the interview, you should be prepared to ask about them.

There are numerous questions which are safe to ask during a first or second interview. Some questions are simply best left unasked until a job has actually been offered to you. Each of the following questions could be appropriate at any time:

Would you describe your management style?

How would you describe the corporate culture (environment)?

What types of people seem to do well in this department/company?

Why is this position available?

Where is the person who had this position before? (If the person was promoted, ask where the person is now; if the person was fired, ask why.)

How many people have held this position in the last three years? (If it seems like there has been a high turnover, ask for an explanation.)

What are the opportunities you see for this department/company in the next year?

What are the challenges that have to be faced?

What do you like about working for this company?

How would you compare this company to others you've worked for?

What would you change about this organization if you could?

Do you see growth opportunities for yourself?

How well do departments interact with each other?

How would you rate top management?

Is the company primed to deal with technological changes in the next five years?

Will the company continue to be competitive? How?

Is the company quick or slow to adopt new technology?

What type of growth do you foresee in the next few years? Why?

Where in the company do you hope to be in five years? (This is a good way to sense potential growth.)

What would you say drives this company—sales, marketing, engineering, or finance?

How does the company promote personal and professional growth?

Notice that all of these questions are basically neutral. They do not reveal a preference on your part, you simply want to know. This is unlike questions such as: "Is there a lot of overtime?" "Is there a lot of travel?" "Am I likely to be relocated?" These questions raise red flags about you. Even if you are unlikely to be relocated, merely asking the question raises a question about your flexibility and ambition.

INTERVIEWING STYLES WHICH DAMAGE YOU

Interviewees often develop styles of interviewing which are counterproductive. Three styles which hurt many job seekers include an unwillingness to reveal their true selves, a tendency to be "meek and mild," and a tendency to take charge and dominate an interview.

Unwillingness To Reveal Yourself

The person who carefully measures every response and who seems fearful of revealing anything which could possibly be construed as negative quickly creates a negative impression. The interviewer becomes frustrated by this total lack of self-disclosure. After the interview the employer knows about past job titles and duties, but has no sense of the person—he or she remains an unknown quantity. While it's important to be careful in what you say, you must also come across as genuine and real. Striking the right balance between openness and discretion is a matter of preparation. If you know the points you want to sell about yourself, if you are prepared to answer all of the typical questions, and if you are prepared to handle any difficult questions with tact and discretion, you will be able to relax more and be your true self.

Meek And Mild Doesn't Make It

Some people are so concerned about appearing to be bragging that they are unwilling to say anything positive about themselves. Their attitude seems to be, "I probably won't get the job, but at least I didn't toot my own horn like a lot of people." This is a self-defeating attitude. If you don't say positive things about yourself, who will? Interviewing is all about selling yourself. To sell yourself you need to believe that you're a pretty good product and that any company which hires you will be fortunate. If you tend to undersell yourself, it's especially important that you take a good look at your accomplishments and identify the skills you demonstrated in those accomplishments.

To avoid the appearance of bragging, simply talk about your experiences. In this way, you can let the experience speak for itself. If the interviewer wants to be impressed, he can be, if not, he won't. If the interviewer is not impressed, you haven't hurt yourself because you did not create huge expectations. The worst thing you can do is state that you are fantastic in a certain area. Even if you provide a good, solid example, the interviewer may be disappointed because expectations were set so high. It's better to respond in this way:

Employer:	Are you effective at completing projects on schedule?
You:	I'd have to say I'm very effective. Last year I...

or

I would say so. In June I...

or

That's one of my top strengths. I've worked on numerous projects that had very tight deadlines. One of them was already three months behind when I took it over, and I had only six months to complete it...

In the beginning of each of these statements, the person sounded fairly modest but also confident. I don't believe that anyone would think the person was bragging. So, go ahead and feel confident. As your story unfolds, it will speak for itself.

Taking Charge Does Not Work

Some interviewees feel compelled to take control of the interview. They dominate the conversation and take it in directions the interviewer never intended. Generally, this approach makes an interviewee seem arrogant. A client recounted how he began interviewing an applicant, and was still in a rapport building stage, when out of nowhere, the applicant said "Well, let's roll up our sleeves and really get to it." This created an instant feeling of dislike. The applicant did not get the job. Another applicant entered the room, took off his coat and announced, "Let's get comfortable." The results were the same.

THINGS TO AVOID

To be effective in interviewing you not only need to know what to do, but also what not to do. The following tips will make you more effective.

I've-never-done-it-but

Avoid saying, as if it is all one word, *I'veneverdoneitbut.* Rarely will you need to confess, "I've never done it, but..." Instead, concentrate on what you've done that is similar. For instance, if the company uses dBase for a data-base manager, and you've only used RBase, you would not say "I've never used it, but I'm sure I could learn." Instead you would say, "I do have excellent experience with relational data bases (which dBase is), primarily using RBase. I became highly proficient with RBase in about four weeks. Having had four years of heavy experience with data bases, I'm sure I could master dBase in two or three weeks."

In this case both dBase and RBase are what are known as relational data bases. That means that while the commands they use may be different, the way they operate is quite similar. Knowing one will make it easier to learn the other. In fact, you could even say that they are similar in more ways than they are different. In this case, the person should go on to describe some of the uses that were made of RBase so the interviewer can see how closely the skills really match those he is looking for.

If the interviewer wants someone who has done grant writing, a job candidate might sell the fact that she publishes a newsletter for her professional association and has raised money for the Boy Scouts. By combining her writing and fund raising experience, she may still have a shot at the job.

Always start with the assumption that you have done something similar to what the employer is looking for. If you assume it, you will usually find it. Don't apologize for the fact that it is not a perfect fit. Just go with what you do have and sell your experience the best you can. Even if the interviewer concludes that the skills or experience don't match what she needs, she will at least respect you for your effort and will have enjoyed a good story.

Do Not Let A Person Feel Threatened By You

Occasionally you'll get a sense that an employer feels threatened by you. This most often occurs if the person is not competent, has less knowledge than you in your speciality, or has not been in the job long enough to have gained the full confidence of upper management. Books on management typically discuss the importance of hiring the best person possible, even if that person knows more than you. The idea is that you can't be promoted until your replacement has been trained. People who are secure seek the best because those employees will make them look good and help them get promoted. In spite of this management premise, some employers will consciously or unconsciously not want to hire someone who is more knowledgeable or capable than they are.

If you sense that your interviewer feels threatened by you, tone down your experience and results a bit. This is the only circumstance in which you might intentionally undersell yourself. If you determine that you are more knowledgeable than the interviewer, do nothing to give an impression that you feel superior. Avoid discussing things the interviewer may know little about. Do not correct him if you detect an error in something he has said. Of course, you should always be careful about correcting anyone during an interview.

As always, do your best to sell yourself into the position. Once you get the offer, determine whether you want to work for this person. Do your best to talk to people who have worked for him before. As one might suspect, incompetent people rarely make good managers and often seek to sabotage those around them. If you find, upon further investigation, that this person is incompetent, you must take this into account as you decide whether to accept a position in the organization. If such a person is entrenched in the organization, he may make it difficult for you to get promoted because he will rarely get promotions himself.

Avoid "Foot-In-Mouth Syndrome"

To prevent saying something you might regret, practice telling your stories and giving answers to the common interviewing questions. This will give you a clear sense of how they come across. I once interviewed for a claims adjuster position with an insurance company. In the middle of the interview, I was asked why I wanted to leave my present claims position. Taken by surprise, I stated, "Mainly because they give us too many assignments." As soon as I said it, I knew it didn't sound right; the look on the faces of both interviewers confirmed this suspicion. I'd stuck my foot in my mouth, and I spent the next five minutes extricating it. I must have done a pretty good job since I did get an offer. I quickly explained that my company gave us so many claims that we were unable to thoroughly investigate each one. I told them how many claims I handled each week and they determined it was about three times more than their adjusters handled. I came out of it all right, but I certainly learned a valuable lesson. Preparation is the best way to avoid foot-in-mouth syndrome.

Don't Assume The Interviewer Sees Your Qualifications As Clearly As You Do

When you describe accomplishments, most interviewers can discern additional skills even if you don't label each one. They may not discern all of your skills, however, so don't be too subtle. One method which can ensure that your interviewers get a clear picture of your skills is to state which skills you demonstrated in a particular accomplishment. For example, you might say: "I think my greatest strength is my ability to get people excited and motivated about projects. For example..." Then, tell a two-minute story which illustrates your point. Go on to say, "So I really do think I can get people excited about projects and really motivate them. At the same time I can keep people focused and bring out the best in them." Notice that two additional skills were identified and demonstrated in the accomplishment, even though the person started to describe only one skill, the ability to motivate people.

Interviewees often assume and act as though interviewers should be able to magically see what wonderful qualities they possess. While some interviewers are very perceptive, many are not. They will only know those things which you reveal verbally and nonverbally. Thus, it's your responsibility to reveal your strengths and demonstrate why you are the right person for the job.

THINGS TO DO/REMEMBER

Do Something Unique Or Different

Throughout your job search, keep asking yourself if you can do something unique, something creative, or something unexpected, that will make you stand out. Consider what happened to Jason when he used such a strategy. A major software company was interviewing three candidates for a purchasing manager position. Jason's last interview was held on Thursday, and he was told he would be given the decision by Monday. Thursday night after his interview, he wrote a plan for purchasing that would help handle the firm's rapid growth. On Friday morning he had a messenger deliver the proposal. On Monday he was notified he had the job because, "We knew you wanted it." Clearly, the extra effort and creativity Jason applied in this circumstance gave him the outcome he was hoping for.

Check With Your References Before Using Them

Make sure your references are truly willing to speak on your behalf. When asking for their help, give them an out by saying, "If you're really busy, I'll understand." If they don't want to act as references don't use them—they won't do a good job for you. If you've had a major interview, call them and let them know to expect a call. Give them the background of the job and tell them why you'd be effective in the position.

SELL YOURSELF

Knowing how to sell yourself is the key to successful interviewing. Building credibility and projecting a winning personality are the first steps.

Credibility

To interview effectively, you must convey your credibility. You accomplish this by showing that you are truthful, sincere, and genuine. The great benefit of credibility is that, once it's established, whatever you say from that point on tends to be believed. In fact, what you say will be believed unless you give the employer a reason to doubt you. That's why you should do nothing to jeopardize your credibility. Consider, for example, how you might answer the question, "What is your biggest weakness?" Job hunting books written in the 1970s frequently recommended that you work out your answer so that your weakness really comes across as a strength. One recommended answer ran something like this, "I'd have to say that my greatest weakness is that I work too hard. My wife complains that I'm not around enough, and I guess sometimes I work my people too hard too." The employer was supposed to think, "Well, isn't it nice that if this guy is going to have a weakness it would be something like this." The problem is that the answer is so planned and contrived that it is difficult to make it seem sincere. And lack of sincerity can damage your credibility.

Once you lose your credibility, everything you said before and everything you say after will come under greater scrutiny and there will always be an element of doubt about you. This is not the way to start a relationship. So do everything possible to establish credibility, and then do nothing to lose it.

Project And Sell A Winning Personality

On a conscious and subconscious level, employers will be evaluating your personality and asking, "Do I like this person and will we work well together?" When considering two people with equal qualifications, the one with the most pleasing personality will always be hired. A job is similar to marriage—the two of you may "live" together for many years. Work will be a lot more enjoyable if you like and respect each other.

In order to adequately sell yourself, you need to know your personality skills. Such skills include being appreciative, cooperative, and energetic. Employers highly value such qualities. Even someone seeking a CEO position must sell personality skills. Some of the most desirable characteristics or personality skills are friendliness, cheerfulness, tactfulness, sincerity, maturity, open-mindedness, loyalty, patience, optimism, reliability, flexibility, and emotional stability. There are others, of course, but these are among the most important.

During an interview you won't just rattle off claims to each of these characteristics—you will demonstrate each one. In just twenty minutes, a perceptive interviewer can accurately assess you in each area—both by what you *say* and by what you *are*. The famous saying, "Your actions speak so loudly, I can't hear what you're saying," is especially applicable to the ways in which employers assess a job applicant's personality during an interview.

Imagine you are interviewing with a company that just fired an employee because he was uncooperative. You might be asked, "In this organization cooperation and teamwork are absolutely essential. Are you a cooperative person?" You might respond, "Yes, I am very cooperative. When we were developing prototypes I would have to coordinate the project with people from four or five different departments. We always got the project completed on time. None of us got our way on everything. We worked out our differences and we felt good about the results." This example, which would be expanded upon in an actual interview, clearly illustrates that this is a cooperative, team-oriented person.

Your goal during the interview is to reveal as many positive attributes as possible. While your competitors are busy merely *describing* their technical strengths, you will be selling your personality skills as well as your technical skills.

There is a saying that sales are made on emotion and justified with logic. When most of us go to buy something, we start by liking it at an emotional level; we then look for ways to justify spending the money on the purchase. This process can be so subtle that few are even aware that it's taking place.

Hiring decisions are very similar. Your challenge is to get the employer to like you and to begin "leaning" your way. You do this by projecting enthusiasm, potential, and a winning personality. The employer has an emotional reaction—she begins to like you and feel comfortable with you. She senses your potential. Once you have hooked the employer emotionally, she will find a way to justify hiring you.

To identify and become more acquainted with your personality skills, rate yourself on the following 42 key skills. Rate yourself on a scale of 1–10, where 10 is excellent and 1 is poor. Be sure to give yourself a range—not all 8s, 9s and 10s. Avoid over-analyzing here—go through the list as quickly as you can.

Appreciative	Goal-oriented
Assertive	Growth-oriented
Cheerful	Honesty/Integrity
Compassionate	Insightful
Considerate	Joyful
Cooperative	Loyal
Curious/Inquisitive	Open-minded
Decision-making	Optimistic
Decisive	Patient
Discreet	Persistent
Easy-going	Practical
Effective Under Stress	Real
Efficient/Productive	Reliable
Emotionally Stable	Responsible
Energetic/Stamina	Resourceful
Enthusiastic	Risk-taking
Flexible	Self-confident
Forgiving	Sense of Humor
Frank	Sincere
Friendly/Nice	Sound Judgment
Generous	Thorough

Writing about your personality skills will prepare you for interviews. So once you've rated yourself on all these skills, pick out your top ten personality skills and write a short paragraph on each one describing how you are that way. This is a quick exercise; you're not trying for polished writing. Using your own shorthand, list an example for each skill. The example should illustrate your ability to use that skill at a high level. Your descriptions might read something like this:

> Although some may say I seldom get excited, I do have a high degree of <u>enthusiasm</u> in many areas. It is not a gushy enthusiasm, but a strong, deep enthusiasm that comes from conviction. Example: Motivating the team on the Baxter project.

> I am very <u>efficient</u>. This quality has been my worst enemy where I am now working. A difficult, demanding job appears so easy because I am efficient. No one fully recognizes my worth. Example: Cut the time it took to get month-end reports out from 8 days to 3 days.

> I was <u>diplomatic</u> when I had to discuss accounting irregularities with the client's accountants. Example: Especially on the XYZ account, when we suspected fraud.

Selling Personality Skills

Once you've identified and described your personality skills, it's important to consider how you might best sell these skills. There are four primary ways: 1) State the skill and then give an example to back it up; 2) State the skill and describe how you use it; 3) While selling a skill using a specific experience, describe the experience so vividly that some of your other personality skills are clearly evidenced; and 4) *Be* it. That is, demonstrate that you possess the skill.

State the skill and give an example. During an interview you might be asked to describe your strengths. You could respond by saying,

> I'd have to say that one of my strengths is my ability to work effectively under stress. A good example would be when I was working on the Otis account. Out of nowhere our client told us that they needed a new ad campaign for a product that was not doing well. We had only two weeks to develop a campaign that would normally have been a two-month project. My staff and I practically lived at the office, but we got the campaign out. It was a very successful campaign for the customer.

If warranted, you could expand on this by taking two or three minutes to explain the details of the project.

State the skill and describe how you use it. Sometimes providing an example is not possible or not appropriate. Instead of giving an example you might say, "I have a reputation for being reliable. People at work know that if a tough project has to get out on schedule, it should be given to me. When I agree to take on a project, my boss knows it's as good as done. I'll get it done no matter what." In this instance a specific example was not used, but the person did everything possible to prove she is extremely reliable.

Describe an experience so vividly that other skills are evident. You may have indicated that one of your strengths is your flexibility and then offered an example which clearly illustrates your flexibility, but reveals other positive traits as well. When you describe your experiences vividly, even a half-way perceptive person will pick up other positive qualities without your having to label them.

Be it. Don't just say it, show it. For instance, you can demonstrate your energy level through the way you walk and talk, your body language, facial expressions, and your voice inflection. I can sense a person's energy level within the first minute we are together. Cheerfulness, insightfulness, joyfulness, open-mindedness, optimism, self-confidence, enthusiasm, sense of humor, and sincerity are all traits that can be demonstrated.

Practice. Practice telling your stories. Only by doing so can you really hone them down to their most important points. Describe the experiences so vividly that the interviewer forms a mental image. Mental images can last for weeks or months in an employer's mind, mere words may last five minutes.

Sell Exposure

If you know you lack certain skills or experience, look for ways to sell your exposure. In an interview your order of priority is: 1) Sell the experience you have that is identical or nearly identical to what is being sought; 2) Sell your related or similar experience; and 3) Sell exposure. Exposure means you have observed that task or skill being done by others, you worked closely with people who used that skill, or you assisted someone performing that skill on one or more occasions. People don't get hired *because* of their exposure to certain skills, but exposure can tip the balance scale just enough to make the difference. When all you have to sell is exposure to a skill, do not apologize. Rather, move straight ahead and make the most out of what you have to offer.

Let's assume that a person, who is currently a shipping and receiving manager for a medium-sized company, is interviewing for a mangement position with a smaller company in which he would be required to function in a variety of roles. Halfway through the interview he is asked, "Have you ever handled inside sales?" His response might be, "As head of shipping and receiving, I had contact with the inside salespeople every day. By getting out rush orders for them, I saved their bacon a lot of times. Frequently, when customers had a question about a part and the inside salespeople were busy, the call would come to me. I sold a lot of parts that way." This is selling exposure.

Notice there were no apologies and no saying, "Well, no, I've never really done it, but I have observed it." The person unabashedly and convincingly described his *exposure* to inside sales without giving any apologies or excuses regarding his lack of direct sales experience. He comes across as confident and aware.

Safe Answers

As you read my suggestions you may notice that I often recommend safe answers, answers that are not controversial. There is, in fact, a strong case to be made for safe answers, but always within the context of truthfulness. It is important to give the interviewer a sense of your openness and credibility. But this also requires discretion.

Your challenge is to get the employer to make a job offer. You want the opportunity to accept it or reject it and you do not want to give the interviewer any excuses for rejecting you. So discretion is the key. If you are asked why you want to leave your present job, you may have six reasons. Discretion tells you to only mention three of them. The interviewer may ask about your greatest weakness or the biggest job-related mistake you ever made. By all means share a genuine weakness and reveal a real mistake, but it need not be your greatest weakness or your biggest mistake. Revealing either might hurt your chances for a job offer.

This is a tricky topic to cover because I believe in the importance of honesty. With all of this in mind, however, there are times when you must choose not to reveal something. Whatever you say should be true, but there are times when you may withhold additional information. Use this as a principle to determine how you will respond to some of the really tough questions.

The honesty issue and the safe answer issue are not identical, so let's return to safe answers. Controversy will never benefit you and should be avoided. During an interview, an issue might come up that you would just love to go after with all of your views and opinions. Don't do it. In fact, the interviewer may even be baiting you just to see how you will react.

Base your answers on what you have already learned about the job and your prospective boss. Say you have twenty strengths that you are prepared to discuss during an interview, but you quickly realize that four of them would simply not sell you in this particular job with this particular supervisor. Naturally you would choose not to mention those four, but would sell the other sixteen at every opportunity. That is safe and prudent.

You may be a person who relishes independence on the job. Yet when asked what your job-related needs are, you might choose not to mention this because you have sensed that this employer likes to maintain close contact with employees.

*Harry decided this was the time to determine if they
would accept him just the way he was.*

Some might suggest that it's better to clear the air right away. I call this the let-it-all-hang-out syndrome. It is justified by the belief, "If they don't like me the way I am, then I don't want to work there anyway." While this may be a rather noble approach, it does not yield the desired result—a job offer. Get the offer, then decide if you want to work there.

Sell Yourself At Every Opportunity

One principle in interviewing is to always go for it. When the job you are interviewing for is fully described, and it seems to be less than what you really want, go for the offer anyway. People often consciously or unconsciously sabotage their own efforts, and as a result, don't get asked back for a second interview. My belief is that you never know whether you want the job until an offer is made, money is on the table, benefits have been covered, and you have had a chance to negotiate in the things you want in, and to negotiate out the things you want out. People have negotiated for amazing things—and gotten them—but only because they had sold themselves so well that the employers were willing to do almost anything to bring them on board.

Sabotaging your efforts means that, somehow, you have failed to do your best. Consciously or unconsciously, your answers are not as sharp, not as well thought out, the zip in your voice is missing. The interviewer picks up on these cues.

I realize there are times when you immediately know the job is not for you. If this happens, resist the temptation to tune out. Perhaps the interviewer will also realize *this* job is not the right one for you and will offer you a *different* job instead.

You might indicate at the end of the interview that the job is not a good match. If you are highly interested in the company, however, or would especially like to work for this person, say so. There may be nothing else available right now, but the perfect job could materialize during the next six months, and you might be the prime candidate. If the person is impressed, she may refer you to someone else in the company who could use your talents. There is always the possibility that the job could be changed to suit you better. None of these positive things can happen if you stop selling yourself or fail to respond as best you can.

Show What You Can Do For Them

One of the biggest turnoffs for employers is the candidate who seems self-centered and cares only about what the company can do for him or her. Employment is certainly a two-way street and there must be give and take, but during the interview the emphasis *must* be on how you can benefit the organization.

To paraphrase John Kennedy's famous challenge, "Ask not what your company can do for you, but ask what you can do for your company." After the offer is made there is plenty of time to talk money and other things. Until then, emphasize what you can do for the organization.

Answering Ambiguous Questions

Employers often ask questions that can be interpreted in more than one way. Examples could be, "What is the biggest mistake you ever made?" or "What was the biggest crisis you ever experienced?" In both, it is unclear whether the employer wants job-related experiences or personal experiences. It is better not to ask for clarification. Take a direction that is easier for you, safer, or will show you in a better light. Take, for example, the question about your biggest mistake. It may be easiest and wisest to simply mention a personal experience. The employer can always come back and ask the question again if more information is desired. But at least you gave an honest answer. Usually, if you give a good answer, the person will be satisfied and will go on to the next question.

One reason to not ask for clarification on these types of questions is that it breaks the continuity of the interview and can seem awkward. You may seem too cautious and afraid to take risks. I am not saying never ask for clarification. At times you must. If the question is important, and the ambiguity is so great that you dare not take a wrong direction, by all means ask for clarification.

Excite An Employer

You can genuinely get an employer excited about you. You do so by demonstrating that you can do any or all of the following: 1) **make** money for the organization; 2) **save** money for the organization; 3) **solve** problems the employer is facing; and 4) **reduce** the level of stress and pressure the employer is under.

It's fairly easy to show how you have helped a company make money, save money, and solve problems. You do this by describing actual examples. Less obvious, but just as valuable, is demonstrating that you can reduce the stress and pressure your prospective boss is facing. Start by selling your reliability, responsibility, and resourcefulness. By having confidence that responsibilities can be delegated to someone of your caliber, your prospective boss will actually visualize a life filled with less pressure.

Strange Questions

Sometimes you'll get questions which are really hard to prepare for, such as, "If you were an animal, which animal would you like to be?" Don't panic with this type of question. Clearly, there is no right or wrong answer. The interviewer is observing you to see how you handle unusual things. Don't over analyze it. In this case, you would simply think of an animal and explain why you would like to be that animal.

A client of mine was once asked to take the recruiter through a typical day at work. He was asked how he knew what to do, how he knew it was time to go home, how he felt when people doubted him, and what types of people intimidated him. Because these are unusual questions, it is impossible to prepare for them. You need to be so well-prepared and knowledgeable about yourself that you will always be able to come up with a good response, even to questions you didn't anticipate.

ATTITUDES

How you approach an interview and the attitudes you adopt will have a tremendous impact on your success at interviewing. There are three attitudes that can destroy your interviewing effectiveness: being apologetic or defensive, providing inappropriate information, and expressing anti-business feelings.

Apologetic/Defensive
Many job applicants come across as apologetic or defensive. This usually occurs because they feel insecure and believe their background is weak in certain areas. Consider the following responses to the comment, "Ted, we're looking for someone with six years of computer programming and systems analysis."

An apologetic response: "I'm sorry, I only have four years of experience. I wish I had gone to school earlier in my career, then I'd have the six years. I really blew it."

A defensive response: "Well, I don't have six years of experience, I have four years. Every place I go they want more experience than I have. What's wrong with my background?"

Whether apologetic or defensive, Ted's lack of confidence comes through loud and clear. If the applicant lacks self-confidence, how can the interviewer be expected to have confidence in his or her ability?

Now consider Ted's response after he's had some interview coaching: "Mr. Jenkins, I've had four years of programming experience. Because of the variety of my experience, however, it's equal to what most people gain in seven or eight years. During these last four years I've taken on every challenge I could so I'd be ready for this type of responsibility."

Ted has learned the art of overcoming objections. The interviewer was probably impressed with Ted already when the question was asked. The job description specified six years of experience, but the interviewer realized it was not just a matter of years, but of the quality of experience. He was testing Ted, and Ted passed.

Inappropriate Information

Giving inappropriate information in an interview can be disastrous. Let's assume an interview has just started and the two people are still involved in small talk:

Interviewer: Did you see the latest Gallup Poll? It indicated the number-one goal of college students today is to get a good job and make a lot of money. Things sure have changed since the 60s, haven't they?

Sandy: I think they've sold out. Everything now is "what's in it for me?" When I was in school people cared and they took action. Look at what we did with the marches on Washington and the 1968 Democratic Convention.

Job interviews are not the place to discuss religion or politics. Both are emotional issues. You can win in such discussions only if your views coincide with the interviewer's. It's seldom worth taking the chance. In principle, any statements that do not help to sell you should be left out.

It is also inappropriate to be giving your opinions in an interview. Have you known people who are so opinionated that they constantly insist on telling you what they think, whether you want their opinion or not? For instance, it would be very inappropriate to say something like, "Mr. Bertram, it's probably none of my business, but have you noticed how old fashioned your logo looks?" Do you think this person scored any points?

Anti-Business

Especially during the 60s and 70s, many college graduates went into interviews expressing a strong distaste for big business and capitalism. Business people do not feel the need to defend the profit motive, neither do they want to enter a debate regarding investments in South Africa or their record on pollution control. Raising these and other anti-business issues merely raises questions about you.

If you have strong views on various issues, however, there is a solution. Research the company prior to the interview to determine how well it matches your values. If you like the organization and you're called in for a second interview, research the organization more thoroughly. Even if your research doesn't give you a definitive answer about the organization, go to the interview and thoroughly sell yourself. If the matter you're concerned about is an emotional issue for you, it is probably best not to ask questions concerning the issue until the job is actually offered to you. When you do ask your questions, ask in a calm, objective fashion. If the company passes your test, you have an employer who shares your values.

KNOW HOW TO DEAL WITH PROBING QUESTIONS

The key to handling probing questions is to eliminate the necessity of being asked such questions. Probes occur because the interviewer is not satisfied with the information obtained. The interviewer may follow up with another question simply because the answer was incomplete, or because the interviewer believes you may be withholding something. Your challenge is to provide enough information to satisfy the interviewer, but not supply so much information that it hurts you. Probing questions might arise around such issues as your weaknesses, why you were terminated, or why you've had four jobs in the last five years. Clearly, you can't score points with questions like these, so the tendency is to provide an extremely brief answer. If interviewers suspect you're avoiding something, however, they often go for the jugular. An interviewer could ask three or four additional probing questions and use up 10–15 precious minutes doing it.

Several approaches can help you pre-empt probing questions. For example, you should know in advance what questions could potentially hurt you. If you were recently fired, you know what the difficult question will be. When you've decided which questions might hurt you, practice your responses. Avoid sounding evasive, anxious, or defensive in your answers. Provide enough information to satisfy a normal person. Share things which you feel the person might be able to relate to.

QUESTIONS TO BE PREPARED FOR

I see a lot of people who only do a passable job in interviews, and the cause is almost always lack of preparation. Since nearly every conceivable question can be anticipated, you can have a real edge over others by being ready for them.

Below are 76 questions which are frequently asked or cause great difficulty for interviewees. Write each question on a sheet of paper, and then briefly list the points you would like to make in response to them. Do not write out your responses word for word and try to memorize the answers. In an interview you may forget parts and stumble. Besides, your answers would sound "canned." Instead, briefly list the main points you'd like to cover, then practice speaking the answers. This will help prepare you to give thoughtful but spontaneous-sounding answers.

1. Tell me about yourself.

2. What is your greatest strength?

3. What can you offer us that someone else can't?

4. What are your three most important career accomplishments?

5. What is your greatest weakness?

6. What kind of recommendations will you get from previous employers?

7. What are your career goals?

8. Describe your perfect job.

9. What is most important to you in a job?

10. Why do you want to change careers?

11. Why do you want to get into this field?

12. What do you really want to do in life?

13. What position do you expect to hold in five years?

14. Why would you like to work for us?

15. Why do you want to leave your present employer?

16. How long have you been out of work?

17. Why did you leave?

18. What actions would you take if you came on board?

19. How long will it take before you make a positive contribution to our organization?

20. What is your opinion of your present (or past) employer?

21. How long would you stay if we offered you this position?

22. What do you like least about this position? Most?

23. What personal, non-job-related goals have you set for yourself?

24. What do you know about our company?

25. Are you willing to relocate?

26. Can you supervise people?

27. Can you work well under stress?

28. Do you prefer to work individually or as part of a team?

29. Are you a team player?

30. Tell me about your duties at your present job.

31. What frustrates you about your job?

32. Describe your relationship with your last three supervisors.

33. Are you willing to travel overnight?

34. How do you feel about overtime?

35. What jobs have you enjoyed most? Least? Why?

36. What are your supervisor's strengths and weaknesses?

37. What have you learned from your mistakes? What were some of them?

38. What do you think determines a person's progress with a good company?

39. How would you describe yourself?

40. Why did you pick your major?

41. What kind of grades did you have?

42. What courses did you like most? Least? Why?

43. How has your schooling prepared you for this job?

44. Do you feel you did the best work at school that you were capable of doing?

45. Why should I hire you?

46. Who has exercised the greatest influence on you? How?

47. What duties have you enjoyed most? Least? Why?

48. What kind of supervisors do you like most? Least? Why?

49. Have you ever been fired or asked to resign?

50. Why have you changed jobs so frequently?

51. Describe the biggest crisis in your career.

52. Why have you been out of work so long? What have you been doing?

53. What public figure do you admire most and why?

54. What are your primary activities outside of work?

55. Would you have any concern if we did a full background check on you? What would we find?

56. What qualities do you most admire in other people?

57. Tell me about the last incident that made you angry. How did you handle it?

58. How has your supervisor helped you grow?

59. What did your supervisor rate you highest on during your last review? Lowest?

60. What are the things that motivate you?

61. How do you handle people that you really don't get along with?

62. Describe your management philosophy and management style.

63. What is the biggest mistake you ever made?

64. How many people have you hired? How do you go about it? How successful have the people been?

65. How many people have you fired? How did you handle it?

66. How would your subordinates describe you as a supervisor?

67. Some managers watch their employees very closely while others use a loose rein. How do you manage?

68. How have you improved as a supervisor over the years?

69. What kind of supervisor gets the best results out of you?

70. What have you done to increase your personal development?

71. How do you feel about your career progress?

72. What is unique about you?

73. What types of books and magazines do you read?

74. Starting with your first job out of college, tell me why you left each organization.

75. What is your boss like?

76. How would your supervisor describe you?

In the following material, I've given you principles you can use to answer each of these commonly asked questions. In some instances I have given examples of what could be said. When examples have been provided, it is not with the belief that these short responses are adequate to answer the entire question. Your responses will almost assuredly be longer. Use this material as a guide, then develop your own responses.

1. *Tell me about yourself.* Most people hate this question. By preparing for it, however, and knowing what a wonderful opportunity it is to sell yourself, you should look forward to it. It is the most frequently asked question in interviewing. It usually serves as a bridge to go from small talk to the real interview.

Briefly describing your education or your work history are appropriate responses to this question. Even though the employer has your resume at hand, describing interesting aspects of each job can add a nice touch. Expand briefly on some of your results. This will likely cause the interviewer to select an accomplishment and ask you to tell more about it. That is exactly what you want; you score points every time you discuss results. After bringing the employer up to the present, and if you believe you have maintained his or her interest, describe one of your top strengths. You might summarize by saying:

Basically I'm an analytical person. For example, at Dependable Services, no one really knew how much our services were costing the company. I had taken courses in cost accounting in college, so I figured out the actual costs, taking depreciation of our equipment into consideration. I discovered that one of our services actually cost us 7% more than we charged for it. We raised our fees immediately. That alone earned an additional $17,000.

2. *What is your greatest strength?* The question asks for your number-one strength, skill, or asset and requires you to analyze yourself. Going into the interview you should have several strengths in mind. Share the strength you feel will score the most points. Begin with a brief statement and provide a clear example. A person interviewing for a management position might respond:

I would say it's my ability to train and motivate people. At XYZ there was a severe turnover problem among their first-line supervisors. Even without the benefit of a pay increase, which they deserved, I reduced the turnover from 20% to 7% in just six months and to 5% by the end of the year. My analysis indicated that our foremen were receiving inadequate training when they were promoted to supervisors. Most were unsure of their authority and how to use it. Many quit out of frustration. I developed a training program which really gave them confidence. Once we got the supervisors trained, productivity in the plant rose substantially.

3. *What can you offer us that someone else can't?* Since you can't possibly know what backgrounds the other candidates have, you must respond by describing your known strengths. If you feel certain that you have some valuable or unique experience, you would certainly want to use that as an example.

4. *What are your three most important career accomplishments?* Choose accomplishments that are related to the job you are interviewing for, and ones which your interviewer can relate to. Avoid unnecessary detail. A question like this gives you a fantastic opportunity to sell yourself. Take full advantage of it.

5. *What is your greatest weakness?* This is one of the most asked questions, yet interviewees typically do poorly with it. Avoid trying to score points with this question. If the interviewer asks you this question, it is guaranteed that everyone else will be asked as well. Everyone being interviewed will have to reveal something that is somewhat negative. Some "interviewing experts" advise people to select something which is really a strength and disguise it as a weakness. They suggest statements such as, "I guess I'm a workaholic," or "Sometimes I'm too aggressive." The intent is to get the employer thinking, "That's not a bad weakness to have." Most interviewers readily see through such a ploy, however, and the interviewee immediately loses credibility. Show

yourself to be genuine and willing to reveal things about yourself.

Be prepared to discuss personal weaknesses as well as technical weaknesses. A personal weakness could be a tendency to procrastinate, while a technical weakness could be a lack of experience with Lotus 1–2–3.

When asked this difficult question, it is best to state a genuine weakness, but choose one which will not automatically disqualify you. It cannot be a trivial weakness, however, such as a manager saying he or she is all thumbs when it comes to typing.

Usually you would indicate that you have known about this weakness for some time and have taken definite steps to overcome it. You don't need to demonstrate that you have totally conquered it, but show that you've made major progress with it. Examples of weaknesses that people have used successfully include: "I'm not good at working with repetitive details," "It's hard for me to get to know people at first," and "Sometimes I'm not assertive enough." There are many possibilities, but it may take time to come up with one which is safe to use. In interviewing you can score anywhere from minus ten to plus ten on any question. On this question you are trying to remain in the minus two to plus one range. Something in the minus six range can seriously damage you, while trying to score plus five or better will jeopardize your credibility and sincerity. The goal is to provide a short answer which satisfies the interviewer, and allows you to move to other questions that you can score points on.

Any other weaknesses besides the fact that you crack your knuckles?

Fred was ready for the "What's your biggest weakness?" question.

After you decide which weakness to use, begin developing a response. Your response must show how it is a genuine weakness. In other words, you need to show how it has hurt you. Numerous clients have used their perfectionism as their greatest weakness. That will work, but you must show how perfectionism has caused problems for you. When I asked one client during a practice interview how perfectionism had hurt her, she replied, "Well, I guess it hasn't, but I just know that I shouldn't be so much of a perfectionist." I responded, "Then give me a real weakness." She had not convinced me that perfectionism was a genuine weakness, so when I asked for a real weakness she got flustered and did poorly throughout the remainder of the interview. So, you can see how important it is to answer this question properly.

Perfectionism can work, but let me show you how it might be used to better effect than the situation described above:

> I think probably my greatest weakness is my perfectionism. It seems that I want everything done just right, and it's hard to let go until it's almost perfect. Sometimes that means I'll spend too much time on a project when I really should go on to other things, since it's probably just fine the way it is. But then I'll look at it again and realize that it could be better with just a little fixing up. Sometimes I'm through in an hour, but other times I might dig into it again and spend another day or two on it. Last year that happened on a project, and because of it, another project had to be rushed and it was definitely not the quality it should have been. So now as I'm finishing up a project I'll just tell myself, 'It's fine as it is, just put it to bed.' Or I'll have a coworker look at it and if she thinks it's fine, it's usually easier to wrap it up. I know that I'll always be a perfectionist, but I think I've got it pretty well under control.

Where do you think she scored? I would put her around zero, or neutral, which is right where she should be. She came across as sincere and genuine. She was willing to open up and show that her perfectionism gets her in trouble at times, but she also demonstrated that it is almost under control. Undoubtedly an employer would have been satisfied with her response and would have gone on to other questions.

In addition to showing how the trait has hurt you, you can also show how it sometimes benefits you. In the case of our perfectionist she might add:

> Of course, as a perfectionist I'm also very thorough. Last year we were having a quality problem with one of our cold cream products. Customers were calling and complaining that when they got the product home, the oil had separated and risen to the top. Our chemists and manufacturing engineers were unable to find out what the problem was and we were getting ready to shut down production. As the marketing manager for that product, solving a production problem is not my area, but I did

not want to lose the market share that we had gained in the last two years. I starting researching the problem. One day I was chatting with a purchasing agent and asked him if any of the ingredients had been changed in any way. He said no, but then something clicked. I asked if we had changed any suppliers in the last four months. It turned out that we had started buying an emulsifier from a new vendor who claimed the product was identical to what we were using, but cost about 20% less. We checked the emulsifier, and sure enough it was substandard. We immediately returned to the previous vendor and the problem was solved. So I guess sometimes my perfectionism and thoroughness can pay off.

This example demonstrates that there are always two sides of a coin: The very quality that causes problems in one situation, can be very useful in another. When sharing a genuine weakness, it is fair to show the other side of the coin as well.

Another way to share a weakness is to describe one which has almost been overcome:

I absolutely hate firing people. In the past I held on to a couple people longer than I should have just because I hoped they'd turn around. I was just plain avoiding the inevitable. To prevent that from happening in the future I've been holding extensive interviews with the top candidates and performing thorough background checks. That way, I hire only those with the greatest potential. If I don't find what I want, I won't hire second best. I'll keep looking until I find the right person. The last five people I've hired have been really good choices.

You should be prepared to share three weaknesses. If one seems inappropriate for a particular job, you still have two others to choose from. You could also run into an interviewer who loves to ask about several weaknesses.

6. *What kind of recommendations will you get from previous employers?* You should know the answer to this question. Even though companies today are very hesitant to make negative statements about former employees because of possible defamation of character lawsuits, some will still do so. If you have been fired from one of your last three jobs, you would be wise to contact your former boss or the personnel department and ask what they will say. If the termination was justified, but you have since changed your ways, explain that to your former boss. Explain, too, how the firing was actually a blessing in disguise because you really learned from the experience.

If you know you will receive good recommendations you might simply say, "I'm certain each of my former bosses will have only positive things to say about me. We worked well together and I learned a lot from each one." You could also expand and describe some specific points the supervisors might make. In other words, let your supervisors sell you even though they are not present.

You may have had excellent relations with all but one former supervisor. How you would respond to the question, in that case, depends on what you find out when you recontact past supervisors. If you are confident that nothing negative will be said, simply respond by stating they will all say positive things. If you are fairly certain that a particular supervisor would say negative things about you, describe some of your results and indicate some areas where you and your boss differed. Your intent would be to soften or counteract what you believe your former boss may say. Psychologically it has less negative impact when an employer has already heard from you the negative statements that a former boss might make. Of course you need to be discreet about what you mention.

If your relations with that boss were poor, but you know the company has a strict policy about giving out information, do not indicate that your former boss would say anything negative about you. Be sure to read the material covering question 49 regarding having been fired or terminated. Even if you have never been fired or terminated, there are several key points in that section which will help you respond to this question.

7. *What are your career goals?* This question tests whether you've established career goals, and whether your goals match what the organization has to offer. Sound clear and definite about your goals, but express yourself based on what you know about the organization. Mention only those goals that you feel the organization can help you attain. Express them in terms of the experience you hope to receive and the expertise you hope to develop. You could use the opportunity to describe your present level of expertise and then how you want to further develop yourself. You want to leave the impression that you are a growth-oriented person with realistic expectations regarding promotion opportunities.

8. *Describe your perfect job.* Be careful. This is not the place to describe your dream job. Select those *parts* of your dream job, however, that you think could be fulfilled in the job you are interviewing for. If you dream of a job that would take you to Europe twice a year but this job offers no chance of that, don't mention your desire to travel. The greatest danger here is in becoming too specific. If you mention things that cannot be fulfilled in the job, the employer may assume you would soon become dissatisfied.

9. *What is most important to you in a job?* What do you value in a job—challenge, good working conditions, friendly coworkers, a boss you respect? Mention one or two items and explain why they are important.

10. *Why do you want to change careers?* I define career change as a change of fields, such that the skills and knowledge required to adequately perform the new occupation appear *on the surface* to be significantly different from what was required in the former occupation. The key phrase is *on the surface.* Most would agree that moving from teacher to sales representative is a career change. But when you get below the surface, you will see the similarities in these careers. Both motivate—one to buy, the other to learn. Both must be able to simplify and explain difficult concepts. Of course the teacher must develop product knowledge and learn specific closing techniques. But, because of the underlying similarities in these careers, teachers frequently make excellent salespeople.

Here's my point: In most cases, refuse to accept the label of career change. You might say:

> I don't feel I'm changing careers. Basically I'll be using the same skills I've developed during the last eight years of my career. My knowledge base will be somewhat different, but I took several college courses in this area, and during the last three years I've been subscribing to three trade journals and devouring every article in this specialty.

This is not just a question of semantics. The employer has stated that he or she believes you are making a career change. In essence, the employer has raised an objection about you. The employer is actually saying, "You don't have a track record, so how can I judge your ability to perform this job?" Unless you can overcome the objection, no job offer will be made. Respond by saying, "I don't feel I'm changing careers." Avoid defensiveness and sell those skills which are similar to ones required in the new field.

11. *Why do you want to get into this field?* This is different than "Why do you want to change careers?" This interviewer is looking for evidence that you really know what you're getting into. People getting into personnel work often respond, "I enjoy helping people." That is the worst possible response and indicates a total misunderstanding of personnel work. In answering this question, it's important to let the interviewer know that you are aware of positive *and* negative aspects of the field.

12. *What do you really want to do in life?* Sometimes this is a filler question. Most interviewers have received no training in the art of interviewing and many have little experience. Sometimes this type of question is inserted so the interviewer can think of the next question. Still, you want to be prepared so that your every response will demonstrate enthusiasm and potential.

This could be a time to share one of your dreams. Perhaps you want to enjoy a cruise around the world someday. Or you could select a job-related dream. Almost anything will be positive as long as you are genuinely enthusiastic about it.

13. *What position do you expect to hold in five years?* A question like this tests how realistic you are. It's not realistic to say you want to be president in five years when you are five levels below that and there are four hundred people ahead of you. It's okay to have such a goal, but don't express it. Employers seek promotable people, but tend to be suspicious of the person who expects to turn the company upside down. If your interviewer will be your boss or your boss's boss, you might say, "I would like to move up the ladder with you. I realize you have other very capable people in this department, but through my contributions I'll seek to be the person who moves into your position when you're promoted. In five years I'd like to move up two or three notches."

14. *Why would you like to work for us?* If this question is asked at or near the beginning of the first interview, you have an opportunity to describe what you know about the organization. If the question is asked after the interviewer has described the job and the company in detail, you could mention positive points that you had discovered on your own, as well as some mentioned by the interviewer. This might include the reputation of the company or department

16. *How long have you been out of work?* The employer who asks this question may simply be curious, in which case you would merely mention the month by saying, "I left in June." The employer could also be implying that he knows you've been out of work several months and wants to know why you haven't found a job yet. If you had to take care of certain personal or business-related responsibilities before you could get fully into your job search, you might want to mention those responsibilities. If you've had some job offers, mention that and state that they just weren't what you were looking for. Demonstrate that you intend to be selective. Then state that you are excited about the position you're interviewing for because you are being selective.

Do not be defensive when answering a question like this. Emphasize that you've been carrying out a systematic job search and that you've met many interesting people. See also question 52, *Why have you been out of work so long?*

17. *Why did you leave?* When you are asked this, you must overcome another objection, since it often seems safer to hire someone who has a job. Even when a person has been laid off during a recession, the question in the interviewer's mind is, "Most people in her company are still there. Why was she laid off?" The concern is that perhaps you sound impressive, but are not able to produce under pressure. Remember—an objection is *not* a rejection; it is a request for more information.

If you left voluntarily, make that clear and then explain the reason. A resignation due to a personality conflict must be handled carefully. Your explanation should make your leaving seem like a mature and responsible thing to do.

If you were fired, terminated, or laid off, you must handle this question very carefully. Do not become defensive and do not start criticizing your former boss. A good answer will require a carefully considered response. It is wise to know what your former employer will say about it. See question 49 for additional help if you were fired.

18. *What actions would you take if you came on board?* This question is usually asked to determine if you have preset ideas on what should be done. The person with all the answers after one or two interviews is usually not trusted. The people interviewing you consider themselves capable. If they have been studying a problem for months and don't have the answers, they don't expect you to have the answers either. Perhaps you really do have some solutions, but don't sound cocky. You'll be respected more if you admit it will take time to study the situation, than to say you will have a complete set of recommendations by next week.

This question also tests your thought process. The steps you would take to solve a problem can reveal more about your character and your expertise than the actual recommendations you might make.

19. *How long will it take before you make a positive contribution to our organization?* This question tests your self-confidence. A good response might be, "After a brief orientation to your methods, I think I can contribute almost immediately. The duties you've outlined are very similar to the ones I've been performing at Jersey Central." The interviewer will be looking for a realistic, self-confident response. You do not have to come across as a miracle worker.

20. *What is your opinion of your present (or past) employer?* The interviewer does not expect you to speak in glowing terms about your employer, but you should emphasize the positive qualities. If you really like your present organization, your response will be easy. If you hate it, be careful. Start by saying something positive, followed by one or two minor negatives, and finish with a strong positive. This is not the time to blast your employer. If you mention only negatives, the interviewer may assume you are a negative person who is difficult to satisfy.

21. *How long would you stay if we offered you this position?* This is an impossible question to answer. No one really knows how long he or she will stay. The best way to handle it is to lay out the conditions for your staying:

> I hope to stay indefinitely. Everything I know about the company tells me this is an ideal fit. The philosophy of top management matches mine

and I like everything I've seen so far. Advancement and pay are certainly important to me. As long as my responsibilities and income grow with my proven worth, I expect to stay a long time.

Notice how stating the conditions made it seem like a much more realistic and honest response. You are unlikely to be believed if you say that you expect to stay with the company for 20 years and then retire. Furthermore, such a statement may make it seem as though everything you say is designed simply to match what the interviewer wants to hear.

If you have an unstable work history, you must develop a convincing statement which clearly shows that those days have ended. Actually, you should begin dealing with this issue as soon as you can in the interview; don't wait for the interviewer to bring it up. At the first opportunity mention what makes this job appealing. You could also sprinkle in subtle hints that there is more stability in your life at this time and that you would value a stable job as well. These comments will help you emphasize that you are a very reliable, responsible person.

22. *What do you like least about this position? Most?* By asking these questions, the interviewer is trying to get below the surface and force you to make some definite statements. This is a hard one to prepare for because you won't usually know enough about the job prior to the interview to prepare adequately. An effective way to deal with these questions is to describe a minor duty as one you like least and a major duty as one you like most.

23. *What personal, non-job-related goals have you set for yourself?* If you take time to consider your goals in life, both job- and nonwork-related, the answer will be easy. The interviewer will be determining if you are a thoughtful person. Goals related to your family are always acceptable and often preferred because they demonstrate stability. Anything related to personal growth is very acceptable, such as taking night classes, learning a foreign language, building your own home, or jogging.

24. *What do you know about our company?* The employer asks this question to determine your interest, enthusiasm, and initiative. There's no faking this question—either you've done your homework or you haven't. Typically you would describe what you know about their products or services, the reputation of the organization, the size of the organization in relation to its competitors, and any financial information you've picked up. If you've thoroughly analyzed the company's annual report, don't overwhelm the interviewer with financial data. Share any interesting knowledge about the company you've gathered, such as a new product or acquisition.

25. *Are you willing to relocate?* The only response is, "Yes, I'm pre-pared to make a move." If you answer "no," the interview is over. At this stage no harm is done by saying "yes;" you merely keep the inter-view alive. Actually what you're saying secretly to yourself is, "Yes, I'd relocate for a great opportunity." Of course by the time the job is of-fered, you should know whether you would actually be willing to relo-cate.

26. *Can you supervise people?* A positive statement followed by an example works well. "Yes, I supervise people very well. At Somestates Insurance I supervised eight claims adjusters. Through my personal training I was able to teach more effective negotiating tech-niques. As a result, our average personal injury settlement was reduced 4% last year." Relate one or more good examples, always keeping them short and to the point. When appropriate you might discuss your phi-losophy and techniques of supervision.

27. *Can you work well under stress?* You don't have to say that you like stress, but you should provide an example or two demonstrat-ing that you work effectively under stress. Most stress comes from deadlines and long hours. Perhaps the question is asked since in the past people have quit because they could not tolerate the stress. You should know in advance whether this organization, field, or industry typically requires long hours or faces lots of deadlines.

28. *Do you prefer to work individually or as part of a team?* The best response depends on what you know about the job. If the organi-zation is looking for a decisive person, you would emphasize your in-dividualism and independence. If most work is done by committees and task forces, emphasize your ability to work as part of a team. If you are not sure of the best response, describe how you enjoy both aspects.

29. *Are you a team player?* With the question worded in this way you are virtually assured that they are looking for a team-oriented per-son. Describe how you are philosophically committed to working as a team. Indicate that you do not hesitate to state your beliefs, but when the group makes a decision, you willingly go along with it. Show that you are flexible and cooperative. Provide evidence that people enjoy having you on their team. Use an example where effective teamwork was essential to the success of the project.

30. *Tell me about your duties at your present job.* This question provides an opportunity to really sell yourself, yet many miss this op-portunity. Mention only those duties that will help sell you. Sometimes this even means overlooking a major duty simply because that duty would not be related to the job you're interviewing for. As you describe your major duties, describe an associated accomplishment as well.

A good overview will require two or three minutes. Be concise, however. Because people know their duties so well, many go on and on, adding unnecessary details that bore the interviewer. At this point the job sketches you used to prepare your resume will come in handy again. Many people review their job sketches before each interview so they'll be ready for this and other questions. Based on what you know of the job you will be interviewing for, select those duties that you would like to discuss, then practice sharing them concisely and with enthusiasm.

31. *What frustrates you about your job?* Give concrete examples when answering this question. If you feel strongly about a particular frustration, and would refuse future job offers if you would continue to face that frustration, describe that frustration in bold terms. For example:

> When I started in quality control, Acme was producing very high quality drill bits. We applied stringent tests before they passed inspection. Because our new plant superintendent gets his annual bonus based on production, however, during the last year or so he has forced me to approve shipments that simply will not produce the results that our reputation was built on. That's why I'm especially interested in Best Tools. All of our tests on competitors show that you consistently produce high quality drill bits.

If you don't feel so strongly about any of your frustrations, or you wouldn't let them stand in the way of accepting a job, you'll want to choose more minor frustrations. Another quality inspector might say, "There really aren't any major frustrations. I was frustrated a few times when I wasn't allowed to buy new testing equipment when I felt we could use it, but we got by." Your response should sound justifiable, such that your interviewer will think, "I'd be frustrated too, if I were in that situation."

32. *Describe your relationship with your last three supervisors.* This question is easy to answer if you've had great relationships with your supervisors. If the relationships were less than sterling, you don't have to pretend they were wonderful, just accentuate the positive. If you had a hot and cold relationship with a supervisor, stress the things which you know your boss valued about you. It is acceptable to say, "We didn't agree on everything, but we both respected each other a great deal. We learned how to work around those differences. Once decisions were made, I would back her completely, and she valued that." A statement like this shows maturity on the interviewee's part. After all, even your interviewer has probably had four or more bosses. I can guarantee you that not all of them were wonderful. If you try to paint a picture that your relationship with each supervisor was ideal, you will seem less credible to your interviewer.

33. *Are you willing to travel overnight?* The question may be worded as generally as this, or it may be more specific: "This job involves at least four nights on the road each month. Is that acceptable to you?" Prior to the interview you should have an idea of whether the job you are seeking typically involves overnight travel. Even if the amount of travel mentioned in the interview is more than you had anticipated, respond with, "That's no problem." This response will simply keep the interview alive. Later you will determine whether you are willing to do it. If the amount of travel is more than you want, but you believe there are ways to reduce it, keep selling yourself. Get the offer, then negotiate the travel issue.

34. *How do you feel about overtime?* If you've had jobs that required overtime, simply describe how you handled it. If you have not had a job which required much overtime, you might respond, "I'm the type of person who will do whatever it takes to get the job done right." Before accepting the job, however, you will need to know whether you will be expected to work overtime regularly or only occasionally.

35. *What jobs have you enjoyed most? Least? Why?* To prepare for this question, think through and recall each of your positions. Relive them. What brought you satisfaction? What was frustrating? If you have been out of college several years, do not bring up summer or part-time jobs—most people assume that such jobs are unrewarding and frustrating. You need not admit that you hated any of the positions, however. The question only requires that you discuss which jobs you enjoyed least.

36. *What are your supervisor's strengths and weaknesses?* This question could pertain to any previous supervisor. To answer it, concentrate on strengths. Play down weaknesses, even if they were many. Select a fairly minor weakness to discuss.

37. *What have you learned from your past mistakes? What were some of them?* All of us have made mistakes. Often, there were lessons to be learned from these mistakes. So, when you answer this question, share some mistakes, but not any major ones. Determine in advance whether you will discuss personal mistakes or business-related mistakes. The best mistakes to share are those that you were able to recover from. For instance, you might describe a mistake that created a temporary setback for you, or one you recovered from by putting in extra time. If a mistake cost you or your employer money, show how the lesson ultimately benefitted you or your employer. With some mistakes, enough time has elapsed that you are able to laugh about them. Thus, they may offer an opportunity to inject some humor into the interview. In any event, use your mistakes to show how you have matured and grown from these experiences.

38. *What do you think determines a person's progress with a good company?* A survey by Korn-Ferry, the international executive search firm, indicates that senior executives believe that hard work, high integrity, intelligence, and excellent human relations skills got them where they are today. Your answer should reflect those main points plus factors such as the ability to get results and sell ideas.

39. *How would you describe yourself?* To answer this question, discuss only positive attributes and then describe or give examples to show how you typically demonstrate those attributes. Emphasize your personality skills.

40. *Why did you pick your major?* Typically, this question will only be asked of those who have graduated within the last five years. To answer it, try to recall your reasons for choosing your major, and then give only the most positive reasons. The question gives you the opportunity to demonstrate your forethought and planning ability. Indicate that the decision was made only after considerable thought. If you are not using your major—you were a psych major now looking to get into banking—indicate the strengths you were able to develop as a result of your major.

41. *What kind of grades did you have?* If your grades were mediocre, you need to prepare for this question. If, while you were in school, you worked 20–30 hours per week you might say, "I was a good student and worked hard in my classes. I'm confident that if I hadn't had to work nearly full-time during school I could have maintained a 3.0 GPA." If you simply weren't a good student you might say, "I've never been a great student, but I do retain information well and I use a lot of common sense. That's always been my strength."

42. *What courses did you like most? Least? Why?* For courses that you liked, mention those that are most related to the job you're interviewing for. Otherwise simply choose courses which excited you and explain why. It's safe to mention courses having little to do with the job as those you liked least. For instance, business majors can say they least enjoyed science courses and can even admit they disliked accounting.

43. *How has your schooling prepared you for this job?* If your education is directly related to the job you are interviewing for, emphasize that your education has given you a strong foundation upon which to build. If you are a liberal arts major, emphasize your broad education, your written and verbal communications skills, and your analytical ability. If you are seeking a job in private enterprise, discuss any business-related courses you took, such as macroeconomics.

44. *Do you feel you did the best work at school that you were capable of doing?* If you truly worked hard at your studies, you might say,

"I worked very hard and really took my studies seriously. I graduated with a 3.2 GPA (or with honors). Even the classes I didn't do so well in grade-wise really taught me something." Or you might say, "I worked hard and got good grades, but I also wanted to balance my education. I was active in [student government, debate, sports, dorm counseling, etc.]." If you received poor grades you could admit to a lack of focus at the time, adding that you are very focused now.

45. *Why should I hire you?* This question is often asked at the end of an interview and allows you to summarize your strengths. Since this is a summary, you can discuss points that you've already covered and mention new points as well. Sell yourself. This may be one of your best opportunities. Be prepared to take up to four minutes. Try to focus on everything you have learned about the job, your future boss, and the needs of the company. With such limited time, you must cover only those points which will have the greatest impact. You can create that impact by describing a combination of personality skills, transferable skills, and technical skills.

46. *Who has exercised the greatest influence on you? How?* This question is designed to discover what type of person you are and to reveal a side of you that the interviewer might not otherwise see. People will often mention parents, relatives, former bosses, coaches, and teachers as having influenced them. Being asked this question is an opportunity to describe what they taught you. Emphasize that these qualities are deeply ingrained in you.

47. *What duties have you enjoyed most? Least? Why?* Select your favorite and least favorite duties based on what you have learned about the job for which you're interviewing. In general, pick major duties to like and minor duties to dislike. A disliked duty might be one you have done in the past but would not be doing in the job being interviewed for.

48. *What kind of supervisors do you like the most? Least? Why?* To prepare for this question, list all of the qualities you truly like and dislike in a supervisor. When the question is asked, select those that are most appropriate. For your preferred characteristics, select two or more that your future boss appears to have. For dislikes, select qualities that appear not to be true of this person. Be careful with a statement like, "I don't like a supervisor who won't give me enough independence." You may come across as a maverick. Don't just make a statement—explain what you mean. Instead of the above, you might say, "It's frustrating working for someone who can't delegate effectively." See the difference? No one appreciates someone who does not delegate well. You would then go on to describe yourself as one who is highly reliable and self-directing, capable of taking on major challenges.

49. *Have you ever been fired or asked to resign?* This is perhaps the most difficult question of all. Fortunately, many managers have at some time in their career been fired, or have sought new employment while under pressure to do so. Studies indicate that about 80% of firings are over personality issues rather than competence: good chemistry becomes bad chemistry, the company changes but the employee is unable to adapt, or new managers come in with different values and expectations. Being fired is not the kiss of death to a career.

Your goal is to develop a response that demonstrates maturity. If you can handle this question with dignity and maturity you will raise your esteem in the eyes of the interviewer. Cause the interviewer to realize that regardless of the reasons for the termination, you are a person with a great deal of potential. Speak in such a way that the interviewer neither questions your competency nor integrity. For this reason you must never "attack" your former boss or company. Everything you say must be said without the hint of defensiveness or rancor.

Another goal is to go into interviews calmly and with confidence, with no fear of this question being asked. I have worked with clients whose dread of this question was clearly communicated by their nervousness. To overcome this problem, I usually have clients work on the response and the delivery until it becomes merely another question.

If you were recently fired, one approach is to tackle the question head on. Admit that you were fired, and then without any defensiveness, explain the reasons. While explaining the reasons, be sure to describe your strengths and contributions as well. If you believe it was unfair, say so, but avoid calling your former boss names, raising your voice or losing your temper. While not blaming yourself for the outcome, you could mention things that, looking back now, you wish you had done differently. Concentrate on describing the situation and explaining that under those conditions a termination occurred. The key to this approach is explaining things in a totally nondefensive manner. Because of the understandable concern of the employer, your task is to convince the person that this was a one-time occurrence which will not affect your future performance.

It is perfectly acceptable to indicate that you were a top-quality employee who received excellent reviews. You might indicate that you got caught in a political squeeze. In such a case, state that you understand that this is simply part of business. Sometimes you can say you supported the wrong person during a power struggle. Frequently if the boss is fired, the subordinate's termination follows not long after.

You may want to admit that had you been more astute, you would have quit months earlier. You might mention that sometime prior to the termination the organization began experiencing serious problems. Looking back you should have started looking for another job, but out of loyalty to the company and a desire to make things work, you stayed too long. In your answer you can admit that you and your boss differed in management style and philosophy of management. You could say "She's a very good manager, we just had different ways of getting the job done."

If your position has not been filled since you left, that could give you an out. You could explain that the company was having financial difficulties and that you were laid off.

By the way, it is always more positive if you can say you were laid off rather than terminated or fired. It may be beneficial to work out such an arrangement with your former boss or the human resources director.

Generally a past employer has no desire to hurt a terminated employee's career. If that's true in your case, discuss your situation with your former boss and reach an agreement on what both of you will say when asked. Agreement is essential. Your former boss needs to know what you will be saying so he or she can back you up. In these days when people are suing their former employers for defamation of character, your company has every reason to want to help you.

If you were fired from a job several years ago, you should contact your former boss. You might explain that getting fired was the best thing that ever happened because it shook you up and you got your act together. You would go on to explain that you have been successful since that time. You might then suggest some things the former boss could say if contacted by a prospective employer. The former boss will probably be glad to hear from you and will be more than happy to assist you. Surprisingly, the negative things which caused the termination are often forgotten, with only positive qualities now being remembered.

Even if you still hate your former boss, the two of you need to talk. I have had clients who strongly resisted this and absolutely never wanted to see or talk to that person again. Once accomplished, however, I have never seen anyone regret having done it, even when the outcome was a less than total success.

If you've been fired, you **must** know what your former boss is saying about you! The issue is often taken care of in your discussion with your former boss, and can be confirmed by having the person write a letter of recommendation for you. When someone has *written* nice things about you, it is much harder to *say* bad things about you. If the recommendation seems half-hearted, have the person write it again. You are not powerless. One client had her boss revise the letter three times before she was satisfied. Her request was tactful but firm; she virtually forced him to write a better letter.

Having the discussion with your former boss and getting a letter of recommendation may be enough, but often it isn't. Sometimes you just won't trust your former boss. If you have any doubts regarding what is being said about you, obtain the help of someone who can find out. An executive recruiter or employment agency counselor would be good, but a friend or anyone who does hiring could do it just as well. The person should not only write down what is said, but also indicate the tone of voice. The tone of voice can totally change the meaning of what was said. The person making the call may indicate you are being considered for a position and should then ask what type of an employee you were. You should provide the person helping you with a job title and brief description to help make this process more effective.

Often, it is the way a former boss gives a reference, rather than what is said, that makes the reference a bad one. While all the words may be right, the tone of voice can give a completely different message. Imagine someone saying, "Yes, he was a very good employee." Consider enthusiasm coming through in the voice. Then imagine the same words with a couple pauses and a complete lack of enthusiasm. The identical words can create two distinct impressions.

I've had many clients who were fired from positions. One person had been fired from an executive position. Due to his past successes he was highly marketable and began getting interviews throughout the country. He was flown to interviews in several major cities. Although the interviews seemed to be highly successful, he was not offered any of the positions. After three months and interviews for seven high-level positions, he discovered that his former boss was giving him negative "recommendations." He confronted the person and it was agreed that a more favorable person would provide future recommendations. The client then quickly found another job. Numerous opportunities, however, had been lost because he waited so long to find out what was being said about him.

If you know your boss is going to be a bad reference, seek out someone else in the company to provide a reference for you. If the boss who fired you was not always your boss, list a previous boss, even if that person is no longer with the company. Sometimes your boss's boss will do an excellent job, since he or she is not hindered by the emotional issue which may be affecting your boss. Of course, whoever you use, he or she must know what you are doing and must agree to assist you.

Because of their concern regarding defamation of character lawsuits, many companies will not allow managers to give references. In those cases, people trying to check references will be referred to the personnel department where only job titles and the dates of employment will be confirmed. If your company has a strict policy of giving out only dates of employment, your task is made easier and you won't have to be concerned about what your boss might say.

If you were fired from a job years ago and there is no way for a company to discover that, you must decide whether you will reveal the firing or not.

I've given you some principles that should help you answer this difficult question. If your situation is particularly sticky, however, and you just can't come up with a good response, I would recommend obtaining the advice of a career specialist or executive recruiter. If you seek the help of a career counselor, make sure the person has extensive experience with interview coaching.

50. *Why have you changed jobs so frequently?* An interviewer asks this question when something in your background has given the appearance that you're a job hopper. If, at the end of your response, the interviewer still views you as unstable and unlikely to stay long enough to really contribute, you probably will not get the offer. If you have worked for three different companies in the last six years, you have not been the epitome of stability.

To overcome the objection you might begin by stating that there have been good reasons for leaving each position (there's no need to detail the reasons unless specifically asked) and that long-term employment is certainly your goal. Sometimes a person has spent 15 years with one company and then has a string of three one-year jobs. Emphasize the long-term position and indicate that your stability in that job reflects the true you. If there are only three or four changes to account for, do so briefly.

If you have not been stable, you might point out that you are now married, own a home, or any other point that might convince a person that stability has entered your life.

51. *Describe the biggest crisis in your life.* Describe a genuine crisis or difficult situation, not necessarily the biggest crisis you've faced. While the wording of the question will help you determine whether to mention a personal crisis or a work-related crisis, be prepared to describe either. Select an example that will demonstrate positive qualities and one in which you ultimately came out on top. Tell it concisely yet vividly to reveal as many qualities as possible. This is an opportunity to sell qualities such as maturity, perseverance, emotional stability, effectiveness under stress, and sound judgment.

52. *Why have you been out of work so long? What have you been doing?* This question is usually only asked of those who have been out of work for over six months. The concern is that while you seem capable, other employers have apparently discovered something negative enough not to hire you. Prepare for this question by listing on pa-

per what you were doing at each period. Did you take a long vacation or drop out for a while?

One approach is to show that you really have not been looking for long. Numerous things can account for your situation: you were waiting on a job which was promised you but never came through, you took care of a sick relative, you were managing the estate of a relative, or you took a long vacation. You may have worked briefly for a friend who needed help, decided to work on a temporary basis for awhile, or you took a break from work to recover from your last job. You may have spent considerable time deciding what you really wanted to do and just recently made that decision. You might mention only one item that kept you from your job search, or you may mention several. Plausibility is the key to a successful answer here. Explaining the reason for a long period of unemployment, by using an example like those mentioned here, is a form of damage control. In other words, such explanations won't help sell you, but they will reduce the concerns an employer may have about you.

You may have been looking steadily for a job for the past six or nine months. Sell the fact that you have been working hard at the job search just as you work hard at everything you do. You might indicate you have been quite selective and that this is one of the few jobs that has been attractive. If you have had offers but turned them down, mention them.

If you have been looking for over a year without success you should seek out the help of a professional career counselor who can help evaluate any weaknesses in your search and can get you back on track.

Even if you are having trouble paying the rent, do not allow any sense of desperation to show through during your interviews. Emphasize that you are a confident person merely waiting for the right opportunity.

In these situations women actually have an advantage. When women have long gaps in employment, it is assumed that child rearing was involved, even though this may not be the case. If you have chosen to stay home and raise children, however, merely explain it without sounding the least defensive about it. There is no need to defend this choice, even if a fast climbing career was temporarily put on hold as a result.

53. *What public figure do you admire most and why?* Quickly identify two or three people you admire. Generally they should be people who are widely admired but not overly controversial. Political figures are more risky, but can be used effectively. In the late 70s I had a client who indicated he admired both Menachem Begin and Anwar Sadat for the courage they showed during the Middle East peace ne-

gotiations. Another person did a good job with Richard Nixon. He said he did not like everything Nixon ever did, but he admired him for the way he opened up contact with the People's Republic of China. A local figure who is well known would also be an acceptable choice. Usually the question will be worded in such a way that the interviewer clearly wants a living person, so don't use historical figures such as Abe Lincoln. Generally, your reasons for admiring the person are more important than the specific person.

54. *What are your primary activities outside of work?* All of your activities reveal things about you so choose your answers carefully. If you mention one thing, you might balance it with another. For example, mentioning family activities shows certain positive qualities, but might be balanced with mentioning that you enjoy reading trade journals in your field.

55. *Would you have any concern if we did a full background check on you? What would we find?* The immediate response should be a simple, "Not at all." If damaging information would be discovered, however, this might be the time to share it so you can put it in the best light. But be discreet. This is not the time to bare your soul and confess everything you ever did.

56. *What qualities do you most admire in other people?* Pick four or five and explain why you value them so highly. This tells the employer more about you and your character.

57. *Tell me about the last incident that made you angry. How did you handle it?* Pick an example that would have made anyone angry. Describing how you reacted is particularly important. Make sure your reaction was mature, rather than childish. If it was a somewhat childish reaction, describe it in a humorous way so both of you can laugh about it.

58. *How has your supervisor helped you grow?* Whether you have a great supervisor or a lousy one, every supervisor will add to your personal growth in some way. If, for example, your supervisor has no human relations skills, emphasize how the person has helped you grow in technical knowledge.

59. *What did your supervisor rate you highest on during your last review? Lowest?* Emphasize the positive and give a complete explanation as to why your supervisor valued that quality. Undoubtedly there are four or five things that you were rated highly on. Pick the one or two items that will score the most points with this particular interviewer. Of those things you were rated lower in, you might say, "Overall, I was rated quite high in everything. I suppose if there was anything that my boss wanted me to work on it would be to work on my presentation skills. As a result of this, I'm now enrolled in Toastmasters and really enjoying it." When possible, emphasize a technical skill

that your boss simply wants you to work on, as opposed to a personality characteristic. It is always more acceptable to say you need to learn or perfect a technical skill rather than say, "My boss wants me to work on my tendency to be rude to customers."

60. *What are the things that motivate you?* Challenge, creativity, success, opportunity, and personal growth are the motivators most frequently mentioned. You can also mention specific skills that you are motivated to use. These might include troubleshooting, problem solving, planning, implementing, speaking, writing, or helping people.

61. *How do you handle people that you really don't get along with?* If you are one of those fortunate types who get along with almost anyone, tell the interviewer so. However you answer the question, indicate that you work hard to get along with others. Think through how you really do respond to difficult people. The interviewer is using this question as an opportunity to learn about your human relations skills. As a follow-up question the interviewer could ask you to describe an actual instance in which you dealt with a difficult person.

62. *Describe your management philosophy and management style.* To answer this question effectively you need to be clear on both your management philosophy and style. Management philosophy and style have to do with your beliefs regarding participative management, management by objectives, total quality management, methods for training and motivating employees, and dozens of concepts and techniques that are covered in books on management. Philosophy is the theory you follow, while style is the way you actually operate on the job. Spend a short time on philosophy, but what an employer really wants to know is how you actually manage on the job. Emphasize your strengths. If you're a good delegater or a good motivator, describe how those abilities help you to be an effective manager.

63. *What is the biggest mistake you ever made?* If asked in this way, you can decide whether to mention a personal mistake or a job-related mistake. Personal mistakes are a little safer to discuss than job-related mistakes, but be prepared to discuss either. A personal mistake could be that you wish you had selected a different college major or not dropped out of college. As a rule, pick something that happened two or more years ago. This will enable you to discuss what you learned from the experience with more insight and objectivity.

If there is an obvious and glaring mistake in your background that the employer will be aware of, this might be the chance to deal with it. For instance, if you have three years of college but never finished your degree, this question gives you an opportunity to discuss that situation. Since you are providing information about an issue that the interviewer is already curious about, you are also defusing a possible objection before the interviewer brings it up.

Reveal a mistake, but don't feel obligated to reveal the absolute biggest mistake you ever made in your life. Revealing a major mistake may cause an employer not to hire you, more for the lack of discretion than the mistake itself.

64. *How many people have you hired? How do you go about it? How successful have the people been?* By asking this question the interviewer is trying to learn about you and your processes. Describe your methods, but emphasize your results. If you have hired five or more people it is highly unlikely that each of them has gone on to great success. You do not need to claim perfect insight or judgment. You do want to get across the idea that you are very careful in your hiring decisions, that you are a good judge of character, and that you provide adequate training so that employees achieve their full potential.

65. *How many people have you fired? How did you handle it?* Here the interviewer is trying to determine how decisive you are, and how "cleanly" you can fire people. Terminations are the ultimate test of decisiveness. Typically, employers agonize over firing decisions even when it is clear that the employee is hopelessly ineffective. As you describe your termination process, demonstrate that you were decisive as well as humane.

66. *How would your subordinates describe you as a supervisor?* Indicate that you work hard to gain their respect, but that being liked by everyone is not your main concern. You might add, "They would say that they enjoy working for me. I'm fairly tough as a manager, but I'm fair. I give them room for independence and I seek self-starters. They would say I'm an excellent trainer. I'm patient, but they know I can get pretty upset when I see the same mistakes recurring." Here is a chance to share some of your management philosophy. Use this question to demonstrate that you elicit maximum output from your employees.

67. *Some managers watch their employees closely, while others use a loose rein. How do you manage?* You should indicate that you manage your employees neither too closely nor too loosely. Employees should be monitored carefully when new to the job and until they demonstrate the ability to do the job with little assistance from you. Use this as an opportunity to emphasize results you have achieved through those working for you.

68. *How have you improved as a supervisor over the years?* The interviewer is assuming you have improved as a supervisor, which means you can admit to past mistakes. Management is learned through experience, not textbooks, so it is safe to admit that you were far from perfect in the past. You might admit that early in your management experience you had difficulty delegating, or that sometimes you were too demanding. Preparing for this question will give you an

opportunity to reflect and see how you have improved over the years. Once you've done this, you'll be prepared to share some of those reflections with an interviewer.

69. *What kind of supervisor gets the best results out of you?* Base your answer on what you've learned about your prospective boss. If you know this person keeps a tight rein on employees, you would not mention your strong need for independence. Think through and identify several qualities that really help motivate you and be prepared to share two or three. You might answer by saying you prefer a supervisor who is fair, open-minded, and has high integrity. You could also say you prefer a supervisor who leads by example and motivates people.

70. *What have you done to increase your personal development?* The employer is trying to determine whether you are a growth-oriented person. You might mention courses, seminars, or self-study you have undertaken. Whether you were engaged in these activities on your own time or company time does not matter. The things you mention need not all be work-related unless the question was worded that way. You may have started studying a foreign language, taken up karate, or joined Toastmasters. Be prepared to discuss why you started these things and how they have helped you.

71. *How do you feel about your career progress?* If you are not feeling good about your career progress, you could mention that as one of the reasons you're looking for a new position, particularly if career progress in your current company is blocked. Indicate that you have done the right things and have received excellent reviews, but that lack of company growth, or some other factor, is preventing you from moving ahead. Indicate that you know patience is important, but state that your strong ambition to take on more responsibility is also important to you.

If you've made rapid progress in your career, you should acknowledge this and supply the reasons for your progress in terms of your results and accomplishments. Be sensitive to your interviewer's situation, however. If you know that the interviewer has not been promoted for some time, you might want to tone down your own success, so as not to appear to be a threat. In such a situation, you would also have to determine whether your prospective boss's lack of progress could block yours.

72. *What is unique about you?* In essence the interviewer is asking what is special about you. The interviewer is not asking what is absolutely unique about you. None of us is totally unique. Nevertheless, you are being given an opportunity to discuss some of your best qualities. So, reach into your mental check list and pull out some of your strengths.

73. *What types of books and magazines do you read?* This question may be asked to determine whether you are a growth-oriented person. It may also be asked to determine whether you keep up on the technical side of your profession. If you subscribe to any periodicals that keep you up-to-date in your field mention those, along with any recent books you've read which do the same. You can also mention novels, biographies, or other genres, as well as any specific books or authors you've liked. It's fine to mention news magazines, business magazines, or periodicals that deal with a hobby of yours. If you've recently read a book which is highly recognized in your field, you could mention it and describe what you found useful in it. Avoid mentioning trashy novels or other types of reading that would not help sell you.

74. *Starting with your first job out of college, tell me why you left each organization.* Generally, people will have several reasons for leaving a company. Select the most appropriate and acceptable reason for each move. Do not use such negative statements as "I had a personality conflict with my boss," or "It was a lousy company to work for." Learn how to soften your statements. Your answers may require some elaboration since the reasons for leaving are often complex. If you had four or five reasons for leaving, select one or two that will cause the employer to understand and accept your reasons.

75. *What is your boss like?* This is similar to the question regarding your boss's strengths and weaknesses, but with this question you will only discuss your boss's strengths. No matter how bad a boss may be, every supervisor has strengths—concentrate on those.

76. *How would your supervisor describe you?* This is an opportunity to mention positive qualities that you know or assume would be said about you. Discuss the qualities that you received high ratings on during reviews. Also give quick examples that demonstrate why your boss would see such qualities in you.

BE READY FOR ANYTHING

By understanding the principles of these 76 questions, you'll be able to develop effective responses to any question thrown at you, including the ones provided below. You'll be better prepared to think quickly and assess what the employer is after. It is impossible to predict all of the questions that might be asked in an interview. By being prepared for the 76 most common questions, and by having experiences in mind for behaviorally-based questions, you'll be ready for just about anything.

An employer can take any quality or characteristic and turn it into a question by asking whether you are analytical, intuitive, genuine, easy to work with, assertive, aggressive, decisive, etc. To help prepare for these types of questions, review the personality skills covered in pages 316 to 318. The same could be done with the list of 415 transferable skills listed on pages 393 to 399. This doesn't mean that you should develop 415 answers which describe how you possess each of those skills. I only mention these numbers to give you an idea as to the vast array of potential questions an interviewer might ask. Even faced with this limitless number of potential questions, if you are prepared for the 76 questions listed above, and you know what points you want to bring out to sell yourself, you'll be fully prepared.

Reviewing the questions below can also help you get ready. As with the 76 most commonly asked questions, write out each question and then list the points you would want to make, almost in an outline form.

1. Can you establish effective methods and procedures?

2. Describe a typical work day.

3. Can you establish long-term relations with customers (vendors)?

4. Can you quickly establish rapport with people?

5. Can you handle working with people with big egos?

6. We need people who are detail-oriented.

7. We have some very difficult and demanding customers. Can you handle that?

8. We need someone who is resourceful.

9. What personal areas are you working on? (similar to greatest weakness)

10. How do you resolve conflicts?

11. What project that you worked on has been most helpful in your personal growth?

12. What was the most useful criticism you ever received?

13. What is the most important lesson you've learned in the last 10 years?

14. Describe a time you had a leadership role. How did you gain it and why did you take it on?

15. What has been your greatest challenge?

16. Describe a stressful time when you performed well.

17. Describe the type of stress that hurts your efforts and the type that helps. Give me examples.

18. Describe a team project where you are proud of the team's result, as well as your personal contribution.

19. Describe a difficult decision you've made, and the process you went through to reach that decision.

20. What is the biggest change you've made in your life in the last 10 years?

21. Walk me through a project when you demonstrated (human relations) skills.

22. In hindsight most of us can think of some things we wish we had done differently. What are some things you would have done differently, and what did you learn from them?

23. Give me three qualities that are really helping you get ahead, and three qualities you must work on if you are going to achieve your career goals.

24. If you won a $5 million lottery today, what would you be doing a year from now?

25. Describe a time when you were rejected or an idea was rejected. How did you handle it?

26. What is your feeling about job quotas (or any controversial subject such as abortion or gay rights)?

27. Are you tolerant of people with opinions and values different from yours?

BEHAVIOR-BASED INTERVIEW QUESTIONS

Besides the types of questions mentioned above, you must also prepare to answer behavior-based interview questions. They are among the most unpredictable. There are literally hundreds of questions which can be asked. Although the wording will differ, in essence they will begin with, "Tell me about a time when..." While most of the questions will allow you to speak of positive experiences, you will also receive numerous questions that will require you to discuss negative or less positive experiences. You are not being singled out. This is simply part of the process. Virtually everyone will be asked the same questions, including the difficult ones.

The following questions are a sampling of behavior-based questions. Not all behavior-based questions begin with "Tell me about a time when...," but I'm using that phrase as a convenient way to introduce to you the types of questions you can expect.

Tell me about a time when you:

achieved a great deal in a short amount of time.

were disappointed in your performance.

made a major sacrifice to achieve a work goal.

were unwilling to make the necessary sacrifice to achieve a goal.

worked effectively under a great deal of pressure.

didn't handle a stressful situation very well.

really got angry over a situation at work.

felt under a great deal of pressure from an internal or external customer.

were really bothered by the actions of a coworker.

were especially creative in solving a problem.

were not as creative as usual.

organized or planned an event that was very successful.

planned and coordinated a project that was very successful.

were unable to complete a project on schedule despite your best efforts.

really had to remain flexible.

had to deal with a personality conflict with a boss or coworker.

were unable to sell your idea to a key person.

felt really good about a decision you made and the process you went through.

were very effective in your problem solving ability.

used facts and reason to persuade someone to accept your recommendation.

utilized your leadership ability to gain support for what initially had strong opposition.

were able to build team spirit during a time of low morale.

were able to gain commitment from others to really work as a team.

used your political savvy to push through a program you believed in.

were particularly perceptive regarding a person's or group's feelings and needs.

were able to predict someone's behavior or response based on your assessment of him or her.

were particularly supportive and reassuring to a person who needed a friend.

built rapport quickly with someone under difficult conditions.

wrote a report which was well received by others.

were particularly effective at prioritizing tasks and completing a project on schedule.

identified potential problems and resolved the situation before the problems became serious.

were highly motivated and your example inspired others.

found it necessary to tactfully but forcefully say things others did not want to hear.

were particularly effective in a talk you gave or in a seminar you taught.

had to make an important decision quickly even though you did not have all the information you wanted.

had to make a decision you knew would be unpopular.

were in a situation when events and circumstances changed rapidly.

As you can see, these are difficult questions. If you are asked such questions, you may need to take time to come up with an example. The main thing is to stay calm, recall several potential examples, choose one that feels right, consider the ramifications of sharing it, recall a few key points, and begin your story. Your interviewer is likely to give you considerable time to answer the question because he or she knows it is a difficult question that requires a thoughtful answer.

Because these questions can be so difficult, the best preparation is to simply recall dozens of different experiences that you have had, both positive and negative. These experiences need not be major events in your life. They may be experiences that started and ended in five minutes or five days. The best way to recall experiences is to begin with your current job. Just let experiences flow through your mind and as they do, quickly jot down a key word or two so you'll know which experience you're referring to. Pause just long enough to visualize it in your mind for a few seconds.

If this seems like a lot of effort, it is, but if you've ever been in a behavior-based interview and were not able to come up with an example, you'll understand why this process is important.

DISTINGUISH YOURSELF FROM THE COMPETITION

Ultimately there are eleven key things you can do to get more job offers. All of the tips and all of the techniques covered on interviewing are incorporated in these eleven points. Tell yourself that you will do everything necessary to fulfill each of these points on every interview you go on.

1. Demonstrate enthusiasm and potential.

2. Tell vivid stories.

3. Exude confidence.

4. Be prepared.

5. Sell yourself.

6. Come across as a real and genuine person.

7. Listen intently.

8. Show you can solve problems.

9. Be interesting.

10. Know things about the organization.

11. Know yourself.

NEGOTIATING THE BEST SALARY

Like most of the other things you've been learning in this book, negotiating a salary is not difficult, but it does require preparation and practice. By studying and applying appropriate salary-negotiation principles, you can significantly increase your starting salary. You owe it to yourself to get the best salary and benefits possible. Salary, respect, and authority are interwoven.

All jobs have formal or informal salary ranges. Your goal is to receive an offer and negotiate for the high end of the range. To do so you must know the salary range for your geographical area. Your primary information will come from people who are knowledgeable about the field and industry. To get top dollar you must also clearly be the top choice.

As a rule, if you have a solid background and are making a job change rather than a career change, go for a 20% increase in salary. You can do this based on the fact that the employer has decided to look outside rather than promote from within and expects to pay a premium for your experience, fresh ideas, and potential.

KNOW YOUR WORTH

The first principle for getting a top salary is to fully sell your worth to the organization. You do so by demonstrating your ability to make or save money for the organization, solve problems, or reduce the stress and pressure that your future boss has been experiencing. Although companies have formal or informal salary ranges, those ranges often get thrown out the window when someone with unexpected experience or potential becomes available.

At the early stages of your job search, you should determine your overall value in the field you are pursuing. Numerous resources exist to help you. The *Occupational Outlook Handbook* contains salary ranges covering about 300 major occupations. The *American Almanac of Jobs & Salaries,* by John Wright, is updated every two or three years and provides excellent information on an even larger range of occupations. Keep in mind, however, that both of these references provide national figures; salaries in your geographical area may be considerably higher or lower.

Beyond these tools, the most useful resources for determining salaries are people, including professional association officials, head-hunters, and people who currently do the type of work you're interested in. Associations exist for every career field imaginable. They sometimes produce salary surveys for the benefit of their members. Even those which don't can often give you good information about current salary ranges. To find an appropriate association, use *The Encyclopedia of Associations* and *National Trade & Professional Associates of the U.S.* These references are available at most libraries. For local associations ask people in your chosen field what associations they belong to.

Once you locate an association, attend meetings and talk to members. With national associations find out if salary surveys are available and also ask to speak to the person most knowledgeable about salaries.

Headhunters are another good source of salary information and wage scales because they are privy to what people are being offered. Many will take two or three minutes with you to give you some advice. If you choose to call some headhunters, briefly sell yourself and ask if they are interested in receiving your resume as well. Recruiting firms and employment agencies often conduct wage surveys that they make available to the public as part of their marketing. You can call and ask these firms if they have such surveys available.

Talking to people who do the type of work you want to do can also provide excellent insight into salary scales. You can usually get this information over the phone. Explain the purpose of your call, and ask if they have a couple minutes. Then tactfully ask about salary ranges. You might say something like, "I'm not asking what you make, but if you could give me a good sense of how much someone in the Cleveland area might make with four years' experience in shipping and receiving, that would really be helpful." Taking them off the hook by specifically not asking how much they make invariably yields better results.

Complete your salary research at the beginning of your job hunt so you know what your career field is paying today. Then you won't end up turning down what will later look like a very good offer. Many people have turned down offers, only to accept something for even less several months later. This happens most frequently during a recession when many job seekers do not realize that salaries have fallen. By the same token, salaries tend to rise during a boom time, so don't short change yourself if you're job hunting at a time when the economy is strong.

KNOW WHAT YOU NEED

Knowing your worth as well as your financial and psychological needs is crucial. If you are currently paid well but are miserable in your job, you would probably be willing to take a pay cut if you could get greater job satisfaction. The question becomes how much of a cut you could accept.

To determine your financial needs, establish three budgets. If you kept track of last year's expenditures it will be easy. In the left column you would list all of the categories of expenditures that you have. The next three columns would consist of: 1) last year's expenditures; 2) a level of spending that is less but still comfortable; and 3) a bare bones budget that enables you to keep your car and home, but slashes other nonessential items. By doing this you are not saying you want to live on a bare-bones budget. This process will simply give you an idea of how low you could go salary-wise and still maintain a modicum of normalcy.

Next, examine and define what you need in a job regarding your psychological needs. Ultimately, this should lead to producing an ideal job description (described in appendix A). The right job is one that enables you to utilize your top skills and strengths. It also allows you to be and express what you already are, without trying to squeeze you into some pre-existing mold. The right job should closely match your temperament, values and motivators. You should also define the type of organization you want to work for. The organization you work for is tremendously important and can often make the difference between a good job and a great job. Once you have created an ideal job description, ask yourself the lowest salary you would accept if this dream job was offered to you. Assume you are currently working. How much less than you are now earning would you accept?

Create a checklist to help determine how close a particular job is to what you want. Below is Debbie Wilson's checklist. It provided her with a useful guide as she evaluated jobs she interviewed for. You can use Debbie's checklist as a guide for creating your own checklist. Each item is listed according to its importance, with the most important things first. Debbie was looking for accounting management positions. Adapt the items to suit your career focus.

PRIORITIES LIST

	Definitely meets my needs	Somewhat meets my needs	Does not meet my needs	Unsure at this time
Potential for advancement				
Company is financially secure				
Encourages growth in employees and pays for professional development classes				
Teamwork, professional, friendly atmosphere				
Allowed to work independently				
My boss expresses appreciation				
Company has strong sense of direction, purpose, growth-oriented, seeks new opportunities				
Strong integrity and ethics				
Company is doing interesting, valuable work				
Promotes use of new computer systems				
Management is open with staff				
Do hands-on work; not just directing				
Short commute				
Work mainly on projects, with some routine tasks				
Projects that last several weeks and are challenging				
Non-smoking environment				
Use of both mainframes and PC's				
Have my own office				
Analysis of financial data, work with management on financial results and setting up action plans				
Developing and enhancing Lotus spreadsheets				
Establishing financial controls				
Implementing computer systems				
Pay is good				
Complete benefits				
Hours are reasonable, small amount of overtime				
Stable and respected management				
Accounting department is respected and valued				
Management encourages new ideas and frankness				
Procedures to eliminate inefficiencies				
Nice building and physical environment				
Size of company 50–100				
Casual yet professional dress policy				

Debbie found this check list very helpful as she evaluated jobs. Most of the items came right from her ideal job description. The job she currently has gives her almost everything she was seeking.

DO NOT DISCUSS SALARY UNTIL THE JOB IS OFFERED

Discussing your salary requirements before an offer is made hurts your ability to negotiate. For that reason you should avoid asking about salary, and you should deflect probes into your current earnings or salary expectations.

If the job seems challenging, assume it will pay adequately. Even if it turns out that the job will not pay enough, going through the interviewing process will at worst cost you some time. The following four things can happen only if you thoroughly sell yourself throughout the interviewing process and then go for the job offer:

1. The job is excellent and it pays what you want.

2. You succeed in convincing the employer that they need a highly capable person such as yourself, causing them to change the job description and to bump the salary up a couple notches.

3. You're overqualified for this position, but an excellent job in the company opens up a few months later and you are hired.

4. The employer hears of a suitable position with another company and refers you there.

None of these positive things can happen if you prematurely terminate the interview process.

If the job seems challenging, it is best to attend the first interview, learn as much as you can, sell yourself to your fullest ability, and do everything you can to get a second interview. If you are not interested in the position, and you believe it will not pay enough, you can always tactfully decline the offer for a second interview. I would recommend sticking with the process, however, with the intent of getting an offer. Then see where it can go. Any one of the four things listed above might happen.

The problem with asking about pay is that the interviewer will often turn the question around and ask you how much *you* make or how much *you* need to make. When that happens, you're in trouble. Of the three things that can happen, only one is positive. If you provide your income or your expectations, it will either be too high, too low, or about right. If the figure you give is too high, it will generally be assumed you will not be interested in the company's salary range, so the offer won't be extended. If you are making considerably less than they are prepared to pay, the assumption will be that you're a lightweight. This, too, results in no offer. Or, you might get the offer but they may lowball you, knowing that what they're offering you is 15% below the bottom of their range, but 20% above what you were making before. They know you will be hard pressed to turn down their offer.

Deflecting Questions

No matter how you look at it, talking about money before the time is right confuses things. Frequently of course, it's the employer who brings up the issue, so you need to know how to deal with it. Even in the first interview, the employer may ask you "What are you looking for?" "How much do you need?" "What's the minimum amount you'd accept?" or "What range did you have in mind?" Assuming no offer has been made and that the employer has not told you the salary range, your response might be, "Perhaps we should concentrate on determining if I'm the right person for the job." Another response might be, "I always make it a point not to discuss money until a job has been offered." If you're fairly far along in the interview process you might add, "Can I assume you're offering me the position?" Although the employer was not actually offering a position, more than one job seeker has heard, "Well, yea, I guess I am."

Usually these mild deflections work, but some interviewers persist. If the question comes again, tactfully, but assertively state, "If you don't mind, I'd really like to concentrate on making sure I'm the one who can help you reach your goals. When we accomplish that, I'm sure the compensation will be fair." A statement like that will usually work. If not, return to the statement that you have always made it a point not to discuss salary until a job has actually been offered. In using any of these responses it is important to be as diplomatic as possible.

People are often concerned that these mild deflections will get an employer angry. When handled tactfully, that rarely happens. If you detect that the employer *is* getting angry, you could ask what range has been set for the position. If the employer provides the range then indicate whether your needs will fall within that range.

If the employer is unwilling to give you the range, and you really are interested in the position, you might use a wide range by stating, "Probably $28,000 to $35,000 depending on the level of responsibility and benefits." If you make over $50,000 you might use a $10,000 range.

When The Interviewer Supplies A Salary Range

If the interviewer gives you a salary range for the position and asks whether the amount would be acceptable, you owe it to the interviewer to say yes or no. Some managers want to know immediately whether your salary needs can be met and may pose this question to you during the first ten minutes of the first interview. Their rationale is that they neither want to waste their time nor yours. If the range is acceptable you may want to say something as simple as "The range seems adequate." You would not want to sound elated or concerned.

PLAN YOUR STRATEGY

The goal of all good negotiations is to allow both sides to gain most of what they want—this is the well-known win-win concept. During the first interview and immediately after, you will begin determining what you need to feel like a winner in this situation. You will learn a lot about the job, your prospective boss, and the culture of the company. If the job, boss, and company seem relatively undesirable, you might be unwilling to accept it for anything less than 30% more than you currently earn. With a much more desirable job, you might accept only a 5% pay increase. Before deciding whether to accept an offer, many factors will be considered; money will be only one of them. Take notes immediately after the interview, jotting down what you learned, observed, and felt, as well as issues that were raised and questions you would like to have answered.

Between the time you are invited back for a second interview and the time you actually attend the interview, you will continue to research the company to determine how desirable it is. You should also formulate questions that will help you decide whether you would accept an offer. If you have detected some undesirable aspects of the job, determine whether they could be altered, and if so, how. Keep in mind a key concept in negotiating—everything is negotiable, not just money. There is no guarantee you will get everything you want, but everything is fair game for discussion. The worst thing that can happen is that the employer will say no. Raising an issue, even one that ultimately gets rejected, can cause the employer to give in on another issue that otherwise would also have been rejected.

At the end of the first interview, you should ask about the intended process, including how many interviews are anticipated, and how soon they expect to fill the position. That way you'll know when to expect an offer. You'll also know when you need to be fully prepared to negotiate.

BENEFITS ARE IMPORTANT

You won't know if you want the offer until you know the full range of benefits and perks. A health plan that pays 100% of all bills and has no deductible can save you over $1,000 per year. A company car might be worth $4,000 per year. Since many companies do not offer dental or orthodontic insurance, having such a policy may be worth another $1,000 per year. Tuition reimbursement could also save you thousands if you intend to pursue a degree.

As you look at the financial value of a job offer, you must consider its total value. Take into account salary, stock options, bonuses, profit sharing, insurance, tuition reimbursement, and determine the total value for *you*. In other words, tuition reimbursement may be nice, but it's of little use to you if you have no interest in entering another classroom. Likewise, if your kids are grown and married, orthodontic insurance will have little value for you.

A fairly complete list of benefits and perks includes: vacation pay; bonuses; stock options; profit sharing; health, dental, orthodontic, vision, disability, and life insurance; company car or payment for mileage; tuition reimbursement; expense account; professional memberships; country club or health club memberships; relocation expense; free parking; deferred compensation; pension funds; severance pay; outplacement assistance; physical exams; use of corporate plane or vacation property; estate and financial planning; tax and legal assistance.

WHAT ARE THOSE INTANGIBLES WORTH?

There are many intangibles to consider. Perhaps the last company you worked for did nothing illegal, but was always on the edge of doing things that were unethical. As a result, you didn't feel good about yourself and you felt no sense of pride when you told people where you worked. What would it be worth to you to work for a company with a great reputation?

Perhaps your present company watches you like a hawk. What would it be worth to you to work for a company that only hires highly responsible people and then trusts them to do whatever is necessary to get a task done?

These same questions could be posed regarding any of the factors that affect people in a work environment. They like working in organizations where people cooperate, where there is minimal office politics, where people get ahead on merit, where top management listens and keeps everyone informed, where employees receive recognition for doing good work, and where employees are treated fairly and with respect.

While it's hard to put a dollar value on these factors, most people would trade some money to work in a more suitable, positive work environment. Some would trade a lot, others only a little. But clearly, these factors must be taken into consideration when you determine the minimum salary you would accept to work for an organization.

YOU'RE WORTH WHAT THEY'RE WILLING TO PAY

While negotiating, keep in mind that neither you nor your prospective boss knows your true worth. Your worth is whatever someone is willing to pay you. Your challenge is to make the employer want you badly enough so he or she will offer you what you want.

You May Be Worth More Than You Think

When all is said and done, the most important aspect of interviewing is to make the employer want to hire you. Once that happens, good things will follow. The following story demonstrates this idea.

A young woman was interviewing for a position which was really going to make her stretch. She had convinced the employer of her potential, and he really liked her spunk. He asked her how much she wanted, and she responded by saying, "I think twenty-four would be fair." What she was really saying was that she wanted $24,000. The employer paused for a moment and said, "Fine, let's start you at twenty-four hundred. When can you begin?" Do you see what just transpired? She asked for $24,000 but the employer thought she meant $2,400 per month, which is $28,800. It was more than he had intended to pay, but she had created value in his mind, so he was willing to pay it without negotiating. This also demonstrates that she was worth more than she thought. She broke some of the rules of negotiating, but she ended up with far more than she had ever hoped for. The key to her success was that throughout the interview, she sold herself.

People Want What They Want

The psychology of salary negotiations is important to understand. A key psychological factor is that people want what they want. Once people decide they want something, they are virtually always willing to spend more to get it than they originally intended. In 1990 a Van Gogh painting called *Portrait of Dr. Gachet* sold for a record $82.5 million. Art appraisers had assumed it would sell for about $60 million, based on the sale price of a similar Van Gogh the year before, which set a record of $53.9 million. When the bidding got started, it quickly exceeded the $60-million level. The painting was finally sold to a wealthy Japanese businessman. No doubt he had hoped to spend *only* $60 million, but he really wanted the painting. As the bidding kept rising, he undoubtedly said to himself, "I don't care how much it costs, I'm going to have that painting."

Most of us don't go around buying expensive art, but we go through exactly the same process when we shop for a new car. Almost everyone ends up spending more than was originally intended.

So, even if your prospective boss says he or she simply can't go over a certain amount, don't accept that too quickly. Managers have budgets, and if they are willing to cut the budget somewhere else, it may free up some money.

Determine The Causes Of Roadblocks

If you reach a roadblock in your salary negotiations, try to determine the true cause. You might ask the employer, "What do you think is the main issue? Is it a problem with your budget, or will the wage-and-salary-administration folks feel that the job's structure doesn't warrant a higher salary?" By asking a question you will at least get a response. This will also give you something different to discuss for the next few minutes. Once you have a response, even if it's not the full truth, you can begin dealing with that issue. Get the person to agree that your worth is greater, and then help her come up with a creative way to find the money. If the human resources department is the problem, then suggest rewriting the job description to give you more responsibility. This would place you in a higher pay bracket. By helping to clarify the issue, you are also helping the manager decide how badly she wants you. She is psychologically committed and does not want to lose you. Furthermore, she's come this far in the process with you, and she does not want to lose you over $2,000 or some other fairly minor sticking point.

To negotiate in the way I've just described requires confidence that you have something unique or valuable to offer. If you have identified your strengths, and if you are interviewing for a job that will fully utilize those strengths, you will have some unique attributes to offer. If, on the other hand, the employer was ready to flip a coin as to whether to give the job to you or candidate B, you are not in as strong a bargaining position. The employer may have reason to believe that candidate B would accept a lower figure than you. Although the employer wants to hire you, she may be unwilling to go to any great lengths to do so. During the interviewing, and then later during the negotiating, you must assess how much this person really wants you. At a certain point the person will say in essence, "That's as high as I can go, take it or leave it." When that point is reached the decision will be up to you.

The Value Of A Job Is Set By The Responsibility Level

Sometimes a job only has a certain value. While you might be capable of handling more responsibility than the job needs, the worth of the job is based upon the level of responsibility required. You may get the offer, but you will not be able to negotiate for top dollar unless you can get the employer to expand the duties and responsibilities.

You'll Gain Respect By Negotiating

Some people are afraid that by negotiating for salary they may offend the employer. If you negotiate fairly and reasonably, employers will actually respect you more. Almost all initial offers are less than what the employer is prepared to pay you. If you accept the initial offer, it may actually cause the employer to wonder why you were obtained so cheaply. Employers expect to negotiate, so accommodate them. For some it's even a game that they enjoy. Let them have some fun.

Ask For A Shorter Review Time

If you reach an impasse, asking for a shorter review time may break it. Typically, reviews come six months after joining the firm, and then annually thereafter. If you have the confidence that you can become a strong producer in three months, ask for a review at that point. If you are able to negotiate a sizable raise at that time, it will almost be as if you had started at that level.

When The Offer Is Just Right

If the initial amount offered you is perfectly acceptable, you have some quick decisions to make. You could cordially accept the offer and thank the person for making a fair offer. That will make your boss feel good. Or, you could counter with an amount just 5% above the initial offer to see if there is room to negotiate.

Saving Face When You Have To Back Down

Sometimes an offer is made and the employer refuses to budge on the amount, or comes up only a token amount. During the negotiation you were fairly adamant that you wanted a significantly higher starting salary. You realize that you still want the job despite the large gap between offered and desired pay, but it seems awkward accepting what has been offered. Here's a solution: "Mr. Chang, I've always felt that the quality of the job is more important than the pay. This job is very attractive to me. In my mind there's no question that the job is worth $48,000 and I'm worth at least that amount. Let's go ahead and start at your $42,000 figure. It's my intention to quickly prove to you my worth. At my review, if I've demonstrated real value, I'll expect to be paid what I'm worth." At this point all Mr. Chang has to do is affirm that you will be paid based on your actual contribution. You're basically putting Chang on notice that he risks losing you if you are not compensated properly. You haven't actually said it, and you are not threatening Chang, but he's on notice, nonetheless.

You Need To Practice Negotiating

When it comes to negotiating, there is no substitute for actually practicing what you intend to say. In our society we are not used to haggling. The only haggling over price we do is when buying a car or attending a garage sale. For most of us, neither is an everyday occurrence. That's why practice is necessary just to become comfortable with the process of negotiating. Also, practice saying the amount you want. Let's say you want $29,000, although the most you've ever made is $25,000. If the first offer you get from an employer is $26,000, you'll need to counter with $32,000 just to have a chance to get your $29,000. If you haven't practiced saying that you want $32,000, that number will stick in your throat and you won't get it out.

Get The Employer To Redefine The Position

Because no one knows your strengths as well as you do, it's your responsibility to thoroughly present your capabilities and demonstrate the full range of your strengths. A perceptive employer will sense your strengths during the interview. If your background exceeds the scope and salary of the position you're applying for, a smart manager may change the scope of the job without any prompting from you. Others will not be so perceptive, so the responsibility falls upon you to explain how the organization can maximize their investment in you by redefining the position. If you can show how they can get a higher return on their investment, you may be able to extract part of that return in the form of more salary.

BREAKING THROUGH AN IMPASSE

If it's important to you that you truly get what you're worth, you must be prepared to walk away from the bargaining table. You should be clear on the minimum you would accept. If, despite your best efforts, you can't get close to an acceptable salary, you'll be forced to restate your minimum requirements. If your prospective employer indicates those needs cannot be met, you'll shake hands and both express regret that it did not work out.

While you should be clear in the beginning regarding the minimum you would accept, you must remember that you are not just talking dollars; there are also the benefits and the intangibles to consider.

Only you can decide whether the combination meets your minimum needs. As both sides sense an approaching impasse, both parties will begin considering how they will feel if the deal does not go through. Reaching that stage often helps both sides get creative again to come up with a solution. You'll be saying to yourself, "I really do want to work for this person, and I think this company is going places. I don't want to miss out on this opportunity." The employer will be saying, "This is the person who can help me get my promotion. With her drive and past successes, I know she'll be effective. I've got to find a way to bring her on board."

As you sense an impasse approaching, you may choose to adjourn. It may work like this: "Mrs. Barkley, maybe the best thing to do is get back together tomorrow. I would really like working for you and I'm still excited about the opportunities here. From my standpoint, it would really help if you could add $2,000 to the starting pay." Barkley would probably then restate her position. Neither side is promising to budge, but sometimes a good night's sleep can put a new perspective on things.

NEGOTIATING THE SALARY

Salary negotiating is an art. Knowing how to respond can make a difference in your paycheck.

Responding When The Employer Makes A Specific Offer

Note: As you read this next section, you will notice that in some of the conversations the dollar sign is missing. That's because in real conversations people often say, "I was thinking of thirty-seven thousand," rather than "I was thinking of thirty-seven thousand dollars."

Most employers know it is their responsibility to make an offer, so it may begin like this: "John, we'd like to start you out at $28,000 and then review your salary in six months." You must quickly decide whether you will negotiate, since you were expecting at least $30,000 and you want $34,000. In a case like this you might say: "Mr. Russell, I'm glad I turned out to be your top choice. Although money is not the only factor, it is important. In fact, it's the major reason I've chosen to leave my job. When I began this process, I made a decision to take a job at 20% above what I'm now earning. I really don't see a reason to change that decision. If there is any way you can adjust your budget, it would sure help. I never intended to accept anything below 34,000."

Although there is nothing that guarantees that John's worth to his new prospective company is 20% above what he is currently making, it is not unfair for John to want to make more. If he really wants 20% more, he will simply turn down all offers which are below what he wants. He can afford to wait since he currently has a job.

John could also use what I call the straightforward approach when responding. It would go like this: "Mr. Russell, based on my potential I really feel I'm worth $36,000, but if you would make it $35,000, the decision would sure be a lot easier."

The creative approach should sometimes be tried. Remember, the offer was for $28,000. "Mr. Russell, based on the duties you've described, I agree that the job is probably worth no more than $30,000. I'm sure you would agree with me, however, that I'm capable of handling much more. And when I began this job search, I never intended to accept anything below $34,000. But perhaps if the responsibilities were increased you could justify $34,000." Notice what has been done. The offer was for $28,000, and the interviewee is basically agreeing, but then suggests that the job is worth $30,000. Even while agreeing, the interviewee adds a little to the salary, then asks if the responsibilities could be increased.

Another strategy is to use another job offer as leverage whenever possible. You may have received an offer where the salary is satisfactory, but the job is not what you really want. Then you may get another offer where the job is perfect, but the salary is low. You might want to say, "Mr. Stuyvesant, the job itself is perfect, and of course I would really enjoy working with you. The salary is below what I expected, and I already have an offer at 3,000 a year more. If you could adjust your budget, it would make my decision a lot easier."

Employers are human too. No one likes to be rejected. If they feel they cannot match your salary expectations, the employer may decide not to make an offer even though he or she would dearly love to have you. It is important, therefore, to have a feel for the range and let the employer know that you are very interested.

Responding To "How Much Do You Want/How Much Are You Worth?"

When making an offer most employers will specify a certain beginning salary. Some, however, will not, and they may ask, "How much do you want?" or "How much do you think you're worth?" If you get this type of offer you will have to depend on what your research revealed. Your research should provide you with a good idea of what the typical range is for the position you want. If you believe the range is $30–35,000, you might say, "The starting salary is important to me, but not nearly as important as a job that fits me and allows me to make the kind of contribution I know I can make. I believe in three years I should be making at least $42,000." This is a good response. You are giving the impression of being very realistic and flexible. Actually, you have just put the interviewer in a corner. The interviewer may know that the best he or she can hope to do is get you an 8% increase each year. Therefore, to reach your $42,000 goal in three years the starting salary must be the $34,000 you actually wanted. Surprisingly, it is often easier for a supervisor to start you off high at the beginning than to obtain raises commensurate with your contributions later on.

If you believe the range is $30–35,000, you could present a range by saying, "Based on my experience and potential, an acceptable starting salary would be between 32 and 38,000, depending on my full range of responsibilities and other aspects of the benefits package." This is effective because it cannot be interpreted as saying you would accept X amount. The idea is to state a range with the high end of your range slightly higher than what you assume their high end is, and your low range slightly higher than what you assume their low end to be. Or you might state a single figure about 5% above what you believe the top of their range is. If you think the top of the range is $35,000, you would look the employer in the eye and say, "I was thinking about 37,000." The employer will probably reject that amount. Don't let it bother you. Simply ask, "What's the *best* you can offer?" Because of your confidence and the potential you have demonstrated, the next figure will probably be very close to the top of their range.

Of course, the employer could respond, "We were thinking close to 30." Perhaps you misjudged the range. For this company $30–32,000 may be the top of their range. Or you may not have completely sold the employer on your potential. Your response might be, "I feel I'm worth more than that. However, working for the right organization is really more important than the starting salary. I'd say 35,000 would be fair. The employer may still not go for it, or may come up to $32,000. If the employer counters with $32,000, you would counter with $34,000 and probably end up at $33,000. Not all negotiations, of course, end up with each counter proposal neatly meeting in the middle.

Wrapping It Up

How tough you negotiate depends on how strongly you feel about your worth. Once you have negotiated for the best salary possible, other factors must still be considered, particularly if the salary offer is below what you expected. If, for example, the employer offers a six-month salary review, ask for a three-month review. Other factors you will continue to negotiate at this point include: cost-of-living increases, moving expenses, tuition reimbursement, flex-time, an extra week of vacation, or anything else that is important to you.

In any negotiations, a final point is eventually reached. You know you've reached the end of negotiations when the two sides are close, yet neither side will go any further. At this point someone has to make the final compromise and say, "Let's call it a deal."

Salary negotiations are usually not long and drawn out. For entry-level to middle management positions the whole process may take less than two minutes.

Observe the following, typical negotiation:

Employer: Bob, I'd like to have you join us. I'll start you out at $28,000 and then review your performance in six months.

Bob: I appreciate the offer. As I'm sure you could tell, I'm really quite excited about the position. I'll be honest though; I had thought the job would be worth considerably more. I had figured on something closer to $36,000.

Employer: (Pause) Bob, I know I'm not going to be able to match your figure, but I'll tell you what, let's start you at $30,000.

Bob: That certainly helps. I really do want to accept the position and money is not the only issue. I feel that there are going to be excellent opportunities with this company. I still feel the job is worth 36, and I know I'm worth that much, but I would definitely consider 35.

Employer: Bob, I'm sure you realize that any firm like ours has to place minimums and maximums on salaries at various levels to keep everything in the company balanced. I suppose I could offer you 32, but that's as high as I can go.

Bob: Make it 33 and you've got yourself an employee.

Employer: All right, you've got a deal at $32,500. Agreed?

Bob: Agreed. Thirty-two-five and a review in three months.

Employer: Do you really think you can prove yourself in three months?

Bob: I think so.

Employer: Okay, thirty-two-five and a review in three months. But I'm not promising a pay increase, you've got to earn it.

Bob: I understand. I think you'll be pleased with my results.

At the executive level, however, negotiations may take a half hour or several days, as both sides propose and counterpropose. If one of the negotiation issues must be decided by someone else in the organization, it may take several days to conclude the negotiations.

The ability to negotiate for a higher salary is one of the most valuable skills you can develop. Once you understand the principles, the practice is up to you.

NOW YOU CAN DECIDE IF YOU WANT THE JOB

Once salary and benefits have been negotiated, you are almost ready to decide whether you will accept the position. You need time to consider the decision. Your emotions are strong at the moment, so you need an opportunity to step back and be objective. Just as the employer did not make the hiring decision after the first interview, you need time to consider everything. Employers realize that it is never an easy decision to accept a new position or to leave a current position. The employer had time to consider several people and to check references prior to making you the offer. The employer had a chance to sleep on it and make the decision with a proper frame of mind. You need the same opportunity.

Ask for time by saying something like, "I think the salary is going to be adequate and I think we're going to work very well together. How soon do you need a definite decision?" They should give you at least three days. If you have another offer pending, you might respond with, "Today is Thursday. How about if I confirm everything by next Wednesday?" If you're going to need more than a week you should be prepared to explain some of the reasons. If you have another job offer pending, but won't know anything definite for two weeks, you'll probably need to explain the situation. You might explain that if that job comes through, you feel you owe it to yourself to be able to weigh all factors. If you've established solid rapport with your prospective boss, the person won't like it, but will understand. If the employer cannot wait that long, you may be forced to make a decision sooner than you would have liked. When you ask for the time to make the decision, do not say, "I'll have to discuss it with my wife (husband)."

RESEARCH AFTER AN OFFER IS MADE

Once you've gotten the job offer, negotiated salary and benefits, and reached an agreement, you still need answers to your remaining questions. Some of the questions you did ask may not have been adequately answered, and there were other questions you did not ask at all because they seemed too sensitive. Now is the time to ask those questions. To the interviewer you might say: "Mrs. Torgeson, I'm glad you had the confidence in me to offer me the position. The salary is about right and I'm really looking forward to working with you. I do have just a few questions that I would like clarified so that I can make the right decision." Then proceed to ask every question you have, even those sensitive ones you did not ask earlier. As long as it is asked tactfully, almost any question regarding you, the job, or the organization is reasonable.

Having asked for time to decide, you now have two important tasks to complete: 1) Make a final, all-out effort to discover more about the company from inside sources; and 2) Contact those other organizations which have expressed interest in you.

Complete Your Employer Research

During the next several days learn everything you can even though you've basically decided to take the job. Perhaps you would turn it down only if another company made a better offer or if additional research uncovers serious problems concerning the organization. Many people regret their failure to do this final bit of research; I wouldn't want you to be one of them.

Throughout your research you learned a lot. During the interviews you learned a great deal more. After the offer was made you asked even more questions, including the sensitive ones you had postponed. The answers to those last questions probably cleared away all of your doubts. You may have been tempted to accept the job on the spot. Fortunately you didn't. On your way home from this interview, begin asking yourself if there are still any matters that need more clarification. Determine what sources might answer your questions. If you haven't talked to any competitors yet, this would be a good time. It's also the time to talk to employees and ex-employees of your prospective employer. Ask your contacts if they know anyone who works for or has worked for your target organization.

Things are not always as they appear. The boss who seems so understanding and likable in the interview may be completely different on the job. The company that seems so peaceful may be experiencing political infighting. Or the company that seems so stable may be ready for bankruptcy. Organizations often hide serious problems. As a detective it's your job to discover what those problems are.

Maintain a healthy skepticism. Talk the job over with your mate, a friend, or a career counselor—anyone who will be more objective about it than you are. It's amazing what a second party can see that you may be blind to.

Suppose the offer was made on Thursday and you agreed to give your final answer by Monday afternoon. Through several insiders you picked up some information plus a few rumors that need to be clarified. On Monday morning you might call your boss-to-be and ask for an appointment that afternoon: "Mr. Bradley, this is Paul Johnson. I've been doing a lot of thinking and I have essentially decided to accept the position. I still have a couple questions to ask you though, and it might be good just to meet with you for a few minutes this afternoon."

With some questions you will simply ask and then evaluate the response. If the answer is not complete enough, you may have to ask a follow-up question. When asking about any rumors, be tactful.

Get Additional Offers

After a job is offered, your second task is to contact those organizations that have interviewed you for definite openings. Your call might go like this:

> Ms. Esparza, this is Sandy Hogan. We talked last week about your scheduling coordinator position. You indicated it could be two weeks before I would be asked back for a second interview, but I thought I'd better call to explain my situation. I've just been offered a really good scheduling position with another company. But, based on our conversation, I would really rather work for you. What do you suggest I do?

If you aren't being considered for the job, the employer will suggest you take the position already offered. If the employer is really interested, another interview may be quickly arranged. Do your best to get one or two additional offers. It may not work, but it is definitely worth the effort. It is extremely helpful to have two or more job offers to consider at one time.

If the other job is really the one you want, this effort may cause the employer to speed up the decision making process. What might have taken another week or two, may be reduced to two or three days if you really were the number one choice.

SELF-AWARENESS
THROUGH SELF-EXAMINATION

In order to select an appropriate career field or to obtain the job which is just right for you, you must know yourself well. The following exercises have been designed to give you the insight you need in order to make good career decisions. These are powerful exercises: they get you thinking about yourself in ways that very few exercises can and they provide you with tremendous insights.

I would encourage you to work on each exercise. Although each one is independent of the others, they are brought together and they culminate in the creation of your ideal job description. The exercises include: Accomplishments, Transferable Skills, Prioritizing Skills, Work Content Skills, Temperaments, Motivators/Values, and The Ideal Job Description. The exercises should also be done in this order. In the accomplishments exercise you will be asked to write about your top twelve accomplishments. Those twelve accomplishments will also play a role in the Transferable Skills, Temperaments, and Motivators/Values exercises.

The best thing to do is simply get started. You will find the exercises interesting and insightful. When you rate yourself on skills, temperaments, or motivators, rate yourself quickly. When you write about yourself, write quickly without being concerned for spelling, grammar, sentence structure, or polished writing. None of those things matters. Seeing yourself from a new angle does.

You will be rating yourself using a 1–10 scale. Do not struggle over how to rate yourself on a particular skill or motivator, trying to determine if you are a seven or an eight. The ratings are intended to get you thinking about yourself and are not intended to frustrate you by struggling over whether to give yourself a six, a seven, or an eight. Today you may give yourself a seven, tomorrow you might think you're an eight, and next week you may be sure that you're really a six. But all of this won't matter because it really isn't the ratings which provide the insight. The ratings simply cause you to see new sides of yourself and to also confirm things that you already know about yourself.

With each of the exercises you will be asked to do some writing. While you may not enjoy writing, I guarantee that you can do it. I have worked with every type of person imaginable and they were all able to write sufficiently well to gain high levels of insight.

Begin by merely looking at the exercises, scanning the lists, and examining the examples. This will give you a good overview of the journey you are about to begin.

Involve someone in this process. It could be a friend, relative, or spouse. Best if you can find a person who is in the same situation, so you can go through this process together. Each of you will be able to give considerable insight to the other.

People have obtained help from others in numerous ways:

1) Have a person help you identify skills in the accomplishments exercise. That person will see skills that you missed completely, or for some reason, were unwilling to give yourself credit for.

2) Although you will be writing about your accomplishments, have someone listen to the full story. Telling the story out loud will help your recall the experience even better and will give you good practice for interviews. The person will also pick up skills that would have been missed if the person had merely read what you wrote. People find it enjoyable to talk about their accomplishments and to receive positive feedback from someone they respect. As you speak, the person should write down any skills which come to mind and then give you feedback when you're through. Rather than simply reading back what was written, the person should expand on it and describe what convinced him or her that you have that skill.

3) When rating yourself on temperaments or motivators, have someone who knows you well also rate you. Compare the differences and try to determine why there were differences. You may be surprised that in almost each case the other person was within two points of your rating. That actually indicates that you both see you in a similar way. If you gave yourself an eight on something, and the other person gave you a three, that is quite a difference. Since you invited the person to help, you must remain nondefensive. Even if you disagree strongly with how the other person rated you or what the person said, practice your active listening. Practice allowing yourself to receive feedback without reacting or trying to defend yourself. On most of these things there are no right or wrong answers anyway.

If at anytime you get stuck, help is available. See Appendix F.

RECALLING YOUR ACCOMPLISHMENTS

Knowing your accomplishments and identifying the skills used to achieve each accomplishment is one of the most important tasks of an effective job search.

The experience of recalling and reliving your accomplishments is a powerful one. Recalling these peak experiences increases one's self-confidence, allowing possibility thinking to take place. Recognizing your accomplishments and identifying the skills used in those accomplishments is one of the most important tools you will have for selecting the right occupation, and then effectively selling yourself in interviews.

Accomplishments can be big or small, very impressive or rather simple. An accomplishment is anything you 1) enjoyed doing; 2) did well; 3) gained satisfaction from; or 4) are proud of. Many accomplishments include all four aspects, while some may include just one or two. Accomplishments often involve solving problems. With some accomplishments you may receive recognition or compliments from parents, friends, or supervisors, while at other times you may be the only one who knows what you did. Some accomplishments are achieved through great effort, while others come easily. Many of your accomplishments were totally enjoyable, and are fondly recalled.

Other experiences are genuine accomplishments, but they may be "bittersweet." It may be an accomplishment simply because you overcame many adversities. At the time you may have been extremely frustrated. Even thinking about the experience may bring back those feelings of frustration, anger, or hurt. It's okay to remember the negative parts, but concentrate as much as you can on the positive aspects of the experience. In other words, concentrate on the result.

Accomplishments are best thought of as specific experiences. Most of your accomplishments should be things that occurred during a relatively short period of time. It could be something that occurred from start to finish in 15 minutes. More typically, accomplishments are experiences which occurred over days or weeks. Although some accomplishments may take place over years, those long-term accomplishments can be broken into sub-accomplishments. For example, graduating from college is certainly an accomplishment. Although you should list an accomplishment like that, step back and consider all of the smaller accomplishments that enabled you to achieve the larger accomplishment. In the case of graduating from college that would include the key papers you wrote and the projects you worked on. Those papers and projects should be listed as well.

Now review the list. Notice how some of the accomplishments are impressive, while others seem rather common and ordinary. That's the way it is with most people. Many have four or five rather impressive accomplishments and then it falls off dramatically from there. That's to be expected.

Jobs

I received a $600 award from Boeing for suggesting a money saving idea.

I became the first woman engineer in the firm.

I earned my way through college painting houses.

I figured out a faster method of estimating the cost of our printing jobs.

My advertising jingle is credited with increasing sales 15%.

My plan for flex-time has really reduced absenteeism.

I made a sale to a firm which had refused to deal with us for 15 years.

I increased sales in my territory 39% in two years.

I added 24 customers to my paper route.

I wrote a report on a hazardous waste program that was adopted by the state.

I received three promotions in four years.

I became one of the youngest store managers ever in the chain.

I produced a videotaped training program for our tellers which cut training time of new tellers about 20% and significantly reduced the errors they made.

I developed a plan to purchase a fleet of trucks to handle our own deliveries. The plan cut our costs about 5% and provided better and more reliable service to our customers.

School

I learned Russian so I could read War and Peace in the original language.

I got a B in chemistry after failing the midterm exam.

I got an A in chemistry from the toughest prof.

I wrote an outstanding paper on the causes of World War II.

I was elected senior class vice president.

I was committee chairperson of the junior prom decorations committee. Some teachers thought they were the best decorations in years.

Hobbies/Activities

I planted a garden, fought the weeds, and got 15 bushels of vegetables.

I hitchhiked from Paris through France, Italy, Greece, Turkey, Iran, Afghanistan, Pakistan, and India. (A woman, aged 23, who traveled alone in 1972)

I planned and built a 400 square foot deck.

I won honorable mention in a county bakeoff for a unique potato salad.

Sports/Physical Activities

I learned to ski at age 44.

I got third place in a cross-country track meet.

I scored a game winning basket.

I won first place in a kite flying contest.

I climbed Mt. Rainier.

I competed in my first 10 K race at age 36.

Volunteer

As president of PTA I increased membership 36%.

I was elected secretary of my local accounting association.

As chairman of fund raising, I raised more money than any other Bay Area Lions Club in 1979.

My team built a very effective irrigation system during my Peace Corps tour.

I administered CPR to a man and saved his life.

Family

I raised three mischievous boys and trained them to become well adjusted adults.

I quit smoking.

I planned and arranged a three-week vacation in Europe with a tight budget.

After reviewing the list, read some of the expanded accomplishments on page 386, and notice how we identified skills. The real purpose of this exercise is to identify as many skills as possible, and especially to identify all of your "hooks." A hook is a special skill, or a skill described in such a way that it "hooks" an interviewer. Hooks get remembered. Typically in interviews all you need to do is know your hooks, and be prepared to give an example or two to back each one up. Knowing how to identify your hooks, and then learning how to use them in interviews, will be among the most important parts of your work.

Before you actually begin identifying your accomplishments, be sure to read all of the instructions. There are important points throughout that you need to know and understand before you begin.

WRITING ABOUT ACCOMPLISHMENTS

1. Write a list of at least 30 experiences that you would consider to be accomplishments.

a) List the experiences as they pop into your mind. Don't filter them out, just list them. They do not need to be "knock your socks off" types of experiences. Try to list 40 or more, but list at least 30. Once you get started listing them, one accomplishment should trigger another.

b) Include at least two accomplishments from each five year period of your life since age ten. This acts as a reminder that many of your top skills today, began to develop early on.

c) Include at least ten work-related accomplishments, with at least three coming from your current or most recent job. If you're frustrated in your current job it's easy to assume there haven't been accomplishments, but there have been. Sometimes it merely takes a little more effort to identify them. Remember, an accomplishment is merely an experience where you did something well or got satisfaction from it.

d) You have dozens of accomplishments. Don't screen them out because they seem insignificant. Each positive experience that you've had reveals something about you—your talents, your personality, your interests.

e) By the time you list your twentieth accomplishment, go back over your list to see if you have identified the top 12 accomplishments in your life. If not, make sure that in your remaining 10-15 accomplishments, those extra special experiences are included.

2. Write about your top experiences.

a) Determine your absolute top twelve lifetime accomplishments. One way is to decide which have had the greatest impact on your life. Another way is to ask yourself which ones will reveal the most skills. Some accomplishments are quite important to a person, but there simply aren't a lot of skills to be identified. Sometimes a slightly more modest accomplishment is better to write about because it may reveal more about you. Select some because of the variety they will supply. They may reveal a different side of you or will enable you to see a set of skills that are somewhat different from the other accomplishments. As you begin to write, be sure to leave a three inch margin on the left so you can identify skills.

b) With six of your accomplishments write approximately 200 words, the other six about 100. If you get on a roll, feel free to continue writing until you've said all that you want to say. For some people that might be 250 or 300 words.

c) Begin by describing the situation. Give some background. What were the circumstances? What were the problems you faced? How did you analyze the situation? Write as completely as you can and give enough details so any reader would have a good understanding of what you did. If the accomplishment is job-related, avoid acronyms or any technical jargon.

d) Describe your role. Many accomplishments are achieved through a group effort. You can still claim it as a personal accomplishment; simply concentrate on what your role in it was.

e) Describe the result. Every experience, every project, has a result. The fact that you are calling this experience an accomplishment means it had a positive result. To describe the result, think about what your goal was. Did you achieve it? One of the best ways to think about results is to consider what you did, and then add the words, "which resulted in." An example would be: "I trained all year for cross country which resulted in my placing sixth in state, the highest finish ever for someone from my high school."

f) Quantify your accomplishments whenever possible. It may mean estimating, but that's fine; you, and whoever you choose to show your accomplishments to will be the only ones to see them. Did your accomplishment increase productivity at the office? If so, how much? 10%, 40%, 65%? As a manager, did you decrease turnover? If so, how much? As a committee leader for a volunteer organization you may have increased membership, attendance at monthly meetings, or revenue on fundraisers. For more on results, see pages 140 to 152.

g) As a conclusion, tell us how you felt. Were you elated, tired but satisfied, glad it was over?

h) Write as fast as you can. After all, this is an experience you lived through. Memories will jump into your consciousness. One memory will lead to another as you recall what occurred in the accomplishment. Try to make your pen keep up with your brain. Do not be concerned about spelling, grammar, sentence structure, or polished writing; do get your thoughts on paper. This is not a philosophy report where every word must be perfect.

3. Identify skills.

a) One of the most important things you're going to do now is identify the skills you used. Identifying skills is important, and is probably the most challenging part of this assignment.

b) The best thing to do is study the sample accomplishments to see how skills and qualities are identified. Skills are important, but personal qualities and characteristics are just as important. As a skill you might say, "produce highly effective marketing plans." As a quality you might say, "extremely reliable," "work well with people," "hard worker," or "able and willing to take on greater responsibility." In actuality, these characteristics are skills.

c) Identify skills and qualities using phrases. Again, study the examples. In almost all cases a phrase has more impact than a single word. "Persistent" is a good word, but it doesn't have the same impact as, "I never give up until the job is done right." "Organizing" doesn't have the same impact as "Effectively plan and organize projects and obtain high quality results." Use words like *excellent, effective, effectively*. Words like that remind you that you didn't just do it, but that you did it well.

d) Be objective. Pretend you don't know this person. Assume you are an employer who has requested that people send descriptions of accomplishments rather than resumes. Assume also that you are going to make a hiring decision without ever meeting any of these people. If that were the situation, you would really read between the lines to learn as much about each person as possible. You would be saying to yourself, "If this person did this, what does that reveal about abilities and character?" Hiring decisions are first made on emotion and then justified by logic. The employer not only must be convinced that you have the basic abilities, or the potential to learn, but also the right set of personality and character traits. The employer has to like you. Much of that realization can come from accomplishments.

e) Identify as many skills as you can, even if you feel the same skills were identified in other accomplishments. This is important because you are looking for patterns. If a particular skill has been used in several accomplishments, that tells you a lot about yourself. Probably it is a skill that you are not only very good at, but also enjoy using. It is not an accident that you have frequently relied on that skill. Probably you would want to use that ability in your next job.

f) One way to identify skills is to pull them right out of your descriptions. Often you can take a phrase almost word for word out of your accomplishment.

g) Don't skip the obvious skills. Sometimes a skill is so obvious to a person that it doesn't seem valuable or important. Go ahead and quickly write it in.

h) Don't skip a skill just because you think everyone can do it. Even if it is a common skill, it should still be listed. Often, however, a person only believes everyone can do it. This happens because the person has been skilled at it for a long time, and in fact, cannot remember a time when he or she could not do it. Because of that, it's easy to assume that anyone can do it. Don't get caught in that trap.

Able to bring consensus in areas that had been chaotic

Achieve the unachievable

Effectively get people to review a concept objectively

Get people to value consensus and to be willing to compromise

Effectively organize large educational seminars

Excellent at resolving disputes among diverse interest groups

Excellent at marketing programs and getting excellent attendance

Excellent writer

Effectively organize committees

People enjoy and value the events organized

Gain the support and involvement of people who are naturally defensive and hesitant

Develop innovative methods and techniques

Effectively analyze profitability of products and services

Able to analyze a complete product line, take it apart, and put it back together with greater profitability

Develop highly effective computer generated reports

Gain the confidence and absolute trust of people

*   For three years, beginning in 1982, I held a volunteer office with the Rocky Mountain Ski Instructors Association. I was elected to this position by the association's 3,000 ski instructors to reorganize and simplify the current methodology used for teaching skiing.

This had long been disputed because there were so many systems of teaching and a widespread misuse of terminology. This became a critical issue because state licensing and certification was necessary for ski instructors to teach on U.S. Forest Service land at state ski areas.

To accomplish this I organized several large educational seminars each year to educate both candidates and certification examiners on a simplified American teaching system. As many as 500 people attended these two-day events. Many hours and days were spent in various levels of committee meetings disseminating information and resolving disputes among these diverse interest groups. As a result of these efforts, a unified ski teaching method was developed.

*   I led a research group in studying the profitability of installment lending at U.S. Bancorp. I analyzed gross yields, handling costs, and loan losses for the various types of loans. I developed a consistent and accepted method for measuring handling costs among the several loan categories. My analysis gained credibility with the senior lending managers. I worked with the installment lending department and obtained their help in the project. The analysis revealed that some of the types of loans had very high handling costs and were not profitable. My analysis helped initiate a move away from unprofitable loan categories. After discussions with a senior executive at the bank, I developed a computer report for easy monitoring of the rates, maturity, and size characteristics of new loans. This process helped ensure that we kept profitability high.

Develop effective systems that increase sales and efficiency

Persuasive

Develop sales incentives that really work

Leader—motivate staff

Conduct useful meetings

Able to instill a need for planning and organization into staff

Conduct motivating sales meetings

Always create a winning team

Get people believing in themselves

Give people the tools to help them succeed

Have strong goals and act on them
Able to find solutions to tough problems
Willing to tackle difficult situations
Wiling to work hard
Enjoy learning new skills
Unwilling to get discouraged and give up
Very persuasive
Able to get people to believe in us
Excellent at modifying blueprints
Excellent at selecting the right contractors
Get contractors to want to give us their best
Supervise contractors well
Know how to get our money's worth
Making excellent purchases
Excellent time management
Plan projects thoroughly
Obtain excellent results

* In 1985 I was promoted from agent to district manager for New York Life. For the first month I hardly knew what I was supposed to do because there were no procedures or systems in place. Then I attended a seminar on insurance management put on by the Kinder brothers. They taught that you needed a system for everything. I learned a lot.

When I returned to the office I began to write a recruiting and training system. It really helped new agents get off to a fast start and those early successes increased their motivation and self-confidence. I developed good campaigns with wonderful awards to motivate the achievers on the staff. We had training meetings which were always great occasions. I spent a lot of time with my new people and really got them going. I made mistakes but I did enough things right that it started to show. In 1986 we finished number three in the region and number one in 1987.

* After renting a house for six years my wife and I decided we wanted a home of our own. We did not have enough money for a downpayment so we decided to build our home ourselves. I took some courses in carpentry, wiring, and plumbing. I figured we could build an $80,000 home (1979) for $36,000, plus $11,000 for land. I had to go to seven banks before one of them would finance it.

My wife and I bought blueprints and then made some alterations. I began ordering everything from concrete to lumber to kitchen cabinets. We used four subcontractors and I made sure we got our money's worth. We worked three nights a week and all day on Saturdays. We moved in after four months and completed all the work in ten months. It was worth the effort. Today we have a beautiful home that is worth three times what we paid for it.

Taking on challenges

Good detective

Getting valuable information from people

Able to get to the right people

Quickly gain people's confidence

Persuasive

Excellent long-range planning

Making the most out of a small success

Strong product knowledge

Able to build on past successes

Make excellent presentations

Know how to get repeat sales and expand sales

Provide outstanding customer service

* Fifteen years ago Pacific Dynamics was our best customer. Somehow we shipped some defective equipment and Paul Sanders, the owner, never forgave us. No one could even get through to him. I decided to take on the challenge, but with a new strategy. Through some research I learned that Pacific was planning a new product and our micro gears would be perfect.

I avoided Sanders and got to know the project manager who had been there less than a year and knew nothing of the feud. I gave him some of our gears for testing and he was ecstatic. Through his recommendation I made the sale. We are now selling over 60 different products to Pacific, and in just two years they have become our third best customer.

Learning From Your Accomplishments

Now that you've written about your accomplishments and identified many skills, it's time to step back and determine what you've learned from them. Begin by asking yourself some questions. When you were really effective at what you were doing, what types of activities were you doing? Do you see some trends? Are there certain skills and certain activities that you find yourself attracted to? Are you usually successful when you use those skills or do those activities?

Identifying trends is particularly important as you begin to select a career field to pursue and as you define what it is that you really want in a job. The right career and the right job will allow you to spend most of your time working on activities that you are good at and enjoy.

Even now it's not too soon to begin thinking about your ideal job. Do you imagine using some of the skills and doing some of the activities that showed up in your accomplishments? Probably so. As you have spare moments, think about the types of things you enjoy doing and are good at. Even jot them down. There may be no single occupation that would allow you to do all of those things, but there is probably an occupation that would enable you to do many of those things. At this point don't be concerned with specific job titles or career fields. That will come later. For now all you need to be clear on is what you do well and what you enjoy doing.

As you move on to rating yourself on dozens of transferable skills, you will find the pieces of the puzzle beginning to come together.

IDENTIFYING YOUR TOP SKILLS

"I don't have any marketable skills." How often have you heard someone say that? Or, maybe you've said it yourself. The fact is you have dozens of skills, but society has not taught you to recognize or value them. A failure to recognize your many skills and to realize how those skills can be used in different occupations, explains why many people feel trapped in their present work. They do not believe they are capable of doing anything else. Or, if they personally believe they could perform a new occupation, they have no confidence that they can convince someone to give them a chance to do it. Many people feel trapped in their jobs because they fail to recognize the transferability of skills they already possess—skills which are useful in many occupations.

All skills can be classified as *Personality Skills, Transferable Skills,* or *Work Content Skills.* Personality skills and transferable skills are highly transferable, while work content skills are usually transferable only when making changes in closely related fields. Personality skills have been defined and listed on page 317.

TRANSFERABLE SKILLS

Transferable skills include finger dexterity, figuring out how things work, visualizing in three dimensions, and motivating people. Transferable skills develop early in life, with growth and improvement potentially occurring throughout life. Many have traced their most valued transferable skills back to pre-teen years. Jan, a graphics artist, began drawing realistic animals at age six. Bill, an engineer, began designing and building model airplanes at age eight. Keith, an electronics technician, began fixing radios at age ten.

Work content skills, or people's specialized skills, are built upon transferable skills. Without the prerequisite transferable skills, a person will never develop competence with a work content skill. If a person lacks finger dexterity or eye-hand coordination (transferable skills), that person will probably not succeed as a typist or a surgeon.

Knowing your transferable skills will help you select just the right occupation. As you read about occupations or talk to people about what they do, assess what transferable skills are most important in that career field; then determine whether you possess them at an adequate level. Also determine what you could do to raise your skill level high enough to be effective.

WORK CONTENT SKILLS

Work content skills are the specialized skills and knowledge developed throughout life. They are those skills people actually get paid for using. They are primarily learned in vocational schools or colleges, through apprenticeships, by watching experts, by practicing, or by self-study. A surgeon memorizes parts of the body, learns to recognize symptoms, watches operations, and then practices surgical procedures. A mechanic memorizes the parts of an engine, learns how to diagnose problems, and practices overhauling the engine.

Work content skills are the least transferable of the three types of skills. A car mechanic's knowledge of automobile engines would provide little benefit if he or she were required to repair a jet engine. However, should the mechanic choose to study jet engine mechanics, his/her manual dexterity and ability to figure out how mechanical devices work (transferable skills), and his/her inquisitiveness and resourcefulness (personality skills) would all be great assets.

While there are thousands of work content skills, there are far fewer transferable skills. Since every work content skill can be broken down into its transferable components, you can calculate with considerable accuracy whether you can develop a specific work content skill. You would do this by rating yourself on the transferable skills needed for a specific occupation. Typing requires finger dexterity, a sensitive touch, and fast reflexes (transferable skills), as well as knowledge of spelling and punctuation (work content skills). A portrait artist requires a steady hand, eye-hand coordination, depth perception, ability to imagine in three dimensions, and a sense of color combinations (transferable skills), as well as knowledge of how to mix paints and knowledge of human anatomy (work content skills).

RATING YOURSELF ON TRANSFERABLE SKILLS

1. Rate yourself on all 410 transferable skills. Rate yourself quickly and spontaneously. Do not take time to analyze yourself. Achieving the desired level of self-knowledge will occur best if you rate yourself almost instantly.

2. Rate yourself using a scale of 1–10. A 10 is one of your absolutely top skills, while a 1 is a skill you have tried to use but failed miserably.

3. With the transferable skills, give yourself *at least* fifteen 10s, twenty 9s, and thirty 8s. Don't count, just make sure you give yourself approximately the right number of 8s, 9s, and 10s. The main thing is that you give yourself some 10s.

4. Basically you are comparing yourself only with yourself. You are trying to identify *your* top skills.

5. If you are a very capable person and have a lot of self-confidence, the tendency is to give yourself all 8s, 9s, and 10s. If so, you should consciously force yourself to also include some 5s and 6s. It is perfectly acceptable and common not to have any 1s, 2s, or 3s, or to have only a few.

6. If your self-esteem is very low today your tendency will be to give yourself all 3s, 4s, 5s, and 6s. Avoid that and follow the directions above in #3. Give yourself a good number of 8s, 9s. and 10s. Or, put the exercise away and do it when you're feeling more like yourself.

7. If you come to a skill which you don't understand, or you have never used, or you simply can't relate to, just place a dash in front of it to note that you at least read it. Rarely should you need to do this with more than a few skills.

8. Twenty-three skill clusters have been identified. Virtually every transferable skill imaginable will fall into one of the 23 clusters. There are at least 1,000 identifiable and distinct transferable skills, but the distinctions between some of them are so slight that we have selected only the 410 most important ones.

9. As soon as you have rated yourself on all of the Human Relations Skills (the first skill cluster), give yourself an overall rating for that cluster. Do the same with each cluster. When giving yourself an overall rating, <u>do not average the scores</u>. Within a cluster it's possible to have a dash or two (skills you haven't used before) and even a few low scores, yet still give yourself an 8 or 9. The reason is that the skills in which you gave yourself low scores, may simply not be critical skills. Example:

__9__ Human Relations Skills *1, 3, 6, 7, 9, 10, 12*

9	Sensitivity to others
8	Treating people fairly
10	Listening intently
9	Communicating warmth
7	Establishing rapport
6	Understanding human behavior
9	Empathy
10	Tactfulness
8	Cooperative team member
8	Avoiding stereotyping people
8	Feeling comfortable with different kinds of people
9	Fun person to work with
9	Treating others as equals
10	Dealing effectively with conflict
7	Helping clarify misunderstandings
9	Creating an environment conducive to social interaction

USING ACCOMPLISHMENTS WITH TRANSFERABLE SKILLS

1. You have already written about your top twelve accomplishments. You will use those accomplishments to help verify which are your top skill clusters. Write all twelve accomplishments on a sheet of paper, using just a short phrase so you know which one you're referring to. Assign 1 to your top accomplishment and 12 to your twelfth most important accomplishment. It might look like this:

1. Discovered error in manufacturing process
2. Cut defective products 20% at ExcelPro
3. Convinced president to buy new equipment—increased productivity over 25%
4. Built morale after it had fallen really low
5. Economics paper on the effects of the Great Society Program 1964-1968
6. Developed, improved inventory control system at Datec
7. Set production record at Datec
8. Reduced defects at Datec over 35%
9. Customized 1956 Chevy
10. Ran first marathon at age 42
11. Coached son's Little League team to 2nd place
12. Learned enough Spanish so I could travel in Mexico for three months

2. Review the skills in the Human Relations Skills cluster. Did the use of Human Relations Skills contribute to your success with your top accomplishment? If so, put a 1 to the right of the skill cluster title. If accomplishment number two had only some rather insignificant people contact, which contributed little to the overall accomplishment, you would not include it. Go on to number three and continue with all twelve accomplishments; then move on to the next cluster. Make quick decisions so you don't get bogged down. In the example above it was concluded that Accomplishments 1, 3, 7, 9, 10, and 12, made significant use of human relations skills.

3. When you are through you will have a graphic presentation of your top skill clusters. A skill cluster that you rated 8 or above, and was used with eight of 12 accomplishments would indicate it is one of your top skill areas.

You have used virtually all of these skills. Some you have used on jobs, others were used in school, in hobbies, in volunteer activities, or just in everyday living.

TRANSFERABLE SKILLS

_____ Human Relations Skills

Sensitivity to others
Treating people fairly
Listening intently
Communicating warmth
Establishing rapport
Understanding human behavior
Empathy
Tactfulness
Cooperative team member
Avoiding stereotyping people
Feeling comfortable with different
kinds of people
Fun person to work with
Treating others as equals
Dealing effectively with conflict
Helping clarify misunderstandings
Creating an environment condu-
cive to social interaction

_____ Helping Skills

Helping people
Patient with difficult people
Responsive to people's feelings
and needs
Counseling/Empowering/Encour-
aging people
Assisting people in making deci-
sions
Enhancing people's self-esteem
Working effectively with those
often ignored or considered
undesirable
Letting people know you really
care about them
People sense you feel what
they're feeling
Helping people help themselves
Encouraging others to expand and
grow
Facilitating self-assessment and
personal development

_____ Training/Instructing Skills

Instilling the love of a subject
Perceptively answering questions
Explaining difficult ideas and con-
cepts
Creating a stimulating learning
environment
Enabling self-discovery
Encouraging creativity
Effectively using behavior modifi-
cation
Teaching at the student's or
group's level
Training people at work
Developing training materials that
enhance and speed up learning
Keeping classes interesting
Presenting interesting lectures
Creating the sense of being part of
a caring group
Assessing learning styles of indi-
viduals and tailoring training
Presenting written or spoken infor-
mation in a logical step-by-step
fashion that builds a solid foun-
dation for future learning
Sensing when people aren't "getting" it
Being able to rephrase points so
people do "get" it
Quickly establishing rapport with a
group
Developing and effectively using
audio-visual aids
Maintaining productive group
discussions

_____ Leadership Skills

Leader
Motivating/Inspiring people
Getting elected/Getting selected
as a group leader
People believe in you/trust you
Causing change
Stirring people up

Making difficult decisions

People are motivated to follow your lead and recommendations

Fighting the establishment or unfair policies

Accepting responsibility for failures

Decisive in crisis situations

Sound judgment in emergencies

Settling disagreements

Open to other people's ideas

A person of vision

Getting others to share your vision

Recognizing the need for change and willing to undertake it

Perceived as a person with high integrity

Recognizing windows of opportunity

Recognized as one worthy of taking the lead

Sensing when to compromise and when to fight

Reputation for being highly reliable and taking on new responsibilities

Giving credit to others

_____ Managing Skills

Seeing the big picture

Completing projects on time

Setting priorities

Breaking through red tape

Organizing projects and programs

Managing projects

Establishing effective policies/ procedures

Negotiating and getting desired results

Working closely and smoothly with others

Gaining trust and respect of key people

Making effective recommendations

Anticipating problems and issues and preparing alternatives

Taking the initiative when opportunity appears

Effectively overseeing a myriad of details

Handling details well without losing sight of the big picture

Responsive to others' needs

Finding and obtaining the resources necessary for a task

Making those above me look good

Getting people at all levels to support and implement decisions which have come down from the top

Implementing new programs

Working effectively with superiors and people in other work units

Gaining the cooperation of people or groups even when not possessing authority over them

Turning around negative situations

Obtaining allies

_____ Supervising Skills

Getting maximum output from people

Understanding human motivation

Developing a team that truly works together

Training and developing staff

Encouraging people to seek personal and professional growth

Developing a smooth functioning organization

Effectively disciplining when necessary

Creating an environment for people to trust and respect each other

Supervising difficult people

Delegating work effectively

Knowing the strengths and weaknesses of others

Consistently recruiting and hiring good promotable people

Holding profitable meetings

Increasing morale

Staying in touch/communicating with staff

Mediating

Effectively cross-training staff

Encouraging people to want to do their best
Helping people achieve their potential
Reducing turnover
Minimizing complaining and back-biting

_____ Persuading Skills

Influencing others' ideas and attitudes
Mediating between groups
Obtaining consensus among diverse groups
Effectively selling ideas to top people
Getting people to change their views on long-held beliefs
Getting people to value something not previously valued
Getting departments or organizations to take desired action
Getting people/clients/customers to reveal their needs
Really listening to people and sensing their true needs
Developing a strong knowledge base so questions can be answered
Selling products
Selling services
Selling ideas to others
Selling yourself
Closing a deal
Gaining support from those impacted by decisions/changes
Helping people see the benefits of a course of action

_____ Speaking Skills

Holding the attention of a group
Strong, pleasing voice
Clear enunciation
"Reading" a group
Impromptu speaking
Thinking quickly on your feet
Telling stories
Using humor
Handling questions well

Getting a group to relate to you
Coming across as sincere and spontaneous
Making convincing arguments
Providing clear explanations of complex topics
Presenting ideas in a logical integrated way

_____ Numerical Skills

Solid ability with basic arithmetic
Multiplying numbers in your head
Figuring out "story" problems
Adding long columns of figures
Figuring out percentages
Recognizing patterns and relationships in numbers
Gaining lots of valuable information from graphs, tables, and charts
Quickly spotting numerical errors
Sensing when an answer or number could not logically be correct
Storing large amounts of numerical data in your head
Making decisions based on numerical data
Making rough calculations/estimates in your mind
Analyzing statistical data

_____ Financial Skills

Developing a budget
Staying within a budget
Finding bargains
Estimating costs
Eye for a profit
Recognizing money making opportunities
Ability to buy low and sell high
Managing money/making money grow
Setting financial priorities
Developing cost cutting solutions
Negotiating financial deals
Understanding economic principles
Gut feeling for financial trends
Ability to get financing

_____ Office Skills

Making arrangements
Scheduling
Expediting
Concentrating on details
Efficient with paperwork
Using the telephone to get things done
Knowing how to get information
Organizing an office
Organizing records
Creating systems for data storage/ retrieval
Memory for detail
Quickly spotting errors
Thorough understanding of regulations and procedures
Cutting through red tape to achieve a goal
Expert at using and manipulating the system to resolve a problem
Processing information accurately
Pleasant phone voice
Learning office procedures quickly
Operating business machines
Proofreading, correcting

_____ Body Skills

Finger dexterity
Hand dexterity
Eye-hand coordination
Physical coordination
Quick reflexes/reactions
Walking long distances
Standing for long periods
Strong arms/legs/back
Running
Jumping
Throwing
Lifting/carrying
Physical endurance
Steady hands
Sorting things
Depth perception
Sense of rhythm
Working quickly with hands and fingers
Sense of taste

Sense of smell
Sense of hearing
Sensitive touch
Able to see/spot things others miss
Skilled at sports
Control over your body
Enduring pain or discomfort

_____ Mechanical and Tool Skills

Inventing
Improvising with a machine or tool
Assembling/building/installing
Precision work
Operating power tools
Using hand tools
Operating machinery/equipment
Driving cars, trucks, and equipment
Fixing and repairing
Troubleshooting/diagnosing problems
Figuring out how things work
Drafting/Mechanical drawing
Understanding manuals/diagrams
Mechanical ability
Understanding electricity
Reading gauges/instruments

_____ Idea Skills

Imaginative
Conceiving and generating ideas
Improvising
Innovative
Creative
Inventing
Conceptualizing
Synthesizing and borrowing ideas, and creating something new
Seeing the big picture
Developing new theories
Recognizing new applications for ideas or things
Open to new ideas from others

Able to look beyond the way things have been done in the past

Refusing to become fixated on a single idea and looking for better ideas

Seeing things others don't see

Finding ways to improve things

Bringing together two distinct concepts to produce something original

_____ Writing Skills

Overall writing ability

Writing clear concise sentences

Grammatically correct writing

Strong versatile vocabulary

Developing a logical, well organized theme

Vividly describing feelings, people, senses, and things

Stirring up people's emotions

Creating living, real, believable characters

Developing logical and persuasive points of view

Summarizing and condensing written material

Editing, strengthening, tightening someone's writing

Humorous writing

Simplifying scientific and technical material

Making "dry" subjects interesting

Writing
- Letters
- Memos
- Reports
- Position papers
- Research reports
- News articles
- Speeches
- Manuals
- Proposals for funding
- Poetry
- Song lyrics
- Fiction
- Satire
- Slogans
- Advertising

_____ Planning Skills

Planning programs or projects

Setting attainable goals

Determining priorities

Forecasting/Predicting

Scheduling effectively

Making persuasive recommendations

Using facts while trusting gut feelings

Time management

Accurately predicting results of proposed action

Accurately assessing available resources

Anticipating problems before they develop

Anticipating reactions of people and sensing whether they will support a proposal

Finishing projects on time

Sensing whether a project or program will work and making appropriate recommendations

Developing alternative actions in case the primary plan doesn't work as expected

Developing innovative methods and techniques

Predicting where bottlenecks can occur and preparing workable plans to get around the bottlenecks

Considering all the details of a project, even the smallest

_____ Troubleshooting Skills

Anticipating problems

Solving problems

Untangling messes

Bringing order out of a chaotic situation

Determining root causes

Intuitively sensing where the problem is, and usually being right

Recognizing and resolving problems while they're still relatively minor

Able to come in and take control of a situation
Selecting the most effective solution
Improvising under stress
Helping a group identify solutions
Not stopping with the first "right" answer that comes to mind
Handling difficult people
Staying calm in emergencies
People have confidence that now you're here, things will be taken care of

_____ Organizing Skills

Organizing/Planning events
Organizing offices
Organizing systems
Organizing people to take action
Organizing data/information
Making sure people are in the right place at the right time
Organizing enjoyable and memorable happenings

_____ Researching/Investigating Skills

Working on research projects
Researching in a library
Knowing how to find information
Able to sift important information from unimportant
Investigating
Tracking down information
Following up on leads
Organizing large amounts of data and information
Keeping an open mind
Summarizing findings
Designing research projects
Discovering new things or phenomena
Relentlessly seeking an answer
Developing new testing methods
Gathering information from people
Producing surveys or questionnaires
Identifying relationships
Detecting cause and effect relationships

Collecting data
Using statistical data
Weaving threads of evidence together
Developing hypotheses
Extracting pertinent information from people

_____ Analyzing Skills

Interpreting/evaluating data
Evaluating reports and recommendations
Analyzing trends
Accurately predicting what will occur based on facts, trends, and intuition
Designing systems to collect or analyze information
Weighing pros and cons of an issue
Simplifying complex ideas
Exposing nonlogical thinking
Seeing both sides of an issue
Synthesizing ideas
Clarifying problems
Diagnosing needs/problems
Breaking down principles into parts
Constantly looking for a better way
Identifying more efficient ways of doing things
Getting to the heart of an issue

_____ Artistic Skills

Excellent taste
Artistic
Sense of color combinations
Sense of beauty
Drawing scenes/people
Painting
Depth perception
Envisioning the finished product/ sensing how it will all come together
Sense of proportion and space
Envisioning in three dimensions
Spatial perception
Designing visual aids
Calligraphy/lettering

Appreciating and valuing fine works of art

Capturing a feeling, mood, or idea through photography, drawing, sculpting, cartoons, music, etc.

Developing visually pleasing things (charts, reports, manuals, etc.)

Applied sense of color, shape, design

Conceiving visual representations of ideas and concepts

Sensing what will work and look right

Sensing what people will appreciate

Working well with artistic people

Producing high quality mechanical and line drawings

Sensing the difference between good and great art

_____ Performing Skills

Poised and confident before groups

Showmanship

Responsive to audience moods

Making people laugh

Getting an audience involved with you

Getting an audience to relate to you

Powerful stage presence

Getting an audience enthusiastic or excited

Eliciting strong emotions from an audience

Stirring up an audience to take some type of action

Entertaining an audience

Playing musical instruments

Dancing

Acting

Singing

Modeling

Poetry reading

_____ Observing Skills

Intuitive

Highly observant of surroundings

Long memory of scenes once observed

Hearing/seeing/feeling things others are unaware of

Perceptive/sensitive/aware

Picking up on people's feelings, reactions, and attitudes

Eye for fine/small details

Spotting slight changes in things

Recalling names and faces of people

INTERPRETATIONS OF YOUR TRANSFERABLE SKILL RATINGS

To make the most out of the transferable skills exercise, you must interpret what the results mean. The following interpretive guides should help.

1. I gave the cluster a high rating and I used it in several accomplishments.

> *Interpretation:* Consciously or unconsciously you have sought out opportunities to use that skill area. You seem to enjoy the skill area and are very good at it. The use of this skill area may be critical to your experiencing a high level of job satisfaction at work.

2. I gave the cluster a high rating but it was used in only a few of my top accomplishments.

> *Interpretation:* You are skilled in this area, but you may not enjoy using the skill area. This skill area should probably be reserved as a supporting skill rather than one you would build a job around. Or, it could be that you enjoy the skill area but have just had very few opportunities to use it. In this case you would want to determine whether you should obtain further training or experience in that area so you can use it more frequently.

> *Example:* I give myself a 9 in numerical skills even though I only occasionally use the skill on the job. Only 3 of my top 12 accomplishments used numerical skills. Throughout high school I was very good in math and I enjoy working with numbers, but I would never want a job to use numbers more than 10% of the time. When the use of numerical skills is only occasional, I not only tolerate it, I actually enjoy it.

3. I gave the cluster a low rating, and have used it in fewer than three accomplishments.

> *Interpretation:* You lack both the skill and interest in this area and would be wise to find an occupation which seldom requires the use of this skill area.

PRIORITIZING CLUSTERS

Now that you have rated yourself on the transferable skills, the next step is to prioritize your top skill clusters and the top skills within those clusters. Once you have prioritized your clusters, similarly to the ones below, you will have a beginning picture of your ideal job. Spend time interpreting it. What is it telling you? What insights does it offer? What connections do you see? Once you've completed prioritizing your clusters, spend 15 minutes or so interpreting what you have. Jot down your thoughts.

1) Review all of your transferable skill clusters. Determine which ones you enjoy most and which you have the highest ability in.

2) Pick the 12 clusters you feel would be most important to you in your ideal job and rank order them. Rank them according to your enjoyment and skill level. In other words, you are ranking the clusters not just according to your skill level, and not just according to your enjoyment level. You are ranking them according to a combination of skill plus enjoyment. If you're having a tough time deciding between two skill clusters, simply flip a coin; we're not concerned whether a particular skill cluster should be ranked third or fourth. Because you are considering two factors—enjoyment level and skill level—you will simply have to sort out in your own mind the proper order. We are not trying to be scientific about this, nor are we trying to be totally precise—we simply want you to obtain some valuable information and insights about yourself.

3) Within each skill cluster list your top 5-9 skills. There is no need to prioritize them. Use the example as a guide.

MY TOP TWELVE SKILL CLUSTERS

1 Human Relations Skills

Sensitivity to others
Treating people fairly
Listening intently
Empathy
Tactfulness
Counseling/empowering
Communicating warmth

2 Managing Skills

Managing projects
Completing projects on time
Setting priorities
Anticipating problems, preparing
  alternatives
Making recommendations

3 Supervising Skills

Getting maximum output from
  people
Understanding human behavior
Developing a team
Supervising difficult employees
Increasing morale
Holding profitable meetings

4 Idea Skills

Imaginative
Conceiving and generating ideas
Seeing the big picture
Innovative and creative ideas
Conceptualizing

5 Writing Skills

Overall writing ability
Writing clear concise sentences
Strong vocabulary
Developing persuasive points of
  view
Summarizing and condensing
  written material

6 Researching Skills

Working on research projects
Researching in a library
Tracking down information
Investigating

Relentlessly seeking an answer
Developing hypotheses

7 Instructing Skills

Perceptively answering questions
Explaining ideas and concepts
Enabling self-discovery
Developing training manuals
Group facilitator

8 Observing Skills

Intuitive
Highly observant of surroundings
Perceptive
Aware
Eye for small detail

9 Planning Skills

Planning
Determining priorities
Scheduling
Excellent time management
Anticipating reactions of people

10 Problem Solving Skills

Solving problems
Anticipating problems
Untangling messes
Determining root causes
Bringing order out of chaos

11 Numerical Skills

Working complex mathematical
  equations
Fascination with numbers
Quickly spotting numerical errors
Making decisions based on data
Analyzing statistical data

12 Analyzing Skills

Interpreting/Evaluating
Analyzing trends
Weighing pros and cons of an
  issue
Simplifying complex ideas
Exposing nonlogical thinking
Synthesizing ideas
Diagnosing needs/problems

WORK CONTENT SKILLS

Work content skills are skills which you develop through study, observation, practice, apprenticeships, or on-the-job-training. Work content skills are also areas of special knowledge which you develop. For our purposes a work content skill is any skill that you have that some people get paid for. If you know how to ride horses, that is a work content skill because jockeys, horse trainers, and mounted police officers get paid for this skill. Admittedly their skill level may be higher than yours, but you also have the skill, so it should be listed.

Place a check by any of these skills which you have done at least once:

Driving a car	Using a power saw, drill, router
Mechanical drawing	Repairing appliances
Tying knots	Using a compass
Interior decorating	Cooking
Typing	Caring for a sick child
Bookkeeping	Sewing
Filing income taxes	Knitting
Drawing cartoons	Gardening
Training a dog	Painting a house
Reading a map	Tuning an engine
Plumbing	Changing oil in a car
Electrical wiring	Sinking a putt
Framing a room	Fishing
Wallpapering	Skiing
Laying carpet	Riding horses

1. The above list of work content skills was designed to help you make the distinction between transferable and work content skills. Remember, transferable skills are more general and are very transferable. Transferable skills enable you to do the work content skills.

2. There are over 100,000 work content skills. Because of the vast number it is necessary to have you identify as many of your own work content skills as possible.

3. Knowledge itself is a work content skill. Examples include knowledge of the causes of the Civil War, knowing all the bones and muscles in the body, knowing all the cloud formations and what they mean regarding weather, understanding electricity, and visually recognizing one hundred strains of bacteria.

4. Many science-related work content skills are really areas of knowledge—memorizing the periodic table, calculating the results of mixing two chemicals, understanding how photosynthesis occurs, and

memorizing the stages of mitosis. To identify science and math work content skills, recall courses you have taken and then recall the matters which were studied. Don't worry if you don't remember the details, that's to be expected. To list a science or math related work content skill does not require that you can presently explain all of the details. The fact that you knew the material at one time is reason enough to list it. Keep in mind, it's always easier to learn a subject the second time than it was the first.

5. Your hobbies and free time activities are a rich source of work content skills. People have turned hobbies into lucrative jobs. To list a work content skill requires only that you have done it, not that you are an expert. Skill clusters that you might use would include Mechanical, Tools/Equipment, Carpentry/Repairs, Housework, Kitchen, Yard/Garden, Home, Office, Sports, Arts/Crafts.

6. Begin by developing a list of all the skill clusters you will be using. Review the clusters at the end of this section to get ideas. Every part-time or summer job you ever had should have a cluster. The cluster titles might simply be, Bucking Hay, Burger King, Waitressing, Mowing Lawns, Retail Clerk. Then list skill clusters that might come from your education. If you are a college graduate you would at least need to list your major and your minor as separate skill clusters. Then recall some other subjects in which you took several courses. I majored in history and minored in political science, so I would use both of those clusters. I took two courses in economics plus I continue to read a lot about economics, so that would be another cluster. I took an art appreciation course, which I enjoyed, but I have done little reading about art since taking that class in 1971. Because of that I would not create an art appreciation cluster.

Next list your hobbies. If you are a fairly serious photographer, create a photography cluster. People often hesitate to list hobbies because they feel they are not good enough. Just because you are not a graduate of a major photography school, and haven't had a photograph printed on the cover of *Life Magazine,* doesn't mean you should not have a photography skill cluster. If you have read books and magazines on photography, have two or three lenses, and put genuine effort into obtaining high quality photos, you should have a photography cluster. I think you get the idea. I have used photography just as an example. If you work around the home you should have such clusters as Tools/Equipment, Carpentry, Plumbing, Electrical, Automotive, etc.

7. For each cluster list as many skills as you can by listing whatever pops into your mind. Don't eliminate anything because you feel you are not skilled enough in it or feel that you could never get a job doing that. Make a game out of this exercise and <u>identify at least 150 work content skills</u>.

Work quickly when identifying the skills learned in summer jobs or part-time jobs, particularly if you held the job more than ten years ago. I wrote the skill cluster for bucking hay. It took less than two minutes because there just wasn't much to remember. There was no need to wrack my brain coming up with more than five items.

8. Avoid being too general. For example, it would not be adequate for a contractor to simply list carpentry as a work content skill. It should be broken down into its components such as: building concrete forms; laying foundations; building walls; installing doors, windows, and cabinets; constructing roof trusses; installing sheet rock. The list would also include any types of machines, equipment, or tools that have been used.

9. When looking at a past job or hobby, try to list all of the things you learned in that job. One way to identify skills is to visualize yourself doing that job or hobby. What are the things you do and what areas of knowledge do you use? Remember, knowledge is a work content skill. List those things as quickly as they come to mind. Do not filter anything out just because you feel you are not that skilled at it. Don't worry about that because later you will have an opportunity to go through your list and identify those skills you are good enough in to get paid for.

Another way to identify skills is to ask yourself what causes someone who is really outstanding, to stand apart from the rest. That will get you thinking about those special abilities and areas of knowledge.

10. Treat this as a game. The game is to come up with as many skills as possible. When they get through, many people are amazed that they know how to do so many things. List every conceivable work content skill. Some seem mundane or minor, but that's okay, list all the small ones with the big ones.

It can be enjoyable considering all the things you know how to do. You never know when you might list a skill that could have a real payoff for you. It might come down to you and one other person for a particular job. Through the interview process you may recognize a need that the employer has for one of your skills. The skill may not be one which is typically utilized in the type of position you are interviewing for, but you see the value nevertheless. By mentioning to the employer how that skill could come in handy at times, it could just tip the balance in your favor. If you don't take time to assess those skills now, you may not think of them later.

The process of identifying work content skills will help you recognize which work content skills you definitely would like to use in your ideal job. Perhaps you've done a particular thing only a few times, but people felt you showed real potential. With some practice or training, that skill could become very important in your career. Or, you may identify a work content skill (or a set of work content skills) that is so important to you that you could build a job or career around that work content skill cluster.

11. Place a check by those skills you feel you are strong enough in to be paid for doing. Place an X by those skills that with some additional training you feel you could become very competent in.

EXAMPLES OF WORK CONTENT SKILLS

The following work content skills have been provided to give you a clearer idea of the types of skills which should be labeled work content skills. Feel free to use the cluster titles or the skills themselves, but this list is only intended to give you ideas. Look at the kitchen work content skill cluster. In this case the person wrote down kitchen equipment, then indented and began listing all of the types of equipment the person has used. Procedures then became the next category. This is a very useful way to come up with skills.

Also make note of the claims adjusting skill cluster, right after kitchen skills. That example was included to show what a really complete skill cluster might look like. This person did a thorough analysis of what he did on the job

You should also realize that these skill clusters were supplied by many different people.

Kitchen

Equipment
  Microwave
  Blender
  Food Processor
  Ice cream maker
  Deep fat fryer
  Pressure cooker
  Institutional ovens
  Wok, stir frying
Procedures
  Baking—cakes, pies, breads, cookies
  Following a recipe
  Calculating a recipe for a larger group
Modifying/experimenting with recipes
Making—lasagna, spare ribs, home made spaghetti sauce, scratch pie crusts, pastries
Organizing a kitchen
Planning so everything is ready at the same time
Dinner for 30 people

Claims Adjusting

Estimating cost of repairing cars, boats, homes
Read the crash book guides to know how many hours to remove and replace bumpers, fenders, quarter panels, and paint parts
Know all the tools used by body shop mechanics
Know exactly how panels will be straightened and how much time it should take
Know how paint is matched
Know all the preparatory steps to painting

Know how a portion of a panel can be painted and blended with the rest of the panel

Negotiating with body shop managers

Explaining to insureds and claimants why a part does not need to be replaced

Recognizing when there really is frame damage

Being fair but getting repairs done at the lowest cost possible

Knowing how to threaten a body shop manager that I will pull the car and take it to a different shop if he won't get reasonable

Know when to total a car and accurately assess its value

Photographing cars, boats, and homes to best show the damage

Finding witnesses of accidents

Getting good statements from insureds, claimants, and witnesses

Knowing how to settle small injuries quickly and inexpensively to avoid financial exposure

Getting claimants to sign release forms

Knowing how much an injury is worth

Being fair with injured claimants and getting them to trust me and not hire an attorney

Really getting the facts about an accident

Studying the facts so I can be in a strong bargaining position when negotiating with attorneys

Know when to call the bluff of an attorney

Settle even big cases by negotiating fairly but effectively with claimants without attorneys

Know how to take advantage of the fact that I know the case better than the attorney

Write well-written reports for the file

Arts and Crafts

Macrame
Knitting
Crochet
Weaving
Latch hook rug making
Sewing simple and complex patterns
Silkscreening
Stained glass, soldering
Making own clay
Pottery making and firing
Candle making
Understanding how colors work together
Knowing psychological effects of color
Charcoal sketching
Painting—oil, water, tempera, landscapes, portraits, modern art
Making dolls
Drawing cartoons

Tools/Equipment

Hammer, screwdriver, pliers, hand saw, crescent wrench
Grinder
Glass cutter
Generator, compressor
Airless paint sprayers
Socket set
Wire cutters
Soldering iron
Electric drill, hand drill
Table saw
Router
Jointer, planer
Drill press
Chain saw
Level
Skill saw
Keyhole saw
Forklift
Hand truck
Winch
Backhoe
Cat
10 speed two ton truck

Office

Electronic typewriter
Word processors
IBM clones
PBX
Programmable calculator
Dictaphone
Microfiche reader-printer
Offset printing press
Microsoft Word, Multimate, Word
    Perfect
dBase IV, RBase 2000
Excel
Lotus 123
    Creating spreadsheets
    Using macros

Statistics

Probability
Chi-square analysis
Simple regression analysis
Sample selection processes
Confidence intervals
Nonparametric statistics
Prepare frequency distributions
Median, mean, mode
Normal curve
Standard deviation
Standard scores, Z scores
Correlation—Pearson, product-
    moment
Random sample
Null hypothesis
Type I, Type II errors
F distribution
ANOVA

Bookkeeping

General ledger
Accounts payable ledger
Accounts receivable ledger
Write checks
Balance checking account
Check posting
Making deposits
Trial balance report
Keep full set of books
Credit analysis

Collections
Shipping invoices
Receivable invoices
Credit invoices
Debit invoices
Medical insurance forms

Computer

Equipment
    CRT Terminals
    HP 2100
    IBM 8100
    IBM Series 3
Procedures
    CMS (Conversational Monitor
    System)
    JCL (Job Control Language)
    Flow diagrams
    Transfer files from disk to tape
    TYMSHARE—Stat Pak
    Revise and submit computer
    programs
    Edit raw data
    Understand how disk operates
On-line and batch environments
Languages—BASIC, FORTRAN,
    COBOL, C
Unit record equipment—sorter,
    interpreter
I/O devices
    Printer, card reader, card
    punches, tape drive, disk drive,
    diskette drive

Bucking Hay

Driving trucks
Hooking up loader
Using bale hooks
Techniques of stacking bales
Tying bales down

Burger King

Taking customers' orders
Getting customers to say yes to
    fries and cheese on burger
Giving change
Preparing french fries
Making sundaes

Sports/Activities

Waltzing, swing dancing, square dancing
Square dance calling
Horseback riding
  Saddle horse
  Groom horse
  Stay on bucking horse
  Barrel racing
  Calf roping
  Training commands
  Towed trailer
Motorcycle riding
Fire rifle, shotgun, pistol
Shoot bow and arrow
Gymnastics
  Floor exercises
  Balance beam
  Vaulting
  Trampoline
  Horse
  Rings
  Parallel bars
Softball—shortstop, second base, pitcher
  Know all rules of softball
  Umpiring softball
Teatherball
Ping pong
Bowling
Tennis
Tying knots (bowline, half-hitch, clove hitch)
Using a compass
Orienteering

Carpentry/Repairs

Hammer a nail straight
Put together shelves and book-cases
Roofing
Framing
Installing sheetrock
Taping and mudding sheetrock
Installing siding
Installing gutters
Cutting glass and installing win-dows

Installing doors and locks
Installing insulation
Plumbing for a new sink
Installing drain pipes around the house
Building a fence
Built a deck—designed, framed, built stairs
Installed wiring
Installed dimming switch, light sockets
Refinished oak floor
Building concrete forms
Pouring concrete
Finish concrete work

Mechanical

Change oil and tires
Put on tire chains
Charge battery and use jumper cables
Replace spark plugs
Use timing light
Tune engine
Lubricate chassis
Welding
Replace brake shoes
Rebuild engine
Align front end
Wax a car
Fixed grandfather clock
Repaired small electric motor
Fixed a copy machine—bad circuit

Camping

Setting up a tent
Starting a camp fire
Using a kerosene stove
Back packing—packing light
Chopping wood
Recognize poison ivy and poison oak
Keep bears and deer away from food
Recognize edible berries and roots
Making emergency shelter

Selling

Really listening to customers
Identifying needs and problems of customers
Getting customers to tell me the real objections
Establishing rapport with potential customers
Developing strong product

Keeping up-to-date on new products
Always know what the competition is doing
Serving as a consultant to customers
Researching accounts before calling on them
Able to get through to decision makers
Put together thorough bids and proposals
Persistent
Very complete with paperwork
Able to sense buying signals
Know how to close and get the sale

Ceramics

Clay characteristics
Glaze formulas
Firing techniques
  Raku
  High firing
  Bisque firing
  Glaze firing
  Low firing
  Luster firing
Kiln loading
Wheel throwing—centering, opening, lifting, plates, bowls, cups
Handle pulling
Slab building
Texture techniques—ribbing, ruffing, burnishing
Glaze application—dripping, stripping, painting, spraying
Trimming
Drying
Mold use
Wedging

Once you've completed your initial list of work content skills, it's time to examine them. By the way, I wrote "initial list" because you should continue to add to the list as skills and experiences pop into your mind.

If there are any work content skills on your list that you would really like to use in the future, begin considering if the skill is major enough to build an entire job around. If not, ask yourself if you merely want to spend 5–20% of your time using it.

Ask yourself whether you have any skills that you began to develop some time ago, and showed talent for, but which somehow were never fully developed. Perhaps this is the time to identify a career field or job which would make use of that skill. Either you would need to obtain additional training before going into such a field, or you would need to get on-the-job training. The fact that you have some exposure to the skill could help you get hired. Also, remember to place a check by those skills you feel you are strong enough in to be paid for doing. Place an X by those skills that with some additional training you feel you could become competent in.

TEMPERAMENT

Understanding your unique temperament can provide one of the greatest helps in career decision making. Webster's defines temperament as "a characteristic or habitual inclination or mode of emotional response." In other words, in a particular situation, a person will react in a consistent way. Knowing your temperament allows you to predict outcomes and will help you predict your enjoyment of a particular job or career field. If you prefer variety and independence, and your new job will require a great deal of repetitive work, along with strict rules, you will probably find yourself frustrated.

As you read the next several paragraphs, see what you can learn about me. I personally have a temperament of moderation. I seldom take extreme positions or have extreme attitudes. I prefer a considerable amount of variety in my work and become bored and ineffective with repetition. When I was a cost estimator for a business forms printing company in Minneapolis, I once made a simple mistake which cost the company about $2,000. The job had become repetitive and I had stopped checking my work as thoroughly as I should have. Because of that and other experiences, I shy away from repetitive and precise work.

Two years later, while living in Chicago, I interviewed for a position with International Harvester. When I arrived for the interview I was informed that the position I had come for had been filled internally, but that they had another position I might be interested in. Since I was already there I agreed to the interview. The two people interviewing me were very nice, but as they described the position, it sounded amazingly like my old estimating job. I was offered the position but I simply could not picture myself doing it. All I had to do was stay in the position for a year and I could then have transferred elsewhere within the company. Even though I disliked the job I had at the time, I simply could not force myself to take another job with high repetitiveness.

While I prefer variety there are limitations. In my profession as a career counselor I am continually reading, researching, writing, meeting new and unique people, and dealing with a variety of problems. I never get bored. I do have my day basically planned out, however. I know who I have appointments with and I can usually plan my tasks beforehand. A person extremely high in variety prefers to constantly change from one task to another and likes surprise situations. I don't. I like to work on a variety of tasks, but I usually like to complete one and then move to another.

I am both gregarious and solitary, but definitely higher in gregarious. I enjoy meeting people but often feel uncomfortable at large gatherings where I don't know anyone. I love getting to know people on an individual basis. I am also solitary because I enjoy researching and writing. I sometimes spend all day cooped up in my office writing. I love it. At the end of the day I'm refreshed and satisfied. While I enjoy that kind of isolation for a day or two, I would not enjoy it day in and day out.

In just a couple of minutes you have learned a lot about me just by my sharing part of my temperament. Knowing my temperament as I do, allows me to predict whether I would like a certain job.

The value of this exercise is not just in rating yourself on various temperaments, but in thinking about the type of person you really are. Be honest with yourself. If you prefer routine work, admit it to yourself. If you deceive yourself into believing that you prefer variety, you, and the next company which hires you, will suffer. Writing about your temperament is critical. It will lead to much greater clarity.

Knowing your temperament is extremely important. Too many people are in jobs they dislike because they did not consider whether their temperament would fit. Those who are truly excited about their work invariably are in positions which fully utilize their temperament. Determine that you will take whatever actions are necessary to become one of those fortunate few.

Although there are no right or wrong temperaments, having a temperament at the extreme can often cause problems. Being intuitive provides a good example of how your temperament can help or hurt you. At the extreme, some intuitive people have the attitude that they don't want to be bothered with the facts, since they already know intuitively what should be done. Such people often create problems for themselves because they won't even take a few minutes to examine some readily available information. By reading the information the person might quickly realize that they would be better off not taking the action. Then there are the highly objective people who refuse to make a decision because they claim they need more data or another study.

Another important concept is that you possess all of the temperaments. You are higher in some and lower in others, but you have all of them within you. In the temperaments list, planning is paired with doing. Those who are high in planning are usually low in doing, but even a person who is at the extreme in planning, also has some of the doing temperament. In fact, there are people who are excellent planners and excellent doers. They like to take adequate time to plan things out, but for them the satisfaction comes when the thing is actually completed. Just coming up with a great plan is not enough for them.

INSTRUCTIONS FOR TEMPERAMENT

1. Rate yourself on a scale of 1–10 for each temperament. A 10 means you have an extremely strong need to have a job which allows you to express that temperament. If you are rather moderate in your temperament you may not have any 9s or 10s, but will probably have some 8s. A rating of a 10 is extreme. A 10 in variety might be a person who can hardly stand to do the same thing twice. Being a 10, therefore, is not necessarily an advantage. After all, there are not many jobs which offer that much variety. Another way to look at the rating is to say that a 10 represents being in the top 5% of all people, in the need for that temperament. A 9 means you are in the top 10%, an 8 in the top 20%, a 7 in the top 30%, and a 6 in the top 40%.

2. Notice that the temperaments are arranged in pairs, with the exception of persuasive, which is by itself. With the paired temperaments such as *variety* versus *routine*, it is useful to note that you are not all of one temperament and none of the other. We can say with a lot of assurance, however, that if you are high in one temperament, you will probably be low in the other. It is hard to imagine someone who is a 9 in gregarious, and an 8 in solitary. Generally if you are an 8 in one temperament, you are likely to be a 2, 3, or 4 in the other temperament of the pair.

3. Determine which of your top twelve accomplishments utilized which temperaments. If variety was an important aspect of accomplishment number one, place a one in the far left column. Limit yourself to three 1s, three 2s, three 3s, and so forth. In other words, which three temperaments were most crucial in each accomplishment. In the example below, accomplishment 1 primarily used Variety/Versatile, Independent/Self-Directing, and Relaxed Atmosphere. "Variety/Versatile" was rated an 8, and that temperament was expressed in accomplishments 1,2,3,6,8,10 and 12.

①,2,3,6,8,10,12	8	VARIETY/VERSATILE
	3	ROUTINE/REPETITIVE
	2	CLOSE SUPERVISION/DEFINED PROCEDURES
①,4,5,7,9,10,11	8	INDEPENDENT/SELF-DIRECTING
4,6,7	6	DOMINANT
	4	RESERVED
12	7	PERSUASIVE
4,6	6	GREGARIOUS
8,12	6	SOLITARY
	3	STRESS/PRESSURE/DEADLINES
①,8,10	7	RELAXED ATMOSPHERE

2,3,5	6	SUBJECTIVE/INTUITIVE
9	6	OBJECTIVE/USE FACTS
	3	PRECISION WORK/ATTENTION TO DETAIL
2,7,9,12	7	CONCEPTS/SEEING THE BIG PICTURE
3,5,11	7	PLANNING
	6	DOING/IMPLEMENTING

4. Highlight the six temperaments most like you and describe how each is important to you. Write quickly without being concerned for spelling or grammar. Examples:

> VARIETY - I need a lot of variety on a job, but I don't mind some repetitious tasks because they give me a break from some of my more difficult tasks. Ideal for me would be to start a new project every month or so, spending 60% of my time on it. The rest might be spent on the ten or more tasks that I do on an ongoing basis. I couldn't handle working on an assembly line.

> ROUTINE - I prefer learning a job and then being able to do it automatically, without a lot of thinking. I've sorted mail for six years and there's still a challenge to working accurately.

> I am very self-directing in my work. I like a supervisor to give me an assignment, tell me what's required and when it's due, and then leave me alone to figure out how to do it. I hate it when I'm always being checked up on.

Once you finish rating yourself on the temperaments and writing about them, step back and ask yourself what it all means to you. Spend time thinking about jobs or activities which you've enjoyed. You probably enjoyed them because they allowed you to be the person you are. Then think about jobs or activities which you did not enjoy. A big reason you did not enjoy them was probably due to the fact that they conflicted with your temperament.

Spend some time noticing which temperaments were most frequently used in your accomplishments. This should give you a graphic illustration of which temperaments are really most important to you. If you rated a temperament an eight, and it was used in five or more accomplishments, that fact is probably quite significant. That temperament is probably not just a characteristic of you, but should probably be placed in the category of a need. A job which conflicts with that temperament will probably make you miserable.

Recalling your past in this way should convince you of how important it is to have a job which matches your temperament.

Before you begin rating yourself on the temperaments, first read the definitions of temperaments beginning on page 416. Reading about the temperaments will give you greater clarity as you rate yourself.

TEMPERAMENT

Temperament - Characteristic mode of emotional response; tendency to act in a certain manner under given circumstances; dominant distinguishing qualities.

VARIETY/VERSATILE - You like variety; frequently moving from one task to another; enjoy the unexpected; many things going on at once.

ROUTINE/REPETITIVE - You like routine, repetitive work; a regular routine carried out to set procedures.

CLOSE SUPERVISION/DEFINED PROCEDURES - You prefer taking instructions from others with little room for independent judgment.

INDEPENDENT/SELF-DIRECTING - You work effectively alone, completing projects on schedule without supervision.

DOMINANT - You feel comfortable directing and supervising people. You often seek to take the lead on a committee.

RESERVED - You prefer being responsible for your own work, with little or no supervision.

PERSUASIVE - You enjoy influencing people, or seeking to influence people, in their attitudes and opinions.

GREGARIOUS - You are sociable, like the company of others, and enjoy meeting people and making friends.

SOLITARY - You prefer working alone; autonomous; self-reliant.

STRESS/PRESSURE/DEADLINES - You enjoy working under stress; able to focus better as a deadline approaches; self-controlled; calm and level-headed in emergencies or stressful situations.

RELAXED ATMOSPHERE - You prefer working at your own steady pace with few emergencies.

SUBJECTIVE/INTUITIVE - You feel comfortable making decisions without supporting data; trust your hunches and intuitions; may avoid using data even when available.

OBJECTIVE/USE FACTS - You rely on facts and verifiable data; take only carefully calculated risks; utilize rational problem solving.

PRECISION WORK/ATTENTION TO DETAIL - You insist on high quality work; willing to check and double check; love working with many details; enjoy working with small tolerances and margin for error.

CONCEPTS/SEEING THE BIG PICTURE - You have a need to see the big picture. You enjoy conceptualizing and coming up with answers to major problems, but you dislike details.

PLANNING - You like extensive analyzing and planning of programs and projects, and then turning everything over to others to implement.

DOING/IMPLEMENTING - You don't like being bothered with planning. You like to jump right in and get the job done.

DEFINITIONS OF THE TEMPERAMENTS

I have given definitions and examples to help provide a better understanding of temperaments. Reading them should enable you to get more out of the exercise.

Variety/Versatile

Some people need a great deal of variety on the job, and without it are quite frustrated. Variety is in the eye of the beholder, however. As a counselor I have helped hundreds of people analyze their temperament and I have used essentially the same exercise since 1980. Some might say that doing what I do is routine. There is an element of routine with it, but to me there is great variety since each person is different.

I have met people who told me that what they liked about their job was the variety. As I listened to what they did, it struck me as being rather repetitive. But my opinion didn't matter, the person was happy because the right amount of variety was available.

Don't just say you like variety, ask yourself what kind of variety. Some people like jobs with ten main activities that they do almost every day. The person may perform those same activities for 12 years yet never get bored with them. For that person, the variety comes in the form of never having to spend an entire day doing one thing. Other people feel there is adequate variety if periodically they can get out of the office or drive to another facility. Still others find variety by moving from one project to another. They may have the same daily duties, yet they always have at least one project that they are working on.

Routine

People often prefer more routine activities. The problem is that most people don't want to admit they like routine. Our society tells us that everyone is supposed to like variety, and people often put down the assembly line worker. But the point is that many people's temperament is perfectly suited to repetitive work. If you're one, it's important to admit that and be true to yourself. Many people prefer a job that they do well because they've done that thing hundreds or even thousands of times. The activity might require a great deal of concentration or perhaps very little. Repetitive work, such as that of a craftsman, can be very challenging.

Independent/Self-Directing

Many people prefer a boss who defines what needs to be done, provides deadlines, and is available when there are questions. When people first get a new job and are experiencing a steep learning curve, most prefer having a boss close at hand. Then, as they grow more confident, they prefer being given more freedom to make decisions and to carry out a project their own way.

There are different degrees of independence. I met a person who had the ultimate in independence. He worked several hundred miles away from his boss, and rarely talked to him. He did, however, write a quarterly report describing what he was doing and what his results had been.

Salespeople typically have a lot independence. When they are out making calls, usually no one even knows where they are. Although most salespeople work very hard, and usually work a 50 hour week or more, it is possible to take care of personal business during the day, and maybe even knock off early on a Friday. Being self-directing implies the ability to sense what needs to be done, and doing it—without being asked. Some people fail in sales or as independent businesspeople because of the lack of structure. The new salesperson may lack the discipline to make an adequate number of phone calls. The consultant or small business owner may lack discipline, and may waste time doing unimportant functions.

Close Supervision/Defined Procedures

Sometimes it's just easier working with close supervision and having clearly defined procedures for each aspect of the job. No one wants the boss looking over their shoulder all day long, but it can be comforting knowing that someone is close at hand to answer questions or to bounce ideas off of. With clearly defined procedures you don't have to worry about making errors in judgment which you could get in trouble for. Close supervision usually implies that your work is being reviewed frequently and perhaps everything is double-checked by your boss or someone else.

Dominant

A dominant person feels comfortable directing and supervising the work of others. It does not imply that dominant people are domineering. The dominant person often volunteers to take the lead on committees or will seek to be elected. Dominant people are not lords and masters, they simply know how to get work accomplished through others. It does not bother a dominant person to ask or tell someone to do a certain task.

Reserved

Some people prefer not to supervise anyone, and be responsible only for their own work. As they get promoted, however, they will eventually have to supervise a few people. If you have a reserved temperament and would prefer not supervising people, hire only highly independent, responsible, and resourceful people. With that type of person you will spend very little time actually supervising.

Gregarious

The gregarious person likes meeting new people and feels comfortable with new people. The gregarious person is usually a good conversationalist. Gregarious people usually like to be surrounded with others, but also like some alone time, often with a sense of recharging their batteries so they're ready for another intense period of being with people. A person who is a 10 in gregariousness might be one who can hardly stand to be alone. I know a manager who rarely spends more than 30 minutes alone in his office. After 30 minutes he feels an urge to see or talk to someone and will find an excuse to come out of his office and talk to the secretary or a colleague.

Solitary

Preferring to work alone does not indicate that a person is antisocial or doesn't like people. Some people just feel more comfortable working alone. They tend to be autonomous and self-reliant. I have worked with mechanics and most of them prefer working alone and do not like much customer contact. As they work, however, there is often banter going on between them and they spend time talking during breaks and during lunch. Such people also often have a small core of very close friends. The solitary person often feels uncomfortable with small talk and does not view himself or herself as a great conversationalist. Because of their temperament, some people simply enjoy life more when their people contact on the job is less than 20%.

Persuasive

Some people just naturally like to persuade and influence others. They enjoy the activity and derive great satisfaction when someone's view or attitude is changed. Keep in mind, we are talking about the temperament of persuasiveness, not the skill. A person can have a high need to seek to be persuasive, but not be very skillful. Salespeople are usually fairly high in this temperament.

Stress/Pressure/Deadlines

On many jobs the major form of stress and pressure comes from deadlines. Many people believe they work better under the stress of a deadline, and become more focused. Very few people, however, enjoy a life filled with constant deadlines where there is never enough time to do the job right. A person who is a ten thrives in such environments and enjoys such things as handling two or three phone calls simultaneously and putting out several fires daily.

There are people who thrive on stress. People like Red Adair have made a career out of stress. Red makes hundreds of thousands of dollars a year putting out oil well fires. People such as Red always stay calm and level headed during emergencies and instantaneously make the right decisions.

Emergency medical technicians face great stress. They need to think and act fast when they arrive on the scene where someone has just suffered a heart attack, or someone is badly hurt but trapped in a smashed vehicle.

People who are growth-oriented typically handle stress well. They seek more responsibility at work and enjoy learning new things. Although enjoyable and challenging, this creates stress.

Some of the negative stressers include dealing with constant backbiting on the job, having to constantly put out fires, being asked to do great things but being given neither the time nor tools to accomplish them, and working in an unethical environment. Very few people enjoy these kinds of stressers.

Relaxed Atmosphere

I handle stress well, but I really prefer a relaxed atmosphere. Being able to handle it is different from preferring it. I need deadlines also, but I like "reasonable" deadlines. I can easily handle the occasional rush job, but I naturally try to set up systems where that is rarely necessary. I seek out environments where people get along and there is a minimum of conflict. I'm willing to work overtime when the job demands it, but I don't want it every day. I prefer to work at an even pace, one that I can sustain for a long period of time. Once in a while it's kind of exciting to work under a tight deadline or work a 12 hour day. If you relate to what I've described, you'll give yourself at least a six on relaxed atmosphere.

Subjective/Intuitive

Intuitive people feel comfortable making decisions without supporting data. They are prepared to make decisions based as much on gut feelings as logic. They have learned to trust their intuition. Often they will avoid studying data, even when the data is available.

Some jobs are best done by people who are intuitive while other jobs are better handled by objective people. Overly objective people rarely make good actors, while highly subjective people seldom make good scientists. The truly great scientists, however, often have a strong intuitive side to them. It is that intuition and creativity that enables them to look at the same data that their colleagues have, and come up with a different idea or theory.

Being intuitive does not mean that people are just relying on feelings or their gut. In fact, truly intuitive people are pulling in far more information than the average person, they simply don't process it on a purely intellectual level. Intuitive people tend to be highly observant and gather information from many sources.

Objective/Use Facts

The objective person feels most comfortable making decisions when an adequate amount of data is available. In both business and personal decision making the objective person typically gathers large amounts of quantifiable data, develops very orderly plans, and takes only carefully calculated risks. This person also uses a very rational approach to problem solving. To help you rate yourself on this one, ask yourself a question. If you had an important decision to make, and there was valuable information available to you, but it would require many hours to dig it up, would you do it? If the answer is yes, you are probably a seven or eight in objective. If you would go to even greater lengths, and then analyze the data from every possible angle, you would be a nine or ten.

Precision Work/Attention To Detail

Those who love precision work typically have a great deal of patience. Artists and craftsmen usually possess this temperament. Such people are willing to check and double check their work. Accountants, bookkeepers, and proofreaders are examples. The CIA hires people who review satellite photographs of the Soviet Union, Cuba, and other countries. What they do is compare last week's photograph of a small section of territory with yesterday's to see if there have been even the minutest changes. In some jobs it is absolutely essential that every detail be examined, with no detail being too small.

Concepts/Seeing The Big Picture

Conceptualizers differ from detail oriented people. Conceptualizing is generally a more intellectual process and some people derive great satisfaction from the exercise. Conceptualizers like to consider all of the options and assess the results of each option. They tend to think globally. They go to great lengths to avoid the "can't see the forest for the trees" syndrome. Big picture people tend to be very open minded because they often must consider options which others, and perhaps even themselves, oppose. They must recognize the advantages and disadvantages of a given course of action.

Big picture people have a need to see the big picture. Virtually everyone likes to see how their part of a project will fit into the whole, but big picture people have an overwhelming need for it. A Boeing engineer might work on a trajectory problem. Data is analyzed from 20 different angles and may be sent to another group of engineers. The engineer analyzing the trajectory information might never find out exactly what was done with the information. Big picture people are greatly frustrated by that scenario.

Conceptualizers gain satisfaction from coming up with new ideas, and often refer to themselves as "ideas people." Conceptualizers tend to synthesize ideas. They incorporate ideas from numerous sources, and come up with a new twist.

Conceptualizers can often see things that others can't. Architects, artists, and interior designers are often conceptualizers. They can see something in their mind's eye and then can produce it.

Planning

Planners like to plan programs, events, policies, and procedures and then have others carry them out. They are excellent at considering all of the options and putting it all together. In private enterprise there are strategic planners, schedulers, and industrial engineers who spend great amounts of time planning and ensuring that a project gets done right and on schedule. The problem that "pure" planners run into is that they often want to plan and plan, and then plan some more. Often nothing really gets done, especially if they are the ones who are supposed to implement the plan. In real life, not every planner has someone to delegate things to.

Doing/Implementing

Doers typically do not want to be bothered with planning. Their attitude is "when something needs to be done let's jump in and get it done." Doers are very good at carrying out the plans of others. They don't resent the fact that others planned it out, they are just happy to make something happen. Doers like to stay busy. Unfortunately the pure doers often paint themselves into corners. Sometimes just five minutes of planning would have prevented a problem from occurring.

MOTIVATORS AND VALUES

People often fail to recognize the importance of motivators and values when making career decisions. Many jobs, however, create conflicts with your motivators and values, and can substantially reduce your job satisfaction. Take for example the salesman who is on the road five nights a week. His value of *money* attracted him to the position, but the job conflicts with another strong value—his *family*. Another is attracted to the *security* offered by a utility, but turns down the job because it seems to lack the necessary *challenge*. A third person is motivated to *help people,* something she accomplishes as a social worker, but the job conflicts with her value/motivator of *money*.

Values

Values and motivators are similar, but not synonymous. Values are stronger than mere purposes, attitudes, interests, convictions, and beliefs. All values stem from three key words—choosing, prizing, acting. According to Louis Raths, a full value must include all of the following criteria. It must be 1) Chosen freely; 2) Chosen from among alternatives; 3) Chosen after due reflection; 4) Prized and cherished; 5) Publicly affirmed; 6) Acted upon; and 7) Part of a pattern that is a repeated action. Read these points again so you get the full impact.

While all of us hold many beliefs and opinions, using this definition demonstrates that many people have few true values. As Sidney Simon says, "When we realize the extent to which values guide our lives—consciously and unconsciously—it's understandable that people with few values tend to be apathetic, conforming, and inconsistent...The person who has clarified his or her values will perform zestful, independent, consistent, and decisive 'acts of courage'— not necessarily dramatic, much-publicized feats of heroism, but rather acts based on the courage to say what has to be said and to do what needs to be done."

Knowing your values is critical. It is much better to define your values now, when those values are not being tested. In other words, now is the time to consider how much you value your family. But just saying that you highly value your family is not enough. The real question is, how will that value affect your behavior? Would you take a high paying job that put a lot of stress on you (and therefore on your family) and forced you to travel extensively out of state? You might reply that it would depend on the circumstances, and I would agree. Perhaps the high stress would last only a year or two and the travel would subside as well. Making these kinds of value decisions is never easy and they are not necessarily forever. Many people have had their values fully tested. One person left a promising career in the Navy after a family tragedy made it imperative to be home every night.

While clarifying one's values is a major undertaking, you are primarily concerned with how values will affect your career satisfaction. To do things which violate your values or to work for an organization which violates them, will cause problems for you.

Motivators

Motivators have a slightly different connotation. If you are motivated by something, it means you want it badly enough to pay a price for it. Athletes willingly punish their bodies because they are motivated by winning. Your strongest motivators could even be viewed as needs, or driving forces within you. For example, we are all motivated to utilize various skills. One of the skills I am most motivated to use is writing. Although many people hate to write, I enjoy it and find it relaxing and satisfying. One of my motivators is creativity, and writing helps satisfy that need. Every job I've ever had I have looked for opportunities to write. When I've had the opportunity to write, I've excelled, while when I didn't, I was often rather mediocre in my performance.

It is essential that your work provide opportunities to express your strongest motivators. You need a job which allows you to be who you already are. It is much better to have a job which fits you, rather than trying to mold yourself to the job. That only results in frustration. Without a release or expression, these motivators build up inside and sometimes explode. Creativity is a good example; it requires an outlet.

Let's look at what happens when a strong motivator is constantly squelched. Gretchen has a strong need for creativity yet her clerical job simply does not provide it. Several times she has tried to be creative by making company reports more visually attractive by utilizing the advanced desktop publishing features of her word processing program. Each time, however, her boss demanded that she redo it exactly as reports had been done in the past. You can imagine how frustrated she is.

Consider Sam. Sam is motivated to improve systems or procedures. Early in his new position he came up with several good ideas but each time his boss nixed them by saying they wouldn't work or by claiming the present system worked fine. Because of those experiences Sam tried a fait accompli, and made some changes without telling his boss. His boss really laid into him for that. One of three things will happen to a person in Sam's situation: The person will 1) quit out of frustration; 2) try more changes and as a result get fired; or 3) suppress the need. For most the only viable option is to look elsewhere within the organization for a more compatible boss, or to look for a different company. In Sam's case, if he suppresses his need he will become so frustrated that the quality of his work will suffer, and although he may not get fired, he may not get promoted either. He will also be heard complaining a lot.

Everyone is motivated by money to some extent. The desire or need for money causes people to take certain actions. An artist may work 20 hours a week in a restaurant to bring in the $10,000 per year which is needed just for survival. But her passion is painting, which takes up 40–50 hours per week, but may add only another $4,000 in income. This person obviously has a low motivation for money, but is strongly motivated by creativity and independence. This very smart and talented person could probably make $30,000 a year in another endeavor, but has sacrificed money for a greater motivator.

People often sacrifice money for prestige or prestige for money. A university professor may make only $40,000 per year but have very high prestige. A garbage collector has low prestige, but may make over $40,000 per year.

The key point is that to get one motivator or value often requires sacrificing another. You may want lots of job security and lots of money, but the two usually don't go together. Jobs where you can make a lot of money usually carry high risks. Only you can decide which is more important.

The goal in this exercise is to clarify what is most important to you in a job. A good job is one that allows you to obtain those things which motivate you and which you value, and does not conflict with any of them in a major way. As you consider various occupations, and then begin interviewing for specific jobs, you'll have a sharper eye for potential conflicts. On the positive side, you'll be able to spot occupations and jobs which represent a good fit for you.

When assessing how important a motivator or value is to you, it is helpful to ask yourself what you would trade for it. Money is a great trading item, so it is useful to use it as a guide. For example, if you had two job offers, and the two jobs were identical except that Job A would pay $1,000 more, but Job B would give you greater satisfaction in terms of helping people, which would you accept? What if Job A paid $5,000 more? Although you'll never have two job offers where everything is identical except for one variable, it does get you thinking. People who obtain satisfaction from helping people would undoubtedly sacrifice the $1,000 and take the job with greater opportunity to help people. However, for an additional $5,000, many would seriously consider the higher paying job. People face these issues frequently. There is no single right answer—you must decide what is right for you.

Everybody likes some time freedom—setting your own hours and coming and going as you see fit—but what would you trade for it? Suppose Company A demands that you arrive at work at 7:58 a.m., take 15 minute breaks at set times, take lunch from 12:00 to 12:30, and leave promptly at 5:00. Company B gives you wide latitude. Company B knows its people work hard and most work over 40 hours per week, but receive no overtime pay. Perhaps Brenda has a friend in from out of town, and although it is only 11 a.m., tells her boss that she is taking her friend to lunch and then for a spin around town, and should return about 3 p.m. Her boss simply tells her to enjoy herself. Does this sound appealing? Or suppose you have just finished a major project and you've been putting in 55 hour weeks for the last four weeks just to get it done. It is now 2 p.m. on *Thursday*, you're beat and you really don't feel like starting another project so you hand the assignment to your boss and tell her you'll see her on *Monday*. Your boss thanks you for your efforts and wishes you a pleasant weekend. You walk out with no funny looks from your boss or coworkers.

Okay, it seems attractive, but how much money would you trade for the opportunity?

Keep in mind there are two types of motivators. First, some of your top skills motivate you. Consciously and unconsciously you are constantly looking for ways and opportunities to use them. You examined your motivated skills by identifying your skills within your accomplishments, and by identifying your top transferable and work content skills. The list which follows covers another set of motivators, such as recognition, success, and creativity. If you feel that there are additional things which motivate you, don't hesitate to list them.

When you are truly motivated, you work harder and smarter, and often longer. You're more dedicated and disciplined. Many positive things happen when you're motivated. It is important, therefore, to have a job that allows you to spend most of your time doing things that motivate you.

INSTRUCTIONS FOR MOTIVATORS

1. Rate yourself on a scale of 1–10. All of the items may motivate you, but some are significantly stronger motivators or stronger values than others. If you are moderate in your motivators and values you may not have any 9s or 10s, but will probably have some 8s. A rating of 10 is extreme. A 10 in job security could mean that you would choose to make one-third less money, and work at a job you dislike, if that meant you could have a job with a company where no one has been

laid off in 97 years. Another way to look at the rating is to say that a 10 represents being in the top 5% of all people, in the need for that motivator. A 9 means you are in the top 10%, an 8 in the top 20%, a 7 in the top 30%, and a 6 in the top 40%. Remember, it is very likely that you will not have any 9s or 10s, since those scores mean you have an extreme need to exercise those motivators and values.

2. Determine which of your top twelve accomplishments utilized which motivators and values. If helping people, inner peace, and creativity, were the three primary motivators used in accomplishment number one, you would place a one in the wide column, to the left of helping people, inner peace, and creativity. When you have done that with all twelve of your top accomplishments a pattern will appear. Not only will you have rated certain motivators higher, but you will see that you have acted on certain motivators more frequently than others. By analyzing both your rating, and the number of times that motivator has been important in your life, you will get a much better sense of what is really important to you.

3. Select your top eight motivators/values and write a paragraph about each one. Describe how you value each item and how it motivates you. Writing about your motivators and values will help you to be more clear on what is important to you. Examples:

> Money is absolutely my top motivator right now. I really don't enjoy my job that much, but I do make good money. I would quit my job only for one that paid better. Satisfaction is nice, but it can't replace money.

> IMPROVING/PERFECTING - At every office I've ever worked, I have improved something—the filing system, the bookkeeping system, or a procedure. I have designed new business forms and written new procedures manuals. I like to make things more efficient.

> FAMILY - My family is very important to me and I would never sacrifice them for anything. I would never take a job where I had to work swing or night shift or had to work most weekends. I am willing to work overtime occasionally, though.

> INTEGRITY - I believe one of the most important things a person has is her reputation for integrity. Perhaps my honesty has cost me a few sales, but I believe it has brought me many more customers than I have lost. I know that I have received a lot of referrals because of my reputation for integrity.

MOTIVATORS AND VALUES

Money/Acquiring Things

Helping People/Society

Creating Peace and Harmony in a Group

Adventure/Excitement/Risk

Attention/In the Spotlight

Appreciation/Recognition

Prestige

Success

Job Security

Inner Peace

Power

Shape/Influence/Control — material, policy, people

Beauty/Aesthetics

Improving/Perfecting

Causes

Challenge

Family

Health/Safety

Integrity

Lifestyle

Time Freedom/Flexible Hours

Creativity

Being the Best

Striving for Your Full Potential

Mastery — subjects, skills, equipment, objects

Pioneering/Exploring/At the Forefront

Developing/Building — company, department, something ne

Combat/Prevail — over adversaries, opposing ideas

Perfection

Once you finish rating yourself on your motivators and values, and write about them, step back as you did with temperaments. Recall experiences where your motivators and values have been important to you. Recall jobs or other experiences that you enjoyed. Probably those experiences allowed you to experience those things which motivate you. Then recall jobs or experiences which you disliked. In most cases what frustrated you was an inability to express yourself through your top motivators and values.

MOTIVATORS AND VALUES DEFINED

I have defined the various motivators and values to give you a better understanding of how they affect you.

Money/Acquiring Things

Everyone is motivated by money. Some are so motivated by it that they will sacrifice their family, work 70–80 hours per week, and even do unethical things. Others will work only until enough money has been accumulated to stay fed and keep a roof over their head. These are two extremes.

It's important to know how strong a motivator money is. Money is our primary source of trade and we often trade it to get more of our other motivators and values. If money is truly a motivator, it means you are willing to do something extra to get more of it—take greater business risks, work harder, or work more hours. A salesperson who is on the road three weeks a month may make $55,000 per year but that person pays a real price for it. Perhaps the sales rep could make $50,000 a year in sales while staying close to home but refuses to do it because of an unwillingness to take any cut in pay. Many others would be more than happy to take a $5,000 cut in pay to be able to spend more time with the family.

As you rate yourself, consider the long term. In other words, unemployed people will often rate money much higher than if they were working, because at that moment, money, or the lack of it, is foremost in their minds.

One way to look at money as a motivator is to determine how much you would need to feel comfortable. Most of us would like to make $200,000 per year, but would be satisfied with less. If you could basically be satisfied on a combined family income of $35,000, then your money motivation is probably moderate. If you're making $25,000 per year now, but you need an income of $60,000, your motivation is probably high, but the real test comes when you consider what you're willing to do to get it.

The money issue is so important that you need to take a good look at it. Remember, if it is a true motivator, you're willing to pay a price to get it. You need to be clear enough so that you can sense whether a job is going to be in conflict with any of your motivators.

Most teachers are not highly motivated by money. They're probably more motivated by creativity, helping people, and shaping people. They like new cars and nice homes, but are willing to sacrifice them if other needs (motivators) are met. These days many are leaving the profession because they no longer feel they are really able to help people. Some are seeking sales positions because of the higher pay. The attitude is, "If I'm not getting any satisfaction in this lower paying job, then maybe sales won't be any more satisfying, but at least I'll make more."

Some people are highly motivated by money, but primarily for the security that comes with it. I heard a comedian say, "I've had money and not had money, and overall its better to have money." It does bring with it a certain level of security. It's nice to be able to go out for dinner at a nice restaurant or to be able to impulsively buy something, without worrying about where the money will come from. It seems that people can sometimes increase their creativity when they are not constantly worrying about money. These people who like the security which comes with money are often modest spenders—they keep the car five or more years and they buy a Ford rather than a BMW, even though they could afford the BMW.

Helping People

Some people experience great joy and satisfaction from helping people. To them helping people is not just a nice experience, but a need. Counselors, teachers, and nurses are noted for this motivator. At the end of a school year a teacher can point to several students and know that they blossomed during the year because of the extra attention provided or an added dose of encouragement.

To be motivated by helping people does not require that you get into one of the "helping professions." Some people find that as a department manager they get a great deal of satisfaction from helping people in their department. The person could be the accounting manager—certainly not a typical helping profession—yet derive much satisfaction from helping people grow and develop. This person is also very sensitive and understanding, and may lighten the load of someone going through a divorce or dealing with a death in the family. The person is always there for advice and counsel. Or it may be a person who has almost no contact with people on the job, but as a volunteer is very much involved with helping people.

Helping Society

There is a difference between helping people and helping society. The nurse can point to specific people who have been helped. Others, such as people like Ralph Nader, are probably not as motivated by helping people as they are by helping society. Ralph Nader gets satisfaction from his belief that society is a better place for what he has done. A community activist works hard to get a volunteer-staffed medical clinic established in a poor neighborhood and feels a genuine sense of satisfaction.

Creating Peace and Harmony in a Group

Some people are born diplomats. They feel uncomfortable when there is disharmony and will do whatever is possible to get people or groups to work together more effectively. They typically are good moderators and mediators. Both parties trust them because they give evidence that they are not choosing sides but are trying to get both sides to understand the views of the other.

Adventure/Excitement/Risk

Do you have a need for adventure, excitement, or risk on the job? Most people can obtain an adequate amount of adventure on weekends when they hang glide, ski, scuba dive, or rock climb, but some need these on a daily basis. Some jobs do offer high levels of excitement and risk—lion tamer and Wall Street trader might be two examples. With excitement and risk comes adrenalin, and some need greater doses than others.

Attention/In the Spotlight

Some people clearly crave the spotlight. Others are more subtle, but the need is just as great. They enjoy being the recognized expert when presenting a seminar. They like being the center of attention. This is another example of a motivator where you must be completely honest with ourselves. Society may have taught you that you should not desire the spotlight, but if in fact this is a strong motivator, you must be true to yourself. If you are an 8, but accept a job in which there is no opportunity at all to ever be the center of attention, you will be frustrated.

Appreciation/Recognition

This is perhaps the most universally valued of all the motivators on this list. Virtually everyone wants appreciation and recognition. At some organizations managers virtually never thank or praise their employees for having done a good job. That attitude of managers is often formed by the concept that employees are being paid to do a good job and should not receive praise for it.

If you know that appreciation and recognition are important to you, your selection of companies and bosses is important. In some companies it simply is not part of their culture to show appreciation, so it is important to find that out in advance. Or you might be interviewing with a company which tries to give recognition, but your prospective boss is simply not one of those people who gives more than one compliment a decade. Try to sense what this person is like. During an interview with the hiring manager, ask the person to describe his or her management style. This is an excellent question because it is open-ended and gives no clues about what you hope to hear. Listen carefully to determine if this is the type of person who will show appreciation.

Prestige

Some occupations and some organizations have more prestige than others. If you're highly motivated by prestige, choose your career path carefully. Will it meet your need for prestige? Will you feel proud telling people what you do when they ask at a party?

Success

Before you can determine to what extent you are motivated by success, you must first define it. Some people define success purely in terms of money or fame. Others would define it by family successes. To me, a person who has achieved fame and fortune, but can barely communicate with his or her 22-year-old son, has not been successful in life. To help you define success for yourself, ask what you must achieve in order to say on the day you retire, that you have been a true success. List the items quickly and then prioritize them.

Job Security

The only problem with job security is that it hardly exists anymore. With mergers and buyouts, even highly competent people can find themselves out on the street. Even government and utility jobs are not as secure as they once were. Granted, some companies and some industries offer more security than others, but it is still hard to find these days. The greatest security comes when you are among the top 20% in your field and you know how to conduct an effective job search. Then when the rumors start flying about a merger, you can stay calm while others are panicking. You'll know that you will probably be retained, but you will nevertheless revise your resume and start utilizing the contacts that you have been so carefully cultivating.

I once had a client who gave herself a 10 on security. I was very surprised because she had recently divorced her husband of 23 years and had quit a very secure job and started her own business. When I pointed out the contradiction, she realized that although she desired security, she was clearly willing to give it up in order to obtain other motivators.

Sometimes people will rate security quite high because they have not felt secure for a long time, or they are unemployed and the lack of security bothers them. In such a situation it is important to consider whether the need for security is only temporary, or whether it is a true and longstanding motivator.

Inner Peace

It's tough to have inner peace where there is backbiting on the job and the company's practices are unethical. Being personally asked to do illegal or unethical things makes matters even worse. Some companies are so filled with office politics, intrigue, and backstabbing, that many people find it difficult to work in such an environment. Inner peace is that quality that allows you have a clear conscience and enjoy life.

Power

Lord Acton once said, "Power corrupts, and absolute power corrupts absolutely." Since that statement was made, power has had a bad name. I personally don't believe that power inevitably corrupts. I think of power as the ability to change things or make things happen. Money and position create power. Knowledge is said to have power. Certainly U.S. Senators, presidents of Fortune 500 companies, and multi-millionaires have power, but so also do teachers, counselors, secretaries, and supervisors. All exercise power in different ways, but all possess it. The question is, are you motivated to obtain more power? Do you enjoy exercising power? If you desire to become the president of a major company or own your own company, ask yourself why. Is it for money, control, power, or independence?

Shape/Influence

These terms are almost the same as power, but their connotations are a little different. Teachers have a level of power, but more importantly they have the ability to shape and influence. All supervisors and managers possess a degree of power, and inherent in that is the ability to shape and influence the lives of people. Some derive great satisfaction from this ability.

Beauty and Aesthetics

People who are highly motivated by beauty and aesthetics would choose a job with less money if their surroundings were aesthetically pleasing. You might desire an office building with a campus-like setting, geese in the pond, and thickly carpeted offices with nice art work throughout. Another person would be just as happy with an old gray metal desk and a view looking out over the dingy backside of another building. For some people beauty and aesthetics implies that their jobs involve working with beautiful things such as art, sculptured wood furniture, or designer clothes.

Improving/Perfecting

For some people it is in their blood—they are always looking for ways to improve or perfect things. This quality is highly sought after by employers because these people are always looking for a new procedure or process which will make something work faster or better. This quality shows why it is so important to determine in advance if you will be allowed to do what you are motivated to do. When you are highly motivated it means you have a strong inner drive or even a compelling drive, to do something. If you are motivated to improve things, you are always looking for ways. A problem occurs, however, if your prospective company believes "if it ain't broke, don't fix it." Improvement by definition means change, and people tend to resist change. If you know you are motivated to improve things, ask what the company does to keep up with technology or the competition.

Causes

Some people are highly motivated by causes. It might be a person who devotes her life to a single cause or a person who feels strongly about several causes. Being cause-oriented can definitely influence the occupations you should choose. If civil rights, the homeless, nuclear power, or the greenhouse effect, are causes you feel strongly about, there are occupations you should pursue and others you should avoid. Some organizations would be good for you, while others would prove to be a real mistake.

Challenge

Some people are always looking for another challenge. Challenges get their creative juices flowing and they need one challenge after another. Others prefer a bit of a break before tackling the next big challenge.

Family

Most view family as a value rather than a motivator. Your challenge is to determine to what extent you value your family and how it will affect your behavior. Everyone says they value their family and they really do, but the issue is how it affects them on a daily basis. A major challenge occurs when people really like their jobs. For them it's easy to work a 55-hour week. It is not drudgery and they have the energy to do it. The major career issues for family people are how many hours they are willing to work, whether they will work weekends, whether they are willing to travel, and whether they will relocate. All of these are issues of degrees. Some are willing to work occasional overtime, but basically want to work nine to five. Others will put in the overtime anytime the task or boss demands it. Some are willing to work an occasional Saturday, with the emphasis on occasional. Others will come in almost every Saturday morning just to catch up on paperwork. Some simply cannot take part in overnight travel. Others are willing to be on the road Monday through Friday. Some would relocate only for a really fantastic job. Others will relocate at the drop of a hat. Take the time now to decide what you are willing and not willing to do for your career.

Health and Safety

How important is your health and safety to you? Would you take a good-paying job which endangers your health or safety? Would you consider working around toxic chemicals or in an environment in which accidents are likely to happen? Do you smoke and fail to exercise adequately?

Integrity

As an individual you may operate with total integrity, but organizations rarely meet that standard. The issue then is, what are you *willing* to accept? In your private life you may refuse to ever exaggerate or do anything that would mislead. So, how demanding are you going to be of an organization? Can you work for an organization as long as you are not personally asked to do anything unethical? Would you quit your accounting job if you learned that the sales department had shipped a used product but sold it as new, or if they frequently exaggerated the capabilities of a product? If you give yourself a 10 I would interpret that to mean that you operate personally with absolute honesty and would demand that of your next employer. If you really feel that way, by all means give yourself a 10. It only means that you will have to work harder in order to find the right employer.

Lifestyle

For most people lifestyle is not a major issue in employment because their lifestyle fits in with most occupations. Some lifestyle issues which could affect work include: you enjoy coaching soccer and baseball; you have a cabin in the mountains and go there about 30 weekends a year; you travel to Europe almost every year; you like to dress casually; you like to work hard and play hard; some days you feel creative and some days you don't. The coach needs predictable hours, the cabin owner needs to be able to refuse overtime, the traveler needs more vacation time than most companies allow, the casual dresser needs a casual company, the hard work/hard play person and the creative person need high amounts of time freedom. If your lifestyle might be an issue, ask yourself how important it is. Are you willing to compromise? What would you do if the perfect job were offered you, but it was just a little bit short in the lifestyle area?

Time Freedom/Flexible Hours

Everyone likes some time freedom, but how important is it to you? Perhaps you would just as soon get to work at a set time and leave at a set time. Everyone has those special occasions when they need time off—a school recital, a doctor's appointment, or a sick child. People with flexible hours are able to accommodate those types of things. People with a strong need for time freedom will need a job where they basically set their own hours. When they're in a groove they may work 16 hours straight, while at other times would leave early.

Creativity

People who are especially motivated by creativity need an outlet to express it. Creativity is not limited to artistic expressions, but includes creative thinking and creative problem solving. If you are highly motivated by creativity it is imperative that you be able to express it.

Being the Best

Striving to be the best implies that you are highly competitive. Competitive people are usually competitive in everything they do, even playing a game of croquet. This person is only satisfied with being the top salesperson in the district and is working on the number one spot in the region. Contests and competitions can highly motivate this person. Striving to be the best does not always necessitate being number one. An economics professor may be seeking recognition as one of the top ten economists in her specialty of economics— the type that gets quoted in *The Wall Street Journal.*

Striving for Your Full Potential

Seeking one's full potential is somewhat different from seeking to be the best. Full potential implies a person who simply wants to become all he or she is capable of, with very little thought given to "winning." The difference between being motivated to be the best and striving for one's full potential, can be likened to two friends running a 10K race together. One person is consumed with either winning the whole race, or at least beating the friend. The other person is more concerned with knocking ten seconds off her best time and cares little about beating the friend.

Mastery

Some people lose interest in something if they cannot totally master it. This person will give up golf, not because he doesn't enjoy it or isn't good at it, but simply because he does not feel he will ever truly master the game. There are subtle differences between this person and the person who is motivated to be the best.

Pioneering/Exploring/Being at the Forefront

Being a pioneer requires one to pay a price. Being out ahead of the rest is not only lonely, but also necessitates a thick skin. A lot of people take potshots at pioneers. Pioneers are often criticized or laughed at by all the people who say it can't be done. In spite of this there is something exciting about exploring new territory. Achieving something that has never been achieved before is pretty heady stuff. Pioneers can achieve both fame and fortune and this often drives them on. Sometimes the stronger motivation is just to prove all those people wrong.

Developing/Building

A special feeling comes from developing or building something, whether it be a company, a department, a team, or an invention. Some people like to build tangible things such as skyscrapers, dams, or computers. There is a special satisfaction from seeing or handling the thing. Whenever the skyscraper is seen, the architect or contractor feels a moment of pride as some memories instantly come to mind.

Others like to build things such as a company or a department. A special feeling comes from watching something grow—today there are 12 employees but next year there may be 20. Some managers derive great satisfaction from building a team. They recruit and train the members and enjoy watching and helping them grow.

Combat/Prevail

Some people are naturally combative. They don't really get feisty until they see a major challenge or fight on their hands. They may enjoy defending the downtrodden or gain satisfaction from defeating the big guy or bully. Such people have the ability to go for the jugular. Trial lawyers often possess this quality. A great spectacle is to watch two great lawyers parry in the courtroom as they each seek the total defeat of the other.

Perfection

Are you driven by perfection? People who have a temperament geared toward precision work and attention to detail, often have perfection as a motivator. They are typically not satisfied with the good or even the excellent—it must be perfect. If you are motivated by perfection it is important that you work for a boss who rewards perfection. Perfection always requires extra effort and cost, and some companies are simply not geared for it. Those companies who strive for perfection charge a premium for their product or service so they can afford to put in the extra time. The problem some perfectionists have is that they are compulsive about it. It controls them rather than them controlling it. The key thing the perfectionist must learn is to know when perfection, or near perfection is desired, and when it is important to wrap it up when its quality approaches excellent. A person who is a perfectionist about some things, but not about most, could easily be an 8, possibly a 9, but not a 10.

WRITING ABOUT YOUR IDEAL JOB

Your ideal job description is designed to bring together all of the data you've collected about yourself through the various exercises. Because of all your thought and your writing, you know things about yourself that were not as clear before. Now it's time to let your imagination go and visualize the activities and the organization that would make going to work each day a pleasure.

In one sense there is no such thing as an ideal job. With every job you are bound to experience frustrations. For example, an actress may love performing, but dislike waiting between scenes. While recognizing that the perfect job does not really exist, we can say assuredly that some jobs are better suited to you than others. Some jobs match your skills and personality better than others. Some jobs pay more than others and offer more variety or security than others.

Visualizing your ideal job increases the likelihood that you'll find it. There's nothing magical about it—it just works. When you clearly visualize what you want and match the vision with intense desire, you will take certain conscious and unconscious actions to make it happen. Opportunities which might have been overlooked in the past, are now seen for what they truly are—opportunities. It takes vision to recognize opportunity—it rarely comes with "opportunity" written all over it. That's why I often say that opportunity doesn't knock—it floats by like a butterfly. Too often it is out of reach by the time you recognize it as an opportunity.

The question is—what do you feel a passion for? What gets you excited? What gets your creative juices flowing? What kinds of things do you so enjoy doing that you become oblivious of time? If you can identify some things, you'll be able to identify occupations and industries where those needs can be met. If you already know what occupation you want, or you're already doing it, this exercise will help you clarify precisely what you want out of your next job.

Start by reviewing all of the exercises and everything you've written. You are not just lightly reading, you are analyzing, pausing to think, and pulling the pieces of the puzzle together. Since each of the exercises was basically independent of the others, you need to synthesize and bring many ideas together. Continually ask yourself, "What does this reveal about me?" Pause. Reflect. Consider. Take your time. This process can take 1–3 hours.

1) Read over your accomplishments. What skills did you use most frequently and which did you enjoy most? List the 20 most valuable and enjoyable skills identified.

2) Review the skills exercises. Read over your transferable skills. Concentrate on your top 12 skill clusters and quickly review in your mind one or two experiences when you used each one. Place a check by your top four skills in each cluster.

3) Read your list of work content skills. Do you think you will want to incorporate any of your work content skills into an ideal job? Remember, you don't need to be an expert in the work content skill in order to use it on a job. You may only need some exposure in the skill area, or perhaps you simply need to know a little more than your co-workers. In the long run, desire to use a work content skill is much more important than your current skill level. Place a check by any work content skills that you would definitely like to use in your ideal job. At this point do not be concerned with whether it would be possible to use them all in any one job. You are checking them at this time only because you would enjoy using them.

Now it's time to go on to temperaments, motivators, and values. Review your ratings and read everything you've written. An ideal job will allow you to be what you already are. It will not ask you to be someone different than who you are. In an ideal job there are few conflicts with your temperament, motivators, or values. Instead there will be almost a total match. The question becomes, which temperaments, motivators, and values are absolutely critical to you?

Once you have completed your review, find a quiet place where you can thoroughly relax. Close your eyes and imagine yourself on an ideal job. Picture the physical environment and sense the psychological environment. What is your work space like? What kind of people are you working with? Imagine a typical day or week. What activities will you be involved in? Although you ultimately need a quiet place to pull it all together, you can also visualize your ideal job while you are driving or walking. If you visualize while driving to work, jot some ideas down as soon as you park. Once you have begun to picture what this job would be like, it's time to develop an ideal job outline.

DEVELOPING AN IDEAL JOB OUTLINE

In the ideal job outline you'll be covering these topics: skills, functions, characteristics of the job, temperament, motivators, values, characteristics of the organization, and subjects of interest.

Functions

The biggest question regarding the ideal job, and the hardest to answer is, what functions or activities do you want to devote most of your time to? One thing that makes it difficult is that up to this time you have concentrated on identifying skills you want to use on a job. The problem is that skills and functions are not usually identical. This is because each function of a job is made up of one or more skills. In other words, a function is bigger than a skill. Your challenge is to translate skills into functions.

An example should help. Listening is a skill, but we would not usually think of it as a function or duty. On the other hand, counselors, doctors, diplomats, and supervisors are all more effective when they possess strong listening skills. We'll assume that listening is one of your top transferable skills. Now at this point you should start considering how you would use the skill on a job. Since you are an excellent listener you might come to the conclusion that as part of your job you would like to counsel and advise people in the capacity of a supervisor. A portion of your ideal job description might read like this:

> In my ideal job I will be supervising 3-6 employees. I will hire only self-motivated people who are resourceful and reliable. I will provide excellent training and I will teach them everything I know, but I don't have much patience for people who need to be told several times how to do something. I enjoy listening to people and functioning as a counselor and advisor to those who report to me. I don't want to become their confessor, but I do want to empower them to become all they are capable of. Through my active listening skills I often pick up on things that others are unaware of, and I want to use that to my advantage.

The process of getting to this point was to list listening as one of your top transferable skills. Then you considered how you might want to use that skill on a job.

To help you grasp the concept of identifying functions, review the outline example. For your own outline the best thing to do is just get started. Think of functions that you might enjoy. List them as they pop into your mind. There will be time to prioritize them later. Also, don't be concerned whether it is possible to perform all of those duties on any single job. Perhaps it isn't, but you will use all of your creative energy to figure out a way.

Try not to have a specific job in mind as you list your functions. Your functions list should be general enough that several occupations and jobs would closely match it. Yet your functions must also be specific enough so they have meaning. In other words, saying you want to work with people is too general. The question then would be, in what ways do you want to work with people?

If you do have a job title in mind, determine those aspects that make it appealing, and include them in the ideal job description. In that way you will not limit yourself to that one occupation.

In your outline determine the approximate percentage of time you would like to devote to each function. This is merely an approximation to show the relative importance of that function to you. It's a good way to force you to consider what you really want. When you actually write your ideal job description there is no need to include percentages, although you certainly can. In the outline example you will notice that not every item was assigned a percentage. This was because some of the functions were closely associated with others and giving them a percentage would represent overlap.

Characteristics

Characteristics of a job are those aspects you want in the ideal job which are not functions, temperaments, motivators, or values. To say "I want to work with my hands" is a characteristic whereas "I want to use hand tools and power tools to make things" is a function. Other characteristics would be working independently, setting your own schedule, working with a small group of compatible people, working on projects that require creativity, and having a job where you can get out of the office several times a week. List characteristics as they pop into your mind.

Temperaments, Motivators, And Values

For purposes of the outline, merely list what you feel are your four most critical temperaments, your four most critical motivators, and your three most critical values.

Subjects

Undoubtedly you have a variety of interests. Simply list some of the subjects or things that appeal to you. It may seem to you that there is no way that you could possibly get a job in that subject area, but this is not the time to concern yourself with that. If it interests you, list it.

Every job involves a subject. Examples will best explain what I mean. A person who wants to be involved in research needs to choose a subject—it could be bacteriology, market research, electronics, or sociology. A person who wants to manage will usually have one or more industries in mind such as insurance, electronics, sports, or energy. A person who wants to be involved with training and development will usually have a preference for topics such as time management, sales training, and customer service. A person who wants to use machines and tools will usually have a preference for working with plastic, metal, wood, or fiberglass.

Organization

Before you begin listing items under organization, read *What You Should Know About An Organization* on page 447. Reading it should stimulate some ideas on what is truly important to you. Think about organizations you have worked for in the past. Whatever you liked and valued should go on your list. Then consider things that have bothered you in the past. Merely turn those things into the positive and list them. Then just let your imagination go and ask yourself what would be some dream characteristics.

WRITING YOUR IDEAL JOB DESCRIPTION

Once your outline is complete it's time to flesh it out in paragraph form. Initially you listed things just as they came to mind. I encouraged you not to filter anything out. Now it's time to prioritize points and in some cases group them together. Not everything you listed is of equal importance to you and it is essential to know what is critical and what is merely nice. In other words, you might love six weeks vacation per year, but three would be quite adequate, and of course, much more likely. Some people, on the other hand, really do need six weeks per year. They are those whose lifestyle may include one or two major vacations per year and they really desire that amount of time. Some are able to negotiate for three weeks of time off without pay and are more than willing to give up the money in order to maintain that lifestyle. Now is the time to determine what is critical.

One way to look at your writing assignment is to realize that every item you have in your outline could be expanded into a paragraph. That never happens, however, because some of your items will just naturally group together with others. By that I mean that three items might be quite similar and they really belong together in one paragraph. Other items, once you examine them more closely, may simply not belong in the ideal job description.

Clearly this is an exercise which requires and deserves a lot of time and effort. The vision you are able to create for yourself will largely determine the success and satisfaction you will enjoy in the future. For a few, this exercise is easy and it just flows together. The majority of people, however, struggle and sweat over it. Trust me though, it is worth every drop of sweat. Clearly visualizing your ideal job will keep you on target and ensure your ultimate success in obtaining it.

MY IDEAL JOB

Functions

Reading/Researching 15-20%
Synthesizing ideas
Statistical analysis 2-6%
Planning research projects 3%
Writing articles/training manuals 20-25%
Counseling/Advising 20%
Helping people find answers within
Teaching/Giving seminars 15-20%
Developing seminars and materials
Turn complex ideas into principles
Make difficult concepts easy
Public speaking 2%
Managing projects 5%
Managing a department/people 5%
Training new people 3%
Finding ways to train quickly

Characteristics

Several key duties
Always working on a project
Able to select most of my projects
Lots of independence
Recognized for work I do
Opportunity to try new things
Emphasize helping relationships
Allows me opportunity to achieve lofty goals
50% intense people time, 50% total alone time (to concentrate)
Private office with a nice view

Temperament/Motivators/Values

Variety
Independence
Conceptualizing
Relaxed atmosphere
Helping people
Creativity
Appreciation/recognition
Improving/Perfecting
Family
Honesty/Integrity
Lifestyle

Subjects

Psychology
Human development
Human motivation
Peak performance
Nutrition/Health
Furniture
Poverty
Racism

Organization

Allows me and encourages me to grow
Allows me to express my strong values
Small company
Growing organization
Management truly cares for people
Rules and regs are people oriented
Encourages teamwork
No backbiting
Promotion by merit
Flexible hours
Environment that encourages motivation
No discrimination
Trains well and promotes from within
Impeccably honest
Respects environment

MY IDEAL JOB

For my ideal job I need variety, many duties, and a great deal of freedom to do what I feel is important. In certain areas I have strong values and strong opinions and must be able to express them. Working for the right organization is as important to me as having the ideal duties.

My main duties should include helping relationships (mostly counseling), teaching, research, and writing. I would like to run the whole organization or have a great deal of responsibility and authority to run my department, or work directly with others to work out problems and improve the operation. Such administrative duties would take me away from counseling, teaching, writing, and researching, but organizing, problem solving, and results are very important to me. My tendency would be to try to do everything myself, but I value free time so I would have to delegate various important responsibilities. Since I believe strongly in having freedom, I'll have to remember to give freedom to those under me.

I enjoy counseling because I enjoy helping people find answers within themselves. Sometimes I will give people an "answer" but usually I want to stimulate them to find the answer or truth for themselves. I enjoy being perceptive and understanding of what people are trying to say. I like people to trust me, feel comfortable with me, and open up to me.

I really enjoy teaching a subject to people who truly want to learn. I like to mix speaking with discussion and answering questions. I don't believe I will ever give the same class twice since I like to vary things and experiment. As a teacher I enjoy the role of being an expert and having others come to me for information and advice. I also am constantly learning from other people's examples and experiences.

As a teacher I like to simplify everything so principles are easy to grasp. I have always been one to ask "why" or "how do you know" so I like to anticipate many questions and answer them in advance. I like to take difficult concepts and break them down into easily grasped components. I like to provide the "big picture" so people understand how all of the pieces fit together.

Teaching and counseling require being with people and I enjoy that. I also enjoy time alone. I am constantly reading and learning. I could probably spend four hours per day reading and enjoy every minute. Because of my varied interests I always felt I should be a generalist, but now I want to combine broad general knowledge with a specialty.

I am very good at reading the ideas of many experts and pulling out all of the best ideas and putting it back together as something rather unique, but not entirely original. I am a synthesizer.

I could spend days in a library and enjoy it, but I wouldn't want to do it every day for a year. I need people contact. I also enjoy research projects which require planning and statistical analysis. I like identifying problems and then figuring out a research methodology for solving or learning more about the problem.

Besides teaching, counseling, and research, I want administrative duties. I would want to be actively involved with marketing and public relations. I don't see myself selling much of the time, but I can sell whatever I strongly believe in. I definitely want to train new employees and develop procedures and manuals to help them learn their jobs better and faster. I also want to do the hiring and firing, although I would keep that to a minimum by thoroughly analyzing each person and by adequately training each employee.

I will need to have a private office. It doesn't need to be large, but I want it to be nicely decorated and I would like to have a nice view. The room must be conducive to work and to counseling. The furniture need not be luxurious, but must be of high quality.

I want to be part of a growing organization. I would like to be involved in training and supervising new personnel. I believe good training is essential and would go out of my way to help people develop and learn. I would share my "secrets" and "tricks of the trade." I believe before I can advance I must be able to train my replacement.

As a person in authority I want to constantly remember how I wanted to be treated when I was at the bottom. I want to help build a strong organization with top quality people and one which rewards its achievers. I would want it to have some form of profit sharing. I will ask for suggestions and really listen and recognize the merit in each one, even though in the end, I may not use it. I want the organization to have a free and open, and positive atmosphere. Nothing and no one is sacred.

The organization will be fairly small—under 20 people—but all very competent, friendly, and positive. All will be friendly at work but they won't necessarily socialize after work. We will work together as a team. Whatever competition and rivalry does exist, will be positive and not harmful to the organization. Promotions and raises will be made strictly on merit. There will be plenty of room for individualism, but the overall good of the team will generally be most important.

The organization will have flexible hours. Since everyone will work at least 40 hours per week, no one will question the whereabouts of others or check on what time they go home. I will care only about results and will develop ways to measure our results.

I firmly believe that an organization cannot motivate a person, but it can provide the environment that encourages high motivation. I would want to work for an organization which uses all of the effective means available.

I want to work for a progressive organization. There will be no discrimination—women and minorities will have equal opportunity to rise through the ranks. Promotion should largely come from within, and everyone, including secretaries, should have promotion opportunities. The organization will be impeccably honest and will respect the environment.

This ideal job description became a true vision for the person who wrote it. Within two years the person entered a graduate program and has now been a counselor for several years.

WHAT YOU SHOULD KNOW ABOUT AN ORGANIZATION

Choosing the ideal occupation is easy compared to locating an ideal organization. There just aren't many really good organizations to work for. That's why employer research is so important. Going to work for a new company is always a risk. Your goal is to reduce those risks and find an organization that matches your needs. I've described some of the factors you'll want to know about before accepting a position. Failure to consider these factors and to learn as much about the organization as possible, can lead to frustration and even grief. Suppose you're a person who needs a very stable work environment, yet you go to a company which is experiencing a reorganization, a shakeup in top management, or is being absorbed by a larger company? What if ethics are very important to you, yet your company misrepresents its ability to make delivery dates? You owe it to yourself to learn as much as possible about these factors. I've tried to stimulate your thinking so you can determine what is important for you.

Advancement

What is the potential for advancement? Some positions are dead ends. There is simply no place else to go. Ask where people in that position have moved to in the past. For advancement the best jobs are with fast growing organizations in fast growing industries. As the organization grows and new positions are created, everyone moves up. Determine whether promotions are given by seniority or ability.

Atmosphere

How does the place feel? Is it light and jovial or do you feel a heavy, serious atmosphere? Are people friendly or is there backbiting? You'll need to use your intuition and sensitivity for this one. Some clues might be a gruff receptionist or people passing in the hall without smiling or saying hi. Don't judge an entire organization by just observing it for a few minutes while waiting in the lobby for your interviewer, but make the most out of what you observe. If you like what you see, look for supporting evidence that your brief glimpse was accurate. If you don't like what you see, gather further evidence to either confirm or change your initial impression.

Benefits

Does the health insurance cover 100% of hospital, doctor, check up, and prescription costs? Many health plans only cover hospitalization and even then only 80%. Do you receive dental insurance and a life insurance policy? Do you receive disability insurance? Do you pay for any of your own coverage or pay extra for family members? Do you get three weeks of vacation after five years, as is common, or must you be there for ten years? Some organizations will allow you to accumulate sick leave and even pay you for a portion of that time after you retire or leave the organization. For executives there are additional benefits or perks, such as a reserved parking space, a company car, a decorating allowance for the office, stock options and a full year's salary if terminated. If it's important, you can inquire whether you could have an additional two weeks off each year at no pay.

Bonuses

Some organizations offer bonuses or profit sharing. Sometimes profit sharing is extended only to management. Bonuses range from twenty-five dollars at Christmas time to several thousand dollars and can be distributed many ways, including formulas or by performance. When formulas are used it might be by number of years with the company or a percentage of income. In profit sharing a formula will determine the total amount to be distributed, although department managers are sometimes given a lump sum to distribute as they see fit.

Dress Code

Some organizations have dress codes, either stated or unstated. IBM male employees, with their dark suits and white shirts, are an example. If you might be bothered by working for an organization with a dress code, check it out. When you go for an interview observe the clothing to determine if there appears to be a formal or informal dress code.

Employee Suggestions

Do you like to offer suggestions and have them adopted? Part of your success will depend on the openness of your boss. During your interviews you'll want to assess this quality in your boss-to-be. Some organizations have formal suggestion programs and give financial awards to people offering money-saving suggestions. Boeing has a program where the cost savings are computed and the employee receives 10% of what will be saved during the first year, up to $5,000.

Environment

Are you happy in a cramped office with no windows and drab walls, sitting at an old, gray metal desk? If so, physical environment will hardly be an issue for you. You'll be satisfied almost anywhere.

Some people need a much different environment. It could be open spaces, sizable offices, bright colors, lots of windows, clean, fresh air, the absence of odors or loud noises, paintings, wall hangings, sculptures, a fountain, beautifully landscaped grounds, a pleasant eating facility, and quiet places to eat or talk outside.

Ethics And Integrity Of The Organization

You will want to determine ethics and integrity at several levels: top management, your immediate boss, your coworkers, and those who have direct contact with customers. First you need to be clear on your own ethics. Here are some of the things that often bother people: the organization does not keep promises, sells known defective products, bribes politicians and purchasing agents, postpones paying its bills as long as possible, tells customers the product has been fixed when it really hasn't, constantly looks for shortcuts which also decrease quality, backs out of commitments, misrepresents or misadvertises its products, doesn't back up its warranties adequately, abuses its employees, terminates employees unfairly, lies to customers, overbills customers whenever possible. These are just a few examples.

Family Owned Company

Family owned companies seem to be some of the best or worst companies to work for. Dynamic family owned companies can make quick decisions, take risks that would be impossible for a publicly held company, and can be exciting, rewarding places to work. Stagnant family owned businesses which have been handed down through two or more generations can be very frustrating places to work. Some company owners are so autocratic and filled with "yes men" that they are almost impossible to work for. The real question is not whether the company is family owned, but how well managed it is.

Flexible/Rigid Structure

Is everything done by the book or is there flexibility? A flexible organization can change plans or policies when the situation requires it and cares more for results than tradition.

Goals of the Organization

What are the organization's goals? Is the organization trying to increase its market share, hire more minorities, develop three new products each year, decrease its defective products, expand into new geographic areas, or decrease turnover? Knowing the goals of an organization or a department can be very valuable in determining whether you want to be a part of it.

Growth Potential

Where can you go with the organization? Advancement is part of growth potential but there are other ways to experience personal growth: attending company sponsored seminars, taking company paid college courses, being given new responsibilities, or working on projects that expose you to new ideas or experiences.

History Of The Company

Just knowing that the company lost money last year does not tell you a great deal. Overall the company may have a very good profit history. Where has the company been and where is it going? Has it been involved with mergers, has it bought out other companies, how long has it been in business, is it making the same types of products it started with, have there been any major shakeups in the company, how did the company fare during the last recession?

Innovative

Innovative organizations seem to be more fun to work for. There's usually more challenge as they try new things, whether it's developing new products or implementing new management techniques.

Location

How far are you willing to commute? Does the organization have multiple local offices where you could be transferred to? Is it located in a safe or dangerous area?

Management Philosophy

Douglas McGregor developed the concept of Theory X and Theory Y companies. Each organization has a personality of its own which is usually determined by the management philosophy espoused by top management. Basically, Theory X companies believe that people don't like to work and must continually be pressured with threats, discipline or monetary incentives. They must continually be watched and their production must be monitored. Managers tend to be autocratic and domineering. Rarely will they listen to criticism or implement ideas that originated in the lower ranks. Theory Y companies operate on the assumption that people have a psychological need to work, that they enjoy work, and given the right environment, will rarely miss work, will work hard, and will produce high quality products or services. Managers tend to be democratic and use participative management to obtain greater results. Theory Y managers encourage cooperation and working out problems together.

Management Structure

The major distinction is between centralized or decentralized management. In centralized management all major decisions are made at the home office. With decentralized management a district office or a manufacturing plant is allowed to make all but the most major decisions without prior approval from home office. There are advantages and disadvantages to both methods.

Office Politics

Some companies are famous for their Byzantine intrigues. Often the backbiting, fighting for position, and rallying of allies is actually encouraged by the president who purposely plays off one executive against the other. Such infighting is never beneficial to the employees or shareholders. Competition within an organization can be healthy, but it can easily cross over into backstabbing and empire building. Essentially you want to determine if the organization is experiencing infighting and dirty politics. Most will want to avoid those organizations and the only way to discover it is through insiders. Government agencies and non-profit organizations can be among the worst.

Parent Company/Subsidiaries

Small- to medium-sized companies usually retain their name even after they've been bought out by a larger company. *Who Owns Whom* is an excellent resource to discover if a potential employer owns subsidiaries or is owned by another company. As part of long range planning, working for a subsidiary is one way to eventually move up with the parent company. If your potential company has just recently been acquired, it may face some real shakeups in the coming months. That can be positive or negative. Negative if the job you're hired to do is considered redundant or expendable by the parent company, negative if the boss who hired you (for whom you really wanted to work) is replaced by a less desirable boss, negative if the overall management philosophy changes from one you felt comfortable with. In exactly the opposite ways, such changes could be positive. Very frequently being bought out involves nothing more than cosmetic changes plus an inflow of available cash to expand into new markets or develop new products.

Problems

Most companies have some kinds of skeletons in their closets. Your goal is to discover them before you start the job. Recently the vice president of a major company was hired away to become president of a somewhat smaller company, only to discover that he had been lied to about its financial strength. The company was near bankruptcy. It demonstrates that presidents making $500,000 a year can also be taken. An accountant was hired as controller of a company only to discover that funds had been misappropriated by company officers several years before. The three previous controllers, each of whom had stayed only about six months, had bailed out while they could. This controller unfortunately was still around when federal investigations began and his reputation was tarnished, although he had nothing to do with the scandal. Existing or potential problems might be takeovers or mergers, bankruptcy, scandals waiting to be discovered, old outdated products which will soon lead to decreased sales, union problems, or a lawsuit which could ruin the company.

Products/Services

Find out everything you can about a company's products. Annual reports are one of the best sources because they generally describe each subsidiary's products and also show pictures. By researching the products you can determine your interest. Can you relate to the product or services? Do you believe they have value?

Profits/Sales Volume

Knowing both the profits and sales volume of a company can be very enlightening. Annual reports, *Moody's,* and a clipping file will give you the answers. A highly profitable company can afford to take risks and try new things. A company which has lost money for several years has retrenched and usually cares more about survival than its employees.

Progressive

Progressive firms are trying new things. If you have a hard time adapting to change, stay away from them. Progressive firms are at the forefront of hiring and promoting women and minorities, improving pollution controls, contributing some of their profits for the betterment of their community, demonstrating concern for employees, and trying new methods such as participative management, management by objectives, flex-time, profit sharing, and total quality programs.

Relocation

All national companies relocate managers from time to time but they have varying policies. With some you can refuse one or more relocations with no stigma. At others, turning down a relocation may mean no hope for future promotions, termination, or making life so miserable for you that you'll quietly find another job and move on.

You'll want to know how soon a relocation might occur, how frequently they may occur, and where you might be sent. Most relocations involve promotions but not always. You also need to know what you can expect from your employer. Will they make it worthwhile?

If it's a promotion you should not only receive a raise but also an increased standard of living. When moving from Biloxi, Mississippi to New York, the difference in the cost of living is tremendous. More than one executive has found that the same house he just sold for $290,000 costs $440,000 in the new city. Find out what the company will do if you can't sell your home. The progressive firms will buy it from you at a fair market value and then sell it themselves.

Learn as much as you can about relocation without having to ask your interviewer. Invariably this requires inside information. Until you've been offered the job, don't ask about relocation. Most employers will explain their policy, but if not, you definitely need to know before accepting the position.

Reputation

Every organization has a reputation. Local companies have local reputations and national companies have national reputations. Consumer product companies have reputations based primarily on their products. Even companies you've never heard of have reputations. Your best source of information is insiders. For feature articles look in the *Readers Guide to Periodical Literature* and the *Business Periodicals Index*.

Research

What percentage of sales is being plowed back into R&D? Dollars alone won't create new discoveries and new technologies, but it sure helps. Several years ago a cartoon showed a board of directors meeting, with the chairman pointing to a chart indicating a steady decline in sales and saying, "I don't understand it, we make the best buggy whip in the country". The firm had obviously not been pumping any money into R&D and now was reaping the results. Only companies with a vision will invest a high percentage of their sales dollars into R&D. A shortsighted president, or one who doesn't expect to be around long, will concentrate on the short-term profit picture, to the detriment of future profitability. Learn where the company you're researching stands compared to others in the same industry.

Size

Large and small companies each have their advantages. Large companies may offer higher pay and more security but may cause you to become overspecialized. Smaller companies typically offer greater opportunity to handle varied responsibilities and work on a project from start to finish. Companies under 20 employees account for only about 20% of all employment, but nearly 70% of the new jobs created in the last ten years. Don't be fooled by stereotypes or even your own experience. Don't say "I'll never work for another big company, you're just a number." Even big companies are divided into divisions, branches and departments. What you experienced may have been peculiar to *that* company, and would not be true of other large companies.

Stability

Stability and security go together. Large, more established firms tend to be stable. In times of recession they have good lines of credit to help survive the rough times. Stability can be measured in many ways: How regularly has the company made a profit? Has it always paid dividends? How many chief executive officers has the company had in the last 20 years? Have there been wild fluctuations in profits? Are employees loyal and do they work for the company for a long time? The number of CEO's a company has had tells a lot. Charles Revson, the owner of Revlon, was famous for canning CEO's every 2–3 years over personality clashes. Such changes can have a tremendous effect on long-range planning and policies: one CEO believes in dress codes, the next one doesn't, one CEO insists on total corporate secrecy while the next tries to keep employees informed, one CEO hates unions with a passion while the next accepts them as a force to be reckoned with.

Training

Some companies are famous for their training programs. Merrill Lynch, for example, trained a high percentage of the stock brokers in this country. Going to work for a company which provides thorough training can be especially helpful in your career. Employers will recognize you received solid training and this will make you more desirable. While valuable, don't assume that such formal training is the only factor to consider. Smaller companies may not be able to send you to the San Francisco headquarters for three weeks of training, but they may provide excellent on-the-job training.

Training that is intended to help you advance is valuable. This can take the form of tuition reimbursement at local colleges, sending employees to training centers run by the company or a national training firm, sending employees to local seminars, bringing in outside consultants for trainings or utilizing in-service trainings. Commitment to training is a good way to test a company's commitment to its employees and to its own future.

Tuition Reimbursement

It's nice to work for a firm that invests in its employees. Some companies will pay for tuition only if the course is directly related to the job, while others are more liberal. The amount can range from 50-100%, usually on the condition that you pass the course. Some companies strongly encourage their employees to use the program while others are rather reluctant.

Turnover

Greater than average turnover can signal serious problems with the job or the organization. Find out how many people have held your position in the last five years and where they are today. Twenty to thirty percent annual turnover is not unusual. If five people have held the position and two were fired and three quit, I think you might have reservations about the job. Find out why they were fired and what caused the others to quit. Why weren't any of them promoted? Generally you would save your question until the second interview and then simply ask, "How many people have held this position in the last five years?" If the employer simply gives a number, without elaborating, follow up with, "Why did they leave?" If several have been promoted within the company that's obviously a good sign. If more than one person was fired, ask for the reason. You may determine that the factors causing the others to be fired, might get you fired as well. Suppose the employer says, "They just didn't learn the job quickly enough." At that point it might be best to drop the subject, but make a mental note of it. Later, when you're offered the position, ask the employer to elaborate on the cause. A little probing might show that the training program is ineffective and that two very intelligent people were fired due to no fault of their own. Perhaps the company has exceedingly high demands and quickly drops people if they don't demonstrate rapid progress. If you're the type of person who learns thoroughly, but perhaps more slowly than most, what are your chances?

APPENDIX B

Reprinted by permission of the Washington State Employment Security. Being There was produced by the Washington State Employment Security, in cooperation with the Washington Mental Health Association and Life/Work.

BEING THERE
(Handling Unemployment)

Unemployment steals our self-respect, damages the quality of our lives, changes our personal relationships, and undermines our faith in society, our friends, and ourselves.

It's a crisis that can't be fully understood until you experience it personally. As it continues, your situation worsens; and the more important it becomes that you somehow learn to cope.

BEGIN BY ACCEPTING A FEW FACTS

Emotions of anger, depression, fear, guilt, despair, and isolation are normal.

Your situation is not unique. Your problem is shared by millions of others who are unemployed. Many of those cases are not as critical as yours. Others are worse.

Your situation is not static. If you persist in your search for work, you *will* find a job.

How well you cope in the meantime will depend on the quality of your attitudes, feelings, and actions.

You have the ability to control your attitudes, feelings, and actions.

KNOW THE PITFALLS

Immobilization

Immobilization is the inability to move or to act toward changing your situation. It's staying at home; sleeping a lot; putting off until tomorrow what you don't see much sense in doing today; not making the phone calls you meant to make; and going around in a daze. Immobilization is putting everything on "hold." People who are unemployed are sometimes immobilized to the point of not being able to file for unemployment insurance benefits or other services, even though they desperately need the help and know they are eligible to receive it. And they don't even know why they don't do what they don't do. Immobilization is a symptom of severe depression.

Depression

Depression doesn't necessarily mean crying all the time. Frequently, the depressed person seems to be functioning normally with the possible exceptions of seeming a little withdrawn or being in a bad mood. Of all the pitfalls, depression is probably the most dangerous because it starts feeling comfortable. You can begin to like it. Sometimes, your depression nets you some attention you otherwise would not have received. And there's another reason it's dangerous. It gets better; or it gets worse. Unless and until you turn it around, it gets worse; and the worse it gets the more difficult it is to turn around. That's bad enough, but there is a face-saving factor here too. After all, how can you—after going around for days, weeks, or months with a long face—suddenly give all that up and start smiling again? How? You just do it. You make a conscious decision to alter your frame of mind. It's difficult, but it's better than the alternative of going through life depressed.

Paranoia

Paranoia is difficult to avoid at a time life has dealt a dirty blow. It's easy to convince yourself that you're the victim of some big conspiracy because you're too young, or too old, or a woman, or a man, or a minority, or too tall, or too short, or too smart, or not smart enough, or too outspoken, or too soft-spoken.

While all of the above would be more interesting reasons for unemployment, it is probably more realistic—and undeniably more productive—to assume that you are not being singled out. You're unemployed because of the economy; because there aren't enough jobs to go around; because you had the misfortune of being in the wrong place at the wrong time; or for any of a million other reasons all of which are beyond your control.

But *some* paranoia is justified. Unfortunately, your family, friends, and associates are not psychologists. More often than not, they aren't very good at dealing with someone who is unemployed. Consequently, they seem to develop the knack of saying all of the wrong things, like, "Maybe if you didn't do this, or change the way you do that..." Things that ultimately translate to a rejection of who and what you are.

Or they may avoid you. They don't mean to; and they don't even realize they're doing it. On a subconscious level you frighten them and threaten their sense of security. They don't know what to say to you. They are afraid that any of their good fortunes—no matter how insignificant—might depress you.

It is important for *your* sake that you understand their behavior. Expect it. Accept it. Forgive it. Then, focus your energy on changing it.

Let your friends know that you have no intention of becoming a recluse, and that you welcome invitations. Discuss your unemployment openly and frankly; and whenever possible, use your sense of humor about it.

Anger

Of course you're angry. You have every right to be. You want to work, but you don't have a job. And chances are you're not even sure at whom to direct your anger.

While anger is a negative emotion, there is a great deal of energy behind it that can be put to positive use. That same energy can stimulate your imagination and put some innovation in your search for work. That same energy can be used to better organize and accelerate your work search. It can be directed toward a multitude of positive, productive accomplishments.

Isolation

Isolation can be a by-product of anger, paranoia, depression, or immobilization. And not having any money can isolate you, too. But there are other reasons we become isolated when we're unemployed.

We're embarrassed, so we avoid people. Obviously, we assume the blame and the shame for our unemployment. In addition to being counterproductive and futile, this kind of unnecessary guilt trip is, in all probability, totally without justification.

Sometimes we keep to ourselves out of a misguided concern for others, in that we're afraid our presence is depressing; or because we want to avoid making others feel uncomfortable.

The key word here is "misguided." Your family, friends, neighbors, and contacts are more important now than they've ever been. You need their help and support.

A Sagging Self-Image

A sagging self-image seems inevitable at this juncture. You have no money, and no paycheck to remind you that somebody thinks you are worthwhile.

This is one area that requires constant work. You had a job before and you will find one again. Concentrate on your strengths and assets. Review them daily. Write them on your bathroom mirror, because those strengths and assets will be your survival.

Loss Of Identity

After asking your name, they want to know what you do for a living. When you were working, that was easy. Now, what do you say?

This situation won't be so painful if you prepare a response. Without hesitation, look them straight in the eye and say, "I'm a very good mechanic and I'm looking for a job." Or, "I used to be a secretary, but I'm looking for something in sales." Don't be at a loss for words or apologetic about your situation. Instead, seize the moment to promote your job search.

Fatigue

Fatigue is the direct result of any or all of the above, from immobilization to loss of identity. Other contributing factors might include a subconscious desire to escape through sleep; worry and anxiety over your situation; insomnia (caused by worry and anxiety over your situation); or just plain boredom.

And drinking too much, smoking too much, eating too much, or doing anything too much tends to fatigue, also.

A healthful diet (even though you've lost your appetite), physical exercise (despite the fact you have no energy), and restful sleep are the obvious prescriptions. Keep busy, even if it requires forcing yourself; but make sure your agenda includes recreational activity.

But if you've been getting your eight hours sleep (not four and not sixteen), eating right, exercising, keeping busy, and you're still fatigued, don't overlook other health-related possibilities.

DEVELOPING A COPING PLAN

Organize and take charge of your life. Live by a schedule as rigid and as disciplined as you would if you were working; with set times to get up, eat, and sleep. Pursue your work search during certain hours as though it was a job. Include special projects in your schedule. Try to accomplish something every day, including learning new things. You'll find that having a routine and following a schedule focuses your energy and puts some direction in your daily life.

Organizing your life and taking care of yourself will enhance your self-image and make you feel good about yourself. You'll feel healthier; have more energy; and, more important, you will increase your odds of finding a job.

Get Help

Financial help is probably the first kind of help you need. Find out everything you might be eligible to receive and apply for it—unemployment insurance, food stamps, public assistance, medical coupons, social security—don't overlook any possibilities. And should it be necessary, remember there are food banks in your area, too.

Beyond that, don't forget family and friends. Ask for help if you need it. There are people out there who would appreciate the opportunity to help because they have a sincere desire to be useful. Accepting their generosity will undoubtedly help you both.

Free help in finding a job is available too. Inquire at your local Job Service Center about Job Search Assistance Workshops. Find out if you're eligible for programs that will give an employer tax credits for hiring you; or training programs; or retraining programs. Investigate all possibilities and follow up.

Psychological Support

Psychological support can come from many sources. Frequently, all we need is to talk to someone—anyone—to let it all out. For that kind of therapy, family, friends, or a member of the clergy can give the support you need. Medical research confirms that people who have positive, supportive relationships are physically and mentally healthier. A friend to talk to, a shared laugh, a word of encouragement, and a hug can be more valuable than any prescription.

Another resource is support groups comprised of people in similar situations who understand and can relate to everything you are going through. Call your local Mental Health Association to find out about support groups in your area.

If you feel your situation is severe, professional help might be the answer. Again, contact the Mental Health Association for referral to the resources in your area.

One of the best antidotes for depression is doing something to help someone else. You have time, talents, and skills that could mean a great deal to your family, friends, an elderly person in your neighborhood, a youth group, or a volunteer agency. You'll find that helping someone else helps *you* more than it helps them.

And there are other antidotes. Give yourself a treat now and then. Certainly, unemployment infringes on your lifestyle but don't abandon all of life's pleasures. An occasional movie, ballgame, or evening out is as important as meeting your other basic needs.

Don't forget to laugh. Humor can protect you from some of the pain, and it can help those around you through this, too.

Accomplishments are great medicine because they make us feel good about ourselves—even minor ones like cleaning out a drawer, working in the garage, darning a sock, or writing a resume. Make sure you accomplish at least one task every day.

Pursue New Opportunities

While unemployment is inevitably a time for worry and a certain amount of grief, it is also a time for reflection, change, and growth. Your new freedom may have been thrust upon you, but take advantage of it. It's an opportunity to evaluate where you've been and where you're headed; and determine whether or not you should change course. This could be the time to start a new career. After all, you might be placing unfair limitations on your potential if all you want is your old job back.

Finally, have faith. Whether you put your faith in yourself, the future, or a greater power, a hopeful outlook will do more for you than any of the advice herein.

You are an important person. You can do anything you want to do or have to do. Every day you survive makes you stronger.

And remember, this too shall pass.

APPENDIX C

A WORD TO SPOUSES

You will have more impact on your spouse's success in the job market than any other single person. A friend, relative, or associate may ultimately provide the lead which will result in a job, but on a day-to-day basis, no one will have as much impact as you. You could be the greatest help to your spouse, or the greatest hindrance. It depends on you.

Your main role in the coming weeks is to listen and support. Your spouse needs someone who will simply listen without advising, cajoling, or criticizing. When your spouse asks for advice, give it, but give it in a spirit of love and concern. This demonstration of love and concern may help your spouse to remain open with you, when the tendency is to become closed and isolated.

Because of the nature of the job search process, your spouse is likely to experience a variety of intense emotions. Your spouse may go from the highest highs, to the lowest lows. During the lows, let your spouse know that you are available to talk. Also be prepared, however, to allow your spouse a day or so to recover from any bad news he or she receives, such as discovering that the job which seemed perfect went to someone else.

I often encourage people to feel bad for a few hours, or even a day, in the wake of a disappointment. But then it's time to get on with life and the job search. The best antidote for depression is activity. If a person has several job possibilities cooking at the same time, it's not so devastating if one of the possibilities falls through.

Do everything you can to help your spouse conduct a consistent and systematic job search. Do not place undue pressure on your spouse or load him or her up with tasks to do around the house. When a spouse is out of work, it is easy to assume that he or she has lots of free time, but that simply isn't so. During a proper job search, an unemployed person should spend approximately 30 hours a week on the job search. I don't ask people to spend more time because I believe hunting for a job is one of the toughest jobs there is. The mental aspects can be draining. Thirty hours a week is all one should expect.

In adding up 30 hours per week of job search activity, I count time spent at the library, writing cover letters and thank-you notes, reviewing the want ads, driving to the library or appointments, the appointments and interviews themselves, and making phone calls. Also, throughout the period of unemployment, people with certain types of backgrounds should devote several hours a week to reading about their field. This keeps people sharp, but should not be counted toward the 30 hours.

There is nothing magical about spending 30 hours per week on a job search, however. Just physically doing something 30 hours a week will not necessarily produce the desired result. *How* the 30 hours are spent are most critical. Because it is so easy to waste time, time management is critical during a job search.

As long as your spouse is putting in 30 hours, treat your spouse just as you would if he or she was still working at a full-time job. If in the past you handled a certain household function, continue doing it yourself. That's not to say that the spouse should not take on any extra responsibilities, especially if you are employed also, but do not add many things. Your spouse's job search is a full-time job, and you should do everything possible to ensure that the unemployment period is as short as possible.

At the end of the day, ask your spouse what he or she felt was accomplished, or what positive thing happened that day. Do not ask when he or she will have a job. That is absolutely the last question your spouse wants to hear from you or anyone else. Your spouse is just as anxious about the situation as you, but he or she simply won't know when a new job will be obtained. Anything your spouse says in response to this question will be pure conjecture.

By asking what was accomplished that day or what positive thing happened, you will be doing several things. You will be keeping communications alive by showing genuine interest in your spouse. You will also be reminding your spouse that things were accomplished and positive things did happen.

Job hunters need a new definition of success. For many the definition of success is getting an acceptable job offer. Unfortunately, however, in a four-month job search, success will occur only one day out of 120. That's a lot of days of failure if you believe success is determined solely by job offers.

I have some alternate definitions of success for job hunters. Success is writing a tailored cover letter which may help get an interview when the standard cover letter would not have. Success is talking to someone who provides a lead, or having a positive meeting with a person with the power to hire.

Successes like these can and should occur every day. By asking your spouse to recount such successes each day, you will be offering your spouse powerful reminders that things really were accomplished and successes did occur. On occasion, your spouse may even claim that *nothing* was accomplished and there were *no* successes. Listen to what your spouse did that day and then tell your spouse what accomplishments and successes you believe occurred. As small as they may be, come up with something.

Be available when your spouse asks for help. If your spouse is writing a cover letter and needs an objective person, read it and supply your counsel. Do not use that time as an opportunity to criticize, however, even if it's justified, otherwise your spouse may not seek you out again.

I am not implying that you treat your spouse with kid gloves or as some fragile thing that can easily break. Just be understanding. Before you say something, even if it is unrelated to the job search, ask yourself whether it will increase or diminish your spouse's self-esteem. If it doesn't build self-esteem, try to modify what you were going to say.

Don't build your hopes up too high. If your spouse is among three finalists for a position, don't assume he or she will get it. If your spouse does not get the position, indicate that you are disappointed for your spouse's sake, not because it now looks like at least four more weeks of unemployment.

Instead, encourage your spouse. Remind your spouse that no matter how good a position may have looked, there is something even better out there. If your spouse wants to talk about what he or she could have done better, listen, but don't judge. A good response might be, "Maybe it would have been better if you hadn't said that (or, hadn't done that), but that probably was not the deciding factor. The person who got it probably just had the perfect background. You'll get the next one. I know you will. After all, you're a very good (<u>your spouse's occupation</u>)."

Although there are often things that can be done in the evening, such as writing cover letters and calling friends for leads, basically the daily job search ends at 5 pm. At that point, your spouse has done everything possible for the day, and there will be more things to do tomorrow. Occasionally, your spouse may finish the tasks for that day by two or three in the afternoon. Rather than asking if there isn't something else that could be done that day, let your spouse call it a day. Job finding is not a straight nine-to-five activity. Some things are best done in the evening, while other things can be done over the weekend. As long as your spouse is putting in approximately 30 hours per week, give your spouse the freedom to figure out when to do it.

Remember, your spouse will find a job. What you're both experiencing is temporary.

SELECTING A CAREER COUNSELOR

In this section I will provide you with objective information designed to help you decide whether to seek out the assistance of a career counselor. I will also give you ideas on how to find a career counselor who will be right for you. Keep in mind I am a private career counselor myself.

Career And Job Finding Counselors

Private counselors usually concentrate on providing one-on-one guidance, although they may combine that with group workshops. It is the intensive, individualized attention you get from a career counselor that distinguishes them from the help you would get at a community college or adult education program.

While working with a counselor you will be asked to complete various exercises. These exercises will help you think about yourself in ways that you would simply not do on your own. When discussing your exercises in a counseling session, all of the attention is focused on you. The counselor is able to help you gain the most from each exercise.

As much as I believe in the value of career planning books, job finding books and career workshops, it is my belief that individualized help is generally more effective. The insight that can be gained is greater. The ability to work through individual problems and issues is greater. The cost is greater as well. Depending on the type of program you select, costs can range from $300 to $4,000.

Not all career counselors do the same things. Some specialize in career and life planning and do not assist with job-hunting activities such as resume writing. Others specialize in job finding and do very little in the career planning area. Still others combine both.

Career Coaches

Another group of counselors practice career coaching. They work with people who may or may not be planning to leave their current jobs. The emphasis is on building an existing career rather than choosing a new one. The work they do together can range from maneuvering through the minefield of corporate politics to generating ideas on how to obtain and work with a mentor. If finding a new job seems appropriate, such counselors will then move you into a full-fledged job search. The career coach may work with a person over a period of several years. Initially, the client and counselor might meet frequently as they determine what the person wants out of his or her career. After that, they may meet only three or four times a year.

Outplacement Counselors

Outplacement counselors are paid by the company that fires or lays off an individual or a whole group of people. The major difference between outplacement counselors and other types of career counselors is who pays the fee. Some outplacement firms also provide job seekers with a desk and telephone, as well as secretarial assistance, services which are rarely provided by career counseling firms.

In the 1960s outplacement counseling got its start and was primarily limited to executives. Traditionally the fees were figured at 10% of the individual's salary. In the 1980s and 90s, firms which had traditionally offered individual career counseling became involved in outplacement. While there are about ten large national firms, there are now hundreds of smaller firms which offer outplacement.

Employers offer outplacement assistance for at least two reasons. First, the more progressive firms believe that they have a share in the problem. If many people are being laid off, the firm feels a responsibility to help former employees get into their next position as quickly as possible and with as little trauma as possible. It is one way of saying "We care about you even though you can't work here anymore." When a person is fired, it is a way of demonstrating that part of the blame for things not working out rests with the company. Perhaps the company did not provide adequate training or support, or perhaps the organization changed directions and the individual was unable to make the transition. Whatever the reason, the company is willing to provide some additional support.

A second reason has to do with avoiding some of the problems that can occur when people are fired or laid off. Wrongful termination suits have become more frequent in the last ten years, and former employees are winning a good percentage of those suits. There are also occasional problems with employee sabotage or giving away company secrets. Outplacement can be seen as a way of decreasing the likelihood that a person would pursue a wrongful termination suit or would sabotage equipment or computers.

Throughout the 80s, companies primarily contracted with an outplacement firm to work with all of their employees who were terminated. Some employers are taking a different approach, however. They are offering a set amount of money for outplacement and then telling the employee to seek out an outplacement firm that he or she feels comfortable with. For the individual, that matter of choice offers some advantages.

There is another thing happening in the market place. I have begun to see situations in which former employees initiate contact with an outplacement firm, and then go back to the company and ask that outplacement assistance be provided. While not all companies agree to pay the fee, many of them do. If the employer had not been requested by the employee to provide the outplacement, it would usually not have happened.

I believe that employers providing assistance to employees in their job searches is a healthy trend in employer-employee relations. I believe that both parties benefit.

Who Should Seek The Help Of A Career Counselor?

I do not believe that career counseling is just for those who have no idea what kind of career they want, nor is it just for those who have had trouble finding a job in the past. When working with a skilled career and job finding counselor, you can become much more clear concerning your values, your personality, your goals, and what careers would bring you the satisfaction you've been seeking. A good counselor can often pinpoint why you've been frustrated in the past and why you left those jobs, or did not do well in them. A good counselor can help you prepare an effective resume and enable you to handle difficult interview questions. If you were fired from a job or if you have other sticky issues to deal with, a counselor can suggest effective ways to deal with them.

If your counselor is working with you throughout your job search, he or she should be available as you face various issues. No matter how good a job finding book is, it cannot anticipate all of the issues you're facing, and it certainly cannot address them as personally as a counselor can. For instance, during your job search, you may have to learn to handle an issue which has caused you great problems in interviews. A counselor could help you develop a plan to neutralize the problem. A counselor can also talk to you after an interview and identify things you're doing right and things you're doing wrong. Without a counselor, people generally just keep repeating their mistakes because they do not get any feedback.

Effective counselors will give you feedback, ideas, and insights. Rarely will they tell you what to do, although that is appropriate at times. They will not tell you that a specific career field is perfect for you. Instead they will encourage you to look at numerous careers. Then when you've narrowed your choices down, they may encourage you to pursue some and discourage you from pursuing others. They will tell you why they think a career field is good for you or not good for you.

Effective counselors will not do the work for you. You will be the one completing the exercises, you will work on your resume, you will develop your responses to interview questions, you will do your employer research, you will gain your own leads, and you will make it happen. There are various ways that a counselor can assist you, but the primary effort in all of these areas will be your own.

Career counselors can help those who want to move ahead faster, as well as those who are really stuck.

How To Find The Right Counselor

Finding the right counselor is a challenge. A particular counselor can be sincere but incompetent, insincere and incompetent, or sincere and competent. I want to help you find the latter.

Unfortunately, there are a few wolves in sheep's clothing in the career industry. A sincere incompetent will often not take much of your money (probably $500 to $2,000) but will have robbed you of time and the trust you placed in that person. The insincere incompetents may pick your pocket for $3,000 to $8,000 and provide you with almost no help. The thing to remember is that not all who call themselves career counselors, executive career counselors, or career coaches, are skilled and knowledgeable enough to help you achieve your goals. And some care more about your money than they do about you.

As in any field, when it comes to choosing a career counselor, let the buyer beware. The following suggestions should help you find not only a good counselor, but the one who is just right for you.

Do your best to get referrals. Ask your friends if they or any of their friends have used a local counselor. If you are able to locate a person who has used a counselor, ask if he or she would recommend the counselor and if so, why. Getting a referral won't guarantee you'll get just the right counselor for you, but you almost assuredly won't end up with one of the wolves. Find out from the person how the counselor operates and get an idea about costs. If possible, get the person to show you the exercises that were completed and learn how the exercises were beneficial. Ask whether the counselor was readily available and willing to help. When you get a referral, keep in mind that the individual is being vouched for, not the entire firm.

Many career counselors possess master's degrees in counseling or social work. That training will ensure that they know the theory of counseling, have a strong knowledge base, and can professionally interpret the results of most personality and career inventories. The degree alone will not ensure that the person knows the local job market or has the street smarts to help you maneuver through the roadblocks you might encounter during your job search.

468

There are also some very competent career counselors who don't have degrees, but who have lots of savvy.

Among those counselors who have a master's degree, some also have the National Certified Counselor (NCC) designation or the National Certified Career Counselor (NCCC) designation from the National Board for Certified Counselors. To obtain that designation, counselors must pass an exam and prove their knowledge and competence in several areas of career counseling. They must also abide by some very high and strict ethical guidelines, as well as take continuing education courses each year in order to remain certified.

Request a list of references from any counselor you're considering using. Although even the wolves will be able to supply you with references of satisfied customers, it is wise to check out those references anyway. Of course, no counselor is going to supply you with the names of dissatisfied people. Once you get the names and phone numbers of people, call them and ask what the program was really like. Ask what they liked best and what they would like to see improved. By probing a bit, tactfully of course, you should be able to find out a lot about the person who may become your counselor.

Study any materials the counselor has written or published. These materials can give you a good idea of the philosophy and beliefs of the person. Determine whether you agree with and will feel comfortable with that philosophy. Since most firms offer a no-cost first appointment and will give you materials to read, take advantage of the initial appointment, and study, don't just read the materials. If the counselor has written some good articles you will be somewhat assured that the person has the necessary knowledge to help you. Some, however, are great writers but not very good counselors.

Be sure you meet and get to know the person who will be your counselor. With some firms you will begin by meeting a salesperson. The firm won't call them that, but that's what they are because they do no counseling. It's my belief that the counselor should meet with the prospective client from the beginning and should personally sell himself or herself to the prospective client. But if you do meet a salesperson for a first and second appointment, be sure to meet and spend time with the person who would be your counselor before you make a payment or sign a contract. If the firm asks you to trust them that they have selected the best counselor to meet "your particular needs," I would exit immediately, regardless of how good their program sounds.

You can't tell a good firm or counselor by what they charge. A low-cost program offered by someone who is sincere, but not knowledgeable or talented, will certainly not be worth the time and money spent. There is no guarantee, however, that the high-priced firms

($3,000 to $8,000) are any good either. They may simply be good at convincing you that you need their help. The wolves are great at making promises that sound believable. On the other hand, a fee of $4,000 or more could be one of the best investments you ever make if you work with a top-quality counselor.

I've told you some things to be aware of, but now I want to describe how you should select a counselor. These ideas should be followed whether or not you received a recommendation about the person.

In order to work with a particular counselor I believe several things should take place.

1) You should feel comfortable with the counselor. You should believe that you can share almost anything with the counselor and that the counselor will still accept you and respect you. Your career counselor should not be viewed as a psychologist to share your innermost secrets with, or to receive extensive therapy from (unless the counselor is trained to provide therapy), but you should believe that you could share almost anything. The counselor should truly listen to you. A good counselor spends a lot of time listening and asking you questions to help you achieve greater self-knowledge. A good counselor will give you information, will make recommendations, and will guide you, but the emphasis will not be on telling you what to do or giving you answers for everything. Except for technical areas such as composing a resume or answering a difficult interview question, almost all answers must come from you.

Male counselors can provide excellent help to female clients and female counselors can give excellent help to male clients. But if you know you would feel more comfortable working with someone of the same gender, seek out such a person.

2) You should feel a rapport with the counselor. Rapport exists when you hit it off and feel good in the presence of this person. As you have a first and then second session with this person (I suggest two sessions before you sign any contracts) a sense of trust should build based on the counselor's knowledge and the counselor's ability to relate to you. You should have the sense that this person understands you and will exert strong effort to continually understand you better.

3) The counselor should be highly knowledgeable. While the counselor may utilize certain exercises and strategies with almost all clients, the counselor should be aware of other techniques and strategies as well, and use them when appropriate. While competent counselors are always knowledgeable, a good counselor is continually learning from his or her clients, and is constantly assessing what is working well and what is not. A good counselor is probably an active member of a professional association, and seeks to gain new ideas from colleagues, seminars, and personal reading.

4) The counselor should make it clear what kinds of activities you will do and what will be expected of you as you go through the career counseling process. A good counselor will make you work hard at gaining insight into yourself and your career needs. The counselor should not promise to merely tell you about yourself. Once the full process is understood, you should have the belief that the exercises, activities, and job finding strategies will work for you and that you will be willing to try them.

Things To Watch Out For

Some firms will make strong verbal commitments, but the commitments will not be backed up by the wording of the contract. If you see a major discrepancy, watch out. If you like the firm you might ask to have a point or two added to increase your confidence in their service and to clarify what you expect to receive. If your request is reasonable, most firms should have no trouble with your suggestion. Of course, your counselor may have to get it approved by management, and that could take a day or two.

Avoid firms which insist on receiving your entire payment before counseling begins, particularly those charging several thousand dollars. If you don't have the cash reserves, these firms will request that you put it on a credit card or will help get you a personal loan from a loan company or a bank. That's too much pressure and it is unnecessary. The services you are about to receive will probably be provided over a period of several months, so there is no reason to insist on receiving it all at the beginning. Also, there is absolutely no justification for pressure tactics.

Unfortunately, one of the reasons some firms ask for all of the money up front is that the firm has no intention of providing all of the services promised. A counselor friend shared with me that he once worked for a counseling firm that told him to provide no more than 20 hours of one-on-one help even though the verbal promises were for whatever amount of time it took to achieve the agreed upon goals.

Watch out for the firm that says they will handle everything. They often claim that through their great contacts they will mail out hundreds of resumes and the client will merely have to attend a dozen or so interviews before landing a position. Others state that with their great contacts, they will tell the client who to apply to and will be able to arrange interviews. I have yet to see a firm, let alone an individual counselor, who has so many contacts that they can justify this type of claim. Often, their contacts amount to a data base with names and addresses of employers. Many of the names and addresses will be out of date. A good counselor will have developed good contacts over a period of time, and will make referrals when appropriate, but I personally believe that no client should work with a counseling firm solely because of its supposedly great contacts.

As you work with the firm and your counselor, several things should become evident. They should deliver on their promises. In some firms the counselor becomes scarce after a few weeks and will conveniently have a full schedule for the next three weeks. It only takes a few calls like that to make most clients realize that the firm feels it owes them no more time.

How Counseling Firms Operate

Many firms work on a fee basis in which you agree to pay a certain amount in return for certain agreed services. That is fine as long as the fee is reasonable and the firm backs up its agreements. There should, however, be some type of escape clause in the contract to accommodate the person who leaves the program shortly after starting.

Other counselors work strictly on an hourly basis. You will pay only for the time you use. Some will ask you to pay at the end of each session, while others will bill you each month. Paying an hourly rate has some advantages because you have greater control over the services you receive.

Those who use a fee system believe that a client becomes more psychologically committed to the full process once a contract is signed.

An excellent counselor can help you achieve goals that you might not otherwise attain. If you think a counselor may be able to help you, follow these suggestions closely. A carefully chosen counselor can help you achieve your full potential and gain a high level of satisfaction in your career.

THE ONE HUNDRED BEST QUOTES FOR JOB HUNTERS

The man who procrastinates is always struggling with misfortunes. *Hesiod*

Thales was asked what was most difficult for man. He answered, "To know one's self." *Diogenes Laertius*

The only happy man is a man whose work permits him to function to the full extent of his ability. *Oliver Wendell Holmes*

To each is given a certain inward talent, a certain outward environment or fortune; to each by wisest combination of these two, a certain maximum capacity. *Thomas Carlyle*

Learn what you are and be such. *Pindar*

Everyone excels in something in which another fails. *Publius Syrus*

Let each become all that he was created capable of. *Thomas Carlyle*

When you've exhausted all possibilities, remember this: you haven't. *Robert Schuller*

If it's going to be, it's up to me! *Robert Schuller*

Don't kill the dream — execute it! *Robert Schuller*

Nothing great was ever achieved without enthusiasm. *Ralph Waldo Emerson*

All experience is an arch to build upon. *Henry Brooks Adams*

A bad beginning makes a bad ending. *Euripides*

The world stands aside for those who know where they're going. *David Jordan*

If you don't know where you're going, you'll probably wind up somewhere else. *David Campbell*

If you have built castles in the air, your work need not be lost; that is where they should be. Now put the foundations under them. *Thoreau*

An optimist sees an opportunity in every calamity; a pessimist sees a calamity in every opportunity.

Our great mistake is to neglect the cultivation of those virtues a person has, and trying to extract from each person virtues he does not possess. *Hadrian*

God's best gift to us is not things, but opportunities. *Alice W. Rollins*

A good listener is not only popular everywhere, but after a while he knows something. *Wilson Mizner*

Habits are at first cobwebs, then cables. *Spanish Proverb*

When one door shuts, another opens. *Spanish Proverb*

You rarely succeed unless you have fun doing it.

It may be that knowledge is power, but pulling the switch is enthusiasm.

To really be able to persuade someone, keep in mind that enthusiasm usually is more effective than facts.

Clear your mind of can't. *Samuel Johnson*

Life is like a ten speed bike. Most of us have gears we never use. *Charles Schulz*

A definite goal and a specific deadline—these are the keys to achieving one's destiny!

Don't let life discourage you; everyone who got where he is had to begin where he was. *Richard L. Evans*

An obstacle is something you see when you take your eyes off the goal.

It's not the hours you put in; it's what you put in the hours. *Elmer Leterman*

Let your hook be always cast; in the pool where you least expect it, there will be a fish. *Ovid*

The expert in anything was once a beginner.

Knock the T off can't. You can if you think you can.

Dare to open doors to new experiences and step forth to explore strange horizons.

For every problem, there is an opportunity.

Goals should be viewed as dreams with deadlines.

The difference between ordinary and extraordinary is that little extra.

You can have everything in life you want, if you will just help enough other people get what they want. *Zig Ziglar*

It's your attitude and not your aptitude that determines your altitude.

Expect the best. Prepare for the worst. Capitalize on what comes.

Of all the things you wear, your expression is the most important. *Janet Lane*

Whether you think you can or can't—you're right.

Every job is a self-portrait of the person who did it.

You cannot consistently perform in a manner which is inconsistent with the way you see yourself. *Dr. Joyce Brothers*

Character may be manifested in the great moments, but it is made in the small ones. *Phillips Brooks*

If you do the things you need to do when you need to do them, then someday you can do the things you want to do when you want to do them. *Zig Ziglar*

Success consists of a series of little daily efforts. *Mamie McCullough*

People often complain about lack of time when the lack of direction is the real problem.

The only way to reach your long-range goals is through achieving your short-range objectives.

You don't pay the price for success, you enjoy the benefits of success. *Zig Ziglar*

Give me a stock clerk with a goal, and I will give you a man who will make history. Give me a man without a goal, and I will give you a stock clerk. *J.C. Penney*

You measure the size of the accomplishment by the obstacles you had to overcome to reach your goals. *Booker T. Washington*

Outstanding people have one thing in common: an absolute sense of mission.

Desire is the great equalizer.

A goal casually set and lightly taken is freely abandoned at the first obstacle.

In order to succeed, you must know what you are doing, like what you are doing and believe in what you are doing. *Will Rogers*

Success is determined by taking the hand you were dealt and utilizing it to the very best of your ability. *Ty Boyd*

Failure has been correctly identified as the past of least "persistence."

People don't plan to fail, they just fail to plan.

The price of success is much lower than the price of failure.

Success seems to be largely a matter of hanging on after others have let go. *William Feather*

Life is an echo. What you send out—you get back. What you give—you get.

Do unto others as you would have them do unto you.

The more you "pass on" to others, the more you keep for yourself.

All things are difficult before they are easy. *John Norley*

Have faith in your faith — and doubt your doubts. *Robert Schuller*

All people dream, but not equally. They who dream by night in the dusty recesses of their minds wake in the day to find that it is vanity; but the dreamers of the day are danger-ous people, for they act their dream with open eyes, to make it possible. *T.E. Lawrence*

If I had eight hours to chop down a tree, I'd spend the first six sharpening my ax. *Abraham Lincoln*

Whatever women do they must do twice as well as men to be thought half as good. Luckily this is not difficult. *Charlotte Whitton*

If you give a man a fish he eats for a day. If you teach a man to fish he eats for a lifetime.

The harder you work—the luckier you get.

In the middle of every difficulty lies opportunity. *Albert Einstein*

No race can prosper till it learns that there is as much dignity in tilling a field as in writing a poem. *Booker T. Washington*

A diamond is a chunk of coal that made good under pressure.

If you keep on saying things are going to be bad, you have a good chance of being a prophet. *Isaac Singer*

In the long run the pessimist may be proved right, but the optimist has a better time on the trip. *Daniel Reardon*

The game of life is a game of boomerangs. Our thoughts, deeds, and words return to us sooner or later with astounding accuracy. *Florence Shinn*

When you begin moving toward excellence, you will find very little competition. You're competing with only 20% of the population. *Brian Tracy*

What's the use of running if you're not on the right road.

Many of life's failures are men who did not realize how close they were to success when they gave up. *Thomas Edison*

In my practice as a psychiatrist, I have found that helping people to develop personal goals has proved to be the most effective way to help them cope with problems. *Ari Kiev*

When you can't solve a problem, manage it. *Robert Schuller*

There is no pillow as soft as a clear conscience. *John Wooden*

People with humility don't think less of themselves—they just think about themselves less.

Nonverbal communication is an elaborate secret code that is written nowhere, known by none, and understood by all. *Edward Sapir*

There's no traffic jam in the extra mile.

The most successful people are those who do all year long what they would otherwise do on their summer vacation. *Mark Twain*

There is little difference in people, but that little difference makes a big difference. The little difference is attitude. The big difference is whether it is positive or negative. *Clement Stone*

You must have long-range goals to keep from being frustrated by short-range failures.

Consider the postage stamp: its usefulness consists of its ability to stick to one thing till it gets there. *Josh Billings*

A problem well stated is a problem half solved. *Charles Kettering*

And the day came when the risk to remain tight in a bud was more painful than the risk it took to blossom.

Success is the quality of a journey, not the destination.

Every problem has a gift for you in its hand.

Chance favors the prepared mind. *Louis Pasteur*

Don't wait for your ship to come in, swim out to it.

A great pleasure in life is doing what people say you cannot do. *Walter Gagehot*

When an archer misses the mark, he turns and looks for the fault within himself. Failure to hit the bull's-eye is never the fault of the target. To improve your aim— improve yourself. *Gilbert Arland*

Every problem contains the seed of its own solution. *Norman V. Peal*

HELP WITH THE EXERCISES, HELP WITH YOUR RESUME

HELP WITH THE EXERCISES

The exercises have been designed to be self-directed. A great deal of insight should be obtained from your own efforts. If you feel stuck, it can help to talk to a friend or spouse. While that person will not be a trained counselor, you can show your work to someone and they will be able to see things about you that you did not see yourself. Others are more objective about you. They do not have the same hangups you may have about yourself or certain beliefs about yourself that you've been carrying around like old baggage.

I frequently suggest to clients that they involve their spouses. It can be extremely useful to get feedback from a spouse. Have your spouse read over your materials, especially your accomplishments. Your spouse will quickly spot skills that you missed.

If you're having trouble understanding part of the instructions, your spouse, or another person may be able to make sense out of it and help you back on your merry way. I've tried to make the instructions as clear as possible, but I know that for some, they may not be totally clear.

I'm Really Stuck

If you're convinced that you are thoroughly stuck, we can help. I want you to gain as much benefit from these exercises as possible. Sometimes five minutes of talking is all you need to get unstuck.

I Want More Extensive Help

If you would like more extensive help interpreting an exercise or in bringing all the pieces together, we can arrange to work by phone and by mail.

How We'll Do It

Write to us at Career Management Resources, 1750 112th NE, C-224, Bellevue, WA 98004. Enclose a note describing the areas you would like help in. Indicate whether you have a very specific question, and if so what it is. If that is the case, enclose a check for $15 to cover an initial ten minute conversation. By knowing what you want in advance, we can pack as much help into those ten minutes as possible and try to get you back on track.

In your note also provide us with your name, address, and phone number, and the hours and days you can typically be reached. If you can be reached during business hours that will be very helpful.

If you think you might want more extensive help, we would charge $85 per hour. Send a note indicating the type of help you want and enclose a check for $42 to cover an initial half hour consultation.

Either I or one of my three associates will call. Whoever calls will be highly skilled and experienced with the exercises presented in *The Hunt*. Naturally you should feel free to ask them about their backgrounds.

HELP WITH YOUR RESUME

Over the years we have strengthened hundreds of resumes that people have sent in to us for editing. It seems to be a highly valued service. We thoroughly review a resume and look for ways to improve the layout and writing. We will suggest word improvements and will frequently improve entire sentences.

The editing service is $45. Send photocopies of your job sketches, and a double spaced typed version of your resume. We will return your resume within two working days.

If you have specific questions or concerns, list them in a cover sheet. Give us your phone number and times that we can call you if we need to clarify something.

Your job sketches are important for you in writing your resume and they help us in editing.

APPENDIX G

TELL ME WHAT YOU THINK

This book is going to be revised on an annual basis. Each year new material will be added and existing material will be changed and strengthened. I wrote this book because I believe I have some knowledge and experience which is worth sharing. But believe me, I don't know it all and I haven't experienced it all. It has been said before that we career counselors learn from our clients. This is exactly right. Without their feedback and their experience, we would not know what works and what does not work. In essence, our clients pay us so we can learn from them.

I'm a synthesizer. I'm an eclectic. I beg, borrow, and steal ideas wherever and whenever I can. For that reason, I would love to get ideas from you. I invite you to share a personal experience with me. If you tried something creative and it worked for you, write it up and send it to me. Tell me what you learned from it and how it might apply to others. Whether you think it's an idea everyone should use, or if you feel it's appropriate for only certain groups of people, share it with me.

If a technique or strategy from *The Hunt* worked especially well, let me know. This type of information is valuable because it provides some much needed confirmation. It strengthens my resolve to give people the best information possible and to help as many people as possible.

If you find any interesting articles, I would welcome receiving them. I am especially interested in articles that include information about employment research.

Please write and tell me what you think of *The Hunt*. I'd love to hear from you.

Tom Washington
Career Management Resources
1750 112th NE C-224
Bellevue, WA 98004

BIBLIOGRAPHY

Career Planning

    The Three Boxes of Life, Richard Bolles, Ten Speed Press, 1981

    The Truth About You: Discover What You Should Be Doing With Your Life, Arthur Miller and Ralph Mattson, Ten Speed Press, 1989

Job Finding

    Career Satisfaction And Success: How To Know And Manage Your Strengths, Bernard Haldane, 1988, $9.25. Available only through mail order: Wellness Behavior Northwest, 4502 54th Ave NE, Seattle WA 98105

    The Complete Job Search Handbook, Howard Figler, Henry Holt & Co., 1988

    Go Hire Yourself An Employer, Richard Irish, Anchor Press, 1987

    Guerrilla Tactics In The Job Market, Tom Jackson, Bantam Books, 1991

    How To Get a Better Job In This Crazy World, Robert Half, Plume, 1990

    What Color Is Your Parachute? Richard Bolles, Ten Speed Press, 1992

    Who's Hiring Who, Richard Lathrop, Ten Speed Press, 1989

Interviewing

    How To Make $1000 a Minute: Negotiating Your Salaries and Raises, Jack Chapman, Ten Speed Press, 1987

    Sweaty Palms: The Neglected Art Of Being Interviewed, Anthony Medley, Ten Speed Press, 1992

Resume Writing

    Resume Power: Selling Yourself On Paper, Tom Washington, Mount Vernon Press, 1990

    The Overnight Resume, Donald Asher, Ten Speed Press, 1991

    The Perfect Resume, Tom Jackson, Anchor Press, 1981

Headhunters

    How To Get A Headhunter To Call, Howard Freedman, John Wiley & Sons, 1986

Career Building

    Skills for Success, Adele Scheele, Ballantine, 1979

INDEX